BRITAIN, NASSER AND THE
BALANCE OF POWER IN THE MIDDLE EAST
1952 1967

CASS SERIES: BRITISH FOREIGN AND COLONIAL POLICY
ISSN: 1467-5013
Series Editor: Peter Catterall

This series provides insights into both the background influences on and the course of policy-making towards Britain's extensive overseas interests during the past 200 years.

Whitehall and the Suez Crisis, Saul Kelly and Anthony Gorst (eds)

Liberals, International Relations and Appeasement: The Liberal Party, 1919–1939, Richard S. Grayson

British Government Policy and Decolonisation, 1945–1963: Scrutinising the Official Mind, Frank Heinlein

Harold Wilson and European Integration: Britain's Second Application to Join the EEC, Oliver Daddow (ed.)

Britain, Israel and the United States, 1955–1958: Beyond Suez, Orna Almog

The British Political Elite and the Soviet Union, 1937–1939, Louise Grace Shaw

Britain, Nasser and the Balance of Power in the Middle East, 1952–1967: From the Egyptian Revolution to the Six Day War, Robert McNamara

BRITAIN, NASSER
and the
BALANCE OF POWER
in the
MIDDLE EAST
1952–1967

From the Egyptian Revolution
to the Six Day War

ROBERT McNAMARA

National University of Ireland, Maynooth

FRANK CASS
LONDON • PORTLAND, OR

First published in 2003 in Great Britain by
FRANK CASS PUBLISHERS
Crown House, 47 Chase Side
London N14 5BP

and in the United States of America by
FRANK CASS PUBLISHERS
c/o ISBS, 920 NE 58th Avenue, # 300
Portland, Oregon, 97213-3786

Website: www.frankcass.com

British Library Cataloguing in Publication Data

McNamara, Robert
  Britain, Nasser and the balance of power in the Middle
  East, 1952–1967: from the Egyptian revolution to the
  Six-Day War. – (Cass series. British foreign and colonial
  policy)
  1. Great Britain – Foreign relations – Middle East 2. Middle
  East – Foreign relations – Great Britain 3. Great Britain –
  Foreign relations – 1945–1964. 4. Egypt – Foreign relations –
  1952–1970
  I. Title
  327.4'1056'09045

ISBN 0-7146-5397-7 (cloth)
ISSN 1467-5013

Library of Congress Cataloging-in-Publication Data

McNamara, Robert, 1974–
  Britain, Nasser and the balance of power in the Middle East, 1952–1967: from the
  Egyptian revolution to the Six-Day War/Robert McNamara.
    p. cm. – (Cass series–British foreign and colonial policy, ISSN 1467-5013)
  Includes bibliographical references (p.   ) and index.
  ISBN 0-7146-5397-7 (cloth)
    1. Egypt–Politics and government–1952–1970. 2. Nasser, Gamal Abdul, 1918–1970.
  3. Great Britain–Foreign relations–Egypt. 4. Egypt–Foreign relations–Great Britain.
  5. Great Britain–Foreign relations–1945–1964. 6. Arab nationalism. 7. Panarabism.
  I. Title. II. Series.
  DT107.827.M394 2003
  327.41062'09'045–dc21

                                                                            2002041579

Typeset in 10.5/12.5pt Palatino by Vitaset, Paddock Wood, Kent
Printed in Great Britain by
MPG Books Ltd, Victoria Square, Bodmin, Cornwall

Contents

Series Editor's Preface

ON 24 JULY 1952 Harold Macmillan noted in his diary 'In Egypt, a military coup d'etat (which may prove healthy) has intimidated the King, the corrupt old politicians, and the corrupt old generals. It remains to be seen how soon the "Young Egyptian" movement will itself be corrupted.' It is easy to forget, in the light of subsequent events, that the coup, shortly followed by King Farouk's abdication, was not seen necessarily as a bad thing from the British point of view. Egypt may have been central to British policy in the Middle East – straddling as it did the strategically important Suez Canal, the bases protecting which housed some 70,000 British troops – but the relationship with the old regime had been fraught with difficulties. There were disputes over finance, over the Egyptian claim to the Sudan and, not least, the looming requirement to renegotiate the terms on which the British remained in the Suez bases. On his accession to power Nasser and his colleagues thus already found a very full agenda of Anglo-Egyptian problems.

Nasser did, however, bring a rather different ideological approach to that of the old political classes – such as the nationalist *Wafd* – he despised and suppressed. As Robert McNamara argues here, he sought not just nationalist goals such as the removal of the British from Egypt, but pan-Arabist ones which brought him into conflict with other Arab leaders – and through them the British – throughout the Middle East. In this there was a consistency of aim if not of allies. The Saudis, for instance, had no particular reasons to look with favour on the British and were more well-disposed towards Egypt in the 1950s. In the early 1960s, in contrast, Nasser's support for the revolution in Yemen was to help pave the way for a *rapprochement* between the British and the Saudis which, for the former, bore fruit, amongst other things, in the first of a long and continuing series of defence contracts.

Thus the Anglo-Egyptian problems Nasser inherited were replaced by new ones. By July 1954 the Bases Agreement was largely resolved, and with it the related financial disputes, aided by the fact that the British regarded the garrisons as having been rendered essentially redundant in the new situation of nuclear weapons. The British mean-while also found his replacements rather more amenable on the Sudan than Farouk had been. Thereafter, however, as McNamara shows, the disputes between the two countries instead extended to the whole Middle East, exacerbated to some extent by the anxieties that Nasser was some kind of Egyptian Mussolini formed by some British states-men. This account is therefore of importance for much more than the study of Anglo-Egyptian relations. And in explaining these wider Middle Eastern conflicts McNamara has also had skilfully to untwine the interlacing threads and complexities of Anglo-American cold war strategy in the region. Here, for instance, is explained for the first time in detail the hopes – and their eventual frustration – that Macmillan in 1957 entertained of action with the Americans to achieve Nasser's overthrow.

The Suez Crisis of 1956 thus does not emerge as the turning point it was once claimed to be. McNamara instead shows that it was the Iraqi revolution of 1958 that arguably had more of an impact on Britain's strategy in the Middle East, a point also made in a rather different context by Orna Almog's book in this same series. Within ten years Britain's presence in the region had changed from a military and strategic one centred on Iraq and Aden to a much more commercial one focused on the conservative monarchies of the Arabian Peninsula. Poignantly, as McNamara points out, this triumph for Nasser however coincided with the disaster of the Six Day War. As this book powerfully argues, in the end, whilst both were able to tackle with some success the Anglo-Egyptian problems they found in 1952, Nasser's broader attempts to reconfigure the power relations of the Middle East ulti-mately proved as barren as those of his old adversary, Anthony Eden.

Peter Catterall
London

Acknowledgements

THIS WORK grew to a considerable extent out of a doctoral thesis I completed at University College Cork under the supervision of Professor Dermot Keogh. It was subsequently turned into a book while I was carrying out post-doctoral research work for Professor Keogh. I am particularly grateful to him for his help and advice during our association together. The History Department at University College Cork was a stimulating place to be both a student and an employee of and was always open to new ideas and approaches. I would like to take the opportunity to acknowledge the series editor, Peter Catterall, for his preface, for recommending the book for publication and for his helpful comments on the initial draft. I would also like to thank Andrew Humphrys at Frank Cass, for guiding me through the editorial process.

The Boole Library, UCC, the Public Record Office, London, the British Library, the Bodleian Library, Oxford, St Antony's College, Oxford, the Lyndon Johnson Library, Austin Texas, the National Archives, Suitland, Maryland and the British Library of Political and Economic Science, London, all provided access to material, for which I am immensely grateful. Joe Lee, Geoff Roberts, Eunan O'Halpin and George Boyce all provided help and advice at various times. Ivor Sutton, Kate Meighan, Fergal Bell and Kieran McFeely all provided accommodation during innumerable trips to London. Special thanks are due to Marcella McCann for proofreading and company over the past couple of years.

The spur for this study was my father, the late James Declan McNamara, who recounted the time he sailed through the Suez Canal, as a 19-year-old radio officer in August 1956; on the return journey he had to go back home via the Cape of Good Hope, a sea journey of 56 days. This work is dedicated to his memory and to my mother Olive McNamara. It could not have been completed without their support.

Abbreviations

BIOT	British Indian Ocean Territory
CIA	Central Intelligence Agency
CIGS	Chief of the Imperial General Staff
CO	Colonial Office
COS	Chiefs of Staff
DOPC	Defence and Overseas Policy Committee
EEC	European Economic Community
FLN	National Liberation Front (Algeria)
FLOSY	Front for the Liberation of South Yemen
FRG	Federal Republic of Germany
GDR	German Democratic Republic
GNP	gross national product
GOC	General Officer Commanding
ICBM	intercontinental ballistic missile
IMF	International Monetary Fund
JIC	Joint Intelligence Committee
MI6	Secret Intelligence Service
MOD	Ministry of Defence
MOSFA	Minister of State for Foreign Affairs
NATO	North Atlantic Treaty Organisation
NEA	Near Eastern Affairs
NLF	National Liberation Front
NSC	National Security Council
OAU	Organisation of African Unity
OLOS	Organisation for the Liberation of the Occupied South
OPD	Overseas Policy Defence
PSP	People's Socialist Party
RCC	Revolutionary Command Council
SAF	South Arabian Federation
SCUA	Suez Canal Users' Association
SOS	Secretary of State
SOSFA	Secretary of State for Foreign Affairs
UAR	United Arab Republic

UKMISNY	UK Mission New York
UN	United Nations
UNEF	United Nations emergency force
UNOGIL	United Nations Observer Group in Lebanon
UNSG	United Nations Secretary-General
YAR	Yemen Arab Republic

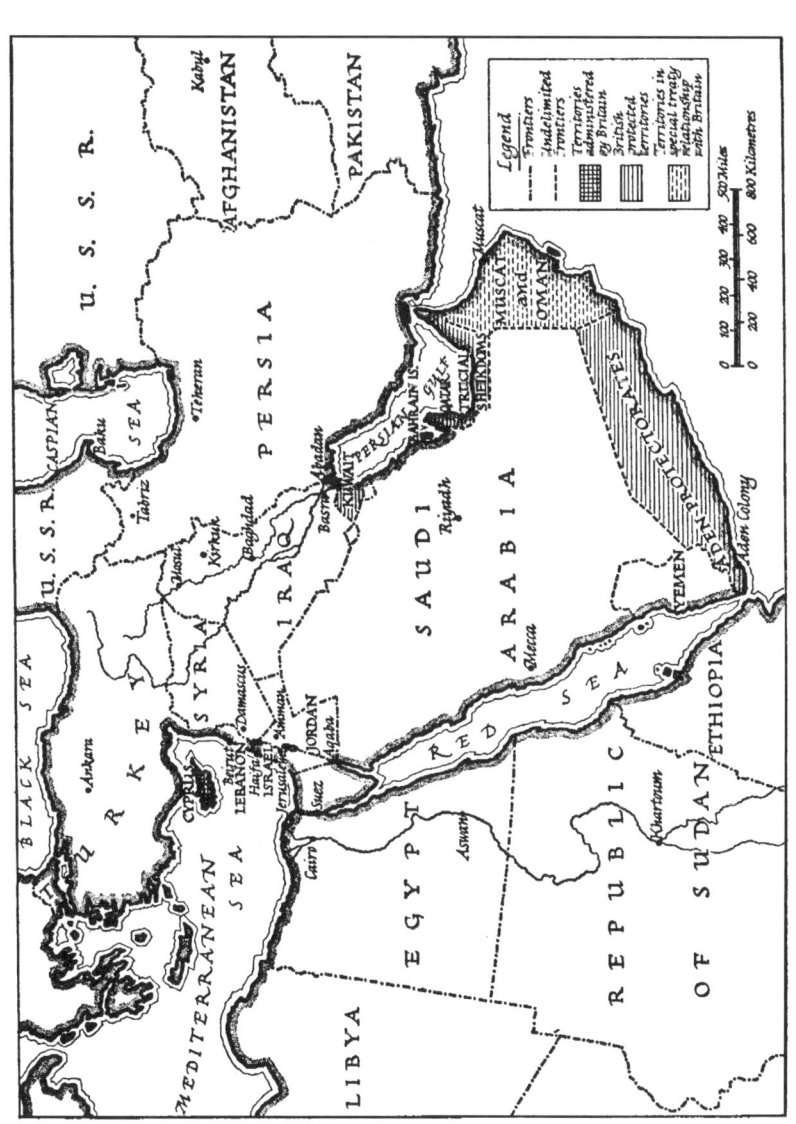

Map 1: The Middle East in 1956

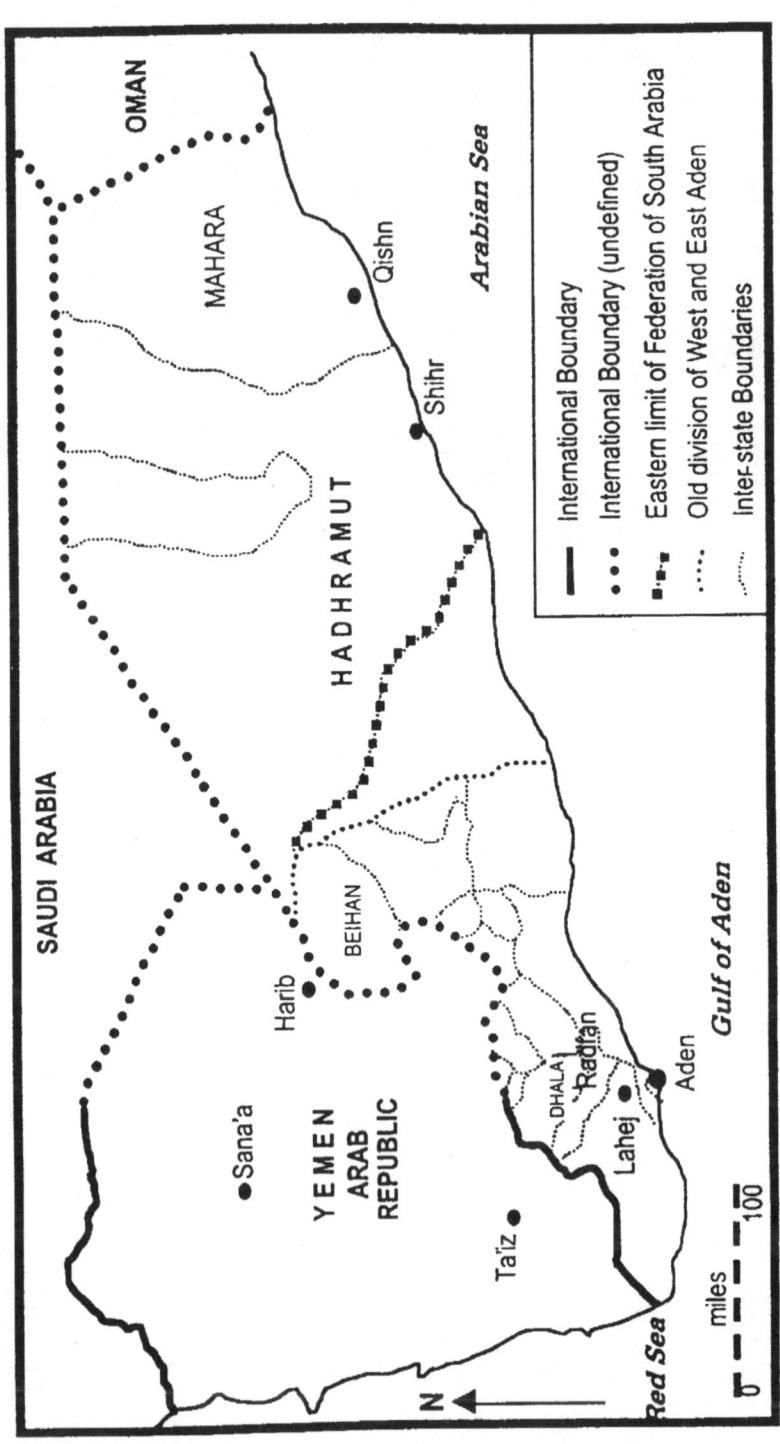

Map 2: Saudi Arabia and Yemen

Chronology of Events

1882	Britain occupies Egypt.
1898	Anglo-Egyptian Condominium (joint control) established in Sudan.
1914 (Dec.)	Egypt, nominally Ottoman province, made British province at the outbreak of war with Turks.
1915	Hussein–McMahon correspondence on British support for an Arab state.
1916	Sykes–Picot agreement on establishment of Franco-British zones of influence in Middle East.
1917 (Nov.)	Balfour Declaration stating Britain in favour of Jewish homeland in Palestine.
1918 (Mar.)	Birth of Gamal Abdul Nasser in Egypt.
1918 (Nov.)	End of First World War and collapse of Turkish power in Middle East.
1919–22	Widespread unrest in Egypt after deportation of (*Wafd*) nationalist leaders.
1920 (Apr.)	San Remo conference allots mandates: Syria and Lebanon to France, and Palestine and Iraq to Britain.
1922 (Dec.)	Allenby Declaration promises limited independence for Egypt.
1936	Anglo-Egyptian Treaty signed granting UK wide-ranging base rights in Egypt.
1939–45	Second World War.
1942	Farouk forced to appoint pro-Allied Prime Minister under threat of abdication; defeat of Axis at El Alamein preserving British power in Egypt and Middle East.
1946	Collapse of Anglo-Egyptian talks on new treaty.
1948–49	State of Israel established: Arab armies, including Egypt, defeated.
1951	Egyptians launch guerrilla attacks in attempt to force Britain from Canal base.

1952 (Jan.)	Black Saturday Anti-British riots in Cairo.
1952 (July)	Free Officers seize power. General Neguib President and Prime Minister.
1953 (June)	Egypt proclaimed republic.
1954 (July)	Establishment of militant radio station, 'Voice of the Arabs'.
1954 (Oct.)	Anglo-Egyptian agreement signed.
1954 (Nov.)	Neguib replaced as President and Prime Minister by Nasser.
1955 (Feb.)	Eden and Nasser meet in Cairo.
1955 (Apr.)	Britain accedes to the Baghdad Pact.
1955 (Sept.)	Nasser announces arms deal with Eastern Bloc.
1956 (Mar.)	After failure of ALPHA mission designed to bring about Arab–Israeli peace, Americans embark on OMEGA strategy to 'cut Nasser down to size'. OMEGA strongly supported by British who wish to go further and topple Nasser.
1956 (June)	Last British troops leave Egypt.
1956 (July)	Nasser announces nationalisation of Canal.
1956 (Oct.–Nov.)	Suez War after collusion between Britain, France and Israel.
1956 (Dec.)	Anglo-French forces withdraw from Egypt.
1957 (Apr.)	Crisis in Jordan – King Hussein removes pro-Nasser government.
1957 (Sept.–Nov.)	Crisis in Syria.
1958 (Feb.)	Creation of United Arab Republic by merger of Egypt and Syria.
1958 (July)	Iraqi monarchy toppled; US troops in Lebanon, UK troops in Jordan. UK and US forces withdraw in October.
1959 (Mar.)	Anglo-Egyptian Financial Agreement signed.
1959 (Dec.)	Anglo-Egyptian relations restored at chargé d'affaires level.
1960 (Sept.)	Nasser and Macmillan meet at United Nations in New York.
1961 (June)	Kuwait crisis necessitates deployment of UK troops there.
1961 (Sept.)	UAR collapses after military coup in Syria.
1962 (Sept.)	Yemen revolution – UAR troops deployed.
1963 (Feb.)	UK Embassy closed in Yemen after UK refuses to recognise republican regime. Qasim regime toppled in Iraq.
1963 (Mar.)	Pro-Nasser coup in Syria.

1963 (Oct.)	Macmillan resigns; Home becomes Prime Minister.
1964 (Feb.)	Nasser launches anti-British propaganda and subversive campaign.
1964 (Mar.)	British retaliatory raid on the fort at Harib in the YAR.
1964 (May)	Revolt in the Radfan province of South Arabia.
1964 (Nov.)	Harold Wilson Prime Minister UK.
1965 (Dec.)	UAR severs relations with Britain over Rhodesian crisis.
1967 (May–June)	Crisis over Straits of Tiran leads to third Arab–Israeli war.

— 1 —

Introduction: Delusions of Grandeur in the Middle East

OWING TO a combination of historical and economic factors, Britain remained the most important European power in the Middle East until well into the 1960s. While British influence certainly faded, particularly between 1955 and 1962, when a combination of disastrous misjudgement at Suez and straitened economic circumstances forced a retrenchment, it remained a significant military and political power in the region. Furthermore, after 1962, British governments became more determined to hold on to their remaining positions in the Persian Gulf, as the value of Gulf oil continued to increase in significance. Britain remained the most visible outside opponent of Arab nationalism whose most important exponent was President Nasser of Egypt. Nasser was committed to driving Britain out of the region. As a result, between 1955 and 1967, Britain and Egypt engaged in diplomatic, political and military confrontation in the Middle East. Egypt, perhaps with the exception of the Soviet Union, was arguably Britain's most persistent foreign policy opponent of the period. Anglo-Egyptian relations of this period, except for a brief interregnum (1959–62) of détente, were constantly strained and tense. An irreconcilable conflict akin to a cold war existed.[1] On four occasions after the Suez crisis of 1956, British governments considered military action against Nasser.[2] British statesmen, especially prominent Conservatives, saw the figure of Nasser behind every anti-Western and anti-British activity in the Middle East. They were convinced Nasser was attempting to wrest Britain's Middle Eastern position, threatening its oil and economic security. While the United States saw Nasser as a minor danger in comparison to the Soviet Union in the Middle East, British leaders viewed him as their most dangerous regional enemy. None of the five British prime ministers of the period, Winston Churchill, Anthony Eden, Harold Macmillan, Sir Alec Douglas-Home and Harold Wilson, were able to establish a reasonable *modus vivendi* with Nasser for any significant period of time. To Harold Macmillan, whose premiership

dominates this study, the Egyptian leader was the 'Mussolini of Egypt
... determined to foster discontent and promote trouble in every Arab
State'.[3] Peter Clarke notes that 'Nasser seems to have stalked the pages
of the [Macmillan] diary like an over-promoted understudy for Hitler'.[4]
It is telling that diplomatic relations were severed under both a
Conservative government (over Suez) and a Labour government (over
Rhodesia) despite the avowed intention of the latter to improve
relations. The Conservatives and Labour may have had differences of
emphasis in their foreign policy platform but the aims and the results
were broadly the same.

The focus of this study is British policy towards Nasser's Egypt from
the Egyptian revolution to the aftermath of the Six Day War in 1967.
The period is dominated by two wars, Suez and the Six Day War. The
former was to make Nasser the great Arab nationalist champion –
whilst providing Britain with probably its greatest post-war foreign
policy failure. The Six Day War was to switch the focus of Nasser's
foreign policy from attacks on British bases and conservative Arab
regimes to battling rather unsuccessfully for the return of Egyptian
territory lost to Israel. Indeed, he was reduced to asking his most
reactionary Arab foes, the Saudi royal family, for a subvention to allow
him to continue the struggle against Israel and, by 1970, the Soviet
Union was providing thousands of troops for the air defence of Egypt.
Ironically his career began with thousands of British troops occupying
Egyptian bases and ended with thousands of Soviet troops doing
likewise. For Britain, the Six Day War provided final illustration of its
Middle Eastern impotence, as it was unable to keep the peace despite
the vast expenditure in bases and infrastructure for just such a purpose.
Furthermore, this military presence failed to prevent an Arab oil
boycott after the war, demonstrating that a military presence in the
Middle East could not secure the primary object of British policy in the
Middle East – the free production and transit of oil to Britain. At the
beginning of 1968, with sterling devalued, Britain decided to withdraw
from the Middle East.[5]

The literature on Anglo-Egyptian relations based on primary British
and American documents for the period until 1956 is excellent. Suez is,
perhaps, the most studied post-war British foreign policy event.[6]
Afterwards the material, especially on the British side, is less rich. Nigel
John Ashton, and Professor Ritchie Ovendale have written the best
accounts of the period based on British documents.[7] Both are more
concerned with Britain's wider Middle Eastern policy than British
policy towards Egypt – which is the central focus of this study. They
do, however, make considerable use of post-Suez British documentation. Both of the studies end in the early 1960s. My study encompasses

a wider period, 1952 to 1967. I have also been fortunate in the release of previously classified material in the United Kingdom Public Record Office and the United States National Archives under recent governmental initiatives, which were not available to the above authors. Particularly interesting material is published here for the first time on the Syrian crisis of 1957, the Yemen crisis of 1964 and the Six Day War. This study also utilises the large number of memoirs, biographies and diaries of presidents, ministers and diplomats.[8] Equally some valuable studies of Britain's disengagement from the Middle East in the 1960s have been written. While many are excellent, they are not document-based.[9] The different release procedures for American archives have seen a vastly greater output of material on American policy. American-based studies are focused on the position of the United States in the Middle East and its policy towards Egypt. Most tend to play down the role of the British, or focus on an aspect of the Middle East, such as the Arab–Israeli conflict, which Britain kept out of as much as possible, particularly after 1956.

President Nasser is perhaps unique in modern British history in that he seemed to vex the British Conservative Party establishment far more than he ever became a figure of hate among the British public. To many Conservative MPs, he never advanced beyond the rank of colonel. George Brown, the Labour Foreign Secretary, complained in July 1967 about this disrespect in a debate on the recent Six Day War: 'Not one spokesman on the opposition side of the House has managed to refer to "President" Nasser. The most polite called him Colonel Nasser; the least polite called him Dictator Nasser.'[10] Despite the feelings and exaggerated fears propounded by some Conservatives, Nasser, unlike Hitler and Mussolini, never quite entered the popular pantheon of villains.[11] Other Conservative ministers, such as Ian Gilmour and Anthony Nutting, were on good terms with him. Nutting resigned over Suez and went on to be a very sympathetic biographer of Nasser. The four Conservative prime ministers who were in office during his leadership mistrusted and feared him to a degree that might surprise contemporary observers. The names of Saladin, Mussolini and Hitler were used consistently and with little historical basis to describe Nasser by senior ministers such as Anthony Eden, Macmillan and Selwyn Lloyd. Kennedy Trevakis, a British High Commissioner to Aden in the 1960s, and a consistent advocate of strong measures against Nasser, perhaps best encapsulates the problem of Anglo-Egyptian relations in the 1950s and 1960s:

Once we had left Suez, we had been told we could expect Nasser to welcome partnership with ourselves and the west. But it was not

partnership that he wanted. It was Britain's position of paramountcy … Having emerged as a leader of the neutralist world at
the Afro-Asian Conference at Bandung in April 1955, Nasser in
effect declared a cold war on Britain, with the object of removing
her from the Middle East.[12]

While in general, after Suez, Britain abandoned its own bid for
regional paramountcy, it remained resolute in its determination to
oppose Nasser's ambitions to gain its former position. It was the Tory
broadsheet, the *Daily Telegraph*, that held him in most contempt right
up until his death, and indeed received a request from the Foreign
Office to moderate its coverage of Egypt in 1960.[13] Liberal and left-wing
opinion in Britain had a more ambiguous relationship with Nasser.
Richard Crossman was a good example of this, holding him in some
regard as an anti-colonial figure, whilst being a passionate supporter
of Israel.[14]

Paradoxically, Nasser seemed to appropriate the language of one of
the most famous foreign policy statements of that most Conservative
hero, Winston Churchill. In a speech in Belgium in 1948, Churchill had
spoken of Britain being at the centre of three interlocking circles of
Commonwealth/Empire, the English-speaking alliance and Europe.
Churchill claimed that

> These three majestic circles are co-existent and if they are linked
> together there is no force or combination which could overthrow
> them or even challenge them. Now, if you think of the three inter-
> linked circles you will see that we are the only country which has
> a great part in every one of them.[15]

British foreign policy until the 1960s was dominated by an attempt
to both balance and maintain these pre-eminent roles. Rather
coincidentally, Nasser outlined in his pamphlet, *The Philosophy of the
Revolution*, that Egypt too lay at the centre of three overlapping though
not necessarily conflicting circles – an inner Arab, an African and a
broader Islamic circle which encompassed the greater part of the first
two. This policy was only formulated into a foreign policy doctrine
after Nasser had seized power for himself in 1954.[16] It will be a central
argument of this book that these similar, yet mutually incompatible,
'geopolitical conceits'[17] were one of the primary reasons for tension in
Anglo-Egyptian relations for the following decade. They became part
of the vital national interests of the two countries. For Britain, the three
circles were equally important until the late 1960s, when the European
circle became dominant, while Nasser always emphasised the

importance of the Arab circle. The Arab circle had the potential to allow resource-impoverished Egypt to become a strong player on the world scene. During abortive Arab unity talks in 1963, he spelt out such a vision:

> With the inclusion of Iraq in a union of Egypt and Syria the unified state would secure the oil wells and pipelines in the east to the Suez Canal, from Asia to Africa. The Iraqi army would be brought up to Israel's borders. Its possibilities would be greater than those of France, commanding a population of fifty million.[18]

A shared history and past were also of the utmost importance. Nasser emphasised the suffering at the hands of Turkish and Western oppressors that Egypt and the other Arabs had been through:

> There is no doubt, the Arab circle is the most important and the most closely connected with us – its history merges with us, and we have suffered the same hardships, lived the same crises and when we fell prostrate under the spikes of the horses of conquerors they lay with us.[19]

Despite the Anglo-Egyptian agreement of 1954 and the end of the British presence in Egypt, the need to expel Britain from the Arab world was an overriding concern of Nasser. The English-speaking alliance with its wish to bring the Arab states into the Western alliance system threatened Nasser's ambitions in the Arab circle whilst the Commonwealth/Empire circle with its oil requirements in the Gulf, communications through the Middle East and the sprawling British African Empire impinged on both the African and Arab circles. The Egyptian newspaper, *Al-Ahram*, pointed out the incompatibility of the British and Egyptian foreign policy philosophies in the starkest terms, arguing that: 'Nationalism and Imperialism were as incompatible as darkness and light.'[20]

Nasser also shared with all contemporary British prime ministers from Churchill to Wilson a 'delusion of grandeur', that their respective countries had the ability to 'punch above their weight' in international affairs, forgetting that it was past fortune that had gained Britain the Empire and an accident of geography that Egypt lay on the Suez Canal adjacent to the Arab world. The British felt that they needed to maintain their global role for economic reasons. Conversely the vast expenditure on men and material to defend possessions against foes such as Nasser merely fed Britain's need to dominate the strategically and economically important Middle East. Even when Britain in the early 1960s abandoned its formal empire with almost unseemly haste, it attempted to maintain its influence through the 'east-of-Suez' role.[21] Nasser, likewise, in his attempt to dominate the Arab circle overextended his reach in Syria and the Yemen, and most spectacularly in his final bid to seize leadership of the Arab world in the build-up to the Six Day War. Between 1955 and 1967, Britain felt bound to oppose virtually all of Nasser's bids for regional leadership. To this end it allied itself with an at times unpleasant crew of Arab allies (Nuri, King Saud, Qasim and Yemeni royalists).[22] This disparate group was united only by the threat posed to them by Nasser and a desire to frustrate the Egyptian leader's bids for regional dominance. Similarly, Nasser felt bound to oppose Britain's attempts to maintain initially its paramountcy and latterly its influence in the Arab circle through regional pacts and military bases. It was a recipe for continuous conflict that was only resolved by the final abandonment by both nations of their attempts to maintain leading roles in their circles in 1967. Then both delusions of grandeur would be shattered almost simultaneously with the catastrophic defeat of Egypt by Israel and by the devaluation of sterling and the abandonment of the global role by the Labour government in Britain. It was the shattering of these illusions that have meant that British and Egyptian relations since 1967 have, on the whole, been excellent. Britain has maintained strong economic and political ties to the Middle East. The most notable would be the huge armament contracts signed with the Saudis in the 1980s and Britain's part in the coalition against Saddam Hussein – another dictator compared to dictators of the 1930s.

There were other factors such as the intense dislike for Britain felt by Nasser and Egyptians engendered by 70 years of British domination. It was almost impossible for an Egyptian nationalist like Nasser growing up in the 1930s to have anything but feelings of loathing and fear towards Britain. Many are recorded by his biographers.[23] This hatred of the British was almost certainly caused by the arrogant behaviour of many of the British rulers and diplomats displayed towards the Egyptians. This arrogance was not just in the Egyptian mind either. There was a firm conviction among most of the proconsuls which Britain sent to Egypt that they were looking after British financial and strategic interests only. The hidden-hand nature of the British hegemony in Egypt made it difficult for the Egyptians to rebel against it.

In an article published in 1964, Nasser's close confidant and chief propagandist, Mohammad Heikal, viewed the failure to improve Anglo-Egyptian relations in quasi-deterministic terms declaring that 'it is a will of history which imposes a real conflict between the destinies of the two countries'. He went on to claim that 'Egypt cannot feel dignified while the United Kingdom remains in control of the Gulf' as it reminded Egypt of 70 years of British occupation.[24] This burden of history was to cast a serious shadow over Anglo-Egyptian relations. Before Suez in 1956, it was the invasion of Egypt in 1882, the 1942 humiliation of King Farouk, or the events preceding Black Saturday in 1952. As one reads through the documentary material, one is surprised how many times mistakes and loose comments created crises and tensions out of nothing. Colin Crowe, a senior British diplomat in Cairo in the late 1950s and early 1960s, lamented that every step forward in Anglo-Egyptian relations was soon followed by a setback:

> I do not know what spell or curse afflicts Anglo-Egyptian relations, but one there must be. It is extraordinary how often when productive steps have been taken to improve relations, or they have actually been improved for a spell, that something crops up or somebody – on one side or the other, does something stupid and back one goes to square one.[25]

However, the frequency with which these crises occurred suggests that deeper, more fundamental, reasons underlay the Anglo-Egyptian antagonism. This study attempts to trace them.

NOTES

1. See S.J. Ball, *The Cold War: An International History* (London, Arnold, 1998), 1, for this particular definition of Cold War. The idea of a cold war between the radical and conservative forces in the Middle East is not new. Malcolm H. Kerr, *The Arab Cold War: Gamel Abd-al Nasir and his Rivals 1958–1970*, 3rd edn (Oxford, Oxford University Press, 1971) and Uriel Dann, *King Hussein and the Challenge of Arab Radicalism* (Oxford, Oxford University Press, 1989).
2. My study will demonstrate these as the Syrian crisis of 1957, the aftermath of the Iraqi revolution of 1958, the Yemen crisis of 1964 and the blockade of the Straits of Tiran in 1967.
3. Harold Macmillan, *Pointing the Way: 1959–61* (London, Macmillan, 1972), p. 381.
4. Peter Clarke, *A Question of Leadership from Gladstone to Blair* (London, Penguin, 1999), p. 229.
5. The British bases in the Middle East that were evacuated were Aden (1967), the Gulf and Libya (1970–71). Singapore, Britain's main overseas base, was evacuated at the same time. Hong Kong was all that remained of Britain's east-of-Suez role afterwards. The classic study is P. Darby, *British Defence Policy East of Suez, 1947–68* (Oxford, Oxford University Press and RIIA, 1973).
6. While it is clear that a weeding of controversial material was carried out, in British archives particularly, admirably detailed books on Suez have been written using British, French, Israeli and American documentary evidence. A brief selection of the finest are: K. Kyle, *Suez* (New York, St Martin's Press, 1991), W. Scott Lucas, *Divided We Stand* (London, John Curtis, 1991), W. Roger Louis

and Roger Owen (eds), *Suez 1956: The Crisis and its Consequences* (Oxford, Oxford University Press, 1989) and David Carlton, *Britain and the Suez Crisis* (Oxford, Blackwell, 1988). From Israel, Mordechai Bar-On, *The Gates of Gaza: Israel's Road to Suez and Back* (New York, St Martin's Press, 1994) and Selwyn Ilan Troen and Moshe Shemesh (eds), *The Suez–Sinai Crisis: Retrospective and Reappraisal* (London, Frank Cass, 1990) are the most significant. The most recent specialist account is Saul Kelly and Anthony Gorst (eds), *Whitehall and the Suez Crisis* (London, Frank Cass, 2000). Whilst being superb pieces of investigative journalism and getting the story more or less right, older works such as Hugh Thomas, *The Suez Affair* (London, Penguin, 1970) have to an extent been superseded. A number of memoirs also stand out. They range from the excellent: Evelyn Shuckburgh, *Descent to Suez: Diaries 1951–56* (London, Weidenfeld & Nicolson, 1986) to the slightly untrustworthy Selwyn Lloyd, *Suez 1956: A Personal Account* (London, Jonathan Cape, 1978). Anthony Nutting, *No End of a Lesson* (London, Constable, 1967), written by Lloyd's deputy, was a path breaker in our understanding of Suez and in cutting through government secrecy. From the Egyptian point of view are: Mohammed H. Heikal, *Cutting the Lion's Tail: Suez through Egyptian Eyes* (London, Deutsch, 1986) and M. Fawzi, *Suez 1956: An Egyptian Perspective* (London, Shorouk International, 1987).

7. Nigel John Ashton, *Eisenhower, Macmillan and the Problem of Nasser* (London, Macmillan, 1996) and Ritchie Ovendale, *Britain, the United States and the Transfer of Power in the Middle East* (Leicester, Leicester University Press, 1996).

8. Prime Ministers. Macmillan's deep concern with the Middle East is evident from his voluminous memoirs heavily based on Macmillan's own archive (which is still unavailable for researchers) and hand-written diaries. Harold Macmillan, *Riding the Storm: 1956–59* (London, Macmillan, 1971), *Pointing the Way: 1959–61* (1972) and *At the End of the Day: 1961–63* (1973). His official biographer reflects this: Alistair Horne, *Macmillan*, Vol. II, *1957–86* (London, Macmillan, 1989). Sir Alec Douglas-Home's biographer pays scant attention to the Middle East crisis of 1964. D.R. Thorpe, *Sir Alec Douglas-Home* (London, Sinclair-Stevenson, 1996). Harold Wilson's *The Labour Government* (London, Weidenfeld & Nicolson/Michael Joseph, 1971) makes little mention of the Middle East besides a wholly misleading account of the British government's handling of the Six Day War. Foreign secretaries provide equally variable material. D.R. Thorpe, *Selwyn Lloyd* (London, Cape, 1981) is again more concerned with personality than policy and the vast bulk of the primary research in the PRO is for the pre-1956 period. George Brown, *In My Way* (London, Gollancz, 1971) has some material on Anglo-Egyptian relations. The history of the Wilson government is dominated by R. Crossman, *The Diaries of a Cabinet Minister*, 3 vols (London, Hamish Hamilton, 1975–77) and Barbara Castle, *The Castle Diaries: 1964–70* (London, Macmillan, 1984). Their most important material on the Middle East concerns the Six Day War in 1967. Philip Zeigler, *Wilson* (London, Weidenfeld & Nicolson, 1993) has material on Wilson and the east-of-Suez role, as well as the Six Day War. Denis Healey, *The Time of My Life* (London, Penguin, 1989) while being a little anecdotal at times again has material on east of Suez and defence planning from probably the most significant defence and foreign policy minister of the Wilson years.

9. Diplomatic memoirs of interest include Charles Johnston, *The Brink of Jordan* (London, Hamilton, 1972) and *The View from Steamer Point: Being an Account of Three Years in Aden* (London, Collins, 1964), which provide interesting material on how one of Britain's most important Middle Eastern ambassadors viewed Nasser. The retreat from Aden and the Persian Gulf is recalled in Kennedy Trevakis, *Shades of Amber: A South Arabian Episode* (London, Hutchinson, 1968),

which describes his term as High Commissioner in Aden between 1963 and 1964 and his battle with Egyptian-inspired subversion. It, of course, leaves out all the interesting bits. Humphrey Trevelyan, *The Middle East in Revolution* (London, Macmillan, 1970) is another inside account of the ending of British influence in the Middle East. The best secondary accounts of the British withdrawal from the Middle East are Glen Barbour-Paul, *The End of Empire in the Middle East: Britain's Relinquishment of Power in her Last Three Arab Dependencies* (Cambridge, Cambridge University Press, 1991), which is a scholarly survey by a distinguished former diplomat, and Karl Pieragostini, *Britain, Aden and South Arabia: Abandoning Empire* (London, Macmillan, 1991) which uses some declassified American documents under the Freedom of Information Act.

10. *Hansard*, HOC Debs, 749, Col. 2115, 6 July 1967.
11. In an interview with Sir Robin Day a few months after Suez, Nasser came across as very reasonable and there was no public outcry about this great enemy of Britain being interviewed on television. Kyle, *Suez*, p. 548. This is not to say that he was a popular figure.
12. Trevakis, *Shades of Amber*, p. 68.
13. PRO FO 371/150927, VG 1051/60G, Stevens to Crowe (Cairo), Top Secret. Oddly enough the *Telegraph* published M. Heikal's memoir, *Nasser: The Cairo Documents* (London, New English Library, 1972) after his death.
14. In a conversation with Archbishop Makarios, Crossman said, 'We really hit it off when we discovered that we could say openly to each other how much we liked Nasser as a person, how much we were invigorated by his presence, how imaginative and creative we found him.' 10 September 1966, Crossman, *Diaries of a Cabinet Minister*, Vol. II, p. 30.
15. Joseph Frankel, *British Foreign Policy 1945–1973* (Oxford, RIIA/Oxford University Press, 1973), p. 157.
16. G.A. Nasser, *The Philosophy of the Revolution* (Cairo, Ministry of National Guidance, no date), p. 56.
17. As described by Henry Wilson, *African Decolonisation* (London, Weidenfeld & Nicolson, 1994), p. 155.
18. P.J. Vatikiotis, *Nasser and his Generation* (London, Croom Helm, 1978), pp. 226–7.
19. Nasser, *Philosophy of the Revolution*, p. 56. See also Majid Khadduri, *Political Trends in the Arab World: The Role of Ideas and Ideals in Politics* (Baltimore and London, Johns Hopkins Press, 1970), p. 172.
20. *Al-Ahram*, 17 March 1961. PRO FO 371/155809, VG 1051/110, reported in Beeley (Cairo) to FO No. 25, 17 March 1961.
21. The wider issues of the global or east-of-Suez role are discussed in Darby, *British Defence Policy East of Suez*, J. Pickering, *Britain's Withdrawal from East of Suez: The Politics of Retrenchment* (London, Macmillan, 1998), R.F. Holland, *Pursuit of Greatness: Britain and the World Role, 1900–1970* (London, Fontana, 1990), and the essays in W. Kaiser and G. Staerck (eds), *British Foreign Policy 1955–64: Contracting Options* (London, Macmillan, 2000).
22. The most important studies of the other Arab states and Nasser include the aforementioned Kerr, *Arab Cold War*, T.Y. Hasou, *The Struggle for the Arab World* (London, Routledge, 1985) and Dann, *King Hussein*.
23. Whenever as a child he saw an aeroplane overhead, he used to shout 'O God almighty may a calamity overtake the English.' Robert Stephens, *Nasser* (London, Penguin, 1971), p. 29.
24. *Al-Ahram*, 26 June 1964, as recorded in VG 1051/16A PRO FO 371/178594.
25. Crowe Manuscript, SAC, 59.

— 2 —

The Historical Context of Anglo-Egyptian Relations, 1800–1952

THAT MOST IMPORTANT COUNTRY

EGYPT WAS the 'swing door' of the British Empire.[1] Lying on the Isthmus of Suez, Egypt controlled the shortest overland route from Britain to British India, the Far Eastern possessions and the Australian continent. Command of the isthmus by a hostile power would have endangered Britain's control of these imperial possessions. With the loss of the American colonies in 1783, Britain's eastern Empire, centred on India, greatly increased in importance to it. Napoleon illustrated the centrality of Egypt to British power with his ambitious attempt to capture it and the overland route to India in 1798. While the bid to seize control of the overland route floundered due to Nelson's victory at the Battle of the Nile, it caused near panic in ministerial circles in London.[2] Throughout the nineteenth century, it remained a source of concern to British statesmen, who feared the growing French influence in the eastern Mediterranean.

Egypt was nominally a part of the Ottoman Empire during the nineteenth century as it had been for over 500 years. However, in reality, it was increasingly independent under a succession of powerful Khedives (viceroys). The Khedives were reformist, and sought to transform their country into an industrialised society with the aid of European expertise and finance, partly to increase Egypt's independence from Constantinople. The centrepiece of this industrialisation programme was the building of a canal along the Isthmus of Suez by a French company between 1859 and 1869. Allowing ships to sail through Egypt directly, the canal dramatically increased the strategic significance of Egypt to Britain. Moreover, the modernisation of Egypt was paid for by enormous loans from French and British bankers, which the Egyptian government found increasingly difficult to service.

British investment was driven by the fear that the growing French financial and political influence over Egypt could not go unchallenged for fear that they would gain control over the canal route.[3] In 1875, Benjamin Disraeli, the British Prime Minister, took the opportunity offered by Egypt's need for liquidity to buy, for the British government, the Khedive Ismail's (1863–79) 44 per cent share of the Suez Canal Company. Again the main objective of this purchase was to prevent the French gaining exclusive control. *The Times* commented that: 'We have now an abiding stake in the security and welfare of Egypt.'[4]

However, Disraeli's injection of liquidity failed to solve the huge financial problems of the Khedive. The European powers, led by France and Britain, imposed a financial settlement, on Khedive Tawfig (1879–92), which saw two-thirds of the revenue of Egypt going to service the enormous foreign debt which it had accumulated.[5] By 1881, the financial pressure was becoming too much to bear for an increasingly disaffected Egyptian army which had not been paid for months. In September of that year, a senior officer, Arabi Pasha, carried out a *coup d'état* and made himself Minister for War. Fearing that the Egyptians might default on the huge loans that British and French capital had poured into Egypt and the inability of the Egyptians to protect foreign citizens, the British Prime Minister, William Ewart Gladstone, deployed naval forces to Alexandria in a show of force. Initially the expedition was supposed to be a joint effort with the French. Indeed an Anglo-French joint note was issued in January 1882 as support for the Khedive against Arabi. However, the French withdrew from the proposed mission, letting the British deal with the crisis alone. In May 1882 a naval force was sent to Egypt. This had the effect of inciting anti-foreign feeling leading to riots in Alexandria which left 50 Europeans and 170 Egyptians dead.[6] On 10 July 1882, after rejecting a British ultimatum to disarm forts around the city, the Royal Navy bombarded Alexandria.[7] The bombardment only served to increase the disorder and anarchy in Egypt as well as further threatening the safety of the large community of foreigners. The Liberal government in London decided to order an invasion of Egypt and crush the Arabi regime – actions which went very much against the ethical inclinations of Gladstone's foreign policy. In this case, he appears to have fallen in with the arguments of the Liberal imperialists in his Cabinet such as Joseph Chamberlain who wished to overthrow the Arabi government, not in order to protect the British and French loans and investments, but 'to protect the Canal and exact reparations for the Alexandria outrages'. Gladstone, according to Gallagher and Robinson, was particularly swayed by the argument about the Canal and the need to protect the India route.[8] In the House of Commons, he justified the intervention on moral and *realpolitik* grounds.[9]

The following month, a British expeditionary force, under General Wolseley, defeated Arabi and his army at Tel-el-Kebir and brought the country under *de facto* British control for the next 40 years. Gladstone despatched Lord Dufferin to Egypt to see how the country should be administered in the future. Egypt became an imperial hybrid. It was neither a colony nor a protectorate and outwardly was independent under the Khedive, who remained under nominal Ottoman control. The reality was somewhat different. Egypt was controlled by a British-run civil service and the 'ultimate sanction was in the hands of the British consul and the English advisers in the Government departments'. Milner encapsulates the reality in his description of Egypt as the 'veiled Protectorate'.[10] The personification of British rule was Lord Cromer who held the rather benign and unimportant-sounding titles of British Consul-General and Agent from 1883 to 1907. However, he controlled the levers of power in Egypt, damping down unrest and restoring the country to solvency. Cromer operated in a paternalistic manner, treating the Egyptians and any nationalistic ambitions they held with contempt. Britain made over 66 declarations of its intention to quit Egypt between 1882 and 1919. A.G. Hopkins argues that this did not happen because 'Britain had important interests to defend in Egypt and she was prepared to withdraw only if conditions guaranteeing the security of these interests were met – and they never were.'[11] A further complicating matter was the Sudan which was conquered by the British in 1898. They agreed to share sovereignty with the Egyptians who saw it as part of Egypt.

In 1914 Britain found itself at war with the Ottoman Empire, which finally necessitated that Britain formalise the relationship with Egypt in a protectorate. The reigning Khedive, who attempted to ally himself with the Turks, was overthrown to make way for a more quiescent figurehead. The First World War broke Turkish power in the Middle East. In the middle of the war, Britain and France agreed – under the Sykes–Picot understanding – to arbitrarily divide up the Turkish possessions of the Middle East between them. The League of Nations mandate system gave this shabby exercise in great power cynicism both a retrospective legality and a more progressive ring. The British High Commissioner in Egypt had during the war entered into correspondence with the Arab leader, the Sherif Hussein of Mecca. He wanted and received – subject to a rubric of reservations that rendered it in British eyes meaningless – a pledge of British support for an Arab state that would include most of the Ottoman Empire.[12] The grandiose, but essentially empty, promises of self-determination for subject peoples made, most notably, by the American President Wilson in his Fourteen Points and other speeches further fuelled the sense of betrayal of Arabs.

Egypt shared in the general Arab sense of betrayal by the British, and was shaken by an uprising in March 1919 caused by the decision to deport to Malta an Egyptian delegation (Wafd),[13] which asked that Britain grant the independence that had been promised when Britain needed Arab aid. The disturbances that ensued cost the lives of thousands of Egyptians as the British, in one of their forgotten wars of Empire, crushed the rebellion with great brutality. Field Marshal Allenby, the Commander of British Middle Eastern forces, was made High Commissioner and Lord Milner, the Secretary of State for War, was sent out from Britain to inquire into the disturbances. Strongly supported by Allenby, he chose, surprisingly, considering his record on other imperial questions, to conciliate Egyptian opinion as much as possible. He believed that in order to 'deflate the Wafdist cause, Egypt should be offered independence and a treaty of alliance that would guarantee Britain's imperial interests'.[14] He saw that the key issue was the achievement of an agreement that protected British interest in the Canal. In February 1922, a reluctant Cabinet was persuaded by Allenby to accept his proposals. The Allenby declaration was issued later that month. It conceded formal independence to Egypt and recognised the Khedive as King, but reserved 'absolutely' for the British government the following: the security of the communications of the British Empire in Egypt; the defence of Egypt against foreign intervention; the protection of foreign interests and the Sudan. The Allenby declaration did not mean all that much. It was merely the concession of 'little more than a constitutional nicety'. The Colonial Secretary was at pains to point out to the Dominion governments that it preserved fully the 'status quo with regard to the special interests of the British Empire in Egypt'.[15] The problem of base rights for British troops was not finally resolved until 1936 because neither the Wafd, which had transformed itself into the most powerful nationalist movement in Egypt, nor the royal court was willing to sign a treaty which would be acceptable to the British – for fear that it would lay them open to attacks by the other side.[16] Martin Daly argues that the failure to agree on the unification of Egypt and the Sudan was the key reason that the negotiations failed.[17] Furthermore various small pressure groups, the Muslim Brotherhood (Ikhwan) and Young Egypt used street protest to prevent a moderate compromise.[18] However, the Egyptian government finally gave in 1936. The Anglo-Egyptian treaty of 1936 negotiated by the young British Foreign Secretary, Anthony Eden, gave Britain wide-ranging military rights in Egypt including the occupation of the Canal Zone, an area that is roughly equivalent in size to Wales. Other rights included full use of the naval base at Alexandria and an alliance with Egypt.[19] The flaw in the treaty was that it satisfied British security interests without really raising the Egyptians from their previous status as second-class partners. Miles Lampson, the British Ambassador, continued to interfere regularly in Egyptian internal politics and believed it his duty to maintain a Cromer-style influence despite Egyptian independence.[20]

When the Second World War broke out the British used Egypt as their main Middle Eastern base. Such was its importance that, in 1941, Prime Minister Winston Churchill, in a directive, could state that the 'loss of Egypt and the Middle East would be a disaster of the first magnitude to Great Britain, second only to successful invasion [of Britain] and final conquest'.[21] In retrospect his analysis does not seem that far off the mark. From Egypt, Britain was able to carry out the military campaigns that secured Allied control of the Middle East, and provided the base area from which the British Eighth Army finally defeated the Axis forces in the Western desert and North Africa. Egypt also acted as the chief rear base for other operations in Italy and Greece. Egypt was sullen in its wartime co-operation with the British. It broke off relations with the Axis powers but refused to declare war on them. The well-founded suspicion among British diplomats in Egypt was that high-level Egyptians found fascism and Nazism attractive ideologies and that they hoped for an Axis victory, which remained a distinct possibility until Montgomery's victory over the Italians and the Africa Corps at the Battle of El Alamein in the autumn of 1942.[22] The British particularly distrusted the Egyptian King Farouk. In May 1942, the British wanted Farouk to appoint a pro-Allied Prime Minister from the *Wafd* party. Farouk was reluctant; he had long held a deep antipathy to the *Wafd*. With the royal palace surrounded by British tanks, the British Ambassador, Miles Lampson, confronted Farouk with an ultimatum. The choices offered were unpalatable: install Britain's choice of prime minister or sign a document of abdication. Farouk – more noted for his seedy reading matter than for his heroism – complied with Lampson's demand.[23] While the Egyptian population disliked their notoriously venal king, they were not pleased to see their nation's ruler so comprehensively humiliated. The whole affair had exposed the sham of Egyptian independence. Indeed one observer has argued that the action was counter-productive as it allowed the wronged but still useless King to restore a strong position after the war.[24] Among the many deeply affected by this was Gamal Abdul Nasser, then a junior army officer but later to emerge as arguably the most significant Arab leader since Saladin. He wrote: 'In the army the event wrought a radical change in the morale of the officers, they now spoke of sacrifice and devotion to duty – of readiness to give their lives for the dignity of the mother country.'[25]

POST-WAR RELATIONS

At the end of the Second World War, Britain remained the paramount Middle Eastern power. Its positions in the region appeared even more firmly entrenched than after the First World War. There were over 50,000 British troops in Egypt occupying the major cities of Cairo and Alexandria as well as the Canal Zone. British military planners re-iterated at the end of the war that the region was second only to the British Isles in terms of its strategic value. The Chiefs of Imperial General Staff in Britain argued that, for Britain to remain a great power, it was imperative to remain in control of the Mediterranean and the Middle East. The Egyptian base was to remain a vital cornerstone of British strategy both as a guardian overlooking Britain's vast Middle Eastern responsibilities and in the post-war nuclear age as a potential airbase for launching atomic attacks against the Soviet Union.[26] The Chiefs of Staff emphasised that

> No effective Middle East Defence can be undertaken without a suitable base to support it … Only in Egypt can such facilities be found on the scale required, and nowhere else in the Middle East could existing facilities be expanded to form a substitute except at prohibitive cost.[27]

The problem was that Britain's strategic requirements needed squaring with growing Egyptian and Arab nationalism. The Chief of the Imperial General Staff, Alan Brooke, visited Egypt and the Middle East in the autumn of 1945. In discussions with King Farouk and his advisers, he believed there was a chance that a Middle Eastern defence confederation based on partnership with the rulers might be a promising line of approach. Indeed with Transjordan, just such an approach proved successful.[28] Making deals with the kings and pashas was at variance with the ideas of the Foreign Secretary, Ernest Bevin, who wanted a security arrangement with the Middle East combined with regional economic development to appease the Arab masses.[29]

Bevin was convinced of the value of the Middle East far more than his Prime Minister, Clement Attlee, who questioned in 1946–47 his Foreign Secretary's and the Chiefs of Staff's assumptions about the region. He felt that Britain could not afford the burden of maintaining a massive military presence in the region – nor was it necessary. He produced a paper in March 1946, which Alan Bullock describes as 'amongst the most radical produced by a British Prime Minister in office' and what Corelli Barnett calls the 'most penetrating and percipient written by any British Statesman in the Twentieth Century'.[30] Attlee called for consideration of the fact that the Mediterranean could no longer be kept open in time of war owing to the increasing ability of airpower to close narrow shipping lanes such as the Mediterranean. If the Middle East was now indefensible against Russian attack and India soon to become independent, then the strategic rationale behind British strategic thinking for the previous three decades was redundant. The consequences of Attlee's thinking would have meant a severe truncation of Britain's global role and with key relevance to this argument the abandonment of the base at Suez and the evacuation of Egypt.[31] Britain's perilous economic condition offered another reason for getting out of Egypt. During the Second World War, the British had bought goods and services from the Egyptians, and as a result sterling balances to the value of £400 million were owed to the Egyptians. These remained unconvertible to dollars owing to the British mechanism known as 'blocking', but would eventually be so. Chancellor of the Exchequer Dalton feared that to maintain the base in Egypt – such was the British financial crisis in 1946 – would mean that Britain could find itself 'in the impossible position of borrowing money from the Egyptians in order to maintain our forces in Egypt'.[32] Despite these very powerful arguments, Bevin – 'the most masterful Foreign Secretary of the century' in the words of Peter Clarke – was able to get his way on the issue.[33] Middle Eastern commitments were to be maintained. Bevin had a strategy of sorts to share the burden. William Roger Louis, in his classic study of the British Empire in the Middle East, outlines how he sought to transform formal empire into an informal one while relying on American military muscle to deal with Soviet threats to the 'Northern Tier' stretching from Greece to Iran.[34]

Egypt had replied to Bevin's call for partnership by asking for a revision of the Anglo-Egyptian treaty on 20 December 1945. On 2 April 1946 the British government sent a delegation to Cairo to negotiate. The Chiefs of Staff were willing to compromise that British ground troops could go but that airbases were needed. The Egyptians, however, wanted a full British evacuation. The leader of the British delegation recommended accepting the Egyptians' demand. In May 1946 Bevin and Attlee agreed that they would publicly offer the withdrawal of all British forces from Egyptian territory before sitting down to discuss future defence arrangements.[35] This brought a furious reaction from Winston Churchill on the opposition benches. He accused the Labour government of 'scuttle'. He remained an inveterate opponent of compromise with the Egyptians. Bevin ignored Churchill's concerns and proceeded to withdraw British troops from Cairo and the other major cities to the Canal Zone by March 1948. He also tried to renegotiate a more palatable agreement on future British use of the base. The Chiefs of Staff had laid down in 1946 what the minimum requirements of any new treaty with Egypt should be. These were that base installations would be built up and that the base could be activated as soon as the British decreed that a state of emergency existed. Bevin chose to use this as his minimum position in negotiations against the advice, it must be said, of the Commander of British Land Forces Middle East, General Robertson.[36]

Unfortunately, Bevin's plans for a new partnership with Egypt were stillborn. Negotiations on the base soon were mixed up with the other issue that divided the two sides – the future of the Anglo-Egyptian Sudan. Egypt wanted that country – which was officially governed under an arrangement of joint sovereignty between them and the British – to be unified with Egypt under the Egyptian crown. Whoever controlled Sudan would control the headwaters of the Nile, the lifeblood of Egypt. It would also of course allow a massive expansion of the territory of Egypt. The British felt that the Sudan would be more malleable towards British policy if it were free from the influence of the Egyptians. At the end of January 1947, negotiations on the base broke down over the Sudan issue.[37] According to Bullock, this 'prejudiced any chance of agreement in the Anglo-Egyptian talks'.[38] Of all the many mistakes made in the long history of Anglo-Egyptian relations, this was perhaps the gravest error made on the Egyptian side. If the Egyptians had agreed to these terms Britain would have withdrawn its troops nearly a decade before it eventually did under the agreement negotiated by Nasser. He received no better terms on the Sudan or on the base in 1953–54 than could have been negotiated in 1946–47. For Britain, 20 years of cold war with Egypt were to follow. In between, Britain's image in the Arab world was irreparably damaged with its role in the creation of Israel out of the Palestine Mandate,[39] though the swiftness with which the United States and the Soviet Union recognised the state of Israel may well have meant that Britain's refusal to recognise Israel until after the Arab–Israeli war meant that the maintenance of some British influence in the Middle East was still possible.[40] However, the defeat of the British-supplied Arab armies convinced many Arabs including Colonel Gamal Abdul Nasser that Britain was deeply involved in betraying the Arab nation.[41] Revolutionary and nationalist feelings in the army were given impetus by defeat. According to Vatikiotis, it was 'their firm belief that their defeat in the field had been due mainly to the British control of Egyptian military training and arms supplies and to the involvement of the Palace and the politicians in several arms scandals'.[42] The Tripartite Declaration of 1950 saw the British, French and American governments pledged to control arms supplies to the region to prevent a Middle Eastern arms race. Furthermore, they also pledged to take action immediately to prevent 'violation of boundaries or armistice lines'.[43] By siding with the *status quo* it seemed to suggest to Arab opinion that the West were protecting Israel. At the same time the base issue rumbled on. Bevin seemed to be moving to a position whereby British civilian technicians would run the base in peacetime, which would remain under Egyptian control. British forces could then re-enter in wartime but this was proving hard to sell to hawks in the British military or to the Egyptians.[44] By the time Bevin had to resign, owing to ill health, as Foreign Secretary in 1951, his new imperial policy was in ruins and 'nowhere did it fail as spectacularly as in the Middle East'.[45]

In Egypt the royal regime began to disintegrate after the first Arab–Israeli war. This was partly caused by the performance of Egypt in the Palestine war, but the primary reason was the decision of King Farouk and the newly appointed *Wafd* Prime Minister, Mustafa al-Nahas, to pursue a policy of confrontation with Britain in the autumn of 1951. Nahas demanded the immediate evacuation of British troops and the unification of Egypt and the Sudan. He was provoked by the tougher line taken by Herbert Morrison, Bevin's successor as Foreign Secretary, on a new Anglo-Egyptian treaty. Morrison refused to withdraw British troops without an agreement that guaranteed British rights and tied Egypt into the Western alliance.[46] To the Egyptians, this seemed like an unacceptable ultimatum. Consequently, they rejected the British offer in April 1951.[47] There was a growing sense of anti-British feeling in Egypt during the summer of 1951. Ralph Stevenson, the Ambassador, warned, in a despatch, that the base and the British occupation meant the masses' 'bitter discontent with their lot in general can be easily focussed on an "occupation" which their demagogues have for so long represented as the cause of all the country's ills'.[48] The negotiations continued without any sign of breaking the deadlock. The prospects of a showdown with Egypt became real and imminent. As the Labour government entered its final days in the autumn of 1951 – beset by the Iranian oil crisis and the problems of financing a massive rearmament programme – Nahas decided to begin a confrontation.

The Korean War had spurred the rearmament programme. In Iran the British were faced with a nationalist regime led by Dr Mossadegh, who unilaterally nationalised the Anglo-Iranian Oil Company. In the summer and autumn of 1951, the Labour government was split between those such as Herbert Morrison, the new and maladroit Foreign

Secretary, and Shinwell, the Minister for Defence, who wanted to take military action to restore the British position, and the more realistic and sensible policies of Prime Minister Attlee. One reason given by the hawks was the need to show the Egyptians the ill-advisedness of trying something similar with the Suez Canal. In the end the evacuation of British citizens from Abadan was all that was carried out. Perhaps emboldened by the successful defiance of the Iranians, Nahas unilaterally revoked the 1936 treaty and rejected British proposals for a Middle East defence organisation. Tacit approval was given to fanatical Muslim Brotherhood guerrillas to attack the British base.[49] A US State Department official reporting on a recent trip to Egypt to the American Joint Chiefs of Staff was sure that compromise was impossible. He reported that 'the British are detested. The hatred against them is general and intense. It is shared by everyone in the country.'[50]

NOTES

1. As Anthony Eden described Egypt in 1929. Kyle, *Suez*, p. 7.
2. Lawrence James, *The Rise and Fall of the British Empire* (London, Abacus, 1995), p. 157.
3. J. Gallagher and R. Robinson (with Alice Denny), *The Victorians and Africa*, 2nd edn (London, Macmillan, 1981), p. 64.
4. Ronald Hyam, *Britain's Imperial Century* (London, Batsford, 1976), p. 251.
5. A.L. Sayyid-Marsot, 'The British Occupation of Egypt', in Andrew Porter, *The Oxford History of the British Empire*, Vol. III, *The Nineteenth Century* (Oxford, Oxford University Press, 1999), p. 653.
6. Sayyid-Marsot, 'British Occupation of Egypt', p. 654.
7. Peter Mansfield, *The British in Egypt* (London, Weidenfeld & Nicolson, 1971), p. 43.
8. Gallagher and Robinson, *The Victorians and Africa*, pp. 110–11.
9. Mansfield, *British in Egypt*, p. 47. More recently, Colin Matthew has teased out Gladstone's conflict of interest as a holder of Egyptian government stock. However, there is little evidence to suggest that this was the key factor in the invasion. H.C.G. Matthew, *The Gladstone Diaries*, Vol. 10 (Oxford, Oxford University Press, 1990), p. lxxii.
10. Mansfield, *British in Egypt*, p. 58.
11. A.G. Hopkins, 'The Victorians and Africa: A Reconsideration of the Occupation of Egypt 1882', *Journal of African History*, 27 (1986), p. 388.
12. See Elie Kedourie, *In the Anglo-Arab Labyrinth: The McMahon Husayn Correspondence and its Interpretations* (Cambridge, Cambridge University Press, 1976), *passim*.
13. *Wafd* is Arabic for delegation.
14. John Darwin, 'Imperialism in Decline', *English Historical Review*, 23, 3 (1980), p. 669.
15. Keith Jeffery, *The British Army and the Crisis of Empire* (Manchester, Manchester University Press, 1984), p. 121.
16. John Gallagher, *The Decline, Revival and Fall of the British Empire* (Cambridge, Cambridge University Press, 1982), p. 110.

17. M.W. Daly, *Imperial Sudan: The Anglo-Egyptian Condominium 1934–36* (Cambridge, Cambridge University Press, 1991), pp. 53–8.
18. P.J. Vatikiotis, *The Modern History of Egypt* (London, Weidenfeld & Nicolson, 1969), pp. 365–6.
19. J.C. Hurewitz, *The Middle East and North Africa in World Politics*, Vol. ii (New Haven, CT, Yale University Press, 1979), pp. 487–8.
20. Hola Gamal Abdel Nasser, *Britain and the Egyptian Nationalist Movement, 1936–52* (Reading, Ithaca Press, 1996), pp. 99–100.
21. S.R. Ashton and S.E. Stockwell (eds), *British Documents on the End of Empire (BDEEP)*, Series A, Vol. I, *Imperial Policy and Colonial Practice 1925–1945* (London, HMSO, 1996), Doc. 25.
22. L. Morsy, 'Britain's Wartime Policy in Egypt, 1940–42', *Middle Eastern Studies*, 25 (1989), pp. 25, 68, 82.
23. T. Evans (ed.), *The Killearn Diaries* (London, Sidgwick & Jackson, 1972), pp. 194–216, for Lampson's account of the 'abdication' crisis.
24. M. Kolinsky, 'Lampson and the Wartime Control of Egypt', in M. Kolinsky and M.J. Cohen (eds), *Demise of the British Empire in the Middle East* (London, Frank Cass, 1998), p. 96.
25. E.S. Farag, *Nasser Speaks* (London, Morsset Press, 1972), p. 19.
26. The various post-war military plans involving Egypt as base for atomic warfare are the US plans 'Broiler', 'Speedway' and 'Dropshot'. The First British A-bomb was tested in 1952. See I. Clark and N.J. Wheeler, *The Origins of British Nuclear Strategy 1945–55* (Oxford, Oxford University Press, 1989), pp. 124, 153. The broader contingency plans for defending the Middle East in a world war are discussed in depth in Michael J. Cohen, *Fighting World War Three from the Middle East: Allied Contingency Plans, 1945–1954* (London, Frank Cass, 1997).
27. Michael Mason, 'The Decisive Volley: The Battle of Ismailia and the Decline of British Influence in the Middle East', *Journal of Imperial and Commonwealth History*, 19 (1991), p. 46.
28. Ovendale, *Transfer of Power*, p. 6.
29. He outlined this approach in November 1945 in a speech to the Anglo-Egyptian Chamber of Commerce. A. Bullock, *Ernest Bevin, Foreign Secretary* (Oxford: Oxford University Press, 1983), p. 155.
30. Bullock, *Ernest Bevin*, p. 242, and Corelli Barnett, *The Lost Victory* (London, Pan, 1995), p. 54.
31. Bullock, *Ernest Bevin*, p. 242.
32. Barnett, *Lost Victory*, p. 63.
33. Peter Clarke, *Hope and Glory* (London, Penguin, 1996), p. 232.
34. William Roger Louis, *The British Empire in the Middle East 1945–51: Arab Nationalism, the United States and Postwar Imperialism* (Oxford, Oxford University Press, 1984), *passim*.
35. Ovendale, *Transfer of Power*, pp. 8–9. Bullock, *Ernest Bevin*, p. 251.
36. John Kent, 'The Egyptian Base and the Defence of the Middle East, 1945–54', *Jounal of Imperial and Commonwealth History*, 21, 3 (1993), p. 50.
37. The complexities of the negotiations are documented in great detail in Douglas H. Johnson, *BDEEP, Sudan*, Part I, *1942–50* (London, Stationery Office, 1998).
38. Bullock, *Ernest Bevin*, p. 254.
39. For a recent interpretation that Britain was more pro-Israeli than pro-Arab (as was accepted wisdom), Tom Segev, *One Palestine, Complete* (London, Little Brown, 2000).
40. Harold Beeley, 'The Middle East', in W. Roger Louis and Hedley Bull (eds), *The Special Relationship* (Oxford, Oxford University Press, 1986), p. 286.
41. Stephens, *Nasser*, p. 86.

42. Vatikiotis, *Modern History of Egypt*, p. 375.
43. The full text is in *Foreign Relations of the United States (FRUS), 1950*, Vol. V, 1.
44. J. Kent (ed.), *BDEEP*, Series B, Vol. 4, *Egypt and the Defence of the Middle East*, Part II (henceforth *BDEEP, Egypt*, Part II), Doc. 1, 30 Nov. 1950.
45. Nicholas Owen, 'Britain and Decolonisation: The Labour Government and the Middle East, 1945–51', in Kolinsky, *Demise of the British Empire in the Middle East*, p. 11.
46. The proposals of 1 April called for the phased withdrawal of British troops to be replaced by civilian contractors, the creation of an Anglo-Egyptian co-ordinated air defence system and the return of British forces in the event of war, imminent menace of war or apprehended international emergency. *BDEEP, Egypt*, Part II, Doc. 200, 28 May 1951.
47. Ovendale, *Transfer of Power*, p. 49.
48. *BDEEP, Egypt*, Part II, Doc. 207, 6 July 1951.
49. F.S. Northedge, *Descent From Power* (London, Minerva, 1974), pp. 117–18.
50. *FRUS, 1951*, Vol. V, State/JCS Meeting, 435.

— 3 —

The New Regime and the Base Agreement, 1952–54

ROAD TO REVOLUTION

THE INCOMING Conservative government was prepared to fight back against Egyptian guerrilla activity. The new, if ageing, Prime Minister, Winston Churchill, was a firm believer that all non-white peoples acting up should be faced down with force. This meant a more aggressive policy against the Egyptian terrorist campaign in the Canal Zone. A vicious undeclared war raged between the British and the guerrillas, which by January 1952 had claimed the lives of over 100 Egyptians and 33 United Kingdom servicemen.[1] Churchill gave the British commander, General Robertson, permission to take aggressive measures against the Egyptians. This strategy led to disaster in January 1952. Some 50 Egyptian Auxiliary police were killed when British troops used force to bring about their removal from a police station in the Canal Zone. The next day entered popular parlance as 'Black Saturday', as the Cairo masses rioted, their anger directed against the European population of the city. Numerous British and foreign citizens were killed before order was restored. The Egyptian King and his Prime Minister were deliberately slow calling out the army to quell the disorder on the streets.[2] The feeling in British circles was that the mobs had the tacit acquiescence of the King. Churchill wrote that the 'Egyptians cannot be classed as a civilised power until they have purged themselves'.[3] A plan code-named 'Rodeo' had been drawn up for a full-scale occupation of Egypt in event of the situation getting out of control. However, the plan was not implemented because the growth of fanaticism in all strata of Egyptian society from the streets to the army made such an operation too risky. The Chief of the Imperial General Staff warned that any further operations in Egypt would denude Britain of a strategic reserve.[4] What was most evident was the bankruptcy of British policy. Stephens points to the fact that the forces in the country who had ruled it for the previous 30 years – the

King, the British and the *Wafd* – 'had now between them made Egypt ungovernable'.[5] It meant that the only other force in the land, the army, came under pressure to save the country from what seemed like certain anarchy. Britain, the dominant foreign influence in Egypt for so long, was about to be superseded by other suitors, untainted by 70 years of, often unfriendly, association.

The most significant dissident army grouping was the Free Officers, led by the aforementioned Colonel Nasser. Spurred on by the events of Black Saturday, the group decided to carry out a coup as soon as possible. Kim Roosevelt, the CIA's senior operative in the Middle East, as early as 1951 had been calling for the United States to develop links with not only current Arab leaders but with potential Arab leaders. Within weeks of this October 1951 conference, CIA officials were making contact with the Free Officers.[6] Many of the Free Officers received training in the United States as a result of these contacts. Having failed to convince Farouk in early 1952 that reform was imperative, Roosevelt appears to have tacitly supported the revolution.[7] He met with many of the most senior members of the Free Officers including Nasser prior to the seizure of power and appears to have accepted their analysis that only an army revolution could deal with Egypt's problems.[8] Nasser's original plan appears to have been for an August coup but Farouk was becoming more concerned about army dissent. In July he appointed his brother-in-law as Minister of Defence in preparation for a crackdown. According to Nutting, Nasser was further rushed by news of an impending move against the conspirators.[9] At midnight (22–23 July) about 3,000 troops with tanks seized the army HQ. The Chief of Staff, General Farid, was captured in the midst of a discussion about army grievances, which may have been the signal for a government crackdown on the dissidents.[10] Key points – airports, radio stations, communications centres and crossroads – were seized. Cairo awoke to be informed by Colonel Anwar Sadat that the army had taken power. The King who was in Alexandria for the summer was unable to rally support. On 26 July he was asked to abdicate in favour of his son and leave Egypt for ever.

There was no British intervention. One British diplomat did suggest a show of force to warn the new regime. But by now they had exhausted their tolerance for Farouk. The Minister at the Cairo Embassy believed that the threat and the use of force against the new regime should be kept in reserve. If the Free Officers turned out to be 'gangsters', 'we can still stop them by a clear show of determination and by an immediate show of force at the appropriate moment if they begin to apply their hitherto successful technique of threats to any aspect of the Anglo-Egyptian problem'.[11] The British also took counsel from the State

Department advising them to give the new regime a chance and warning that foreign intervention 'would be disastrous'.[12] Even Churchill, with all his anti-Egyptian views, was 'not opposed to a policy of giving Neguib a good chance'.[13]

THE NEW REGIME

The new regime was led by Neguib, the popular army general, but its ruling body was the Revolutionary Command Council (RCC), which was dominated by the younger, more radical, Free Officers. The Free Officers were politically a disparate grouping. However, they had a number of agreed goals: the elimination of foreign, particularly British, influence; some form of land reform including the breaking up of the big estates; the ending of the monarchy; and the cleansing of public life of corruption.[14] In some of these areas, like land reform, the new regime made some progress. The Americans gave support to the initiative against the arguments of the British who believed it was encouraging extremist elements in the RCC.[15] Land reform helped cement public support for the regime in its earliest days when the still-popular *Wafd* was a threat. In September 1952, a series of show trials, which purported to claim that *Wafd* leaders were plotting with a foreign power, presumably Britain, to overthrow the regime, further discredited that party. With its domestic position secure, the RCC dissolved all political parties in January 1953. A provisional constitution that placed supreme power in the hands of the RCC was proclaimed in February. The first phase of the revolution was completed with the declaration of a republic in June 1953. Internally the RCC was split between Neguib and the younger officers. Neguib, installed as a figurehead, proved to be a surprisingly resilient figure. He maintained the posts of President and Prime Minister. Nasser, indisputably the leader of the Free Officers, was forced to be content with the posts of Deputy Prime Minister and Minister of the Interior. However, Nasser and the RCC began to marginalise Neguib from mid-1953, taking decisions such as the banning of the Muslim Brotherhood without consulting him. In February 1954 Neguib resigned his posts as President and Prime Minister, which Nasser assumed. Neguib, who enjoyed considerable support in the army and on the streets, was able to return to power on the crest of a wave of public disapproval of Nasser's actions. Nasser and his supporters were forced to back down. However, when Neguib proposed the restoration of political life, Nasser was able to rally the army and mobilise popular distrust of the old political classes to regain the initiative. After a general strike in April

1954, Neguib was forced to reappoint Nasser as Prime Minister, a return to democracy was postponed indefinitely and Neguib's power was broken for ever. Six months later in November 1954, claiming Neguib was conspiring with the Muslim Brotherhood, Nasser had him removed from the presidency and assumed the office himself.[16] It was to become one of the defining characteristics of Nasser's career, his determination to be the undisputed leader. He maintained a lifelong suspicion – even a contempt – for liberal parliamentary democracy. From 1954 he had virtually unchecked political power in Egypt until his death in 1970. The template of his regime – the cult of the strong leader – has proved to be a model that most revolutionary, and it should be said non-revolutionary, regimes in the Middle East have followed since. Leaders leave power in a wooden box rather than by the ballot box.

Gamal Abdel Nasser was born at Alexandria on 15 January 1918, the eldest son of a postal worker. Most accounts of his youth tend to focus on his fervent nationalism fuelled by a copious reading of politics, philosophy and history from a young age.[17] He formed the view that the Egyptian nation had two problems – the British occupation and the craven Egyptian ruling class. As a 17- and 18-year-old he was an organiser of demonstrations and street protests against the British and the government. His youthful radicalism, which he always sought to emphasise after assuming power, seems not to have prevented him on his second attempt being accepted for officer training with the expanding Egyptian army in the aftermath of the 1936 Anglo-Egyptian Treaty. Seven of the nine original Free Officers joined the army around the time of Nasser's entry to the military academy in March 1937: Abdul Hakim Amer, Abdul Latif Baghdadi, Anwar Sadat, Hussein esh-Shafei, Zacharia Mohieddin, brothers Gamel Salem and Salah Salem. The other two, Kamel ed-Din Hussein and Khaled Mohieddin, enlisted a couple of years later.[18] All would hold high office under the revolutionary regime. Sadat would eventually succeed Nasser in 1970. The origin of the Free Officers is unclear. It seems likely to have been little more than a social club for young and ambitious officers at first. Nasser, who spent much of the Second World War in the Sudan, was away from the anti-British activities of Anwar Sadat. Sadat, a born conspirator, was arrested for attempting to make contact with Axis agents and was lucky not to have been shot. By the time Nasser was back in Cairo it was clear that Britain and the Allies were not going to lose the Second World War. There was little opportunity and little profit therefore for Nasser to take part in open anti-British activities. The vast numbers of British troops in Egypt in the period would have made any but the most clandestine activities unwise to say the least. There is no evidence that he attempted to carry out any revolutionary activity at this time. His fear and loathing of the British was confirmed by the humiliation of Farouk in 1942. It was the disastrous Palestine war (1948–49) that appears to have set the Free Officers on the road to revolution. Nasser, by virtue of his forceful personality and his distinguished war record in Palestine, became the leader. However, his lack of public visibility necessitated the employment of General Neguib, the sole senior officer to perform well in the war, as figurehead for the revolution.

Upon becoming undisputed ruler of Egypt in 1954, Nasser had a number of priorities in foreign affairs. Number one was the removal of the British from Egypt. A second was the elimination of British power in the Arab world. A review of the totality of Nasser's career would suggest that a personal ambition to lead the Arab world was one reason for the second priority. His clashes with Arab leaders (Nuri, Qasim, King Saud, King Faisal and King Hussein) who sought to oppose Egyptian dominance suggest that imperialist British leaders were but one obstacle on the road to Arab leadership. There is evidence that Nasser believed that he was the charismatic leader that the Arab world wanted and needed – a man of destiny. British policy, which required a divided Middle East primarily to ensure the supply of oil on reasonable terms and to provide the communications and base rights that allowed the British global role, could only be aimed at frustrating this ambition. A clash was inevitable.

After the consolidation of his personal leadership of Egypt in 1955, Mohammad Heikal assembled a slim volume of Nasser's views entitled *The Philosophy of the Revolution*. Written in a portentous style that is a hallmark of Arabic with its claims that Egypt stood at the centre of three circles of influence (Arab, African and Moslem), the document was certainly, at the very least, an ambitious statement of foreign policy goals. However, the evidence that it was a *Mein Kampf*-style blueprint for regional domination is much more tenuous. Ambiguous, indeed unclear, passages in it could possibly be read as claiming the mantle of leadership of the Arab world for Nasser himself. More reasonably they could be read as putting forward the newly revolutionary Egypt as leader of the Arab world.[19] However, this was in the future. Nasser's regional ambitions were not really seen as a major factor or problem by the British until 1954. Furthermore any sensible analysis would have seen that Egypt, which contained roughly half of all Arabs, was bound to have a leading role in Arab councils. The British were not always averse to this. Britain, when Eden was Foreign Secretary, had aided in the creation of the Arab League in 1945 and the headquarters of that organisation was in Cairo – an acknowledgement of Egypt's leading role in the Arab world. In the early 1950s British policy-makers were concerned primarily with an acceptable deal on the Canal Zone base and bringing Egypt around to the West's conception for the defence of the Middle East. It was only when Nasser directly challenged British interests from 1955 that the manifesto of *The Philosophy of the Revolution* took on such an ominous tone.

A further defining characteristic of Nasser's political methods was his opportunistic streak. Often during large set-piece speeches to massive crowds he would unleash a *coup de théâtre*, such as the nationalisation of the Suez Canal, or make a virulent verbal attack on foreign leaders. Of course many, if not all, of these spontaneous eruptions were planned. To many Western observers Nasser seemed to be nothing more than a populist demagogue who would make up for domestic failings with foreign adventures. Dean Rusk, the United States Secretary of State under Presidents Kennedy and Johnson, was one observer notably unimpressed by Nasser whom he felt was too easily 'swept by the emotions of the crowd and the peculiar fanaticism of the Middle East'.[20] Others such as Anthony Eden, John Foster Dulles (depending on his mood) and Harold Macmillan saw him as a throwback to the 1930s and to other demagogues like Hitler and Mussolini. From 1955 to 1960 Nasser's foreign opportunism and adventurism paid off handsomely. After 1960 he began to suffer reversal after reversal. In contrast to his public demagoguery, Nasser, in private, appears to have been a man of considerable charm. Diplomats who had regular dealings with him seem to have viewed him rather better than those in London. The British Ambassadors Humphrey Trevelyan and Harold Beeley and many others seem to have maintained good personal relations with him at times when this might have seemed impossible. One senior British diplomat once told me, with only a mild hint of derision, that it was a common tendency of British diplomats in foreign postings to come to the conclusion that 'their dictator is not that bad after all and that he is invariably kind to children and animals'.[21]

THE LONG GOODBYE

British foreign policy in the 1950s and 1960s was increasingly complicated by the fact that it was encumbered by having to be in tune with the United States. In areas where the British felt that they had overwhelming interest as well as some remaining influence or specialist knowledge that qualified them for a leading role, such as in the Middle East, friction with the United States was to prove to be a considerable problem. In the Middle East, the so-called 'special relationship' was often more special by virtue of its complexity than because of any great warmth.

The Egyptian revolution and the Iranian oil crisis brought the United States to the centre of Middle Eastern politics. The Truman administration for the most part in the late 1940s was prepared to let the British take the leading role in the region with certain exceptions such as Israel (for domestic political considerations) and Saudi Arabia (oil interests). In 1951, these policies changed. National Security Council (NSC) and State Department documents began to call for a separate course for American Middle Eastern policy. Prior to the Anglo-Egyptian clash in the autumn of 1951, the Americans made it clear that they viewed the basic reason for the crisis as the rigid attitude of the British.[22] This policy was driven by the inability of the British to solve the base issue with Egypt, and the growing threat of neutralist sentiment among the Arab states. These developments required the United States to bring forth initiatives that were not necessarily compatible with British policy. Indeed at times in 1951 over Egypt and Iran, the Americans appeared to be leaning on the side of the nationalists rather than the British.[23] The Roosevelt involvement with the Free Officers was another sign of this. The Americans, particularly the CIA, by their closeness to the Free Officers, according to one British official, had removed the one check on extremism – the fear of British intervention. A Mr Bowker, the Foreign Office's assistant undersecretary for the Middle East, feared that the 'universal American desire for popularity should in practice result in encouraging the more extreme elements in Egypt to believe that they can play the Americans off against ourselves'.[24] The American Embassy in Cairo believed that the new regime wanted a working alliance with the United States to the exclusion of the British.[25] Roosevelt, the American Ambassador, Jefferson Caffrey, and the political secretary and CIA agent in the United States Embassy, William Lakeland, all had regular contact with Nasser and the Free Officers.[26]

President Eisenhower, upon assuming office in 1953, continued the Truman policy of divergence from the British. The President and his Secretary of State, John Foster Dulles, distrusted British policy, believing it to be colonialist and imperialist. They feared that association with it would damage the United States in the Middle East. There was also a deep personal antipathy between Dulles and Churchill, which rubbed off on the Foreign Secretary, Anthony Eden. This was not helped by Dulles' prickly personality. He was too humourless, too self-assured and too pompous for the gregarious Churchill and the urbane but highly strung Eden.[27] They lobbied against his appointment as Secretary of State.[28] The former coined the famous phrase 'dull, duller, Dulles' in dismissal of him. Eisenhower was closely involved in making policy with Dulles.

For the British the main problem with Dulles was his apparent duplicity and the opacity of his policy on many matters outside of the Cold War and international communism. Dulles had a regular habit of seeming to agree with the more extreme positions espoused by his allies when it suited and then not providing the support that they believed they had been assured of. This brought well-founded accusations that he was two-faced. His attitude to Egypt and in particular towards Nasser was almost impossible to fathom. Some documents and conversations would suggest that he was reasonably disposed towards the Egyptian leader, while others would suggest that Dulles considered that he was a figure with Hitlerite ambitions. For the British this was worse as his most extreme comments often emerged in meetings with them. Nigel Ashton suggests that his attitude to Nasser can be best understood by looking at Dulles' world-view, which saw the world grouped into a hierarchy of threats with international communism of overwhelming importance. Nasser's neutralism and anti-Western, particularly anti-British, nationalism in the third world were at best a secondary threat.[29] This was a threat that could be ameliorated and appeased by if necessary sacrificing British interests for the greater good of the West. Nasser's diplomatic successes depended on being able to maintain his radical nationalist policies while at the same time retaining the ability to cut deals with the United States which often worked against the interests of other radical elements in the Arab world, particularly communists, whom he was just as opposed to as Dulles. His willingness to do so was most notable in Syria in 1957 and in Iraq in 1959.

Anthony Eden did not share the world-view of Dulles and Eisenhower. Eden was still a relatively young man in the 1950s (57 when he became Prime Minister) but he already had the best part of a quarter-century of the highest diplomatic experience behind him. He had faced the dictators as Foreign Secretary in the 1930s before he was even 40. He resigned over appeasement in 1938 but this was as much down to interference in the Foreign Office by his Prime Minister, Neville Chamberlain, who wished to direct foreign policy from 10 Downing Street. Fortunately for Eden, he abandoned ship at the right moment as the fall of Chamberlain in 1940 restored him to the front rank of politics. By the end of 1940, he was Churchill's Foreign Secretary, heir apparent and still in his early 40s. He was a leading figure in the highest councils of Allied diplomacy during the war. He was inclined to take a more moderate view of the Soviets than Dulles. He had dealt with them after all as allies as well as enemies and was the leading exponent in the British Cabinet of aid to the Soviets after the German invasion in 1941.[30] The return to power of the Conservatives in 1951 seemed to place him on the cusp of the premiership. However, his career was blighted by the refusal of Churchill to give up the top job and by poor health exacerbated by a botched bile duct operation in 1953. This was to lead him to require considerable doses of drugs to control the resulting pain for the rest of his life. The pain might have been more manageable on a less highly strung workaholic than Eden but his demeanour and style added to the stresses. A desperately unhappy first marriage contributed to these workaholic tendencies. He did not even own a house for many years. His biographer identifies two sides to Eden: one that was petty, bad-tempered and petulant and a second that was wise, generous and high-minded.[31] As Prime Minister, the 'bad' Eden seemed to dominate. His second marriage in 1952 to Clarisa, a relative of Churchill, was fortunately a lot happier and an antidote to the break-up of his first marriage. Unhappily it did not ameliorate his increasingly difficult relationships with political friends and colleagues.

Eden was a relative moderate on the base issue and Egypt. He was a strong advocate of the reorientation of British defence policy occasioned by publication of the Chiefs of Staff's Global Strategy Paper of 1952. The paper concluded a base in Egypt was necessary but could be placed under Egyptian control if Egypt joined a Middle Eastern defence organisation. Most importantly, it concluded that, while the Middle East must be defended in war, 'if reduction in overseas expenditure is essential, it would be least harmful militarily, in the Middle East'.[32] Eden seems to have been particularly impressed by this. In October 1952, he told the Cabinet that, as financial considerations might well necessitate the reduction of defence expenditure in the Middle East, progress in the establishment of a Middle East defence organisation would fit in with a solution of the Anglo-Egyptian problem and that the emergence of the new regime in Egypt would offer a better chance of coming to terms with the Egyptians than in the past. He recommended a strategy of keeping the Egyptians in play without giving way on any substantial issues until future British policy was clearer. The bones of a settlement in the future were that the base would be evacuated in peacetime but could be reactivated in a war emergency. Air defence of Egypt was to be in the hands of Britain and Egypt.[33] Reviewing Middle East strategy in November 1952, the Chiefs of Staff committee agreed that the 'only possible location for the main Middle East base *in war* was militarily in Egypt'.[34] The Chiefs of Staff also outlined the negotiating positions for negotiations with Egypt. There were four possible cases (A–D) in descending order of acceptability. Case A would have seen the base returned to Egypt, 7,000 British troops to maintain it and the creation of an integrated Anglo-Egyptian air defence organisation. Case B would have been the base returned to Egypt,

500–1,000 military personnel to assist the Egyptians in maintaining the base and air co-operation as in Case A. Case C would see the base handed over to Egypt, with British civilian contractors to maintain the base. Air defence would be an Egyptian responsibility. The final case, D, and what the Chiefs of Staff described as the 'last ditch solution' was that the base would be evacuated and only put into use in the event of the outbreak or imminent threat of war.[35] However, Eden, while essentially accepting the above criteria, told the Cabinet in January 1953 that there would be no withdrawal until Egypt had indicated a willingness to co-operate in a regional defence organisation.[36]

The world was entering the age of the hydrogen bomb. With its unprecedented destructive power, it seemed to make large bases such as the Canal obsolete. The new strategic realities might be better served by having smaller and more dispersed bases. Secondly, the Labour government had embarked on a huge expansion of defence spending in 1950–51. The Conservatives wanted to cut some of the fat from the defence budget. Defence priorities had undergone considerable changes since 1947. The creation of NATO meant that the defence of Germany and the Rhine Army were now the main pillar of British strategy. This meant the £50 million per annum being spent on the Canal Zone base was the most attractive target for the cutters.[37] Sir Ralph Stevenson, the Ambassador in Cairo, urged that Britain commit itself to withdrawing from the base at the start of negotiations to persuade the Egyptians of the good intentions of the British.[38] Eden warned the Cabinet in February 1953 of the necessity of an agreement with Egypt. In the light of future events it was ironic to say the least.

> In the second half of the 20th Century we cannot hope to maintain our position in the Middle East by the methods of the last century. However little we like it, we must face that fact. Commercial concessions whose local benefit appears to rebound mainly to the Shahs and Pashas no longer serve in the same way to strengthen our influence in these countries, and they come increasingly under attack by local nationalist opinion … In most of the countries of the Middle East the social and economic aspirations of the common people are quickening and the tide of nationalism is rising fast. If we are to maintain our influence in this area, future policy must be designed to harness these movements rather than to struggle against them.[39]

It took Churchill a long time to accept his Foreign Secretary's view that concessions would have to be given to the Egyptians to facilitate an agreement. The Egypt issue was the cause of bitter disagreements between the two men. Churchill's hope was that the Egyptians could be persuaded to turn the Canal Zone base into one occupied by American, British and Egyptian troops and make it the main support area for a Middle East version of NATO. It was a forlorn hope as the Americans had long concluded. On the British side, Churchill's heir and Foreign Secretary, Anthony Eden, realised that no Egyptian government would conclude an agreement that provided for land forces from a foreign power being stationed in the country in peacetime. There was also the added problem that Nasser and others in the Egyptian leadership would not join any Middle Eastern defence organisation.[40] The arguments between the two men were at their most intense in the early part of 1953 with Churchill telling Eden bitterly that he never knew 'that Munich was situated on the Nile'.[41] (Analogy was to be one of the great curses of Anglo-Egyptian relations.) However, hitherto insoluble problems began to resolve despite Churchill's intervention. The British and the Egyptians agreed on the right of the Sudanese to self-determination in February 1953 just before Eden was stricken by his health problems. The new regime in Egypt could be credited with this. After negotiations with the Sudanese parties it agreed on the right of the Sudan to self-determination. Perhaps the reason for this was that Farouk had a royal claim to the Sudan. The Free Officers were unencumbered by dynastic claims. While they believed for strategic and mainly economic reasons on the need for unity in the Nile Valley they were convinced that the Sudanese would accept Egyptian sovereignty. Why Egypt failed to win union with the Sudan is somewhat of a mystery. Hubris is one reason. The Free Officers were convinced that they would win any self-determination plebiscite. The British, also, played a skilful hand in the Sudan and aided the successful movement against union with Egypt,[42] though it might be speculated that Egyptian adventurism might have been subsumed in the Sudan if union had taken place and the British might have had a quieter life in the rest of the Middle East.

Churchill took over the reins of the Foreign Office when Eden fell ill in 1953. Progress to an agreement noticeably slowed with the Prime Minister seemingly intent on a confrontation. He sent Robin Hankey – a Foreign Office official noted for his hawkish views on the base – to Cairo, to stiffen the resolve of the embassy. Churchill wanted Hankey to give nothing away for six months and make the Egyptians make the running in seeking negotiations.[43] He made it clear that Case A was the furthest he was willing to go in making concessions to the Egyptians. A further sign of his intransigent attitude was the appointment of Sir Brian Robertson, C-in-C of the Middle East, as military adviser to the British Embassy on any defence negotiations.[44] He was strongly for

Case A as a minimum position as well. More worrying was the evidence which seemed to suggest that Egypt was planning the resumption of a terrorist campaign against the base under the command of ex-Nazi troops.[45] The CIA under its Cairo station chief, James Eichelberger, had been providing extensive intelligence support to Nasser's internal security forces. CIA Director Allen Dulles made available a number of ominously titled 'German wartime security specialists' to the Egyptian regime. Nasser's relations with the CIA were cemented even further with the appointment of Miles Copeland as CIA station chief in Cairo.[46]

Case A was rejected by the Egyptians when Dulles presented it to them in June 1953. Eisenhower wrote to Churchill suggesting that the British would have to make 'some concessions which will permit a quick start on withdrawal of UK troops and produce an adequate if not ideal arrangement for maintenance of the base'.[47] Churchill, nevertheless, continued to press for Case A. However, he suffered a stroke at the end of June and his capacity for work was considerably reduced until October 1953. Eden was also out of action so Lord Salisbury became acting Foreign Secretary with Rab Butler, the Chancellor, becoming acting Prime Minister. All of this was kept secret with the connivance of the British press.

The Americans, desperate for an agreement, now persuaded the Egyptians to come up with proposals that might have some chance of success with the British in July 1953. Indeed the Egyptian proposals were based substantially on an American draft document. There was considerable liaison between the United States through the CIA and the Egyptian leadership about the negotiations. The proposals were only accepted by a narrow majority in the RCC. Nasser was the key figure in forcing its acceptance. This essentially called for the British base to be manned by technicians in civilian clothes. The base would be available should there be an attack on a member of the Arab nation. The agreement would run for three years.[48] The British rejected the proposals but were forced to agree that they provided a basis for discussion. It is clear that the exclusion of Churchill from the decision-making process saw a softening of the British line. The Cabinet agreed that there was no prospect of joint air defence and that the number of uniformed technicians would be reduced over the ten-year duration of the agreement. It was also felt necessary to have cast-iron assurances about the return of British forces in wartime. The most important British requirement was that a Soviet attack on Turkey would activate the base as well as attacks on Arab countries.[49] This requirement and the duration of the agreement – the Egyptians wanted it to last five years, the British ten – were the key differences between the two sides. The British were willing to reduce their demands on duration to seven years.[50]

Hankey, sent as a hard man to Cairo, developed a certain grudging respect for the Egyptians – something that William Roger Louis suggests eventually rubbed off on Churchill. Later, even General Robertson came around to the idea of pulling British forces out of Egypt.[51] Churchill's attitude is hard to follow, varying between compromise and confrontation. He hated the thought of retreat but saw the economic benefits. So even as he came around to the idea of withdrawal, he retained a sympathy for the hard-line Suez Group – set up in 1953 by among others Captain Charles Waterhouse and Julian Amery (Harold Macmillan's son-in-law) – which opposed any compromise. They strongly believed that British power in the Middle East should be maintained and that the Suez base was necessary for it.[52] However, in Cabinet in September 1953, even Churchill admitted that there was a reasonable chance of an agreement. He was worried about how it would look to the Conservative party and wanted a clause affirming free navigation through the Canal inserted.[53] The possibility of quick agreement was dashed as the Egyptians refused to accept the seven-year duration, which was now the minimum British position, and demanded that the British technicians be in civilian clothes. The British rejected the Egyptian proposals.[54] The negotiations were coming close to complete breakdown. Nasser was reported by the American Embassy to be in 'a black mood'.[55] Neither side wanted a complete breach as of yet so the talks entered a kind of limbo. Hankey became very despondent that any agreement could be reached or that the Egyptians could be trusted to keep it. He warned of the inevitability of future conflict with Egypt:

> [O]nce the Egyptian Government think they have got us out after the conclusion of the projected Defence Agreement, I really doubt if there will be any holding them from venting their very ill-conceived nationalist ideas on our interests. I certainly feel there is little foundation for any optimistic belief that they will not do so. We are unlikely to get the agreement renewed, and it may well be turned into a farce before its expiry. I believe the effect of such a development on our position in the other Arab countries and our whole position in the Mediterranean, in the Persian Gulf and in the Indian Ocean would be incalculable. I feel convinced that it would far surpass the effect of Abadan or Palestine.[56]

Hankey concluded by suggesting that the British maintain their position in the Canal Zone by force if necessary if a satisfactory arrangement could not be arrived at with the Egyptians. The Suez Group was growing more vocal in its attacks on any attempts at compromise.

Churchill noted that the opponents of British withdrawal feared that the Egyptians would block transit of the Canal in such an eventuality.[57] It, therefore, became a key aim of British policy to get the Egyptians to mention free transit in the Canal as part of an agreement. Considerable amounts of time at the December 1953 summit in Bermuda between Churchill and Eisenhower were dedicated to the Egypt problem. In January 1954 the tone of British documents suggested that they thought it was unlikely that agreement could be reached. The choices available were stark: to stay on indefinitely; withdrawal without agreement ('scuttle'); to liquidate the base and redeploy over a long period maintaining rights under the 1936 treaty. The last course was the one favoured by Selwyn Lloyd, the Minister of State at the Foreign Office.[58] Nasser, who was now increasingly in control in Egypt, broke this particular logjam. He refused to make concessions on uniforms but did agree that an attack on Turkey would allow reactivation of the base.[59] Eden proposed that the British should reopen negotiations on the basis that the base be put under Egyptian control, but with a number of British civilian technicians remaining to service the base, so that it could be reactivated relatively quickly in event of an outbreak of war. He believed such an approach presented the only possibility of progress towards a compromise agreement. He did seek the extension of the agreement from seven years to ten.[60] Churchill was still reticent. He wanted the Americans to join the British in any reactivation of the base to cover any retreat. Within the Conservative party and Whitehall, the differing positions on the base issue began to converge. The Foreign Secretary, Anthony Eden, the Foreign Office and the defence staff all saw the base as obsolete and an impediment to better relations with the Arab world. Even Churchill swung from being an advocate of facing the Egyptians down to the position of Eden after he saw the devastation that the American H-bomb test would likely cause to a base like Suez.[61]

In July 1954 Eden recommended that the heads of agreement should be signed, and the Cabinet agreed. The Secretary of State for War, Anthony Head, signed the heads of agreement in July 1954 and the Minister of State at the Foreign Office, Anthony Nutting, resolved the minor points, finally signing the agreement on 19 October 1954. British troops would be evacuated within 20 months and the new agreement would last seven years.[62] British forces would be allowed re-entry if Turkey or an Arab state were attacked. After the signing Nasser spoke that the 'ugly page of Anglo-Egyptian relations has been turned ... There is now no reason why Britain and Egypt should not work constructively together.'[63]

Still against the agreement was ranged the diehard group of

Conservative MPs – the Suez Group – and a few ministers.[64] They were all intensely hostile to selling out to the Egyptians who they believed could not be trusted. They saw any agreement on the base as likely to destroy Britain's leading role in the Middle East. When agreement was reached, Captain Waterhouse, a leading member, spoke of the deal not as a 'sell-out' but as 'a give-away'.[65] Their analysis may have been correct, but for an alternative policy all they could offer was a war of attrition with the Egyptians, which might well have turned into Britain's Algeria. For Anthony Eden, the success of the base agreement was merely the icing on the cake for a momentous year for himself and British diplomacy in general. That year he had overseen the conclusion of the Indo-China conflict with the Geneva accords – on terms that the Americans were distinctly unhappy with – the rearming of Germany, the settlement of the Iranian oil problem as well as the withdrawal from Egypt. Eden, who during the war had found the Americans immensely difficult to deal with at times, believed that the Americans wanted to replace the French in Indo-China and the British in Egypt. 'They want to run the world,' was his bitter summation to his private secretary in 1954.[66] His last *annus mirabilis* as Foreign Secretary may have convinced him that an independent British line was still possible on some issues.

NOTES

1. Mason, 'The Decisive Volley', p. 46.
2. M. Neguib, *Egypt's Destiny* (London, Gollancz, 1955), pp. 101–2.
3. W. Roger Louis, 'Churchill and Egypt', in W. Roger Louis and R. Blake, *Churchill* (Oxford, Oxford University Press, 1994), p. 478.
4. *BDEEP, Egypt,* Part II, Doc. 264, 28 Jan. 1952.
5. Stephens, *Nasser*, p. 102.
6. W.S. Lucas and A. Morey, 'The Hidden Alliance: The CIA and MI6 Before and After Suez', in D. Stafford and R. Jeffreys-Jones, *American–British–Canadian Intelligence Relations 1939–2000* (London, Frank Cass, 2000), p. 97.
7. See G. Aronson, *From Sideshow to Centre Stage: US Policy to Egypt, 1945–56* (Boulder, CO, Lynne Riener, 1986), pp. 39–46.
8. Lucas, *Divided We Stand*, p. 14.
9. A. Nutting, *Nasser* (London, Constable, 1972), pp. 35–6.
10. Anwar al-Sadat, *Revolution on the Nile* (London, Wingate, 1957), p. 116.
11. *BDEEP, Egypt,* Part II, Doc. 315, 28 July 1952.
12. Lucas, *Divided We Stand*, p. 16.
13. Roger Louis, 'Churchill and Egypt', p. 478.
14. Peter Mansfield, *Nasser* (London, Methuen, 1969), p. 78.
15. Lucas, *Divided We Stand*, p. 16.
16. Mansfield, *Nasser*, pp. 84–9, for the account of the struggle for power in Egypt.
17. Nutting, *Nasser*, pp. 5–14, and Stephens, *Nasser*, pp. 22–37.
18. P.J. Vatikiotis, *The Egyptian Army in Politics* (Bloomington, IN, Indiana University Press, 1961), pp. 47–9.

19. See Nasser, *Philosophy of the Revolution*, pp. 61, 78, cited in A.I. Dawisha, *Egypt in the Arab World* (London, Macmillan, 1976), p. 133. Kyle, *Suez*, pp. 54–6, makes a case for Nasser's defence.
20. Dean Rusk, *As I Saw It* (London, Norton, 1991), p. 321.
21. Private information.
22. *BDEEP, Egypt*, Part II, Doc. 212, 16 Aug. 1951.
23. S.Z. Freiberger, *Dawn over Suez: The Rise of American Power in the Middle East* (Chicago, IL, Ivan R. Dee, 1992), pp. 24–5, and H.W. Brands, 'The Cairo–Tehran Connection in Anglo-American Rivalry in the Middle East, 1951–1953', *International History Review*, 11 (Aug. 1989), pp. 434–56.
24. *BDEEP, Egypt*, Part II, Doc. 320, 11 Sept. 1952.
25. *BDEEP, Egypt*, Part II, Doc. 321, 11 Sept. 1952.
26. Lucas and Morey, 'The Hidden Alliance', p. 97.
27. Recent portraits of Dulles include Fredrick Marks, *Power and Peace: The Diplomacy of John Foster Dulles* (New Haven, CT, Yale University Press, 1993) and Richard Immerman (ed.), *John Foster Dulles and the Diplomacy of the Cold War* (Princeton, NJ, Princeton University Press, 1990).
28. David Reynolds, 'Eden the Diplomatist, 1931–56: Suezside of a Statesman?', *History*, 74, 1 (1989), p. 74.
29. Ashton, *Problem of Nasser*, pp. 7–8.
30. Robert Rhodes-James, *Anthony Eden* (London, Weidenfeld & Nicolson, 1986), pp. 254–6.
31. Rhodes-James, *Anthony Eden*, p. 623.
32. *BDEEP, Egypt*, Part II, Doc. 308, 17 June 1952.
33. *BDEEP, Egypt*, Part II, Doc. 331, 27 Oct. 1952.
34. *BDEEP, Egypt*, Part II, Doc. 338, 14 Nov. 1952.
35. *BDEEP, Egypt*, Part II, Doc. 340, 2 Dec. 1952.
36. *BDEEP, Egypt*, Part II, Doc. 355, 14 June 1953.
37. Mason, 'Decisive Volley', p. 46.
38. *BDEEP, Egypt*, Part II, Doc. 360, 14 Feb. 1953.
39. *BDEEP, Egypt*, Part II, Doc. 361, 16 Feb. 1953.
40. *BDEEP, Egypt*, Part III, Doc. 386, 1 Apr. 1953.
41. Martin Gilbert, *Winston S. Churchill, 1945–65*, Vol. 8, *Never Despair* (London, Heinemann, 1988) and David Dutton, *Anthony Eden: A Life and Reputation* (London, Arnold, 1997), p. 357.
42. Churchill opposed this as well. Gilbert, *Never Despair*, p. 799. Documentation on the Sudan can be found in Douglas H. Johnson, *BDEEP, Sudan*, Part II, *1950–56* (London, Stationery Office, 1998). A good explanation of the failure of the Egyptians in the Sudan can be found in G.R. Warburg, *Historical Discord in the Nile Valley* (London, Hurst, 1992), pp. 69–81.
43. *BDEEP, Egypt*, Part III, Doc. 396, 22 May 1953.
44. He was to leave his C-in-C post early. *BDEEP, Egypt*, Part III, Doc. 388, 14 Apr. 1953.
45. *BDEEP, Egypt*, Part III, Lloyd to Churchill, 21 Apr. 1953.
46. Richard Aldrich, *The Hidden Hand: Britain, America and Cold War Secret Intelligence* (London, John Murray, 2001), pp. 476–7.
47. *BDEEP, Egypt*, Part III, Doc. 399, 11 June 1953.
48. *BDEEP, Egypt*, Part III, Doc. 417, 11 July 1953.
49. *BDEEP, Egypt*, Part III, Doc. 426, 18 Aug. 1953.
50. *BDEEP, Egypt*, Part III, Doc. 431, 8 Sept. 1953.
51. Roger Louis, 'Churchill and Egypt', p. 480.
52. Discussions of the origins of the Suez Group include L.S. Epstein, *British Politics in the Suez Crisis* (London, Pall Mall Press, 1964), pp. 42–4, and Sue Onslow,

Backbench Debate within the Conservative Party and its Influence on British Foreign Policy, 1948–57 (London, Macmillan, 1997), pp. 108–24.

53. *BDEEP, Egypt*, Part III, Doc. 432, 8 Sept. 1953.
54. *BDEEP, Egypt*, Part III, Doc. 439, 2 Oct. 1953.
55. *BDEEP, Egypt*, Part III, Doc. 441, 10 Oct. 1953.
56. *BDEEP, Egypt*, Part III, Doc. 450, 23 Nov. 1953.
57. *BDEEP, Egypt*, Part III, Doc. 452, 26 Nov. 1953.
58. *BDEEP, Egypt*, Part III, Doc. 482, 27 Jan. 1954.
59. *BDEEP, Egypt*, Part III, Doc. 483, 27 Jan. 1954.
60. *BDEEP, Egypt*, Part III, Doc. 503, 13 Mar. 1954.
61. For example, Gilbert, *Never Despair*, pp. 994, 1036–8, and Roger Louis, 'Churchill and Egypt', p. 487, among others, support this point. Kent, 'Egyptian Base', p. 50 dissents, arguing that the H-bomb was a cover story, not the real reason. I have a certain sympathy with this view.
62. David Goldsworthy, *BDEEP*, Series A, Vol. III, *The Conservative Government and the End of Empire*, Doc. 42, 23 July 1953. *BDEEP, Egypt*, Part III, Doc. 541, 29 July 1954. The story of the technical problems that took from July to October to sort out is *BDEEP, Egypt*, Part III, Doc. 557, 1 Nov. 1954.
63. Anthony Eden, *Full Circle* (London, Cassell, 1960), pp. 260–1, and interview with Arab News Agency cited in Tom Little, *Modern Egypt* (London, Benn, 1967), p. 157.
64. Twenty-seven Tories defied the whip on the vote on the settlement.
65. Roger Louis, 'Churchill and Egypt', p. 488.
66. Shuckburgh, *Descent to Suez*, p. 187.

— 4 —

Suez, 1956

THE BAGHDAD PACT AND THE GROWING BREACH WITH NASSER

THE SUEZ OPERATION was the culmination of 18 months of growing tension between the British and the Egyptian governments. The hopes that had been nurtured by the Anglo-Egyptian agreement proved to be a mirage. The essential cause of the crisis was the determination of the new British Prime Minister, Anthony Eden, to maintain Britain's paramount role in the Arab circle through the Baghdad Pact, and Egyptian President Nasser's determination to pursue a policy of neutralism and opposition to all Western attempts to retain regional hegemony, which, depending on your viewpoint, blocked Egypt's, or his own, ambitions for Arab leadership. Eden decided that Iraq, Britain's closest ally in the Middle East, should be the Arab power that Britain should base its Middle Eastern defence policy around. Britain had long sought a revision of its 1930 alliance with Iraq, but a 1948 agreement caused riots in Baghdad. The United States for some time had been seeking regional defence co-operation of the Northern Tier of states in the Near East (Turkey, Iraq, Persia and Pakistan). Obstacles to such a plan were removed in late 1954. Anglo-Egyptian relations were moving towards what seemed more friendly waters. Nuri al-Said, the pro-British Iraqi statesman, became Prime Minister once more in August and began consultations with Turkey's leader, Adnan Menderes. The British appear to have seen the wider scheme for a Middle Eastern alliance as allowing them 'a political umbrella' under which they would be able to secure revision of the Anglo-Iraqi Treaty.[1]

Egypt despite being essentially integrated into the Western alliance by virtue of the recent Anglo-Egyptian treaty was still opposed to any regional defence pact that included Arab and Western powers and in December 1954 warned British officials that any pact of the Northern Tier countries would be unacceptable to Egypt and also to the broader swathe of Arab public opinion. The Egyptians gave broad hints that the Saudis would pour money into a campaign to intrigue against Nuri al-Said if he joined such a pact and they might do likewise. The Saudis had a long-standing feud with the Iraqi royal family dating back to the First World War. More recently, they had clashed with Britain over the Burami Oasis on the border with Oman. The British had expelled Saudi forces from the area which was claimed by both Saudi Arabia and the Oman. This dispute was to poison Anglo-Saudi relations for nearly a decade and be a source of continuous strain with Washington. During his meeting with British officials, Nasser was conspicuous by his moderation and he stated that 'it was not Egypt's intention to attempt to hound the United Kingdom out of the Middle East'.[2] It was not the first time that Nasser's soothing words in private would be followed by actions that were detrimental to the British position in the Middle East. Some opinion in the Foreign Office appears to have been cautious about a Turco-Iraqi pact. However, Nuri seems to have been convinced of the need to sign it, which was done on 13 January 1955. At the Arab summit at the end of January, Nasser lambasted Nuri for signing the pact.

In February 1955 Eden set off to the Middle East on a tour to promote a Middle Eastern defence pact. Eden met Nasser in Cairo on the trip. The meeting over dinner was depending on your source either cordial or a disaster. Heikal claimed that Eden treated Nasser with colonial condescension and described it as a 'confrontation'. Eden, by most accounts a man of immense charm, was unlikely to have intended to be gratuitously rude but one cannot be sure. The Heikal account was written long after Suez so it would be unsurprising if bitterness clouded it.[3] However, the meeting even if friendly showed the huge gap between the British and the Egyptians on the question of the Turco-Iraqi pact. Eden's wife mentioned that Nasser was very bitter about the matter and Eden informed Churchill that there was no chance of converting him to the pact.[4] His summation was that 'No doubt jealousy plays a part in this, and a frustrated desire to lead the Arab world.'[5] Interestingly Nasser's objections, according to British accounts, stemmed from Turkish involvement and he seemed amenable to some kind of alliance between Britain and Iraq.

On 24 February 1955, a Middle East defence organisation was formed with Iraq and Turkey signing a treaty that became the basis of the Baghdad Pact. In April, the pact saw the adherence of Pakistan, Iran and Britain. Nasser later saw the pact as an attempt to perpetuate Britain's regional dominance but his initial opposition seems to be that he was convinced that it was part of a Nuri al-Said scheme to isolate Egypt. The pact, he believed, was part of Nuri's long-standing scheme for Arab unity based on Iraq, Jordan and Syria commonly known as the Fertile Crescent project. Nasser feared that he was being excluded and would be left to face Israel alone and would be forced to come to terms with it.[6] Also, since 1954, when he had become undisputed Egyptian leader, he had been developing foreign policy ideas of Arab unity and neutralism that the Baghdad Pact ran contrary to. In an interview with the *Observer* in March 1956, a year later, when relations with Britain were much worse, Nasser outlined publicly the reasons for his hostility to the pact and to the general thrust of British policy in the region and warned that he believed 'that by attempting to keep this area as a sphere of influence Britain will lose her real interests'.[7]

Nasser's reaction to the pact was to pursue policies detrimental to the British almost as soon as the ink was dry on the pact. The famous 'Voice of the Arabs' radio station was set up and was soon broadcasting propaganda all over the Middle East, pouring scorn and abuse on the pact and the rulers who supported it.[8] But it was not merely Nasser who looked upon the pact as a threat. The Saudis and the Israelis feared that the pact might be used against them. As these countries were the key American interests in the Middle East, the United States declined to join, even though they had encouraged the Northern Tier concept, because the pact was no longer about collective defence against the Soviet Union but had become in the words of Eisenhower and Dulles 'an instrument of British policy' and 'Arab intrigue'.[9] Nasser solidified his ties with other Arabs by forming a military alliance with Syria and Saudi Arabia in March 1955. Despite this Stevenson, the British Ambassador, advised that no breach be made with Nasser yet.[10] On 2 April Britain formally joined what was now called 'the Baghdad Pact'. Two weeks later, Nasser was in Bandung at the first meeting of non-aligned states. Nasser emerged along with Nehru, Zhou Enlai and Tito as a key advocate for those countries that had concerns outside the narrow confines of the Cold War. Nasser certainly was more radical after Bandung and when he returned to Egypt he was undoubtedly the Arab leader with the greatest stature.[11]

GROWING BREACH WITH THE WEST

On 28 February 1955, Israel launched an extensive raid against the Egyptian-ruled Palestinian enclave of Gaza, killing 38 Egyptians. It was ostensibly in response to Palestinian guerrilla attacks on Israel. The raid was the start of the countdown to the Suez War.[12] Nasser, who had until this moment been mainly interested in the economic development of his country, now became convinced that he needed a major rearmament programme. The Tripartite Pact seemed to preclude major arms supplies from the Western powers. Britain had also continuously lobbied the United States not to supply Egypt with arms. The lack of Western supplies and the growing aggressiveness of Israel were the major factors in Nasser's decision to evade the pact's limits on the arms trade in the Middle East by buying arms from the Eastern Bloc in September 1955.[13]

In April 1955 Anthony Eden finally succeeded to the premiership. His new Foreign Secretary was Harold Macmillan. Eden on becoming Prime Minister had a number of acute problems both political and personal. By temperament he was an exceptionally highly strung man. This was further exacerbated by his health problems. Politically, he had only one real string to his bow – a lifetime's experience in foreign affairs. If not economically illiterate, he was certainly not well versed in the minutiae of fiscal and monetary policy. The problems he faced were further heightened when one considers that Britain's problems were as much economic as diplomatic. Indeed the two problems were intimately linked. Britain's worldwide role was a drain on the economy, while the faltering economy hamstrung the worldwide pretensions of many British leaders. For much of Eden's 22 months in the highest office, the British economy was under great strain due to the defence burden and a high-risk pre-election budget give-away by his Chancellor, Rab Butler, in April 1955. At the end of 1955 Eden moved an increasingly out-of-his-depth Butler to the Home Office. Macmillan, who was too independently powerful to allow Eden to dominate foreign affairs completely, was moved to the Treasury. This allowed the promotion of Selwyn Lloyd, a provincial lawyer with a good war record and Junior Minister at the Foreign Office, to the post of Foreign Secretary. Lloyd, with only a novice's experience of high diplomacy, was perfect for Eden, who wanted foreign policy made in Downing Street. Lloyd suffered from the feeling that he had been over-promoted and willingly put up with a barrage of interference from Eden. However, it was perhaps not Lloyd who was over-promoted but Eden. As Foreign Secretary, in charge of one department, all his strengths were focused on a single area in which he was expert. Unfortunately, his inability to delegate made him an overbearing and interfering Prime Minister often in areas that he was far from familiar with.[14] All this damaged his relations with his Cabinet particularly Macmillan. Furthermore, within a few months of winning re-election in May 1955, the Conservative press, particularly the *Daily Telegraph*, was orchestrating suggestions that Eden was failing to deliver firm government. Many of his ministerial colleagues, past and present, were of the opinion that he was not up to the job. These included Churchill, Macmillan and Lord Swinton.[15]

Macmillan's tenure at the Foreign Office was short and certainly with regard to the Middle East not a particularly distinguished one. He had been a long-standing hawk on the Middle East, particularly on the subject of the Suez base. His diaries for 1955 reveal him as showing an early conviction that Nasser was a grave threat to British and Western interests in the region.[16] This was most evident when the arms deal between Nasser and the Eastern Bloc was announced. Shuckburgh warned that the entry of Russia into the Middle East was a big blow as it meant the West would now have to outbid them. Macmillan agreed claiming that 'if we lose Egypt we shall lose the rest of the Arab world'.[17] Harold Caccia, a deputy undersecretary at the Foreign Office, reflecting the increasing British disillusionment with Nasser, wrote, 'we may have to get rid of Nasser'.[18] However, the Americans were not willing to break with Egypt yet and persuaded the British not to do anything rash. Dulles and Macmillan discussed the deal at a meeting in October 1955. It was decided to continue with Project ALPHA, an attempt to get the Arabs and the Israelis to agree a peace treaty and to try to prevent the rot spreading to Syria and Saudi Arabia. At this meeting, Macmillan was a moderate on the subject of Nasser and agreed that the arms deal should be criticised 'more in sorrow than anger'.[19] The Americans, particularly through CIA contacts such as Kermit Roosevelt and Miles Copeland, got Nasser to play down the affair. They persuaded him to say that the arms came from Czechoslovakia rather than the Soviet Union. Sir Humphrey Trevelyan assessed that Nasser's internal position was strengthened by the deal. He could not see a realistic alternative to Nasser unless he was assassinated. From November 1955 Trevelyan was in receipt of top-secret reports from a source close to Nasser code-named 'Lucky Break'. These reports claimed that Nasser was intent on a military attack on Israel and was widening his relationship with the Soviets.[20] While Trevelyan was dubious about the veracity of 'Lucky Break', Macmillan was initially, at least, very exercised about the reports.[21] There is dispute about who 'Lucky Break' was. Some Foreign Office reports would suggest that 'Lucky Break' was an embassy contact, while Scott Lucas, who is an authority on intelligence aspects of Suez, is convinced that he was a figment of the imagination of hawks in MI6 who wanted to persuade British statesmen and civil servants of the need to remove Nasser. It is not clear what his evidence for this is, and the MI6 files are unlikely to be released any time soon.[22]

It is clear that British policy towards Nasser began to crystallise at the end of 1955. The Permanent Undersecretary at the Foreign Office, Sir Ivone Kirkpatrick, outlined a package deal that should be offered to Nasser. In return for Nasser turning away from the Soviets, limiting arms purchases and moving towards a settlement with Israel, the Western powers would provide arms, pressure Israel to make a fair settlement, finance the Aswan Dam and help salve Egypt's increasingly fractious relations with Sudan and Iraq. If Nasser rejected the deal, Egypt would be isolated, and refused aid and arms. Ominously, in such an eventuality Britain and the United States would also have to consider 'ways and means of bringing down the regime'.[23]

Meanwhile, the British were more interested in getting other Arab states to accede to the Baghdad Pact. Macmillan, in particular, appears to have had little time for ALPHA, the American project for a comprehensive Arab–Israeli peace. This may be because Eden was determined to control the British involvement in the scheme, much to Macmillan's annoyance. Nasser's attitude to ALPHA was never fully clear. There had been a channel of communication between Nasser and Moshe Sharett, the dovish Prime Minister of Israel since 1954. The first dialogue was interrupted by Israeli attempts to sabotage the Anglo-Egyptian agreement by setting off bombs in Egypt. The purpose of the amateurish scheme – the 'Lavon affair' – dreamed up by Israeli intelligence was to fake incidents that would discredit Nasser, making it look like the Egyptians could not protect Western property, and wreck the Anglo-Egyptian negotiations. The sabotage ring was broken up and two members of it were executed. The Israelis also tried to breach the Egyptian blocking of the Suez Canal to their vessels with the ship *Bat Galim* in September 1954. The Egyptians were outraged. A dialogue of potentially historic significance was ruined when Israel called it off after Nasser refused to commute the sentences of the Israeli saboteurs. It was finished completely by the raid on Gaza. This was launched at the behest at David Ben-Gurion, former Israeli Prime Minister and since the end of 1954 restored to the Defence Ministry. Ben-Gurion was by now convinced that Nasser was a deadly threat to Israel, potentially combining the military leadership of a Saladin and the modernising zeal of an Ataturk. He concluded during the course of 1955, like Anthony Eden would later, that 'his removal was a matter of vital national interest'.[24] The Americans pinned a lot of hope on their belief that the charismatic Egyptian leader was the only Arab with the ability to deliver an Arab–Israeli peace deal. ALPHA was continued throughout 1955 until it was finally finished by the failure of the Robert Anderson mission of March 1956.[25]

In the autumn/winter of 1955, Jordan became the battleground between Britain and Nasser as the Egyptians orchestrated a campaign to prevent another Arab state adhering to the Baghdad Pact. After King Hussein signalled a willingness to join the Baghdad Pact in November 1955, Macmillan was keen to fast-track Jordanian entry against the advice of Dulles.[26] When the British Chief of the Defence Staff, Field Marshal Templer, visited Amman in December, he was greeted by

Egyptian- and it should be said Saudi-inspired riots.[27] This prevented Hussein from acceding to the pact. Eden met Eisenhower and Dulles in January 1956. Disappointed by Nasser's increasingly hostile attitude to ALPHA, Dulles wondered 'whether our whole attitude to Nasser will have to change'.[28]

However, most observers agree that the final and fatal breach with Nasser, on the part of the British, occurred in the spring of 1956. This was sparked by the sacking of Glubb Pasha (General Sir John Glubb), the commander of the Jordanian Arab Legion, in March 1956 while Selwyn Lloyd, the new Foreign Secretary, was in Cairo for talks. According to Nutting, from this moment on, Eden saw Nasser as the most serious threat to Britain's leading position in the Middle East, and he had to be got rid of. A parliamentary debate on the 'Glubb affair' went very badly for Eden. Eden, who understandably felt that he had taken a bold political risk in the base agreement, found the Suez Group seeking action against Nasser, as well as taking the opportunity to lash the Prime Minister for his handling of Britain's relations with Egypt. Eden was also outraged by what he considered Hussein's betrayal and had to be dissuaded from abrogating the Anglo-Jordanian Treaty of 1948 and cutting all aid. The 'Glubb affair' provided Eden with the spur to take a strong line against any further intrigue by Nasser. Co-operation with Nasser was no longer possible. To one observer he shouted out that 'It's either him or us, don't forget that.'[29] Anthony Nutting, the Minister of State at the Foreign Office, still talked about neutralising and isolating Nasser. Eden had now gone far beyond such a policy:

> What's all this nonsense about isolating Nasser or 'neutralising' him, as you call it? I want him destroyed, can't you understand? I want him removed, and if you and the Foreign Office don't agree, then you'd better come to the Cabinet and explain why.[30]

Senior British ministers now began to make the invidious comparisons between Nasser and the dictators of the 1930s – Mussolini and Hitler. According to Lloyd's biographer's account of the meeting between Lloyd and Nasser in March 1956, the latter described in great detail his life history and his future aims: 'They [the British delegation] felt it to be the equivalent of hearing Hitler dilate upon Mein Kampf without omitting any embarrassing footnotes.' Eden now saw him as a figure who wished to control the Arab world like a 'Caesar from the Gulf to the Atlantic'. Macmillan described him as an 'Asiatic Mussolini'.[31] Selwyn Lloyd, the new Foreign Secretary, told Cabinet on 21 March that

It was now clear that we could not establish a basis for friendly relations with Egypt. That being so, we ought to realign our policies in the Middle East: instead of seeking to conciliate or support Colonel Nasser we should do our utmost to counter Egyptian policy and to uphold our true friends in the Middle East.[32]

The Americans were now also convinced that Nasser was inimical to their interests. The failure of ALPHA was the most important factor. A new policy designated 'OMEGA' was instituted. It was designed to strengthen the friendly Arab countries and at the same time use economic and other pressure to modify the policies of Egypt and Syria. Eisenhower approved OMEGA at the end of March. However, the Americans wished to keep open the possibility of wooing Nasser back to a pro-Western line. The British had no such desire. Eden, in particular, wanted Nasser destroyed or even murdered. A number of joint covert operations were put into effect to regain the initiative in the Arab world.[33] The most well known, code-named 'Straggle', was designed to topple the pro-Nasser regime in Syria. The operation was a joint effort between the CIA and Britain's Secret Intelligence Service (MI6). It failed mainly because it was timed by complete accident to take place with the Suez operation. The Syrian plot linked MI6 and the CIA. The sheer recklessness of the plot may have convinced MI6 and Eden that an 'anything goes' policy in the Middle East was now possible. Assassination plots aimed at Nasser were allegedly prepared by MI6. The evidence for assassination plots is by no means definitive and the main source for it remains the claims in Peter Wright's memoirs, which, to say the least, need to be treated with caution.[34] The British Ambassador in Cairo, Sir Humphrey Trevelyan, warned that Britain could not hope to maintain relations with Egypt while working against Nasser in the Middle East. Adam Watson replied that, unless Nasser 'gives up his basic aims which we cannot permit him to realise, we see little prospect of being able to work with him, much as it would suit us to collaborate with a friendly Egypt'.[35]

After the Czech arms deal, the West had sought to re-establish better relations with Nasser. He was seeking Western financial aid to build a high dam at Aswan that would provide electricity for the industrialisation of Egypt. Eden and Dulles, the United States Secretary of State, were initially supportive of the scheme. In line with OMEGA, cutting Nasser down to size meant slowing, if not abandoning, Western support for the scheme. Combined with the fact that the US Senate was proving very unhelpful about providing the aid, Dulles was not willing to invest political capital to help Nasser. On 19 July, Dulles withdrew the offer of finance. It was erroneously thought for years that Britain was upset by the withdrawal of finance for the Aswan Dam but it was the exact timing of the decision to pull out that was all that separated the British and the Americans.[36] The timing of the removal of finance looks like a bad move in retrospect. The main British 'stick' in Egypt – the last few troops of the base garrison – had just been evacuated.

CRISIS[37]

Nasser's riposte was swift. On 26 July, he nationalised the British- and French-owned Suez Canal. Ironically, Eden learned of the act during a state dinner for the Iraqi King and Prime Minister. The latter – Nuri al-Said – urged Eden to hit Nasser hard and fast.[38] Nasser, according to his confidant Mohammed Heikal, expected a British military response when he took the action and was already thinking about how to mobilise world opinion to prevent such an attack.[39] However, it quickly was made clear to Eden by his military advisers that Britain could not launch a rapid riposte.[40] As it turned out the window of opportunity to strike against Nasser – if there ever was one – was limited to the few days after Nasser's action. If Eden had been able to despatch a task force quickly he might have succeeded with gunboat diplomacy on the wave of public revulsion against Nasser, at least in the short term. Eden and certain other members of the Cabinet including the Chancellor, Harold Macmillan, were determined to use force from the start, not only to recover the Canal, but also to topple Nasser. Eden, who was petulant and unstable, suffering from chronic pain, seemed to lose all sense of proportion about the threat that Nasser presented. He and other ministers, who one must remember did not have the chronic illness excuse, became obsessed with the idea that Nasser was a 'throwback' to the 1930s when Eden had last faced the dictators. In this analogous fantasy, the Canal became the Rhineland or the Sudetenland. To call Eden bad or mad overlooks the point that these views were held by a considerable number of Cabinet ministers and it would appear most of the Conservative backbench MPs. The singling out of Eden as some kind of drugged-up lunatic is a little unfair in this context of almost universal fear and loathing of Nasser within the Cabinet and the Conservative party. However, the idea of misplaced historical analogy leading otherwise decent men astray was not the only reason for getting Nasser. The ten years after the Second World War had seen Britain suffer reversal after reversal. That war, while on one level a Manichaean struggle between good and evil, was on another level fought, in the eyes of many Conservatives, particularly those who shared a Churchillian view of the world, for the preservation of the

British Empire. The destruction of Nasser would 'stop the rot', i.e. the slow dismemberment of the British Empire. It would at a stroke restore British power in the Middle East and make any further challenges from the developing world unlikely. As John Darwin suggests, similar claims no doubt were voiced in Vienna as the Habsburgs became convinced that the only way to 'stop the rot' in their empire was to destroy Serbia in 1914.[41] Furthermore, these British aims of destroying Nasser were strongly supported by the French, who wished to preserve their own North African empire. This was on the grounds that Nasser was the main arms supplier to the Algerian rebels, rather than the Canal issue. Mollet and Pineau are rarely indicted to the same extent as Eden mainly one suspects because they were open, some might say brazen, about their role in the whole affair.

In the House of Commons debate on the nationalisation, Eden kept calm and, ironically as it turned out, was more moderate than Hugh Gaitskell, the Labour leader, and Aneurin Bevan, the Shadow Foreign Secretary. Their relative bellicosity was to be used against them when they opposed military force later. In private, Eden was already looking towards military action. With the approval of Macmillan, who was proving the most belligerent of the Cabinet, Eden sent a strong telegram to Eisenhower on 27 July, which took a very uncompromising line on the crisis.[42] This uncompromising line was made clearer to Robert Murphy, the American Undersecretary of State, when he was informed by Lloyd that the whole 'western position in Middle East will be jeopardised if Nasser gets away with his action. NATO, Western Europe and other parts of world will be at mercy of man who has shown himself irresponsible and faithless'. It was made clear that force would be used if necessary.[43] The belief, apparently shared by both Eden and Macmillan, that Eisenhower – their close ally from the Second World War – would support the use of force, or at least would be neutral in such an eventuality, was to prove the most serious misjudgement of the crisis. Dulles can to a certain extent be blamed for putting hope in the heart of Eden. On 1 August he told Eden that 'A way had to be found to make Nasser disgorge what he is attempting to swallow.' This statement was, according to Eden's account, to resonate with him for the rest of the crisis.[44] However, Eisenhower could hardly have been more explicit in his opposition to force in public and in private communication with Eden. In a letter of 31 July he wrote, 'I have given you my personal conviction, as well as that of my associates as to the unwisdom even of contemplating the use of force at the moment.'[45]

Many accounts of intelligence aspects of Suez have concluded, on at best partial evidence, that the intelligence material provided for

Eden contributed towards Eden's decisions to go down the road to war. As Peter Hennessy has recently pointed out, the advice given by the Joint Intelligence Committee (JIC), within days of the Canal nationalisation, which concluded that, should 'western military action be insufficient to ensure early and decisive victory, the international consequences both in the Arab States and elsewhere might give rise to extreme embarrassment and cannot be forecast' proved to be 'remarkably prescient'.[46] Others have pointed to the reckless plots being orchestrated by MI6 in the Middle East, particularly by the senior officer George Young, as evidence that British intelligence agencies were one of the main factors that sent Britain on its road to Suez.[47]

Meanwhile military preparations were continuing apace in close co-operation with the French. The code name for the operation was 'Musketeer'. The plans were for a full-scale land, sea and air assault on Egypt involving 80,000 troops in the middle of September.[48] The size of the operation and the choice of landing area – Alexandria, which is closer to Cairo than to the Canal – all pointed to the invasion having as much to do with toppling Nasser as to regaining control of the Canal. With regard to creating a pretext for military action, it was the French who were making the arrangements that were eventually to lead to collusion. They had been developing close military links with the Israelis for some time previously. Talks were initiated with top Israeli leaders to co-ordinate action against Nasser within days of the crisis.[49] It seems that the French saw the Israeli element as a means of speeding up an attack on Nasser as the Israelis' input would mean fewer Franco-British forces would be needed to be built up on Cyprus.

The Americans were busy trying to find a diplomatic solution for the crisis and it seemed so were the British. A conference of interested parties was held in London (16–23 August). The conference came up with the 18 power proposals for international control of the Canal. It was to consist of an international board that would collect the revenue and be in charge of the administration of the Canal. While Egypt was to be represented under the new arrangement, this proposal would have allowed the Canal to remain under international control in perpetuity.[50] Since the Canal had to be handed over to Egypt anyhow in 1968, the plan was completely unworkable. This puts the whole Suez debacle in perspective. The Canal would legally revert to Egypt in just over a decade no matter what Britain did. The Americans hoped that Nasser would come up with a counter-offer but, before this could materialise, the British insisted that a mission be sent to inform Nasser of the proposals, which now assumed the appearance of a demand. Robert Menzies, the Australian Prime Minister, was despatched to Cairo to talk to Nasser. During the Menzies mission, Eisenhower rejected the use of force to regain the Canal. This was soon followed by Nasser formally rejecting the 18 power proposals on 9 September. 'How could the West deal with a man like Nasser, if they throw their trump cards into the waste-basket?' was the understandable question raised by Menzies after learning of Eisenhower's intervention.[51]

Lloyd informed the Americans that the British wanted to have the dispute considered by the United Nations Security Council, as quickly as possible. Lester Pearson, the Canadian Prime Minister, warned Lloyd that neither Canada nor the United States would allow the UN to be used as a cover for war.[52] It was feared by those countries that, if that failed to see a result, the British and the French would move swiftly towards the use of force. Dulles, to forestall this, announced a new plan called the Suez Canal Users' Association (SCUA). SCUA would collect the Canal tolls and give so much to Egypt for use of the Canal. Eden hoped that a rejection of the scheme by Nasser would see the United States take a harder line. These hopes were dashed at a press conference on 13 September when Dulles announced that even if SCUA was rejected the United States had 'no intention to shoot our way through' the Canal.[53] These comments echoed those of his President two days before. The Americans made clear that they saw retaliatory action as taking the form of the continuation of economic sanctions and a boycott of the Canal. Thus, the second London conference, which established SCUA, could only be a disappointment to Eden. It proved to be little more then a talking shop. The Americans remained convinced that Nasser was a danger. The Canal issue, however, was not the one to take Nasser on over. On 6 October the President vetoed a CIA plot to topple Nasser.[54]

The threat of war appeared to recede as Nasser had predicted. There existed no backing for force from France and Britain's allies. A plan code-named 'Pile-up' to overwhelm the Egyptians with ships and the withdrawal of all the Canal company's foreign pilots backfired and instead of exposing the supposed incompetence of the Egyptians succeeded in demonstrating the efficiency of the new regime. General Paul Ely, the French Chief of Staff, later recalled that by this stage (late September) he thought the crisis was 'very probably buried'.[55] The British had reworked their military plans. The original 'Musketeer' with its grand amphibious assault on Alexandria and bringing the Egyptian army to battle at least had a certain military decisiveness about it. Now code-named 'Musketeer Revise', the new plan appeared to rely on bombing as much as on ground forces and seemed to depend on assumptions that had never been proven. 'Musketeer Revise' called for the waging of an air campaign against Egyptian military and economic targets coupled with a landing at Port Said, which would facilitate the seizure of the Canal. The Chiefs of Staff warned though: 'The new plan is based on the assumption that the air offensive will break the Egyptian will to resist and bring about the disintegration of the army. The validity of this assumption is impossible to check.'[56] Scott Lucas suggests that the revision of the plan was driven by MI6 and speculates about the connections between Macmillan and his son-in-law, Julian Amery, who had the closest of connections with MI6. Macmillan was the chief hawk, who had in August suggested using the Israelis and later misled Eden about American support and the state of Britain's currency reserves.[57]

As September drew to an end, the likelihood of 'Musketeer Revise' ever being carried out diminished further. That tension was lessening was further demonstrated when negotiations at the UN in October seemed to be close to producing acceptable results. The period 5–8 October saw the Security Council discuss the matter without much success. However, when Selwyn Lloyd and Christian Pineau, the French Foreign Minister, and Mahmoud Fawzi, their Egyptian counterpart, engaged in direct negotiations, an agreement based on the so-called 'Six Principles' appeared possible.[58] Lloyd was disturbed by the attitude of Pineau who seemed unwilling to adhere to any agreement. On 13 October, the Security Council voted on an Anglo-French resolution. It was in two parts. The first, which was adopted unanimously, set out the Six Principles. The second part called for the London proposals to be accepted or for the Egyptians to come up with a scheme that satisfied the Six Principles and provide the Canal users with guarantees as good as the London proposals. The Egyptians were also requested to co-operate with SCUA. The Egyptians would not accept the second part and it was subsequently vetoed by the Russians.[59] Lloyd, who was being called back to London for consultations, agreed to continue negotiations with Fawzi in Geneva on 29 October with hopes high for a peaceful solution.[60] However, events had taken a new turn on the other side of the Atlantic.

On 14 October, a French delegation arrived at the Prime Minister's residence at Chequers with what Nutting describes as 'an invitation to a conspiracy'.[61] The acting French Foreign Minister, M. Gazier, and General Maurice Challe, the Deputy Chief of Staff of the French air force, outlined to Eden what was to become known as 'the Plan'. The Israelis were to be invited to attack Egypt across the Sinai Peninsula. When they were close to the Canal, the British and French would order the combatants to withdraw their forces from the Canal area. The British and French would then deploy their forces in the Canal area to separate the combatants. According to Minister of State at the Foreign Office Anthony Nutting's account, the Prime Minister was convinced that the Plan gave Britain the pretext to go to war. This raises the question as to why Eden felt he had to go down this route of clear illegality. The reasons were manifold. Eden considered that a negotiated settlement would enhance Nasser and as a result further weaken his own position. The Conservative party conference, which had taken place on 11–13 October, had seen extremist positions being taken by many members of the party. The Suez Group was able to pass a strong amendment to the government's moderate motion on Suez.[62] One observer sees the Suez operation as the culmination of Eden falling into line with the diehards of the Suez Group. Another suggests that the Suez Group by their militancy prepared the ground for Eden to launch an invasion by their constant writings in the press.[63] Secondly, and perhaps more importantly, Israel had launched a series of heavy raids on the frontier of Jordan. The main threat to peace in the Middle East seemed to be moving from the Suez issue to a potential Israeli–Jordanian war. The problem for Britain was that, if Israel attacked Jordan, Britain would be obliged to intervene on the Jordanian side owing to treaty obligations. British operational plans to fight Israel code-named 'Cordage' were reactivated. The potential outcome could have seen Britain fighting for Jordan against Israel with Nasser supporting from the sidelines.[64] According to Lucas, and his is a convincing argument, the heavy Israeli attacks were part of the deception plans of the Israeli defence forces to fool the Egyptians as to which Arab country was going to be attacked. It was not a Franco-Israel conspiracy but it gave Eden 'the excuse to embark upon a new effort for the overthrow of Nasser'.[65]

Eden was able to secure the backing of Lloyd. At the Cabinet meeting on 16 October (which has either been removed from the minutes or was never recorded), ministers with one or two exceptions agreed to proceed with the Plan.[66] Eden, accompanied by Lloyd, then flew to Paris to meet Guy Mollet, the French Prime Minister, and Pineau. Lloyd in his memoirs claims the meeting merely discussed the possibility of what the allies would do if the Canal were threatened by an Israeli–Egyptian conflict. The two Britons expressed the opinion that the UK would not fight to defend Nasser but would – subject to Cabinet approval – intervene to safeguard the Canal.[67] However, Nutting claims that this account by Lloyd was outright lies and that he was informed that Eden had accepted the whole French plan including co-ordinated preplanning with the Israelis. On 18 October the Cabinet was asked a similar question to the one Lloyd claimed was posed in Paris, i.e. what would Britain do if the running of the Canal was threatened by an Israeli invasion of Egypt? No one in the Cabinet dissented from the notion that Britain should intervene.[68] Britain was then dragged further into conspiracy on 21 October when the French requested that the British send a senior minister over to Paris to meet with the Israelis.[69] On 23 October, under conditions of great secrecy, Lloyd and a secretary, Donald Logan, flew to Paris to meet the French and Israeli delegations in a villa in the suburbs of Sèvres. The delegations included Mollet and Pineau for France as well as the Israeli Prime Minister, David Ben-Gurion, and his army Chief of Staff, Moshe Dayan. The conference hatched what Avi Shlaim describes 'as not just the most famous but also the best documented war plot in modern history'.[70] Lloyd was prepared to say that Britain would intervene to protect the Canal if Israel attacked Egypt. Less palatably, he also pointed out that Israel would receive exactly the same ultimatum as Egypt. The Israelis – on the grounds that they would be portrayed as aggressors – were not happy and it seemed the whole scheme might fall apart, mainly because Lloyd was reticent about the central Israeli demand, which was that the British would destroy the Egyptian air force as soon as possible after war had broken out. He feared that the collusion between the three powers would be all too apparent if this was done. Indeed his main priority was his attempt to continue the fiction that Britain was not instigating the Israeli attack.[71]

Lloyd and Pineau returned to London to consult with Eden on the problem of the timing of the British air attack on the Egyptian air force. The latter – perhaps realising that the point of no return had already been passed – assented to the Israeli demand. Eden sent Patrick Dean and Donald Logan back to seal the matter. The understanding reached was that Israel would attack Egypt on 29 October and threaten the Canal. In return the British would eliminate the Egyptian air force within 36 hours of the start of the invasion. The British representatives were then asked to sign a document, which was essentially a record of what had been agreed. Dean signed the document known as the Protocol or Treaty of Sèvres. When Eden learned of the document's existence he attempted to have all the copies destroyed.[72]

Edward Heath's memoirs are very revealing about the extent that the conspiracy involved all the major British ministers:

I found the Prime Minister standing by his chair holding a piece of paper. He was bright eyed and full of life ... 'We've got an agreement!' he exclaimed. 'Israel has agreed to invade Egypt. We shall then send in our own forces backed up by the French, to separate the contestants and regain the canal.' The Americans would not be told about the plan. He concluded, somewhat unnervingly that 'this is the highest form of statesmanship'. The Sevres Protocol, as it became known, had been signed the day before, in a suburb of

Paris. Sir Patrick Dean had signed on behalf of the Foreign Secretary, Selwyn Lloyd, and Christian Pineau and David Ben-Gurion had signed, respectively, on behalf of France and Israel. Only Lloyd, Macmillan, Butler and myself were to know about it.[73]

Eden – according to the minutes of the Cabinet for 25 October – intimated that an Israeli attack on Egypt was likely and Lloyd suggests he even gave a likely date for the attack as being 29 October.[74] But it does seem that he did not tell the full Cabinet the whole truth about the conspiracy and, according to Heath, they were only told that force would be used as a last resort.[75] The Americans were watching events closely and becoming increasingly worried about what was going to happen. As early as 18 October Secretary Dulles had complained to the CIA Director Allen Dulles that he was 'quite worried about what may be going on in the Near East. He does not think we have really any clear picture as to what the British and French are up to there. He thinks they are deliberately keeping us in the dark.'[76] American suspicions were being aroused by the volume of coded radio traffic between Britain and France. They were also aware – thanks to U2 aerial spy missions – that the French had breached the Tripartite Pact by supplying large quantities of weaponry to Israel. Their fear was that an Israeli attack on Jordan would be used by the British and French as an excuse to attack Egypt. Nobody in Washington appears to have known the extent of the conspiracy that was about to unfold. The British added to the fog by not holding any consultations with the Americans during the week. The new British Ambassador to the United States, Harold Caccia, went by liner rather than plane and was consequently at sea during the crisis.[77] Along with an explosive situation in the Middle East, Eisenhower and his closest advisers were wondering whether events in Eastern Europe (the Polish and Hungarian crisis) were the first signs that the Soviet bloc was about to collapse. On what must have seemed a more mundane and base level, the President was only a few days away from the vote on his re-election.

On 29 October, Israel invaded Egypt. The following afternoon after a cursory Anglo-French consultation, the Israeli and Egyptian ambassadors in London were presented with an Anglo-French ultimatum requiring both sides to pull back their forces ten miles from either side of the Canal. They would also consent to the acceptance of an Anglo-French force landing to protect the Canal.[78] Reaction was swift and condemnatory from both the Labour party and the Americans. Eisenhower sent a message to Eden, which in the coldest language imaginable urgently expressed his 'deep concern' about what had happened.[79] Right from the moment that the Israelis attacked, Eisenhower was unchanged in his determination that the attack on Egypt had to be halted. Dulles felt equally strongly, arguing that all the newly independent countries would turn to the Soviet Union unless the United States opposed its allies.[80]

In the UN the American Permanent Representative, Henry Cabot Lodge, introduced a resolution calling for an Israeli withdrawal and calling on all UN members to refrain from the use of force. The British and French vetoed the resolution to the consternation of world opinion. The Americans, in an unlikely alliance with the Soviets, brought the resolution to the floor of the General Assembly for consideration.[81] In Cairo, Nasser, bolstered by the strong opposition to the Anglo-French ultimatum from all spectra of world opinion, rejected it. Thus on 31 October, the Royal Air Force set about the task of destroying the Egyptian air force. The UN General Assembly debate saw the British and French isolated with a motion of censure passed by 65 votes to 5 on 2 November. Lloyd – in an effort to at least mollify world opinion – persuaded Eden to accept the principle of a UN peace-keeping force to separate the combatants. This created an unexpected problem when the Canadian Foreign Minister, Lester Pearson, began the task of creating a UN emergency force (UNEF) with far greater urgency than the British had thought possible. Having accepted the idea of UNEF in principle, the British then tried to persuade the other UN nations that the Anglo-French force should be the spearhead of UNEF. All the carefully built-up pretexts for invasion were being removed.[82] Meanwhile the Anglo-French force made its way slowly from Malta to Port Said, a voyage that would take five days. (To put this in perspective, fast ocean liners were crossing the Atlantic in three days.) This delay fatally undermined the already faltering expedition.

On 4 November there was even worse news. It seemed the Egypt-ians and the Israelis were on the verge of accepting a UN-brokered cease-fire. This further weakened the pretext for intervention. Eden wanted to proceed with an airborne assault on Port Said the next day. The Egypt committee in the morning was split on the matter, as was a full Cabinet meeting. A substantial minority of the Cabinet led by Butler wished to suspend military action if there was a cease-fire. This led Eden, according to the account of Butler, to threaten resignation. During an adjournment, the Cabinet received news that the Israelis had rejected the cease-fire. The Cabinet unanimously then decided to proceed with the airborne landings that evening and a seaborne assault on Port Said the following day, which were both successfully accomplished.[83] Anglo-French forces had secured the city and the northern end of the Canal when they received the news that the British and French governments had ordered a cease-fire effective from midnight (London time). The Cabinet, meeting on 6 November, was confronted by a number of grave political and financial problems. The most urgent problem was the developing run on sterling. Chancellor Macmillan learned that he would not be able to receive a standby credit from the International Monetary Fund (IMF) to support the currency because the United States was going to block the procedure until there was a cease-fire. They were also threatening oil sanctions. This turned him into an advocate of halting military action. He claims this was the decisive moment in the agreement of the Cabinet to a cease-fire. There is considerable controversy as to whether Macmillan exaggerated the extent of the crisis.[84] At the end of the meeting the Cabinet agreed that a cease-fire had to be accepted.[85] The Americans, particularly the re-elected Eisenhower, were in no mood to let Britain make any gains from the invasion. On 7 November, Eisenhower and Eden communicated by telephone. Eisenhower informed Eden that he believed a proposed summit should be postponed. It was one of the last times that the two men spoke. The United States Ambassador, Aldrich, subsequently commented, 'He [Eisenhower] … wouldn't have anything further to do with Eden at all.'[86] The reason for Eisenhower's change of mind might well be the results of the 1956 American elections. The Suez crisis and Hungary probably convinced any wavering voters that Eisenhower was a safe pair of hands in a time of crisis and helped him in the presidential election but congressional election results saw the Democrats make large gains. This would not have become clear until a couple of days after the presidential results. His first conciliatory phone call was made in the warm glow of electoral success, the second in the harsh glare of electoral reversal.

The American President exploited the weakness of the British to the full. Using the threat of economic sanctions, he demanded Anglo-French compliance with UN resolutions, called for their forces' withdrawal and their replacement with the UNEF. He maintained this pressure until he had got what he wanted, ignoring all entreaties from the British to let them at least achieve some of their objectives. In early November Eden left for Jamaica for rest on medical advice, leaving Butler in charge of the government in what might be described as a triumvirate with Macmillan and Lord Salisbury.[87] These three ministers were tasked with negotiating with the Americans the pull-out of the Anglo-French forces from Egypt.

Macmillan, believing that financial disaster faced Britain unless it capitulated to American demands, wanted an early withdrawal to gain access to American assistance. As Corelli Barnett notes, 'the run on the pound had turned to a nasty bout of Egyptian dysentery'.[88] Macmillan emphasised these points in Cabinet during the last four days of November.[89] The Cabinet, relying on the advice of Macmillan, agreed to withdrawal on 30 November after consultations with the French. This was announced by Lloyd in the Commons on 3 December. This involved a final surrender to the Americans, as Lloyd had to make clear that there was to be a timetable for the withdrawal of the Anglo-French force. If this had not been forthcoming, the vital American financial assistance for sterling would have been withheld. Sterling would have to have been devalued, and with this would have gone its role as one of the world's reserve currencies. In agreement with the UNEF commander, the British and French withdrew all their forces by 22 December. Anthony Eden resigned as Prime Minister owing to his continuing health problems. Some suggest that he was primarily removed from office because he could no longer work with the Americans. A number of historians have concluded that Eden's resignation was the result of some kind of conspiracy orchestrated from within his party by Macmillan or by the Americans.[90] Alas, for the conspiracy theorist, most of the evidence in favour of a plot is circumstantial. However, while Eden was not pushed out of office, his position as Prime Minister was fatally undermined – as he was sidelined from having any input into the decisions of the triumvirate of Macmillan, Butler and Salisbury, which negotiated the British retreat from Suez. With his health shattered, and his presence as Prime Minister an obvious embarrassment to his party, it would have taken an extremely determined figure to continue on. That he chose not to hardly suggests a conspiracy. His successor was Harold Macmillan.

THE SIGNIFICANCE OF SUEZ

Most of the studies on Suez view it as the decisive moment in British policy towards Egypt and the wider Middle East. Scott Lucas claims that, with Suez, Britain left the Middle East 'not with a roar, but with a whimper'.[91] This is not the case, as Nigel Ashton admirably demonstrates in his study. He offers the fall of the Iraqi regime two years later as the decisive event in ending Britain as an arbiter of Middle Eastern affairs. Michael Mason says the decisive moment in Egypt was 1952 and the events of Black Saturday.[92] The main theme of a recent collection is that the demise of the British position in the Middle East was prior to 1955.[93] The fault with the Lucas argument is that Suez did not destroy Britain's alliance with Iraq. It did destroy British hopes of an alliance with an Iraqi–Jordanian axis but even this became a brief reality again under the Arab Union scheme of 1958. What Suez did create was the legend of Nasser as the *Rais* (leader). His grip on power was secured in perpetuity. His survival and his unrivalled ability to mobilise Arab public opinion made him a far more dangerous opponent after Suez.

The use of force on the scale of the Suez operation was an aberration in post-war British policy. Britain has defended its interests when challenged since Suez, notably against Indonesia and Argentina. But in these latter cases the operations were not as ambitious or as foolhardy as Suez, and nor were they as legally or as morally dubious. Similar interventions to Suez were considered against troublesome opponents in 1951 against Iran, and in the following year against the Egyptians under Operation Rodeo. Both were rejected because of a lack of American support. After Suez, military action was considered and rejected on a number of occasions, again on similar grounds. Later in this study we shall see how a 'Suez-style' operation was considered in the lead-up to the Six Day War and again rejected. Suez was the exception that proved the rule that Britain's ability to launch military action without the support of the United States was severely circumscribed. It removed the bluff that Britain could use force against third world despots with impunity. The threat of British retribution was never a serious one again. This was the decisive lesson of Suez for the British and the Egyptians. One of the many lessons of the aftermath of Suez was that American support for anti-Nasser operations was unlikely to be forthcoming.

Nigel Ashton plays down the influence of Suez, perhaps a little too much. He argues that Lucas is mistaken in arguing that after Suez 'Britain paid the price of permanent subservience to American policy' and then proceeds to set about proving Lucas's point.[94] The problem with the Ashton thesis is that, if the Iraqi revolution was so much of a watershed, why was Britain still hanging on grimly to positions in the Middle East until 1968? That there was a post-Suez 'moment' in the Middle East is exemplified by the revision by Elizabeth Monroe of her classic account of 'Britain's moment in the Middle East' to include the period until 1971 (when the last British troops left). On that basis, it could be argued that the Six Day War, with its exposure of Britain's inability to keep the peace despite all its forces, and the devaluation of the same year were more decisive in the ending of British influence. Perhaps searching for watershed moments in history is a waste of time. Suez, the Iraqi revolution and the Six Day War are perhaps better viewed as part of a pattern of British decline and disengagement from the Middle East and a worldwide military role, with the troublesome British economy being the most important factor.

The aftermath of Suez does show Macmillan being constrained by American policy for the most part. It will become clear that Macmillan, in both 1957 and 1958, would have pursued a more radical anti-Nasser strategy if American support had been forthcoming. It was not, and Suez was the primary reason that Macmillan for all his anti-Nasser fulminations would not challenge American leadership in the Middle East. Britain remained willing to challenge Nasser on a more covert level. In 1964 the Americans prevented serious British retaliation against the Egyptians in the Yemen–South Arabia crisis, but could not prevent low-level covert operations.

There is no denying that British attitudes towards Nasser remained exactly the same after Suez. Why would they change? He had, after all, humiliated Britain. Echoes of this anti-Nasser attitude reoccur as late as 1967 in Foreign Office memoranda. Attitude is, however, different from policy – which was directed and implemented in Washington not Whitehall. Therefore Suez remains the ultimate moment when British power and treasure were exposed as not even sufficient to defeat what many in Britain considered little more than a jumped-up Arab Mussolini – which was not a compliment. F.S. Northedge argues that the impact of Suez on policy should not be exaggerated – Britain's Middle Eastern position did not collapse, the Commonwealth survived and the Anglo-American relationship was restored within months.[95] David Reynolds emphasises the psychological effects of Suez, which in his opinion were far more damaging than the material:

> British policy makers had known for years of their underlying weaknesses, but the public image, accentuated by 1940, 1945 and post-war recovery, was of a country that was still a major power. For an Egyptian ex-colonel to twist the lion's tail and get away with it, was a palpable and lasting blow to national self-esteem and international prestige.[96]

The ultimate failure of British policy towards Nasser from the Baghdad Pact to Suez is neatly measured by Dekmejian who notes that the events of the years 1955–56 'propelled the Egyptian President to a position of universal visibility unprecedented in Egyptian–Arab history since the rise of Salah al-Din'.[97] This was hardly the intended effect of the Suez operation and British Middle Eastern policy in general.

NOTES

1. *BDEEP, Egypt*, Part III, Doc. 561, 9 Dec. 1954.
2. *BDEEP, Egypt*, Part III, Doc. 562, 11 Dec. 1954.
3. Heikal, *Nasser*, pp. 77–81.
4. Rhodes-James, *Anthony Eden*, pp. 397–8.

5. PRO FO 371/115492, V 1073/289, Cairo to FO, No. 269, 21 Feb. 1955. See also Eden, *Full Circle*, p. 220.
6. See, for instance, *BDEEP, Egypt*, Part III, Doc. 593, 6 June 1955.
7. Cited in E. Monroe, *Britain's Moment in the Middle East* (London, Chatto & Windus, 1981), pp. 190–1.
8. Patrick Seale, *The Struggle for Syria* (Oxford, Oxford University Press, 1965), pp. 196ff.
9. See Ashton, *Problem of Nasser*, p. 46.
10. *BDEEP, Egypt*, Part III, Doc. 582, 9 Mar. 1955.
11. Dann, *King Hussein*, p. 23.
12. Kyle, *Suez*, p. 62.
13. See Freiberger, *Dawn over Suez*, p. 101.
14. Rhodes-James, *Anthony Eden*, p. 478.
15. P. Hennessy, *The Prime Minister* (London, Penguin, 2000), p. 209.
16. Horne, *Macmillan*, Vol. I, p. 368.
17. PRO FO 371/1133674, JE 1194/152G, Shuckburgh Minute, 23 Sept. 1955.
18. PRO FO 371/1133674, JE 1194/152G, Caccia Minute, 23 Sept. 1955.
19. *BDEEP, Egypt*, Part III, Doc. 602, 3 Oct. 1955.
20. E. Thornhill, 'Alternatives to Nasser: Humphrey Trevelyan, Ambassador to Egypt', in S. Kelly and A. Gorst (eds), *Whitehall and the Suez Crisis* (London, Frank Cass, 2000), p. 14.
21. Kyle, *Suez*, pp. 84–5.
22. W.S. Lucas, 'The Missing Link? Patrick Dean, Chairman of the Joint Intelligence Committee', in S. Kelly and A. Gorst (eds), *Whitehall and the Suez Crisis* (London, Frank Cass, 2000), p. 119.
23. *BDEEP, Egypt*, Part III, Doc. 610, 30 Oct. 1955.
24. A. Shlaim, *The Iron Wall* (London, Penguin, 2000), pp. 134–5.
25. See Freiberger, *Dawn over Suez*, pp. 107–32. Kyle, *Suez*, pp. 56–60.
26. Dulles did not reply to Macmillan's decision until after the Chief of the Imperial General Staff had been despatched to Jordan to negotiate the deal. See *BDEEP, Egypt*, Part III, Doc. 614, 6 Dec. 1955, and accompanying minutes by Shuckburgh and Kirkpatrick.
27. Dann, *King Hussein*, pp. 26–30.
28. Cited in Scott Lucas, *Britain and Suez: The Lion's Last Roar* (Manchester, Manchester University Press, 1996), p. 23.
29. Nutting, *No End of a Lesson*, pp. 31, 34, 35, Rhodes-James, *Anthony Eden*, pp. 431–3, and Shuckburgh, *Descent to Suez*, p. 346.
30. Nutting, *No End of a Lesson*, p. 34.
31. Thorpe, *Selwyn Lloyd*, p. 199. Shuckburgh, *Descent to Suez*, p. 327.
32. *BDEEP, Egypt*, Part III, Doc. 635, 21 Mar. 1956.
33. See A. Gorst and W.S. Lucas, 'The Other Collusion: Operation Straggle', *Intelligence and National Security*, 3 (1994), pp. 576–95.
34. Peter Wright, *Spycatcher* (New York, Viking, 1987), pp. 160–2.
35. *BDEEP, Egypt*, Part III, Doc. 639, 12 May 1956.
36. See K. Kyle, 'Britain and the Crisis', in Roger Louis and Owen, *Suez 1956*, p. 110, for a general discussion of Britain and the Aswan deal.
37. As said earlier, this is not an attempt to provide a blow-by-blow account of Suez. Kyle, *Suez*, and Lucas, *Divided We Stand*, already provide comprehensive treatments.
38. Thomas, *Suez Affair*, p. 31.
39. Heikal, *Cutting the Lion's Tail*, p. 118.
40. Rhodes-James, *Anthony Eden*, p. 454.
41. John Darwin, *Britain and Decolonisation: The Retreat From Empire in the Post-War*

World (London, Macmillan, 1988), p. 214.
42. Horne, *Macmillan*, Vol. I, p. 396.
43. *FRUS 1955–57*, Vol. XVI, Doc. 24, 29 July 1956.
44. Eden, *Full Circle*, p. 487.
45. *FRUS 1955–57*, Vol. XVI, Doc. 35, 31 July 1956.
46. Hennessy, *Prime Minister*, p. 232.
47. Lucas, *Divided We Stand, passim.*
48. Kyle, *Suez*, pp. 167–77.
49. For a first-hand account of Franco-Israeli co-operation around Suez, Shimon Peres, *Battling for Peace* (London, Weidenfeld & Nicolson, 1995), pp. 120–2.
50. Robert R. Bowie, 'Eisenhower, Dulles and the Suez Crisis', in Roger Louis and Owen, *Suez 1956*, pp. 202–3.
51. Kyle, *Suez*, p. 221.
52. Thorpe, *Selwyn Lloyd*, p. 224.
53. Eden, *Full Circle*, p. 483.
54. Stephen Ambrose and Richard Immerman, *Ike's Spies* (New York, Doubleday, 1981), p. 240.
55. D. Carlton, *Anthony Eden: A Biography* (London, Allen Lane, 1981), p. 420.
56. Kyle, *Suez*, pp. 236–8.
57. Lucas and Morey, 'The Hidden Alliance', p. 108.
58. See Lloyd, *Suez 1956*, App. I.
59. Kyle, *Suez*, pp. 288–9.
60. See Nutting, *No End of a Lesson*, p. 90.
61. See Nutting, *No End of a Lesson*, pp. 90–100.
62. Epstein, *British Politics in the Suez Crisis*, pp. 46–7.
63. Onslow, *Backbench Debate*, p. 253. M.D. Kandiah, 'British Domestic Politics, the Conservative Party and Foreign Policy Making', in Kaiser and Staerck, *British Foreign Policy 1955–64*, p. 66, disagrees with this assessment.
64. See Carlton, *Britain and the Suez Crisis*, p. 61.
65. Lucas, *Divided We Stand*, pp. 228–36.
66. See Richard Lamb, *The Failure of the Eden Government* (London, Sidgwick & Jackson, 1987), pp. 231–2.
67. Lloyd, *Suez 1956*, p. 175, and Kyle, *Suez*, p. 302.
68. PRO CAB 128/30, CM 71 (56), 18 Oct. 1956.
69. Lloyd, *Suez 1956*, p. 180.
70. Shlaim, *Iron Wall*, p. 171.
71. Carlton, *Anthony Eden*, pp. 436–7.
72. Rhodes-James, *Anthony Eden*, p. 532.
73. Edward Heath, *The Course of My Life* (London, Hodder & Stoughton, 1998), p. 169.
74. PRO CAB 128/30, CM 74, 25 Oct. 1956, and Lloyd, *Suez 1956*, p. 188.
75. Heath, *Course of My Life*, p. 170.
76. *FRUS 1955–57*, Vol. XVI, Doc. 352, Editorial note.
77. Stephen Ambrose, *Eisenhower the President* (London, Allen & Unwin, 1984), p. 353.
78. Carlton, *Britain and the Suez Crisis*, pp. 69–71.
79. D.D. Eisenhower, *The White House Years: Waging Peace, 1956–61* (New York, Doubleday, 1965), pp. 76–7.
80. W. Roger Louis, 'Dulles, Suez and the British', in R. Immerman (ed.), *John Foster Dulles and the Diplomacy of the Cold War* (Princeton, NJ, Princeton University Press, 1990), p. 153.
81. Carlton, *Britain and the Suez Crisis*, p. 71.
82. Carlton, *Britain and the Suez Crisis*, pp. 73–5.

83. PRO CAB 128/30, CM 79, 4 Nov. 1956 and Lord Butler, *The Art of the Possible* (London, Hamish Hamilton, 1971), p. 193.
84. Macmillan, *Riding the Storm*, p. 164. The controversy is explored in Kyle, *Suez*, p. 464, and D. Kunz, 'Did Macmillan Lie over Suez?', *Spectator*, 3 Nov. 1990.
85. Rhodes-James, *Anthony Eden*, p. 574. Carlton, *Britain and the Suez Crisis*, pp. 77–9.
86. Rhodes-James, *Anthony Eden*, p. 55. Aldrich is quoted in Carlton, *Anthony Eden*, p. 456.
87. As Macmillan described it to Aldrich, Kyle, *Suez*, p. 505.
88. C. Barnett, *The Verdict of Peace* (London, Macmillan, 2000), p. 502.
89. Kyle, *Suez*, pp. 510–11.
90. Carlton, *Britain and the Suez Crisis*, p. 31. Lucas, *Divided We Stand*, pp. 309–23.
91. Lucas, *Divided We Stand*, p. 330.
92. Mason, 'The Decisive Volley', p. 46.
93. M. Kolinsky and M.J. Cohen (eds), *Demise of the British Empire in the Middle East* (London, Frank Cass, 1998).
94. Ashton, *Problem of Nasser*, pp. 100–1.
95. Northedge, *Descent from Power*, pp. 140–1.
96. David Reynolds, *Britannia Overruled: British Policy and World Power in the Twentieth Century* (London, Longman, 1991), p. 205.
97. H. Dekmejian, *Patterns of Political Leadership* (Albany, NY, State of New York University Press, 1975), p. 180.

Issues and Stakes in the Aftermath of Suez, 1957

NEW GOVERNMENT, OLD ATTITUDES

MACMILLAN ASSUMED the office of Prime Minister on 9 January 1957. It would not be too much of an exaggeration to describe him as the only Briton to gain from Suez. The actual succession was decided by the advice given by the senior party elders, Lords Kilmuir and Salisbury, to the Queen.[1] Harold Macmillan, rather than Rab Butler, was the choice. Macmillan was considered more likely to be decisive then the notoriously vacillating Butler and that attribute was something that the Tories needed more then anything else in the dark days of early 1957.[2] At the time of his departure from office Macmillan was viewed by many commentators as an indifferent premier at best. His reputation has steadily risen since thanks particularly to the advocacy of his official biographer, Alistair Horne.[3] His rise to the highest office in the land was nothing short of extraordinary. For while he came from a rich – if upper-middle-class rather than upper-class – background he had as an MP for a northern working-class constituency (Stockton) since the 1920s been on the left of the Conservative party and consequently was never considered for office in the national government. Clement Attlee claimed that he was close to joining the Labour party in the 1930s.[4] He even outlined his beliefs in an interventionist state in a book, *The Middle Way*. His career may also have suffered because of his well-known marital difficulties, which left him prone to depression. While his contemporary, Anthony Eden, effortlessly climbed the ministerial ladder in the 1930s, Macmillan seemed destined for backbench obscurity. Macmillan's stand against appeasement and Munich was his first breakthrough, as it caught the eye of Churchill, and when the latter became Prime Minister he at last achieved lowly ministerial rank. His real rise to prominence came in the autumn of 1942 when Churchill appointed him as British Minister resident in the Mediterranean with Cabinet rank at Allied Forces Headquarters in Algiers until the end of the war. There he forged long-term relationships with, among others, General Eisenhower, de Gaulle and Robert Murphy, his American counterpart. As head of the Allied Control Commission in Italy, he was virtually viceroy of the Middle East. A victim of the Labour landslide in 1945 he managed to get back into Parliament almost straight away thanks to the fortunate –for Macmillan at least – death of a Conservative MP in the safe seat of Bromley. He became a leading advocate of reform in the Conservative party after the war, helping its tilt to the left of centre. Churchill made him Minister of Housing in 1951, where his success in reaching the target of building 300,000 houses a year propelled him to the front rank of the Conservative party. His next two appointments, Minister of Defence under Churchill and Foreign Secretary under Eden, were unhappy due to frequent interference from above and were anyway so brief that he had no opportunity to impose himself on either. His time as Chancellor was equally unhappy.

Macmillan's role in the Suez crisis deserves some scrutiny. He had been one of the strongest advocates of strong measures against Nasser – yet was the first to jump ship when sterling hit the rocks on 6 November. Brendan Bracken, the newspaper proprietor and influential Conservative, wrote critically and accurately about Macmillan on 22 November:

> Until a week ago Macmillan whose bellicosity was beyond description, was wanting to tear Nasser's scalp off with his fingernails. He was like the character in O'Casey's play who cried: 'Let me like a hero fall. My breast expanding to the ball.' Today he might be described as the leader of bolters. His Treasury officials have put before him the economic consequences of the Suez fiasco and his feet are frost bitten.[5]

'First in, first out' was the right-on-the-mark comment of Harold Wilson. Macmillan was no change from Eden in his approach to Nasser and the Suez Canal. Indeed there is plenty of evidence to say that he was even more hawkish on the subject than Eden ever was. From his time as Minister for Housing, when he was a critic of the Suez base agreement, to his tenure as Foreign Secretary when he was an advocate of expansion of the Baghdad Pact, Macmillan was a firm believer in the need for Britain to maintain its leading role in the Middle East. There is every reason to think that until the denouement of 5–6 November, he shared Eden's view that the region was the one area of the world where the British could still carry out independent action without having to look to the Americans. During the crisis, examples are readily available showing his role as the leading Cabinet hawk. As early as August, at an Egypt committee meeting, he was suggesting involving the Israelis some two months before the 'Challe Plan' was put forward by the French, drawing an ironic rebuke from Eden. To the American diplomat, Robert Murphy, he said, 'Suez was a test that could be met only by the use of force.' He was also an advocate of the more ambitious military operations that would have seen the occupation of Egypt and the replacement of Nasser with a more malleable alternative. Most seriously, Macmillan misrepresented the views of Eisenhower in September 1956. He cabled Eden after a meeting with him, claiming that the American President was intent on bringing Nasser down, something denied by the other witness at the meeting, the British Ambassador, Roger Makins.[6] This may well have been Macmillan's gravest error as it copper-fastened Eden's thinking about American attitudes to force.

Thus in no way can it be claimed that the new government was different in attitude to the previous one on the subject of Nasser. The rhetoric in private that continued to be used was certainly no different. The continuation of old attitudes was reinforced by the hawkish views of the extremely influential private secretaries that Macmillan utilised: Philip de Zulueta and Frederick Bishop. As Selwyn Lloyd was a weakened and wounded Foreign Secretary thanks to the Suez affair, Macmillan and his private secretaries were the key shapers of British foreign policy until Lord Home replaced Lloyd in 1960. De Zulueta and Bishop had a function that was more akin to American national security advisers than mere private secretaries. De Zulueta, inherited from Eden, was to prove particularly hawkish on the Middle East. A further demonstration that Macmillan was willing to appease the hard-liners was the appointment of Julian Amery as Parliamentary Undersecretary for War.[7] He was a son-in-law of the Prime Minister and a leading member of the Suez Group. He was to send a number of lively minutes to his father-in-law over the next few years urging the adoption of strong-arm tactics against Nasser. The new government was not one that was going to apologise for the follies of the old.

The aftermath of the Suez crisis confronted Macmillan with what must have seemed like an irresolvable series of problems. The most urgent were the Anglo-American schism and the Canal/Sinai problems. He also had to find some way of restoring Britain's severely damaged position in the Middle East. Iraq, Britain's chief ally, was unhappy. Jordan had requested the termination of the Anglo-Jordanian alliance under pressure from its population, enraged by Suez, and the Saudi Arabians had broken relations with Britain during the crisis. These were just some of the minor problems. Macmillan, a month after he had taken office (9 February), saw the Canal, Egypt and the Middle East as potential breakers of his government.[8]

The lack of diplomatic relations between Egypt and Britain meant all discussions went through intermediaries such as the United Nations Secretary-General, Dag Hammarskjold – whom Macmillan disliked intensely – or the Americans or the Canadians. The prospects for a restoration of relations did not look good as both countries had massive financial claims with the other. A further problem was that Israel was unwilling to evacuate the territory it had seized in the fighting without certain guarantees. The Americans were determined to force their withdrawal. At the United Nations, Henry Cabot Lodge, America's Permanent Representative, was vigorously demanding they withdraw from Sinai and refusing to agree to Israel's demands for concessions and safeguards. Macmillan's greatest fear was that Britain would be forced to vote on an anti-Israel resolution that would force Britain into a conflict of honour and interest, though one might have thought that honour had gone out the window at Sèvres.

The events as they unfold will demonstrate the weakness of the UK position and the ultimate failure to get what it wanted from Egypt with regard to the Canal. The UK government did not resolve its conflict with Egypt but decided to sweep it under the carpet because in the end it was powerless to get its own way. This also demonstrates the collapse of an independent British policy in the Middle East. After Suez, British policy was forced to a large extent to follow the lead set by the United States. Macmillan and his party were determined that Suez should be forgotten about, at least in public, and hoped that any lasting damage to the Conservatives or the country could be avoided. As the official biographer of Macmillan points out, even the most diehard supporters of intervention, the right-wing Suez Group, was 'prepared to write off Suez provided retreat could be made to look like a victory'.[9]

The behaviour of the United States towards Nasser during the Suez crisis was incomprehensible to many in Britain. They had, according to this line of argument, abandoned their closest ally for a third world dictator with neutralist, if not communist, leanings. Considering this was the most ideological American administration, in terms of its rhetoric, of the Cold War, US behaviour requires some explanation. Many in Eisenhower's administration felt a strong dislike for British colonialism that was only exceeded by their anti-communism. John Charmley and others have pointed out that it was a great fallacy of British post-war foreign policy to place so much faith in the Americans when it was clear that their attitude was often unhelpful and at times in total opposition to key British aims.[10] Fortunately, in this case, British hopes of a rapid Anglo-American *rapprochement* were helped by Nasser. The Americans to their surprise, notes Eden's biographer, did not receive as much praise as they had expected.[11] Nasser, to the Americans' chagrin, appeared to credit the not very important intervention of the Soviets with their threat of rocket attack on Paris and London as the decisive moment in the crisis. This made the American abandonment of its closest ally look like a misjudgement. It should then be of little surprise that American policy towards Nasser began to revert to its former hostility as soon as the British and French began their withdrawal.

Another reason for the apparent contradictions in American policy was the continued inconsistent attitude of the Secretary of State, John Foster Dulles, even after the crisis. In two meetings after the crisis he made strange comments to British ministers and officials about the crisis at variance with his actions during it. The first was a visit to Dulles' hospital bed by Selwyn Lloyd and Harold Caccia, the new British Ambassador to Washington, on 18 November 1956. Dulles at this meeting said, 'Selwyn … Why didn't you go through with it and get Nasser down?' The same comments were reiterated later to Harold Caccia.[12] They have often been interpreted as a sign that Dulles was in favour of Suez. However, these are more than balanced by contradictory comments that he made during the crisis and its aftermath. Just to add to the confusing picture for British policy-makers and for the historian, Dulles continued to be prone to making off-the-cuff comments about getting rid of Nasser and using force in the Middle East. It is clear that soon after the end of the Suez crisis American opinion was returning to the views held before the Canal was nationalised when there was agreement with the British under plan OMEGA on the need for 'cutting Nasser down to size'. As one observer points out, the Americans 'differed with the Suez invaders on methods only, not on objectives'.[13] The State Department, even at the height of the Anglo-American schism at Suez, was urging that the United States help restore British power in the Middle East, a point echoed by Eisenhower to Hoover, the Deputy Undersecretary of State, on 25 November.[14]

With or without the aid of the British, the Americans were determined to take action in the Middle East. They feared that, in the aftermath of the Suez War and the Israeli military success, the whole Middle East might fall under the sway of the Soviet bloc. Eisenhower, in his memoirs, states that the Soviet Union's objectives in the region included control of the Canal and cutting the oil supplies of the European powers. This would gravely 'weaken Western Civilisation'.[15] Nasser was also a danger. The United States did not consider him a communist but they did wonder whether, in his desire to rid himself of Western imperialism, he would merely exchange it for the Soviet brand. It was considered in a State Department report that 'Recent relations with Egypt appear to indicate that the United States cannot successfully deal with President Nasser.'[16] America had to pursue a new policy in the Middle East. After rejecting joining the Baghdad Pact, Dulles suggested a programme authorised through Congress to build the United States' position in the Middle East.[17] Eisenhower believed that only America could 'save that area' by filling the vacuum that the humiliation of Britain had caused.[18] America's new policy appeared to be based on the premise that Nasser had to be kept away from the Saudi Arabians, America's closest regional ally. This was to be achieved by calling up the bogey of international communism. This would have the key objective of isolating Nasser. The anachronistic, quasi-feudal figure of King Saud – rather than Nasser – would be the United States' choice for leader of the Arab world. The Eisenhower Doctrine, as it came to be known, was enunciated to a joint session of Congress on 5 January 1957. Eisenhower asked Congress for the power to extend economic and military co-operation and, if necessary, to have the power to deploy American troops to any nation in the Middle East that requested help against communist-instigated subversion.[19] Eisenhower's other purpose – besides warning the Soviets from expansion in the Middle East – was to put Nasser on notice that revolutionary activity that threatened the West's oil supplies would not be tolerated. Macmillan was derisive.[20] Caccia saw the doctrine for what it was, a unilateral American act.[21] It actively supplanted rather than complemented British power. In the Senate hearings on the Doctrine, Dulles played up the unilateral nature of the Doctrine with his comment: 'If I were an American boy, I'd rather not have a French and British Soldier beside me.'[22] Caccia, in his assessment of the remark, commented that it and others critical of the British had 'been said under pressure and the words have not been deliberately chosen. But after all allowances, they do show a cast of thought which we should ignore at risk.'[23]

The question of relations with Egypt was another major topic of debate in the Foreign Office in the early months of 1957. There were indications that Nasser was going to make few or no concessions to Britain on any of the key issues that divided the two countries. If all of Nasser's demands were foisted upon the British, it would ignite serious trouble on the backbenches of the Conservative party. Right-wing die-hards threatened the government's majority even if their enthusiasm for Suez was diminishing. A major rebellion would threaten the survival of the government. If there was one thing that the Conservatives did not want, it was an election fought in the immediate aftermath of Suez. The Conservatives needed to rebuild their reputation and allow Macmillan to gain time to set up another election victory. There was still a British domestic politics element in relations with Nasser's Egypt. It would be some time before this element was removed.

The analysis of this information in Whitehall was confused and there were many different reactions ranging from the restrained to the bellicose. Even though it has been well documented that many in the Foreign Office were deeply dismayed by the Suez operation, few if any memorandums survive reflecting this.[24] In fact the advice being proffered in the months after the crisis reflects the government line to a large degree. Within the Foreign Office there was some division of opinion among the officials. Some voiced strong opposition to any attempt to mend fences with Nasser, while others pointed out the enormous practical reasons for as rapid a *rapprochement* as possible. As early as 3 January 1957, Pierson Dixon at the United Nations was urging a move towards relations of some kind with Egypt in order to 'extricate ourselves from the grip of the United Nations and its Secretary General on our Middle Eastern policies'.[25]

Sir Humphrey Trevelyan, who had been British Ambassador in Cairo during the entire crisis, outlined these practical considerations in a coherent and moderate analysis in the same month as to why relations with Egypt should be restored. The overriding reason was that Egypt held over £200 million sterling in British public and private property.[26] As well as this massive potential loss of British assets, there was also the danger that UK citizens unable to get satisfaction from the Egyptians would lodge claims against their own government. To put this in perspective, £200 million would have been over 10 per cent of the British defence budget in 1957 and nearly 1 per cent of GNP. Trevelyan claimed that the potential downside – that Nasser's prestige would rise and that it would decrease the likelihood of a coup – was invalid, as it was Nasser who broke off relations not the UK, and that restoration of relations would in fact 'increase the chances of a coup against Nasser'. The conclusion reached was emphatic: 'It is in our interest that relations should be restored as soon as possible.'[27] Trevelyan's advice was not accepted in the first months of 1957. As regards his comments about a coup there is some second-hand and primary-source evidence that the British were still interested in bringing down Nasser by such means. Among the British plots that there is some evidence for was Salamander. It was allegedly an MI6-backed plot to use the pro-British elements in the Egyptian army to overthrow Nasser. These plots, which are known to have taken place prior to Suez, may well have continued afterwards. In December 1957, at the ceremony to mark the evacuation of British forces, Nasser announced what was called the 'Restoration Plot'. In February 1957, Mahmoud Khalil, an Egyptian army officer, was called by British intelligence to a meeting in Rome. In the next nine months, he claims that he was paid a total of £162,000 to finance a coup. All the time, though, he kept his superiors informed about what was going on. The plot was revealed at an opportune moment by Nasser.[28] Corroborating the veracity of this plot or something similar is that the British mentioned at the Bermuda Conference the existence of a coup plan to the Americans and asked them to support it. At the meeting Eisenhower noted in his diary that the British spoke of

> the existence of a secret Egyptian plot for executing a coup to dispose of Nasser. They apparently thought we knew a great deal about it and wanted us to make some public statement against Nasser in the hope that this would encourage the dissident Egypt- ians. Manifestly anything the British said against Nasser would only make him stronger in the area.[29]

The consensus from much of the documentation was that the Foreign Office believed in following a slow path to the restoration of diplomatic relations with Egypt in the misplaced hope that the Nasser regime might fall. It must also be remembered that civil servants are just that and they have to tailor their work for the taste of their political masters. It would be a considerable period of time before the Foreign Office was able to regain a degree of control over British policy toward Egypt. Archibald Ross outlined a strategy of this sort on 19 January. He argued that Nasser and the Egyptian government would have to do the chasing if they wanted relations restored. If that happened Britain should be 'coy and very expensive'.[30] In other words any restoration of relations should be on terms that were acceptable to British interests and would involve the Egyptians losing face. Ross, a few days later, sent another memo outlining much the same position but with firmer recommendations on what action to take. It emphasises that he (Ross) desired the restoration of relations but again stresses that Egypt should make the first move. It ends with the warning that the British should be on their 'guard against well wishers who try to push us back into Egypt prematurely'. In a hand-written comment on the end of the memo Kirkpatrick, the Permanent Undersecretary, concurred with the advice that Ross had proffered.[31] Kirkpatrick – who had enthusiasti- cally fed Eden's analogies between Nasser and fascist dictators – was not about to change his opinions. He remained utterly convinced that Nasser had malign intentions for Britain and the Canal.[32] The former Oriental Counsellor of the Cairo Embassy, Trefor Evans, was among the most resolutely opposed to having anything to do with Nasser:

> There is little doubt that British interests in the Middle East would be furthered by the disappearance of the Nasser regime. This

should be our main objective. The re-establishment of diplomatic relations with Nasser would I believe be interpreted as willingness on the part of HMG to tolerate his regime and would be represented by the Nasser propaganda machine as failure of HMG's policy ... As long as there is a reasonable chance of a change of regime in the near future, we should not, therefore proceed with re-establishing diplomatic relations.[33]

What is clear is that the advice being given to ministers and the Cabinet was along the lines of the memorandum quoted from above. This may have been influenced by the fact that any Foreign Office advice to Cabinet urging the restoration of diplomatic relations would have received a swift rejection from the Prime Minister and the Foreign Secretary whose antipathy towards Nasser has been previously documented.

The rejection of détente with Egypt was despite the fact that there were indications that the Egyptians were interested in a *rapprochement* as soon as it was practicable. The British government, no doubt for very sound political reasons, was as yet unwilling to enter into any substantial and meaningful discussions with Egypt on the matters that separated them. Even in March, Ross wrote that the only communication with Egypt was through the Secretary-General of the United Nations and that dealt solely with the question of an 'interim solution of the Canal problem'. The Cabinet was more interested in setting up a radio station in the Middle East to get Britain's propaganda message across more forcefully.[34] There remained a surprising belief in the highest circles that propaganda over the airwaves could change the hearts and minds of Egyptians and other Arabs about the relative merits of Nasser and Britain. A policy of confrontation was to be continued. Furthermore, before contemplating relations with Egypt, the British government had to confront a much graver problem. The continued Israeli presence in Sinai was threatening British relations not only with Egypt but with the entire Arab world.

THE PROBLEM OF SINAI

Israel's occupation of the Sinai Peninsula was the major military consequence of the war. Among other spoils, this gave Israel command of the strategically vital areas of the Gaza Strip and Sharm-el-Sheikh. The former was a small strip of land that had been part of the Palestine Mandate. After the first Arab–Israeli war, Egypt had occupied the area under the terms of the armistice. It had become one of the biggest refugee camps in the Middle East. Soon after the 1949 armistice, Palestinians in Gaza embittered by the failure of the war turned to guerrilla attacks on Israel. The *Fedayeen* – as these guerrillas were called – became an increasing source of irritation to the Israelis. It became a key Israeli security objective to halt these attacks. The latter area, Sharm-el-Sheikh, was the commanding position covering entrance to the Gulf of Aqaba. The Egyptians used their control of this position to block shipping from the Israeli port of Eilat, and had done so since the end of the First Arab–Israeli war. This meant that all Israeli shipping had to come through the Mediterranean, which interfered with Israeli trade with Asia and the Pacific region.

While Ben-Gurion told his Cabinet prior to the war that Israel only intended to open the Straits of Tiran and pacify the border, he changed his view in the aftermath of the war.[35] In the Knesset on 7 November, Ben-Gurion made a tough speech declaring that Israel would retain all of the conquered areas. The 1949 general armistice agreements were dead and could only be replaced by a full peace treaty based on a new territorial settlement.[36] The United States had other ideas. There was a steely determination within the administration that under no circumstances were the Israelis going to benefit any more than the British or French had from the aggression of October. Eisenhower, Dulles and the United States Permanent Representative to the United Nations, Henry Cabot Lodge, were all determined to force the Israelis to withdraw to the pre-war cease-fire lines. Eisenhower was clearly willing to deploy sanctions if he did not get his way over this matter.[37] The Republican administration was not as heavily under the influence of the politically important Jewish lobby as the previous Truman administration had been. In 1953, for instance, Eisenhower had forced the Israelis to retreat from a plan to divert the waters of the Jordan. On 7 November 1956 Eisenhower wrote to Ben-Gurion warning that he would end all co-operation between the United States and the Israeli government unless Israel pulled out of Sinai. He also warned that Israel could be thrown out of the United Nations.[38] Under this strong American pressure Israel slowly pulled back from most of Sinai throughout December and January 1957. But its government remained resolute in its determination to hold on to Gaza and Sharm-el-Sheikh until it had received acceptable guarantees from the United States on free passage in the Gulf of Aqaba and a UN administration in Gaza. The Israelis attempted to obtain as much security assurance from the position they held as possible. To this end they sent an *aide-mémoire* in January to Hammarskjold calling for Gaza to be placed under United Nations control with an Israeli civil administration. This remained contrary to the policy of both Hammarskjold and the United States. It appeared that President Eisenhower would be forced to face down US public opinion (and the Democratic-controlled Senate which was threatening to block the Eisenhower Doctrine because of the President's apparently uncompromising attitude towards Israel) and vote for sanctions against Israel at the United Nations.[39]

The problem for the British was the potential effect of an affirmative vote in the United Nations for the imposition of sanctions on Israel. If Britain voted for it, it would be seen as a sell-out to the Egyptians and another sign of subservience to the United States. Secondly, it would bring Britain into opposition with the Israelis and they might mention the Sèvres collusions – the Israelis had documentary proof of the agreement. The fallout from such a revelation is incalculable but it was probably a factor in the British government's thinking. The paradox was that the opposite course of action – abstention or a vote against such a resolution – would bring the condemnation of the entire Arab world upon Britain and would destroy any hope of rapid rehabilitation of Britain. It would also delay for a very long time British use of the Canal. Michael Wright, the British Ambassador in Iraq, warned that the question of Israeli withdrawal was particularly critical as it was 'the focus for all the emotions which Suez generated and secondly, because it is ostensibly the reason why the Syrian government will not permit the pumping of oil to be resumed'.[40]

Getting the Americans to moderate their uncompromising attitude was a thankless task. Ambassador Caccia warned that British advice on the issue would not be welcome as 'the United States have let us know as clearly as they can that they do not wish yet to be associated with us too closely in Middle Eastern affairs'.[41] The British hope was that the United States would prevent any sanctions resolution coming to a vote. If not possible, Britain would canvass the United States and Commonwealth to vote against it.[42] However, the United States was determined to force Israel to accept its demands and by circumstance place the British government in an exposed position – torn between supporting its new (and somewhat unwanted) ally and its economic interest. After the Israeli government rejected American guarantees on freedom of navigation in the Gulf of Aqaba contained in a memorandum on 11 February as inadequate, because it did not refer to the future administration of Gaza, Eisenhower acted.[43] In a broadcast on 17 February he addressed the American people. After reassuring the Israelis that he did not seek to confront them and supported what they wanted, he warned that his patience with Israel was not infinite. He declared that he 'would be untrue to the standards of the high office for which you have chosen me if I were to lend the influence of the United States to the proposition that a nation which invades another should be permitted to exact conditions for withdrawal'. If Israel did not see reason and withdraw, the United States would 'have to adopt measures which might have far reaching effects on Israel's relations throughout the world'.[44] Eisenhower was telling Israel to agree to his demands or face United States and United Nations sanctions. When Dulles made it clear to Caccia that the United States would vote for the sanctions resolution, Lloyd commented, 'Mr Dulles' attitude is disappointing.'[45] The Head of the Levant Department, Archibald Ross, pointed out to Macmillan that public opinion would not stand for a vote against Israel. However, a vote or abstention with Israel would 'endanger our relations with the Arabs and in particular imperil our vital oil supplies'.[46] Macmillan tried to persuade the Israeli Ambassador, Mr Elath, that a compromise on their part would swing public support back to them and Britain. Whilst 'we were faced with a situation which presented great difficulties but which also, if wisely handled, afforded an opportunity for turning the tables on Nasser', if 'we could get over the present difficulties we should not only have all the oil our countries needed but the finger of criticism would be pointed at Nasser instead of at us'.[47] In his diary on 21 February, Macmillan wrote on the dilemma: 'Our honour and our interest are in conflict.'[48]

The conclusions that the Cabinet agreed upon were that Britain would abstain in a vote on sanctions. The Cabinet's hopes rested on the Americans backing a more moderate Canadian resolution, which was being floated. Only then would the situation be resolved to all parties' satisfaction.[49] The United Kingdom through its diplomatic representatives would do its best to bring this about. In the House of Commons four days later, Macmillan made a statement backing Israeli navigation rights in the Straits of Tiran.[50] He could not have foreseen that his words would be very relevant ten years later when there would be another Arab–Israeli crisis over freedom of navigation in the Straits.

Despite Macmillan's statement, the resolution of the crisis was a demonstration of the decreasing influence of the British in the Middle East. The solution to the crisis was brokered not by the British but by the United States and the French. Firstly, Dulles agreed an *aide-mémoire* with Abba Eban. He promised backing for Israel's freedom of navigation in the Straits.[51] A solution to the more difficult problem of Gaza arrived on 26 February when the French Prime Minister and Foreign Minister, Guy Mollet and Christian Pineau, made a proposal that proved to be the catalyst that ended the crisis. Pineau summarised his proposals under the following headings:

1. The UNEF and a UN administration should be established in Gaza for an indefinite duration, with the tacit acquiescence of Egypt.

2. Israel should reserve its rights with regard to the termination of this arrangement.

3. Other countries should take note but neither approve nor disapprove of it.

4. It would be recommended to both parties that they undertake negotiations for a peace settlement.[52]

The French plan left much undone. The key phrase regarding Gaza is 'tacit acquiescence' and demonstrates the fragility of the agreement. Nasser's motivation for his tacit acquiescence was that while he 'tried to ensure that Egypt gave away as little as possible of her sovereign rights he was aware of the danger of losing international sympathy by a too protracted and stubborn bargaining'.[53] The success of the agreement depended on all sides pretending they were receiving everything they wanted. For Israel, this was freedom of passage in the Gulf of Aqaba and tranquillity on its southern border, and, for Egypt, there was the return of its territory. Eban, the Israeli Ambassador to the UN, agreed that this formula in conjunction with the previous American promises on free passage in the Straits would be sufficient to guarantee Israeli withdrawal. He telegraphed Israel calling for immediate acceptance. Even the most militant Israelis, such as Moshe Dayan, were willing to accept the deal. Israeli politicians warned that any breach of the deal would be considered an act of war.[54]

The crisis was not quite over. Cabot Lodge made a speech which mentioned Egypt's right to occupy Gaza under the terms of the 1949 armistice. The Israelis began to fear that the United States was backsliding on the *aide-mémoire* that had been agreed on 24 February. They wanted a clear American statement on UN control in Gaza and recognition of Israel's right to self-defence in Gaza. Furthermore, they asked the United States to prevent the UN Secretary-General from formulating his proposal that UN troops would be stationed on the Israeli side of the armistice line. Eisenhower sent a letter to Ben-Gurion supporting the Israeli position on this issue and the questions of Gaza and the Gulf.[55]

The letter was a turning point in the relations between the Eisenhower administration and Nasser. The former had given their word to support the Israeli position in Gaza and thus, when Nasser ignored American calls for him to leave the UN in administrative control over Gaza, they felt betrayed. On 10 March, three days after the Israeli withdrawal, Nasser announced the appointment of a new Egyptian Governor of Gaza, breaking the spirit of the agreement to which Nasser had assented. This was a critical blow to Nasser's credentials in Washington as it raised the possibility of a renewed Israeli attack and invasion if Nasser attempted to move troops into the area. Eisenhower notes his disappointment in his memoirs: 'Nasser ... failed to seize this opportunity for true statesmanship, thereby depriving his country of the assistance of and the co-operation of all self-respecting Governments.'[56] Another war scare erupted as a result of Nasser's provocation. A flurry of diplomatic correspondence flew between the State Department, Whitehall and the Quai d'Orsay when the French Defence Minister, Bourges-Maunoury, told the American chargé d'affaires in Paris, Charles W. Yost, that France in concert with Britain would provide the air cover for an Israeli reoccupation of Gaza if the Egyptians broke the deal that had been agreed in the UN.[57] The British denied all knowledge.[58]

A FINAL RETREAT FROM SUEZ

Harold Macmillan's diary and memoirs provide plenty of evidence of his great fear that failure to get an acceptable agreement with the Egyptians on the use of the Canal by British shipping would reactivate the Conservative 'diehards' of the Suez Group and threaten the survival of his government.[59] The best hope of achieving an acceptable solution was for the Western powers to make common cause in a united front against Nasser. Such a united front might force him to agree to some sort of compromise. However, putting such a front together was nearly impossible. The Americans, while anxious to help the British, were extremely worried about becoming involved in wasteful arguments with the Egyptians about relatively technical matters such as methods of payment for use of the Canal. Many of their proposals to the Egyptians appear to have been half-hearted.[60] The British were determined to impress on the Americans just how serious the issue was to them. The United States Ambassador to London, Whitney, reported the Lord President of the Council, Lord Salisbury, as saying that British public opinion was '"simmering" ready to explode if the Egyptians demanded direct payment of tolls'. This was more than likely bluff. British ministers seemed to know that the eventual outcome would be a complete capitulation to the Egyptians. The Middle East committee meeting at the end of February agreed that an account for transferable sterling (called No. 3 Account) would be necessary to pay port dues and duties in Egypt. The Economic Measures subcommittee was to consider whether this account should be used to 'receive other payments to Egypt'. This was a reference to Canal dues and the first hint of the coming British capitulation.[61] United Nations or even SCUA support were not likely.

The Minister of Transport pointed out that 'the difficulties of obtaining the co-operation of Governments on less controversial questions have already become apparent in SCUA'.[62] Commercial considerations rather than loyalty to Britain and France would dictate the actions of the users. Essentially, Suez had made Britain completely dependent on the willingness and the ability of the United States to force the Egyptians to compromise. The Americans, though, as Eisenhower pointed out, had 'no magic means to compel Egypt to accept what we desire'.[63] His mood towards the British was not improved when they publicly leaked American proposals that called for some involvement of a neutral broker in the payment of Canal tolls. The Americans had secretly communicated these to the Egyptians through Hammarskjold, hoping that Nasser might adopt them in a gesture of good will. The British leak had portrayed the proposals as a demand and finished what slim hope they had of success.[64]

By March the British knew that they were running out of time. The Egyptians were close to opening the Canal for use and British ship owners would be soon demanding the right to use the Canal. The British economy – already a European laggard – could not really afford the cost of giving Britain's competitors the advantage of using the Canal while it routed its ships around the Cape. The French, much less dependent on the Canal, were sticking to their hard-line views. In a meeting with Guy Mollet on 9 March 1957, Macmillan pointed out that the worst course of all would be 'to start a boycott which subsequently failed and from which we would have to retreat'.[65] The British Minister of Transport, Harold Watkinson, had already assessed from consultations with the ship owners that there was little or no chance of an international boycott garnering enough support to succeed. Even British ship owners warned that they would not be able to boycott the Canal for long after it reopened for traffic.[66]

On 17 March 1957, the Egyptians issued confidentially to the United States a draft communiqué on the future operation of the Canal. When the British saw the document they were most displeased. 'Canal dues are to be paid in advance to the Suez Canal Authority either in Egypt or elsewhere as determined by the authority' was the key phrase for Britain. Britain's best hope of saving face, the neutral broker proposal, was specifically excluded by the Egyptians. On other points the declaration was more positive. Egypt was willing to abide by the Constantinople convention and would set aside certain percentages of the dues for Canal improvements.[67] The Foreign Office reaction was overwhelmingly negative, criticising its unilateral character, its failure to mention the Six Principles of October 1956 and the lack of co-operation between the Egyptians and the users. The Head of the

Levant Department, Ross, described the draft as 'a hands down victory for Nasser at a very undesirable moment'.[68]

The release of the draft communiqué coincided with the Anglo-American summit at Bermuda which it was hoped would re-establish a working relationship between the two powers. The British had a long shopping list of requests that required the acquiescence of the Americans. This list included American support over the Canal as well as general support for the British position in the Middle East. Other issues included Britain's growing need to cut back its defence budget. This was to be done by switching from conventional to nuclear weaponry.[69] The 1957 Defence White Paper was being drafted at this time by Duncan Sandys, the Minister of Defence. He was given *carte blanche* by Macmillan to make the savings required. These included the ending of peacetime conscription and the reduction of the Rhine Army from 80,000 to 50,000 men. American help was needed to help develop delivery vehicles for the British atomic deterrent. The new all-professional army was supposed to be more mobile and able to react to a crisis like Suez much faster.[70] Sandys' January visit to United States Secretary of Defence Charles Wilson was an important catalyst in setting up the Bermuda meeting. Their discussion on nuclear co-operation brought an offer on 22 January from Eisenhower to meet Macmillan in March on the British island of Bermuda. This seemed to symbolise the willingness of Eisenhower to make the British feel comfortable rather than make them come to Washington for what might seem like an audience.[71]

The British had a firm agenda for the summit on the Middle East. They wanted: American support for an interim settlement of the Canal problem that did not leave Nasser a free hand to do whatever he liked to the major users, i.e. Britain; to look at means of ensuring that the oil supplies of the Middle East remained under the control of the West or friendly countries; and economic development for the Middle East. An agreed policy towards Britain's main Middle Eastern foes, Egypt and Syria, was to be sought.[72] The State Department, in considering how to approach the conference, outlined the British position as they saw it in a number of papers. These considered that while Britain was no longer on a par with the superpowers, it did possess many positive attributes that made it an essential ally for the United States. It recommended that the United States should help to strengthen Britain by developing joint policies in areas of the world where their interests coincided. This would be achieved by encouraging regular consultations and by helping the United Kingdom to fulfil its responsibilities for the maintenance of world peace and stability and by moving it towards European integration.[73]

On the subject of the Middle East, the American position paper argued that, although Britain had damaged its position and the West's in general in the region through the Suez misadventure, 'the maintenance of the British position in the Middle East, to the extent feasible, is in the interests of the free world'. Suez's main effect was that the United States would have to assume a larger role in the area then it had to do pre-Suez. Despite the British insistence that Nasser was untrustworthy and that it was impossible to do business with him and thus all the problems that Anglo-American co-operation could expect, the key aim of United States policy in the Middle East was to restore close Anglo-American relations. To this end, the United States would join the military committee of the Baghdad Pact but not formally join the actual pact, so as not to upset Saudi Arabian sensibilities. British nuclear and defence requests would be looked upon favourably. With regard to Nasser, the paper recognised that he was unlikely to fall from power in the near future and, although the United States would be happy to deal with a more reasonable Egyptian government, they would take no part in 'attempts to unseat him'.[74] On the eve of the conference, Eisenhower and Dulles came to the conclusion that they would have to do business with Nasser to secure an acceptable Canal settlement even if this had the incidental effect of building him up. It was assessed that confronting him in an attempt to get rid of him could lead to him being more hostile over the Canal 'which could be very damaging for the British'.[75]

The Bermuda Conference began on 20 March 1957. Informal talks that night agreed on the need 'for an acceptable Canal settlement'. Macmillan shared the concern of the Americans that inducements aimed at securing a settlement of the Canal would build Nasser up. The major sanction that the British and the Americans had in place against Egypt was the blocking of its sterling and dollar balances. Macmillan feared that the unblocking of the dollar balances to secure a settlement would put pressure on the British to unblock the sterling balances. To give up this last sanction against Egypt would leave the British with nothing to bargain with over the question of frozen British assets.[76]

The first formal plenary session began the next morning with Macmillan making the first speech. In it, he outlined in suitably portentous rhetoric Britain's determination to remain part of the Western alliance and to play its part 'in defending freedom'. Interestingly, despite the importance of the defence problems, the American version of the meeting says Macmillan 'identified the most important [matter] as the problem of Nasser and the Canal'. Concerning the Canal, Macmillan wanted the United States to help with the problem, with most importance being attached to the method of payment of the dues. He wanted the United States to acknowledge plainly if the eventual outcome was unsatisfactory, condemn it as such and not claim a victory. Failure on the part of the United States to this would cause a 'real rift' that would take longer to repair than world needs would allow. Macmillan seemed to be determined to show to the Americans that he was just as intent as Eden had been to continue the fight against Nasser. His personal notes on Nasser for his address are couched in much the same way as those of his predecessor. Nasser was again compared to Mussolini. 'Let's make it clear that we'll get him sooner or later' was another phrase used.[77]

Eisenhower was rather taken aback by the British attitude. Nevertheless, at the summit, he was as helpful as he could be, promising aid on the issue of the Canal and for the United Kingdom's swollen global responsibilities. It was decided to consider whether SCUA could be brought into the negotiations on the Canal in an effort to strengthen the pressure on Egypt. Lloyd asked for the American views in the Egyptian draft communiqué. The British agreed that method of payment was the key issue in any interim settlement. With regard to the question of using inducements on the Egyptians to get a solution, it was felt that they 'might be better reserved for use in securing a final settlement of outstanding issues with Egypt'.[78]

The afternoon session began with Selwyn Lloyd justifying the Suez operation and disingenuously suggesting that it was not quite the flop it obviously was.[79] Lloyd continued that Britain now intended to consolidate its position in the oil-producing Gulf states and 'above all in Kuwait … [Britain] could not, however, ignore the possibility of a coup d'état in Kuwait engineered by Nasser. If he could lay his hands on its oil his financial problems would be solved.' Britain was not going to give up its support for the Omanis over the Burami Oasis dispute. Macmillan was unyielding on this point and declared 'that he could not accept a solution [of Burami] which involved betraying our friends'. At the end of the conversation, Eisenhower suggested setting up a standing group of officials to consider all their common problems, planning as for 'a battle'.[80] What is most noticeable about these conversations was that Anglo-American views were quite diverse on many matters with regard to the Middle East. A group of officials had been designated to see what actions could be taken to put pressure on Nasser. The British were happy to settle for the American proposals that had been sent to Egypt via Hammarskjold who was in Cairo. These called for the reaffirmation of the Six Principles and that half of the Canal dues should be held by a neutral body 'pending and subject to definitive settlement'. They reaffirmed the decision to bring SCUA into the discussions. If a solution was unattainable, consideration was to be given to various sanctions.[81]

The conference was a success – in the sense that the direct breach over Suez had been healed. There existed, though, clear differences in approach to the Middle East. Britain's views on Nasser were far more extreme than the American view. As one study of the conference has pointed out, Bermuda had not resulted in 'many major substantive agreements: indeed the two governments had differed over a number of issues in the Middle and Far East and these continued to divide the two during the summer'.[82] The real fruits of the conference would not be seen until later in the year when the British and the Americans would meet at Washington. That meeting would see the 'special relationship' perhaps reach its post-war apogee.

Two days after the conference – on 26 March 1957 – the Egyptians issued a second draft declaration on the status of the Canal. It contained a number of amendments to the first. The main point in its favour was that it reaffirmed the Constantinople convention of 1888. It also made clear that Egypt would be willing to negotiate on future toll increases. Hammarskjold had failed in his attempt to get Nasser to agree to anything other than these most minor amendments. Nasser had no intention of negotiating with Britain and France but would have no objection to the United States making representations on their behalf. The Bank of International Settlements was designated the body for collecting the tolls. Nasser was willing to accept the comments of interested nations on the draft before he would proceed to the next stage.[83] The British complaints remained that the method of payment of tolls was unsatisfactory and that the unilateral character of the declaration meant that the Egyptians could amend it at any time.[84] However, these objections could only be transmitted through the United States. Dulles despatched to Egypt a version of the draft memo with some amendments that Nasser might be persuaded to adopt.[85]

An issue of national importance, which threatened the survival of the United Kingdom government, had passed entirely into the hands of the United States. This national humiliation was increased by the fact that the Canal was not an issue of vital national importance to the United States in 1957. Harold Caccia and the new Permanent Undersecretary at the Foreign Office, Frederick Hoyer-Millar, must have realised this when they met Dulles on 30 March 1957 at his residence. They were under instructions to persuade the United States to 'get to grips with Egypt directly' and displayed a willingness to see a relaxation of United States economic pressure to get a satisfactory outcome.[86] The meeting discussed the Egyptian draft declaration and what the British wanted the Americans to do on their behalf with the Egyptians.

The British wanted any settlement to be a binding international treaty preferably based on the Six Principles of 13 October 1956. If these demands were not met, the British wanted the United States to put into effect its proposal for double-blocking the Egyptian dollar balances. The meeting agreed that the British hopes for getting the Four Power proposals into the Egyptian declaration were 'unlikely to succeed'. Caccia said that London was considering bringing the matter before the United Nations Security Council even though it was little more than a 'sign of protest' since the Soviets would wield the veto against any practical solutions that might be brought forward in that forum. The British were willing to wait until the results of the United Nations negotiations with Egypt were known, unlike the French, who wished to move quickly towards a confrontation in the Security Council.[87]

On 1 April 1957, Hammarskjold's financial adviser, John McCloy, attempted to persuade Nasser of the need to secure international acceptance of any declaration. He warned that the Suez Canal was a wasting asset unless international co-operation was agreed. Nasser rejected the argument, saying that he did not want to give up Egyptian sovereignty for another thousand years.[88] The British Cabinet meeting on 3 April 1957 agreed to continue to rely on the United States.[89] The fact was that the British were merely playing for time. The Americans were informed the following day that the British were going to set up an account to pay Canal dues in transferable sterling. The matter was now one of timing rather than principle. On 8 April the Cabinet looked at the prospects for settlement again. There was a fear that the negotiations might lead to the unfreezing of Egyptian assets and that reference to the Security Council might lead the Egyptians to retaliate by refusing the British and the French the use of the Canal or forcing them to pay the Canal dues in dollars. The conclusion that the Cabinet came to was that, since negotiations with Egypt on a final settlement were going to take a considerable period of time, they would have to find a mechanism that would allow British shipping to use the Canal without prejudging the final settlement. SCUA would be used as cover for the surrender.[90] Macmillan wrote in his diary the same day that 'Our real problem is how to use the Canal with the minimum short term loss of face.'[91]

The State Department was becoming concerned that an unsatisfactory outcome of the negotiations might lead to charges from the British and the French that they (the United States) were capitulating to Nasser and that this could be damaging to relations. To avoid the possibility of this happening the United States endeavoured to keep in as close contact as possible with the British and French. On 8 April 1957, Caccia informed the State Department that the British position was that there should be one more conversation with Nasser where, if no concessions were made, the matter would be brought to the Security Council. Nasser and his Foreign Minister, Mahmoud Fawzi, and the United States Ambassador, Raymond Hare, met on 10 April to discuss a third draft of the Egyptian declaration. Hare's attempts to get the Six Principles included in the new draft were rejected forcefully by Nasser on the grounds that they were the

> product of Security Council meeting in which British and French had participated at a time, when speaking in terms of peaceful solution, they were planning [the] forceful seizure of the Canal. Furthermore, [the] real thinking of British and French had been clearly revealed in vetoed part of [the] October 13 resolution. Against this background he saw [the] insistence on inclusion [of the] six principles as a trap of [the] West which would result in his being hailed before I[nternational] C[ourt] [of] J[ustice] 'every day' on one pretext or another.

Nasser did not want any more discussion of the users having some input into the canal. He 'would never consent to anything that would allow outside management and control'.[92] Despite this rhetoric, Nasser had gone a long way to meet the demands of the international community. As Lloyd and the British pointed out, the Egyptian declaration did correspond to at least five of the Six Principles. Ambassador Caccia reported to the United States Undersecretary of State on 11 April 1957 the Cabinet decision to pay the Canal toll and that negotiations were to be held with representatives of the National Bank of Egypt on the setting up of a payment mechanism.[93] Even the Security Council appeal that was still to take place was admitted by Pierson Dixon at the United Nations to be nothing more than a smokescreen and face-saving device.[94] Britain's energies were now directed at getting the Egyptians to accept payment in sterling and making surrender look like a tactical retreat. The Security Council appeal was to be the cause of tension with the United States who feared that such an action would alienate the Egyptians and risk the forfeiture of the concessions that had been secured on the declaration. The only justification for continued United States support for the British at the Security Council was the undertakings given to Macmillan by Eisenhower of support. One State official wrote that recourse to the Security Council could see the United States 'stand to lose much more than the United Kingdom stands to gain'. Caccia desperately attempted to keep the United States on side.[95]

The Cabinet committee assessing the latest Egyptian proposals agreed that they did not fall much short of the Six Principles. Pierson Dixon's main point would be to condemn the document as a unilateral document. The British were to avoid entering into any formal agreement with Egypt 'because whatever its nature it will be denounced as a surrender'.[96] The Egyptians issued the final declaration on 24 April 1957 along with the news that the Canal was to be reopened. It was a document that set out at some considerable length the new position regarding the Canal. Dixon carried out the government's wishes at the Security Council with a mild speech, moderately condemnatory of the Egyptians. The meeting broke up without reaching any view of the document beyond that of Lodge who felt that it should be given a trial. The Foreign Office asked for a meeting of SCUA to consider the Egyptian declaration and see if there was any prospect of a continued international boycott.[97] On the same day, a cable was despatched to the National Bank of Egypt with a request for talks. On 2 May, the Egyptians agreed to meet the Bank of England in Basle.[98] At the meeting of SCUA on 30 April 1957, the overwhelming feeling of the members was that no boycott should be organised. Lloyd argued that one should be maintained until the Egyptians had clarified the unilateral nature of the declaration but his proposal received support only from the French who appeared to wish the boycott to continue in perpetuity. Even on the question of bringing the issue back to the Security Council, only the French and the Australians were supportive. The British attitude at the meeting does seem strange since the Cabinet had already agreed that the Canal was to be used by British shipping. The reasoning behind the British stalling became clear later on at the meeting in a conversation between Ambassador Whitney and Lloyd. Lloyd admitted that they were being used to cover secret negotiations that were to take place between the British and the Egyptians in Switzerland to set up a mechanism for the payment of the Canal tolls through transferable sterling. The British hoped that a united front by the users would stop the Egyptians being unreasonable at the talks and making demands such as the unblocking of Egypt's blocked sterling a prerequisite of agreement.[99]

For the United States, the British pressure for another meeting of the Security Council had become a serious irritant. Lodge, who was a known Anglophobe, feared that a Security Council meeting might expose differences between the British and the Americans over the declaration.[100] The London Embassy warned that failure to support the United Kingdom satisfactorily on the Security Council might lead to a situation where 'political forces in Great Britain would seek to place on the United States the onus of an unsatisfactory solution to the Canal question'. Bearing this in mind, Dulles was more circumspect when he discussed the matter with Lloyd on 1 May 1957.[101] He pointed out that a renewed attack on the Egyptians in the Security Council could lead them to be more defiant and that if everybody still used the Canal after such an event 'that would be a loss of prestige for the west and indeed for the United States which he would not want to see happen'.[102] This was reinforced by further American correspondence over the following days. The British – without their major ally's support – capitulated as unanimous support for the British position did not exist within the ranks of the users.

The negotiations in Basle went well. The Egyptians – having achieved their political objectives over the Canal – were happy to compromise on the technical issue of payment. They agreed to the opening of a new account of transferable sterling. They agreed that the blocked Egyptian accounts could be dealt with at a later date at a neutral centre.[103] Watkinson advised Macmillan that the time had come to end the boycott of the Canal.[104]

The overriding point for the government now was to present the decision to abandon the boycott in the 'best light possible'. The Cabinet agreed on 10 May that the arrangements would be made public on 13 May.[105] There was little doubt that the end of the boycott – on terms entirely dictated by the Egyptians – was a serious threat to the stability of the government. Macmillan had long been convinced that this was the moment when his premiership would come to an end. There was a certain understandable nervousness. On the Suez base issue in 1954, 28 Conservatives of the Suez Group had defied the whip. This issue seemed far more damaging. In the Commons, Viscount Hinchingbroke pledged to lead a rebellion while Lord Salisbury – the Tory grandee of his day and according to one historian 'universally regarded as the keeper of the Conservative party's conscience', who had earlier resigned from the government over Cyprus – pledged to organise opposition in the Lords.[106] However, as John Ramsden points out, it helped Macmillan that Salisbury went over Cyprus rather than Suez.[107]

The Hinchingbroke Eight who were the most militant of the Suez Group were bound to abstain. The key task of the Conservative Chief Whip, Edward Heath, was to minimise the drift amongst the mainstream right of the Conservatives. Macmillan was sure that he was going to lose and maintained this feeling till the end of his life. In 1971, he told the *Listener* that the 'opposition ought to have got us out' but it is hard to see what more Gaitskell could have done. He put forward a moderate motion and made a good speech.[108] Macmillan, perhaps, overestimated the moral outrage felt by many Conservative Members of Parliament on the issue. Perhaps most importantly, the kind of Conservative that Labour was trying to attract into the Opposition lobby was the most hostile to them. Such an MP was from the right of the party, and would have held Gaitskell partly responsible for the whole debacle, perceiving him to have formed 'an unholy alliance' with the United States to frustrate Eden. It was easier to shift the blame for the failure of Suez on to the shoulders of the Opposition than on to Macmillan. As Anthony Wedgwood Benn pointed out, such an MP 'blames the Americans, the Russians, the Opposition and everybody else, but not his honourable friend the Prime Minister'. An example of one potential rebel who voted with the government illustrates the above. Captain Waterhouse, a leader of the Suez Group, chose to attack the Opposition and Nasser rather than the government: 'If ever there were an instance of Satan rebuking sin, we have it in the Opposition's amazing motion.' He also declared that 'we have an inveterate foe in Colonel Nasser. We ought to chase him like a pest officer would chase a rat.'[109]

Macmillan was able to claim with some justification that Nasser seemed to be in retreat owing to recent events in Jordan and the break-up of the Arab solidarity pact. 'Egypt is becoming isolated from many who claimed to be her friends and who are now taking every opportunity to free themselves from Egyptian domination and expansion.'[110] Macmillan was also able to announce his plan for supertankers, which would limit Britain's future dependence on the Canal, and the end of petrol rationing. All told, Macmillan was not happy with his performance on the first day of the debate and felt the government was not yet safe. In fact, Richard Crossman, the Labour MP and diarist, went so far as to describe his speech as 'a complete flop'. However, he did not seem to think much of the issue itself, describing it as 'all old cabbage'.[111] The following morning brought relief. Whether by design or good fortune, the newspapers were full of Britain's first successful hydrogen bomb test instead of news of a government in trouble.

If the H-bomb test was by design, it was a masterstroke, as it had the double effect of sating some of the more atavistic Tory right, while causing fractious splits on the Labour benches that were to blight the electoral chances of the party for the next five years. The debate ended with only 14 Conservatives abstaining, giving the government a majority of 49. The government had survived and would win the next election. The debate was the final act in the Suez chapter, and what Aneurin Bevan called 'the lingering stench of Suez' ended at this point.[112] After over a decade of fractious debate over Egypt, the Canal base and then the Canal itself, British domestic politics had heard enough of the subject. Egypt remained a foreign policy opponent for a considerable time but would not have the same public hold over British politicians as previously. Macmillan might retain a strong interest in the Middle East throughout his premiership and a lasting distaste for Nasser, but he differed from his predecessor in that the Suez Canal, at least, would not run through his living room.

NOTES

1. T.F. Lindsay and M. Harrington, *The Conservative Party 1918–1970* (New York, St Martin's Press, 1974), pp. 197–200.
2. Some historians point to Butler's association with appeasement during the 1930s and his supposed flirtation with a compromise peace in the dark days of 1940 as reasons for his failure ever to achieve the premiership. Lord Salisbury had been firmly anti-appeasement as had Macmillan. Richard Lamb, *The Macmillan Years 1957–63: The Emerging Truth* (London, John Murray, 1995), p. 25.
3. Horne, *Macmillan* (2 vols) (London, Macmillan, 1988/89). Recent assessments of his life and legacy are Lamb, *Macmillan Years* and the essays in R. Aldous and S. Lee (eds), *Harold Macmillan: Aspects of a Political Life* (London, Macmillan, 1999).
4. Hennessy, *Prime Minister*, p. 254.
5. R. Cockett (ed.), *My Dear Max* (London, Historians Press, 1990), p. 196. See also John Turner, *Macmillan: Profiles in Power* (London, Longman, 1994), p. 113. Butler on the other hand was far more reticent about the whole affair while remaining scrupulously loyal to Eden and the government.
6. Robert Murphy, *Diplomat among Warriors* (London, Collins, 1964), p. 463. Horne, *Macmillan*, Vol. I, p. 422. His general views on the Middle East before and during Suez are elegantly summarised in Nigel Ashton, 'Macmillan and the Middle East', in R. Aldous and S. Lee, *Harold Macmillan and Britain's World Role* (London, Macmillan, 1996), pp. 38–45.
7. Brendan Bracken in a letter to the press magnate Lord Beaverbrook wrote, 'The so called Canal die-hards think better of him than they do of Eden or Butler.' Lucas, *Divided We Stand*, p. 319.
8. Macmillan, *Riding the Storm*, p. 207.
9. Horne, *Macmillan*, Vol. II (London, Macmillan, 1989), p. 16.
10. See particularly John Charmley, *Churchill's Grand Alliance* (London, John Curtis, 1995).
11. Rhodes-James, *Anthony Eden*, p. 578.
12. Rhodes-James, *Anthony Eden*, p. 577.
13. H.W. Brands, *The Specter of Neutralism: The United States and the Emergence of the Third World, 1947–60* (New York, Columbia University Press, 1989), p. 226. See also Selwyn Lloyd, *Suez 1956*, pp. 238–50.
14. Ray Taykeh, *Origins of the Eisenhower Doctrine* (London, Macmillan, 2001), p. 145.
15. Eisenhower, *Waging Peace*, p. 178.
16. *FRUS 1955–57*, Vol. XII, Doc. 178, 22 Dec. 1956.
17. *FRUS 1955–57*, Vol. XII, Doc. 175, 20 Dec. 1956.
18. *Public Papers of the Presidents of the United States of America 1957*, Doc. 6, pp. 6–17.
19. Ibid.
20. Macmillan, *Riding the Storm*, p. 207.
21. PRO FO 371/127739, V 10345/2, Caccia to FO, No. 30, 7 Jan. 1957.
22. Walter LaFeber, *America, Russia and the Cold War* (New York, McGraw-Hill, 1993), p. 191.

23. PRO PREM 11/1178, Caccia–Lloyd, 26 Jan. 1957.
24. Peter Hennessy, *Whitehall* (London, Secker & Warburg, 1989), pp. 165–8.
25. PRO FO 371/125505, JE 1421/5, Dixon–FO, No. 31, 3 Jan. 1957.
26. The figure that the Foreign Office gave was that the value of UK property held by the Egyptians was worth no less than £210 million excluding the Suez Canal Company. This estimate was whittled to £166 million by the end of the year. See PRO FO 371/125461, JE 1102/10, Brenchley (FO)–Johnston (Treasury), 24 June 1957.
27. PRO FO 371/125444, JE 1052/5, Memo from H. Trevelyan to I. Kirkpatrick, 15 Jan. 1957.
28. See J. Bloch and P. Fitzgerald, *British Intelligence and Covert Action* (Dingle, Brandon, 1983), p. 126.
29. *FRUS 1955–57*, Vol. XXVII, Doc. 271, 21 Mar. 1957.
30. PRO FO 371/125444, JE 1052/8, Ross to Kirkpatrick, 19 Jan. 1957.
31. PRO FO 371/125444, JE 1052/8, Ross to Kirkpatrick, 29 Jan. 1957, Memo on relations with Egypt.
32. PRO FO 371/125505, JE 1421/9, Kirkpatrick minute to Lloyd, 14 Jan. 1957.
33. PRO FO 371/125444, JE 1052/8, T.E. Evans minute, 11 Mar. 1957.
34. PRO FO 371/125444, JE 1052/9, Ross minute, 15 Mar. 1957. For the Cabinet meeting, see PRO CAB 128/31, Cabinet Conclusions, 4, 1 Feb. 1957.
35. Abba Eban, *An Autobiography* (London, Weidenfeld & Nicolson, 1978), p. 228.
36. 'Ambivalent adversaries: David Ben Gurion and Israel vs the United Nations and Dag Hammarskjold, 1956–57', *JOCH*, 27, 1, Jan. (1992), pp. 105–6.
37. See Eban, *Autobiography*, pp. 234–7. Ambrose, *Eisenhower*, p. 386.
38. Michael Fry and Miles Hochstein, 'The Forgotten Middle Eastern Crisis of 1957: Gaza and Sharm-el-Sheikh', *International History Review*, XV, 1 Feb. 1993.
39. PRO CAB 128/31, Cabinet Conclusions, 13, 22 Feb. 1957.
40. PRO FO 371/128131, VR 1081/131, Wright to FO, No. 158, 2 Feb. 1957.
41. PRO FO 371/128131, VR 1081/136, Caccia–Lloyd, No. 295, 9 Feb. 1957.
42. PRO FO 371/128131, VR 1081/143, Lloyd–Dixon (New York), No. 677, 9 Feb. 1957.
43. Eban, *Autobiography*, p. 243.
44. *Public Papers of the Presidents of the United States of America 1957*, Doc. 35, pp. 147–56.
45. PRO FO 371/128134, VR 1081/195, Caccia–FO, No. 387, 18 Feb. 1957 and Lloyd–Caccia, No. 770, 19 Feb. 1957.
46. PRO FO 371/128107, VR 1052/8, Ross Note to Macmillan, 20 Feb. 1957.
47. PRO FO 371/128134, VR 1058/201, Lloyd–Tel Aviv, No. 20, 21 Feb. 1957.
48. Macmillan, *Riding the Storm*, p. 218 – diary entry cited 21 Feb. 1957.
49. PRO CAB 128/31, Cabinet Conclusions, 3, 22 Feb. 1957.
50. Macmillan, *Riding the Storm*, p. 218.
51. *FRUS 1955–57*, Vol. XVII, Doc. 87, 12 Feb. 1957.
52. *FRUS 1955–57*, Vol. XVII, Doc. 159, 26 Feb. 1957.
53. Stephens, *Nasser*, p. 238.
54. Ibid. Eban, *Autobiography*, pp. 248–50. Fry and Hochstein, 'Forgotten Middle Eastern Crisis'.
55. *FRUS 1955–57*, Vol. XVII, Doc. 181, 2 Mar. 1957.
56. Eisenhower, *Waging Peace*, p. 189.
57. *FRUS 1955–57*, Vol. XVII, Doc. 220, 14 Mar. 1957 and Note 4, p. 414.
58. *FRUS 1955–57*, Vol. XVII, Doc. 241, 21 Mar. 1957.
59. Macmillan, *Riding The Storm*, p. 230.
60. PRO CAB 128/31, Cabinet Conclusions, 13, 57, 22 Feb. 1957.
61. PRO CAB 134/2338, OME, 57, 9th Meeting, Min. 4, 1 Mar. 1957.

62. PRO FO 371/125510, JE 1421/67, Watkinson minute.
63. *FRUS 1955–57*, Vol. XVII, Note 3, 9 Mar. 1957, p. 381.
64. *FRUS 1955–57*, Vol. XVII, Doc. 203, 8 Mar. 1957.
65. PRO PREM 11/1786, JE 1421/166G, Record of meeting at Hotel Matignon, 9 Mar. 1957.
66. PRO PREM 11/1789, Watkinson–Macmillan, 12 Mar. 1957. Kyle, *Suez*, p. 542.
67. *FRUS 1955–57*, Vol. XVII, pp. 430–1, 17 Mar. 1957.
68. PRO PREM 11/1789, Adam Watson, 'Proposed Egyptian Declaration on Suez Canal', Minute by Archibald Ross, 18 Mar. 1957. Kyle, *Suez*, p. 542.
69. Michael Dockrill, 'The Bermuda and Washington Conferences, 1957', in Dick Richardson and Glyn Stone (eds), *Decisions and Diplomacy: Essays in Twentieth-Century International History* (London, LSE/Routledge, 1995), pp. 208–9.
70. The Sandys White Paper with reference to east of Suez is discussed in Darby, *British Defence Policy East of Suez*, pp. 101–22.
71. Dockrill, 'The Bermuda and Washington Conferences, 1957', pp. 206–7.
72. PRO FO 371/129328, Sir Patrick Dean memo (not dated). Dockrill, 'The Bermuda and Washington Conferences, 1957', pp. 208–9.
73. Dockrill, 'The Bermuda and Washington Conferences, 1957', pp. 206–7.
74. Dockrill, 'The Bermuda and Washington Conferences, 1957', p. 211.
75. *FRUS 1955–57*, Vol. XVII, Doc. 237, 20 Mar. 1957.
76. *FRUS 1955–57*, Vol. XXVII, Doc. 267, 20 Mar. 1957.
77. *FRUS 1955–57*, Vol. XVII, Doc. 239, 21 Mar. 1957, pp. 452–3. PRO PREM 11/1838, British minutes of 1st plenary session of the Bermuda Conference, 21 Mar. 1957.
78. PRO PREM 11/1838, British minutes of 1st plenary session of the Bermuda Conference, 21 Mar. 1957.
79. PRO PREM 11/1838, British minutes of 2nd plenary session of the Bermuda Conference, 21 Mar. 1957.
80. Ibid.
81. PRO PREM 11/1838, Annex to Bermuda Conference, BC (P), 2nd meeting, 'Joint Report by Officials'.
82. Dockrill, 'The Bermuda and Washington Conferences, 1957', p. 215.
83. *FRUS 1955–57*, Vol. XVII, Doc. 253, 28 Mar. 1957.
84. *FRUS 1955–57*, Vol. XVII, Footnote 2, p. 483.
85. *FRUS 1955–57*, Vol. XVII, Doc. 254, 29 Mar. 1957.
86. PRO PREM 11/1789, FO–Washington, No. 1542, 30 Mar. 1957.
87. PRO PREM 11/1789, Washington–FO, No. 775, 30 Mar. 1957 and *FRUS 1955–57*, Vol. XVII, Doc. 257, pp. 492–3.
88. *FRUS 1955–57*, Vol. XVII, Doc. 262, 2 Apr. 1957.
89. PRO CAB 128/31, Cabinet Conclusions, 29, 57, 3 Apr. 1957.
90. PRO CAB 128/31, Cabinet Conclusions, 30, 57, 8 Apr. 1957.
91. Diary entry in Macmillan, *Riding the Storm*, p. 231.
92. *FRUS 1955–57*, Vol. XVII, Doc. 281, 11 Apr. 1957.
93. PRO CAB 128/31, Cabinet Conclusions 33, 57, 11 Apr. 1957, and *FRUS 1955–57*, Vol. XVII, Footnote 2, p. 539.
94. *FRUS 1955–57*, Vol. XVII, Doc. 286, 15 Apr. 1957.
95. *FRUS 1955–57*, Vol. XVII, Doc. 289, 17 Apr. 1957.
96. PRO PREM 11/1787, GEN 585/3, Meeting, 16 Apr. 1957, and FO–Washington, No. 1911, 20 Apr. 1957.
97. PRO PREM 11/1787, Telegram to all SCUA posts, 27 Apr. 1957.
98. PRO FO 371/125519, JE 1421/474, Summary of meeting at Downing St, 2 May 1957.
99. *FRUS 1955–57*, Vol. XVII, Doc. 307, 1 May 1957, 578–81.

100. *FRUS 1955–57*, Vol. XVII, Footnote 7, 1 May 1957, p. 581.
101. *FRUS 1955–57*, Vol. XVII, Footnote 2, 1 May 1957, p. 583.
102. PRO PREM 11/1787, PMPT 173/57, Lloyd–Macmillan, 1 May 1957.
103. PRO FO 371/125519, JE 1421/478, Laskey (FO)–Beeley (Bonn), No. 895, 6 May 1957.
104. PRO FO 371/125519, JE 1421/485, Watkinson–Macmillan, 6 May 1957.
105. PRO CAB 128/31, Cabinet Conclusions, 36, 57, 10 May 1957.
106. Andrew Roberts, *Eminent Churchillians* (London, Phoenix, 1995), p. 224.
107. John Ramsden, *A History of the Conservative Party: Winds of Change: Macmillan to Heath, 1957–1975* (London, Longman, 1996), p. 22.
108. The motion was 'That this house expresses its concern at the outcome of the Government's Suez canal policy, and deplores the damage to British prestige and economic interests resulting therefrom', *Hansard*, 570, HC Debates, 15 May 1957, cc. 411.
109. *Hansard*, 570, HC Debs, 15 May 1957, cc. 447, 450.
110. *Hansard*, 570, HC Debs, 15 May 1957, cc. 436.
111. Diary entry for 16 May 1957. Richard Crossman, *The Backbench Diaries*, ed. Janet Morgan (London, Hamish Hamilton, 1981), p. 595.
112. Michael Foot, *Aneurin Bevan 1945–60*, Vol. II (London, Davis-Poynter, 1974), p. 535.

— 6 —

Crisis in Syria, 1957

NASSER IN RETREAT

THE CONCLUSION of an interim settlement for the future regime of the Suez Canal had taken place against the background of a series of reversals for Nasser's regime in the Middle East. The most important of these reversals was the overthrow of the pro-Nasser, parliamentary government in Jordan in April 1957. Prior to Suez, Jordan had been one of Britain's closest regional allies, but, by the beginning of 1957, King Hussein, under pressure from his pro-Nasser Prime Minister, Nabulsi, agreed to align Jordan with Nasser's Arab Solidarity Pact. This pact, signed in January 1957, created a military alliance between Egypt, Syria, Saudi Arabia and Jordan. As a consequence of Suez and their adherence to this pact, the Jordanians wished to abrogate the military alliance with Britain. The alliance allowed the latter to station troops in Jordan, but also as we have seen entailed an obligation to come to Jordan's assistance if it were attacked. The British Cabinet was certain by the end of 1956 that a pro-Western government could not be preserved in Jordan. Consequently, they saw the abrogation of the treaty as recognition of political reality rather than a further setback after Suez. When Dulles questioned Lloyd on the future of Jordan in December 1956, the latter replied, 'I don't think it's got one.'[1]

The Cabinet committees – discussing Britain's future strategy in the region in the early months of 1957 – had come to the conclusion that Britain should no longer place prime importance on the assertion of regional dominance. Instead, there was to be a stronger emphasis on the protection of oil resources in the Gulf emirates and Kuwait, as well as the maintenance of the special position that Britain still held in Iraq. The more expensive and not very profitable burdens in Jordan and Libya would hopefully be assumed by the United States.[2] In short, British policy was to avoid bold initiatives and let the United States take the leading role.

With these conclusions in mind, the Jordanian request for the abrogation of the Anglo-Jordanian treaty was acceded to, as soon as

British representatives had negotiated over-flight rights in March 1957.[3] However, within a month of the abrogation of the treaty and the seemingly complete adherence of Jordan to the pro-Nasser camp, King Hussein made an astonishing volte-face. On the night of 10 April 1957, he forced the resignation of Prime Minister Nabulsi. In a blatant attempt to secure American support, he claimed his Prime Minister was allowing communist subversion and propaganda.[4] Hussein's coup was completely successful and broke Nasser's hold on Jordan. The most important effect of the crisis was that it shattered the Arab Solidarity Pact, as the other conservative monarchies of Saudi Arabia and Iraq came out strongly in support of Hussein's actions. Patrick Seale describes the crisis as 'the first major setback for Nasirism in Arab Asia'.[5] From a position of seemingly unassailable strength prior to the crisis, Nasser was left with only Syria as an ally by the beginning of May 1957. The royalist monarchies had evidently come to the conclusion that unity between like-minded regimes against the Nasserite threat was their best hope of survival.

The House of Saud and the Hashemite monarchies of Iraq and Jordan had been rivals since they had thrown off the shackles of Turkish rule after the First World War. Relations had been cool since the Jordanian and Iraqi ruling families, the Hashemites, attempted to take over what is now Saudi Arabia in 1919. King Saud – as a result of this long-standing conflict and the conflict with the British over the Burami Oasis – had been an unlikely ally of Nasser and an implacable opponent of the Baghdad Pact. However, after the Jordanian crisis, Saud was now declaring that the Baghdad Pact was in accordance with the Charter of the United Nations, 'and was of advantage to the Arab world'.[6]

After some debate in Cabinet and the Foreign Office, the British had decided to take no part in the crisis. The Foreign Office initially declared its intention 'to sustain King Hussein against this Syro-Egyptian plot' and briefly considered using British forces still in the kingdom.[7] They inquired to the United States as to what attitude the latter would take in the event that a decision was taken to use British troops to help the King. The American Deputy Secretary of State, Christian Herter, was extremely lukewarm when Ambassador Caccia broached such an initiative. Instead he urged the British to let Iraq and Saudi Arabia help the King. The British Cabinet endorsed this advice and the remaining troops in Jordan were told to maintain a low profile.[8] The British subvention that kept Jordan afloat economically was replaced by the Americans and continued until the Gulf War in the early 1990s.[9] The irony of the whole crisis was that the British played little or no part in this first reversal for Nasser. In the previous year, the

British had used virtually every means at their disposal to combat his growing influence and failed completely. The new policy of keeping their heads beneath the parapet proved to be far more successful than the old one of confrontation. The American strategy since Suez appeared to be working.

ROME NEGOTIATIONS

One of the conditions that the Egyptians had demanded in return for the opening of No. 3 Account, which allowed the British to pay for the Canal, was that they would agree to discuss the release of the blocked sterling balances held in London. These talks were scheduled to take place on 23 May 1957 in Rome. The British approached these talks with conflicting goals in mind. On a simple economic basis the talks were about setting up a mechanism that would allow both sides to discuss the settlement of the huge financial claims against each other arising out of the Suez War. But a relatively hard-nosed, low-policy matter of concluding a financial agreement between Britain and Egypt had become a matter of high policy for both protagonists.

Calculations were being made in Whitehall and in Washington that *not* concluding a financial agreement with Nasser would be a way of weakening his regime – which of course remained a prime British objective. An addition to the opponents of compromise was the now strongly anti-Nasser King Saud who sent a message via Prime Minister Nuri al-Said of Iraq urging no concessions from Britain to Nasser. He argued that the 'right policy was for Nasser to be denied financial and economic help from the west as far as possible. He would then be forced, if he were to survive, to turn to Saud for aid on Saud's own conditions, and could be forced to change his destructive and pro-communist policy.'[10] Saud's advice reinforced the arguments of those who sought to maintain the maximum economic pressure on Nasser. Saud's message was also generally in line with the thinking of the United States, which was becoming increasingly alarmed by the ingratitude of Nasser and what they viewed as the increasing Soviet penetration of Syria in which he appeared to be acquiescing. They were continuing to block the dollar balances of the Egyptians. They were of the opinion that Nasser would require foreign capital to finance his showpiece development projects and to pay for consumer goods. The simultaneous blocking of both the sterling and dollar balances placed an additional burden on the already straitened Egyptian economy. In mid-April, Anglo-American talks on Egypt policy agreed that the Nasser regime was not the 'best Egyptian government we are likely to get', and that, while relations might eventually be restored, the 'policy of cutting Nasser down to size must continue'. Without being overly conspicuous in their hostility, all aid was to be withheld by the West.[11] Lloyd was keen to downplay the importance of the Rome talks to the Americans, describing them as merely 'exploratory'. A message to the Washington Embassy warned the Americans to ignore Nasser's propaganda if it claimed that the British government 'was now running after Nasser'. Britain had 'no intention of giving up the policy of economic pressure on Nasser, or the process of cutting him down to size'.[12] These were hardly the words of compromise.

The British brief for the talks agreed with the above, stating that 'In general there appears to be political advantage in not moving too fast towards normality in our financial and commercial relations with the Nasser regime.'[13] It went on to warn the team that they should stay clear of arguments on the legal basis for the continued blocking of the sterling balances, which the Egyptians were likely to argue contravened both the sterling release agreement of 1954 and the British government's obligations under the International Monetary Fund. The only British response would be to say that it is 'invidious that the Egyptians who have broken so many agreements with us, should claim that we are in breach of our financial agreements'. The brief was not all hostile. The team was told that the 'important thing, however, is to pave the way for agreement about the future rather than indulge in debate about the legalities of the past'.[14] There was an interest in Whitehall in concluding an agreement but on terms that could be made to look like a victory. The only reason for agreement was humanitarian rather than political. It concerned the British citizens who had been expelled from Egypt having lost all their property. They were already clamouring for the return of their property or compensation. If no agreement was forthcoming, the Egyptians might eventually lose patience and make all the sequestrations permanent. If the compensation for this did not come from Egypt, it would have to come from the British government. The British government would probably have been forced to pay for this through the liquidation of Egypt's blocked sterling. This would not have covered the compensation for the evacuees according to the Treasury. It would also have damaged the credibility of sterling, as such an action would have been a breach of IMF rules.

As it transpired, the negotiations were unsuccessful, quickly becoming mired in deadlock, because of the intransigence of both sides. The Egyptians made a number of demands that were obviously unrealistic – such as that the Suez Canal Company should hand over all its overseas assets to them before they would even negotiate with the company for compensation. The British delegation felt that there was a chance of agreement briefly on their proposals that, in return for a resumption of current trade, the Egyptians would desequestrate British assets and allow the owners to return, when a mechanism for the payments of compensation would be set up. There would then be a standstill period of three months after which the British would consider the question of release of blocked sterling. The Egyptian delegation seemed amenable when the British modified the proposals slightly and allowed for the release of a token amount of sterling. However, the Egyptians, after consultations with Cairo, rejected the British offer. They demanded that the British release all the sterling in No. 1 Account before they would agree to desequestration. There was no way that the British would agree to this at this time. The talks were then suspended, apparently irretrievably broken down, on 30 May 1957.[15] The breakdown was a mixed blessing for the British. Whilst it left the problem of the evacuees, it had the advantage that the British did not have to break ranks with the United States on the blocking of Egypt's foreign assets. The importance of this was emphasised by Humphrey Trevelyan upon the conclusion of Anglo-American talks on the Middle East in June:

> I think that we were able to satisfy the Americans that there was no divergence between the policies of the two governments on Egypt and that we were anxious to keep closely in line with them. We should keep in close touch with the Americans on our Egyptian policy and should take great care that they know in advance before we make any move towards agreement with the Egyptians about British property and Egyptian balances.[16]

Western unity was of vital importance, as the gravest threat to peace in the Middle East and the world in general since Suez was about to break in Syria in the late summer of 1957.

THE SYRIAN CRISIS – NASSER RESURGENT

The concern that the British and the United States felt about the growing leftward drift of the politics of Syria has already been briefly alluded to. The British Secret Intelligence Service and the CIA had colluded with Iraq in a failed plot to overthrow the Syrian government in October 1956. It was doomed because of its coincidence with the Suez operation. Suez and Operation Straggle pushed the Syrians further to the left. Nasser himself had become more radical as well. He and the Syrians felt that the 'American interference in Arab affairs in the name of anti-communism threatened to rob them of that local initiative for which they had fought since 1955'.[17] The spring setbacks in Jordan and the collapse of the Arab Solidarity Pact confirmed his suspicion of the Americans. The collapse of the pact had also increased the value of Syria to Nasser. If the Syrian regime fell, Nasser's would be the only radical nationalist regime in the Arab world. The policies pursued by the United States in the summer of 1957 seemed to suggest that the Americans and their allies were determined to destroy the radical regime in Syria.

The Americans were concerned that Syria was about to turn into a base for communist subversion in the Middle East. A number of events fuelled this concern. In the spring of 1957, an American corporation's bid for a contract to build a new oil refinery in Syria was lost to a Czech firm. This was followed by the appointment of Afif al-Bizri – whom the Americans believed to be communist – as Chief of Staff of the army. Then in August came what seemed like decisive proof of the 'satellisation' of Syria: the signing of a trade agreement with the Soviet Union. This was followed on 12 August by the expulsion of three American diplomats accused – with considerable justification – of plotting to overthrow the regime.[18] Eisenhower responded by expelling the Syrian Ambassador.[19] The *New York Times* editorialised on 18 August as to whether the United States and Syria's pro-Western neighbours could tolerate a Soviet satellite in the region.[20] On 19 August the British Ambassador, Harold Caccia, was called in for crisis talks with the President and Dulles. The latter wrote to Macmillan in August suggesting that the increasingly troublesome Syrian regime merited the use of covert action by its neighbours including Britain's loyal ally Iraq. Macmillan, desperate to be at the centre of American planning in the Middle East, was delighted to be able to help.[21] It was agreed that a Syrian working group would be established with the aim of sharing intelligence and to co-ordinate military and political action in Syria.[22] The files available to the historian on the working group are mainly British and incomplete. The sensitive intelligence nature of many of these files is likely to mean that many will remain closed for a considerable period of time. A definitive picture of what was plotted is therefore not yet possible.[23]

The allies' main problem was the lack of justification required to strike at the Syrians. The growth of the communists and the left in Syria was not being orchestrated by the Soviet Union; it was coming from internal sources. More importantly, the real political gains being made in Syria were being made by the radical pan-Arabists (such as the Ba'ath) aligned with Nasser rather than the Soviets. The Soviets were important to the Syrians primarily because they seemed to be the only power able to protect them from the machinations of the West, and not for ideological reasons.

Eisenhower and Dulles attempted to mobilise Syria's neighbours against it. Deputy Secretary of State Loy Henderson was despatched to Istanbul to meet with representatives from Turkey, Iraq and Jordan to urge them to take action against Syria. Cairo Radio denounced him as a plotter planning to overthrow the Syrian regime pointing to his involvement in the Iranian coup of 1953.[24] Henderson described his consultation as covering 'a wide range of possible moves to counter communization Syria including diplomatic activities, possibility [of] utilizing Syrian leaders in exile, assessment of military strengths of Iraq, Jordan and Syria. There [is] possibility para-military action might be required in case unbearable provocation.'[25]

The problem was that unbearable provocation could mean anything. Egypt was discussed. King Hussein rejected the idea of an appeal to be sent to Nasser as that would be 'useless'. On the subject of potential Egyptian intervention, Henderson assured his listeners that he hoped the United States 'would be able make clear [to] them inadvisability any action [on] their part. I added presence certain elements Sixth Fleet in Eastern Mediterranean waters might have a restraining influence as well.' He went on to describe current United States thinking on Syria, which saw the country on the verge of joining the Communist Bloc. Therefore the United States 'would give all appropriate support in the UN and otherwise to Syria's Moslem neighbours in case they were forced to take some kind [of] defensive action in response [to] Syrian provocations'.[26]

The most enthusiastic supporter of action was the non-Arab power Turkey. From the beginning of the crisis, American and French opinion had come to the conclusion that action initiated by Turkey was likely to unite the Arab world against the Turks. The evidence that a plot against Syria was in existence is clear cut. Eisenhower was extremely worried about the crisis. In his memoirs, he frankly admits that he was willing to contemplate general war if the Soviets tried to get involved. The alternative 'to do nothing and lose the whole Middle East to Communism would be worse'.[27] This crisis was taking place at a time of great East–West tension as the Soviets successfully tested their first intercontinental ballistic missile (ICBM) and were only weeks from the launch of Sputnik. The CIA saw the former test as 'an angle of blackmail and possible relation to Syria'.[28]

Macmillan's attitude to the crisis was ambiguous. In a letter to Dulles on 28 August – in which he discussed the possibility of an operation to drive the communists out of Syria – he believed such an operation should be 'undertaken by Syria's Arab neighbours, led if possible by Iraq'. However, Macmillan foresaw problems in finding a reasonable *casus belli*.[29] This bellicosity contrasts with his assertion of moderation in his memoirs where he describes the British role in the crisis as not 'to stimulate but often to restrain the impetuousness of the State Department'. Dulles, Macmillan noted, was advocating measures that a few months ago he would have denounced as 'immoral'.[30]

British enthusiasm with regard to an operation aimed against Syria was tempered to a certain extent by the potential economic consequences of a war in the Middle East. In a Cabinet meeting held on 27 August, Macmillan expressed his concern about Syria but also mentioned his fear that the likely Syrian reaction to a Western invasion would be to blow the oil pipeline from Iraq to the Mediterranean and that this would be done in tandem with the Egyptians closing the Canal.[31] This would be a repeat of the events that had caused such severe economic dislocation during Suez. Admittedly, this time Americans would be economically supportive. Macmillan received a reply to his letter to Dulles the following day. Dulles continued his belligerent attitude. If an 'operation [was] started in circumstances that the US approved, the US would feel committed to make sure that it did not fail'. Caccia was more cautious of the plan, warning Macmillan that 'if anything goes wrong, you may be sure that Mr Dulles will place the blame elsewhere'.[32] In a telegram to the Permanent Undersecretary at the Foreign Office, Hoyer-Millar, he gave a fuller explanation of the apparent conversion of the United States to a forward policy in the Middle East and why it would not necessarily work in Britain's interest: 'In American eyes the use of force by others is justifiable in almost any circumstances when it can be shown to be directed against communism; but that conversely when the connection cannot be clearly shown, there are almost no circumstances in which they can be counted on to support it.'[33]

Macmillan despatched his private secretary, Freddie Bishop, to Washington to liaise more closely with the Americans. The extent of the co-operation was new to Dulles: 'There is genuine, intimate and effective co-operation, stemming directly from Macmillan – this is the first instance in his service as Secretary wherein we have had anything like this attitude.'[34] On 6 September, the British Cabinet discussed the crisis. This and another Cabinet meeting have only recently been declassified. Macmillan informed the Cabinet of the substance of his correspondence with Dulles. Dulles, he said, was inclined to take the view 'that action should be taken now to retrieve the situation before it was too late, despite the difficulties and dangers which such action would involve'. Macmillan advised that it would be necessary to obtain from British experts an independent assessment of the recent developments and then to explore the form and consequences of action with the United States. Macmillan warned of the dangers of reticence and emphasised the benefits of acting in concert with the United States once more in the Middle East:

> It would be important, however, that these discussions should not reflect any reluctance on our part to take advantage of this opportunity to establish between the United States and ourselves a unity of policy and action in the Middle East. Such an opportunity might not recur for a very long time, and it would be unwise to neglect it, provided that the implications of the action envisaged had been thoroughly explored in advance and that both governments were convinced of the joint policy.[35]

The Cabinet met again on 10 September 1957 to discuss whether Britain should endorse a memorandum that the Americans planned to send to the Turks and the Arab states. This memo outlined the support that the United States and Britain would give in event of a clash with Syria and the conditions that would set off this support:

> The United States judges that Syria has become, or is about to become, a base for military and subversive activities in the near east designed to destroy the independence of those countries and to subject them to Soviet Communist domination. If the aggressive spirit which is being inculcalated into Syria by means of Soviet arms, propaganda, etc., should, as seems likely manifest itself in actual deeds – and some such manifestations have already occurred in Lebanon – the United States would hold that a case existed for individual or collective self-defence under Article 51 of the United Nations Charter and that there would be no violation of Article 1 of the NATO Treaty.[36]

The telegram went on to say that the United States would furnish military, diplomatic and moral support to any of Syria's Moslem neighbours that acted pursuant to Article 51. In the event that the Soviets intervened, the United States would, if requested, deploy its own military forces to the region. The Foreign Secretary informed the Cabinet that the 'main choice lay between attempting to contain the situation in Syria or retrieving it by more direct action'. He assessed that the 'right course … would be to support the United States preference for direct action'. The Cabinet agreed to endorse the memo.[37]

With regard to Egypt, a considerable amount of contradiction had entered British policy by the middle part of September. On one hand, the chances of an agreement with Nasser seemed to have improved, while, on the other hand, Macmillan seemed to be looking at the possibility of a military clash with Egypt in the context of the Syrian crisis. The documents describe a confused and contradictory picture. In mid-September, Colonel Hatem, a close confidant of Nasser, was in London, ostensibly on private business. Hatem took the opportunity to meet senior Foreign Office officials. At these talks the real purpose of his trip became clear. He was in London to try to get the financial talks restarted. He seemed to take a more conciliatory line than that taken in May and there appeared to be the outlines of a deal. He said he would recommend the release of the British espionage agents, Zarb and Swinburn, and said that he thought that Colonel Nasser would 'be prepared to issue an announcement that all sequestrated British property in Egypt would be desequestrated and that compensation would be paid for Egyptianised British property'. Most importantly, Hatem seemed to suggest a willingness to trade Egyptian war damage claims against the British stores and base in the Canal Zone. In return, Colonel Nasser would 'expect us to announce our readiness to make releases from the Sterling balances'.[38] On the subject of Syria, Hatem said 'that the Americans were inclined to exaggerate the extent of communism in Syria. In point of fact the Syrians were devoted followers of Colonel Nasser, who was more important to them than communism and who himself was anti-communist.'[39] (This was hardly of great comfort to the British.) In reply to his suggestion that the Egyptians were returning to Rome on 2 October, Macmillan reluctantly gave his approval to the return of the United Kingdom delegation a week later. He recorded in his diary that he was 'not very anxious to get involved in talks with Colonel Nasser. On the other hand ... from the parliamentary point of view I would like to progress with the compensation of our nationals by some means.'[40]

It was decided by the British that the best way to proceed was at least to explore the possibility of agreement. In a meeting with Dulles, Lloyd said that he thought a 'flat rejection of his [Nasser's] approach was undesirable from the point of view of the general situation in the Middle East; and that we would be wiser to keep Nasser hoping'. At the same time, he emphasised that there was no intention of making a bargain with Egypt behind the back of the United States government. Dulles agreed with the proposal for limited contact.[41] However, Macmillan was soon thinking of fighting rather than negotiating with Nasser. He was deeply concerned and excited about the response of Egypt to an Iraqi attack on Syria. If Egypt went to Syria's aid in event of an Arab initiative, as seemed very possible at this stage, the question would arise as to what Britain's obligations under the Baghdad Pact were, and what military aid Britain would provide in such a war scenario. What is strange about this emphasis on Egypt was that a clash with Syria, on the surface at least, was more likely to lead to Soviet action and with it the risk of general war. The question then arises as to why there was such an emphasis on the Egyptians. There is the relatively innocent answer that the war plan for dealing with a Soviet threat was well known and did not require discussion. The other possible answer is that the British knew that the likelihood of Soviet intervention was extremely low – as they were so strategically inferior to the United States. On the other hand, Nasser might be more willing to fight for Syria on the grounds of Arab solidarity. Perhaps there was the potential to drag Nasser into a military confrontation with Iraq, Britain and the United States. With those odds against him, it is hard to see how Nasser could have survived. The evidence of a military plot against Egypt by Macmillan is not conclusive but does have some support in the files. Around the middle of September, there is a growing emphasis in the PREM files on Egypt and the US attitude to military action against it. At a meeting in New York between Secretaries Lloyd and Dulles on 16 September, the Syrian crisis is discussed but the former seems most interested in what the United States would do if the Egyptians blocked the Suez Canal in response to allied action in Syria. Dulles replied that he had not yet taken a position but suggested that the United States 'should use force to the degree necessary to secure the reopening of the Canal'.[42] On 21 September the subject of what to do if Jordan and Iraq, as a result of hostilities with Syria, were attacked by Egypt and requested aid from Britain and the United States came up at a meeting of the two secretaries. Dulles responded by saying that he was

> thinking of telling the Egyptian Government that if they took military action to support the Communist cause in the Middle East it would be regarded by the United States as final proof that they were a Communist dominated State in the sense of the Eisenhower Doctrine. Consequently if Jordan and Iraq were to ask for assurances of United States support against Egypt he thought the United States would be disposed to respond favourably.[43]

Lloyd responded by saying that Britain did not have any obligation to Jordan but as 'regards Iraq, we were by our special agreement under the Baghdad pact under an obligation to go to her assistance if she was attacked. I thought this would apply to an attack by Egypt in the circumstances envisaged, just as much as to an attack by the Soviet Union.'[44]

The sensitive nature of this material is proved by the limited distribution that it was allowed. Only those who were 'in the loop' like Macmillan, his private secretaries and Ambassador Harold Caccia were allowed to see it.[45] On 23 September, the legal adviser to the Foreign Office, Gerald Fitzmaurice, gave his view of the obligations of the British government to Iraq in the event of an attack by the Egyptians. He went through a variety of scenarios and described how Britain would possibly be able to act under the cover of the UN Charter. There was a problem that, because the Baghdad Pact was subordinate to Article 51 of the UN Charter, Britain would not be able to justify military assistance to the Iraqis if they initiated a military attack against Syria 'without any previous Syrian action justifying this':

> If Syria attacks Jordan, and Iraq takes action against Syria in support of Jordan, action against Egypt and/or action in support of Iraq, would be justified in the event of an Egyptian attack on Iraq … However, the case would not be so strong if activities were confined to Syrian territory and no direct attack on Iraqi territory took place. In this case if our action took the form of an attack on Egyptian territory it could be represented as going beyond what the needs of self-defence under Article 51 require.[46]

Sir Gerald had pointed up the weakness of the government's case for military action during Suez.[47] More encouraging than this legalese was the report from a meeting of the working group on 28 September which noted 'that both United Kingdom and United States Governments would be disposed to act against Egypt, if the Egyptians attacked the Iraqis or Jordanians while the latter were carrying out a policy which had been approved'.[48]

Macmillan continued to explore the possibilities of war. Horne cites a top secret personal memorandum drafted at the end of September by Macmillan for the attention of the Minister of Defence. In this, Macmillan, judging by the questions asked, appears to be considering the possibility of a rematch with Nasser:

> In the event of Iraq finding herself at war with Syria and Egypt attacking Iraq, if Iraq calls upon us under the Treaty to come to her aid. What military measures might we be able to take and what military consequences might be entailed? … It would be assumed for this purpose that the United States would also be bringing help to Iraq and would be taking military measures against Egypt.[49]

Sandys gave a short response of what Britain could do in such an eventuality. His and the Chiefs of Staff's assessment was that the

Egyptian potential to intervene against Iraq would be limited to the air. The United Kingdom could respond using aircraft from carriers or from Cyprus against (a) Egyptian airfields, (b) Egyptian aircraft *en route* to or in Syria, (c) Egyptian-based land forces in Syria and of course that particular *bête noire*, Cairo Radio. Sandys pointed out that the consequences entailed in such action would include having to route shipping around the Cape plus the reinforcement of the base at Aden and the various Gulf protectorates.[50]

While the Prime Minister considered war with Egypt, Archibald Ross, head of North and East African affairs at the Foreign Office, urged that advantage should be taken of the recent Hatem overtures 'even though concessions might be necessary on our part'. The implication of a move to restored relations, he warned, was that a policy of letting bygones be bygones would be necessary. Such a policy in the present situation of tension over Syria could raise problems as 'it was no time for us to give Nasser any encouragement or to take steps which might discourage our friends in the other Arab countries and lead them to think that we are weakening in our determination to resist Soviet infiltration'. Ross did acknowledge that 'the recent events in Syria may or may not have been altogether to Nasser's liking, and there may be a chance albeit a slight one, of playing on his suspicions and gradually winning him away from his present dependence on the Russians'.[51] Sir Michael Wright, Ambassador in Iraq, who consequently reflected the strong anti-Nasser views of that country's rulers, was in favour of a deal that would look favourable to the United Kingdom. He suggested that any form of agreement with Britain 'which does not cover war damage, will appear in the nature of a climb down, or at least a return to hard business sense rather than a victory for emotional nationalism'. He warned that a deal which looked like a victory for Nasser would be regretted by Britain's Arab friends.[52] Wright expressed his hope that any sterling releases would not be enough to give Nasser funds for subversion. Within the Foreign Office, at least, there seemed to be a developing consensus that a deal of some description would have to be made with Nasser.

The likelihood of conflict in the Middle East was receding anyway and whatever ambitious plans Macmillan might have desired were unlikely ever to be carried out. The Arab coalition, which was never the most stable, began to have serious doubts about the wisdom of launching a military attack against Syria. King Saud of Saudi Arabia – whom the United States had built so much of their hopes around – was the first to break ranks after a visit to Beirut on 7 September, in which he probably met Syrian officials. On 10 September, the Saudi Ambassador to Damascus announced that his country 'would spare no effort to support, back, and aid' Syria, should it be attacked. After this the likelihood of any of the Arab states taking part in a military attack on the Syrians diminished. Saud by the end of the month was being acclaimed as the 'lion of the peninsula' for his efforts to stop aggression against Syria. The collapse of the Arab determination to confront Syria seemed to be complete when Saud visited Damascus on 25 September followed by the Iraqi Premier, Ali Jaudat, the following day, both pledging non-aggression against the Syrians.[53] Assistant Secretary of State William Rountree commented caustically that 'what the Arabs [are] saying publicly [bears] little or no relation to what they are saying privately'.[54] The British had not yet abandoned all hope of action. On 29 September, Selwyn Lloyd, while admitting that the problems of action must be stressed, warned:

> we must not forget that the danger of complete inaction is probably much greater. We do not want to give the feeling to the Americans that we are driving into some course of action difficult to defend. On the other hand, we do not want to give them the impression that we are dragging our feet and can think of nothing but difficulties.

It went on to note displeasure at the turn of events in Iraq and suggests that greater emphasis should be placed on King Hussein who was 'the only Arab ruler disposed both to say and to do what he thinks to be right'.[55] The telegram also seemed to wonder whether the Turks would have to be used. Nuri al-Said was reported to be so disgusted with the behaviour of his Prime Minister that he was rumoured to be contemplating a coup to topple Ali Jaudat.[56] Ali Jaudat's reluctance for action created an 'unbridgeable gap' between him and Nuri and the royal family and led to him leaving office in December 1957.[57]

By 4 October the British did not rate the possibility of action very highly and suggested that events were moving towards the adoption of a new policy called 'containment plus'.[58] The Syrian working group completed its work sometime around the middle of October and it too came out in favour of this less expansive policy of containment plus. The conclusions of 'containment plus' were that Turkish military action was undesirable but would be supported if they did act. Nasser was to be privately warned not to intervene in such an eventuality. In the event of war involving Egypt, 'the desirability of Israeli action against Egypt should be examined'. A successful coup in any Arab country would spell the end of containment plus.[59] Lloyd discussed Anglo-American policy towards Egypt with Dulles in Washington on 15 October:

Mr Lloyd said that there were three general lines British policy might follow. The British could say they would not discuss anything at all with the Egyptians and maintain a complete 'freeze' on relations with Egypt, they could change their policy completely and say that if Nasser would work with the West he could 'have anything he wanted' from the UK; there was a line of policy in between these two extremes which the British preferred.

Dulles said that US policy was 'coolly correct'. He opined that Britain should not make a deal that would look like a victory for Nasser.[60]

The Syrian crisis would now probably have ended except that the Turks were continuing to apply military pressure on Syria by mobilising their army on Syria's northern frontier. The allies did not want to put too much pressure on the Turks to demobilise for fear that it would look like they were giving in to Soviet military threats. A constant refrain among American and British diplomats was that they did not want to be seen to be enforcing a Munich-style settlement on the Turks. Turkey's eventual demobilisation was bargained away by increased American arms supplies and economic aid.[61]

The beneficiary of the military pressure by the Turks though turned out to be Nasser. At the end of September, it had looked like he had lost out in the crisis, as Saud had seemingly brokered a peaceful solution while the Soviets looked like they had replaced Egypt as Syria's military protector. However, the Egyptian President successfully restored his prestige on 13 October when a contingent of Egyptian troops landed in Syria, ostensibly to protect Syria from Turkish aggression but mainly with the aim of embarrassing Saud who had been calling for an Arab summit in Beirut.[62] Nasser's bold action outflanked everybody. It was, as the *New Statesman* commented, aimed squarely at the 'Arab masses, and is intended to restore the image of Egypt, as the major power in the Arab world, both willing and able to come to the aid of her threatened friends'.[63] The Saudis were shown to be men of words while Nasser was a man of action. He took the opportunity to increase his influence in Syria at the expense of his Arab enemies but also at the expense of his erstwhile allies: the Soviets and their communist allies. The latter policy led to a *rapprochement* with the Americans. Syria had lodged a complaint in the United Nations against Turkey. The Egyptians proved helpful in getting the Syrian complaint to be buried.[64] The crisis ended abruptly on 29 October when Khrushchev pulled back from conflict when he told the Turkish Ambassador that the whole crisis had been a misunderstanding. The Syrians withdrew their complaints soon after.

The British made no comment on Nasser's actions as they were just beginning a renewed round of financial negotiations in Rome. Macmillan noted in his diaries that the Syrian situation is being 'hotted up by the Russians and the Egyptians' on 15 October.[65] The Rome negotiations were proceeding slowly as the British had not 'softened' their position since May. The Egyptian delegation seemed more interested in a deal. The Commonwealth Relations Office suggested this was because Nasser needed sterling for trade and was alarmed at his dependence on the Soviets.[66] A Foreign Office paper at the end of October confirmed a more conciliatory attitude from the Foreign Office towards Nasser:

> In general we should attempt to create a situation in which Nasser was regarded as nothing more then an unfriendly neutral, rather then risk pushing him further into the Soviet embrace by persistent antagonism. At the same time we should continue to do all in our power to reduce Nasser's influence outside Egypt. This is more likely to be achieved by an attitude of disinterested coolness rather than active and flattering hostility.[67]

Others in the Foreign Office, including Caccia, who was a member of the Syrian working group, were more cautious, pointing towards the situation in Jordan where Egyptian-backed subversion continued. He suggested that the line taken be 'there can be no question of relaxing the present Western attitude towards Nasser so long as he pursues, in conjunction with the Russians, a policy aimed against a government friendly to the West on account of that friendship'.[68] The Brenchley paper did not arouse much enthusiasm among the Americans either. Dulles' reply was that unless UK agreement with Nasser extracted substantial concessions from Nasser, 'it might be better that no agreement be concluded'.[69] Judging by the slow progress that the talks were making it seems fair to say that the British were not taking any bold initiatives in the talks. However, the Americans were not averse to changing their minds when the opportunity arose.

On 28 October, Dulles mentioned the possibility that developments in Syria might lead to an improvement in relations with Egypt. William Rountree of the State Department concurred, arguing that the despatch of Egyptian troops to Syria 'was more a reflection of Nasser's desire to bolster Egypt's prestige and to give Egypt a greater voice in Syrian affairs than a genuine act of solidarity'.[70] On 13 November, Eisenhower inquired as to whether there would be any percentage in initiating a drive to bring Nasser to their side. He wanted this to be skilfully done, as 'we don't want to be in a position of "bootlicking a dictator"'.[71]

The Syrian crisis saw Nasser at his best. With considerable diplomatic skill he began to reduce his enemies. Trading relations were restored with France at the end of September. Egyptian newspapers proclaimed desires for détente. On 12 October, *Al-Sha'b* said that Egypt 'is anxious to have good relations with the United States and other states'.[72] All of this wooing of the West from the Hatem mission to the co-operation with the Americans in the United Nations was most likely aimed at securing the acquiescence of the West in letting Egypt take the leading role in Syrian politics. The United States and eventually even the British would realise that, whatever hostility they felt towards his regime, it was infinitely preferable to the prospect of the Soviets securing control of Syria. The plan was completely successful. The United States was, within days of sending Dulles' hard-line message to the British, pursuing an entirely different agenda with regard to the Egyptians. They had watched with satisfaction as Nasser had come down strongly on the side of the radical but anti-communist Ba'ath at the end of November. He contacted the American Embassy through a messenger, whose name remains classified, to let them know that he too feared that the communists were growing too powerful:

> Nasser had investigated recent information that we had given him relative to the communist connections of Bizri and is now convinced [that] Bizri [is] a communist and that something must be done about it. Nasser believes [the] responsibility is Egypt's and that Egypt should tackle it with vigour, and should be able [to] achieve results … [The messenger went on] Only country with capability to succeed, and which can do so with minimal repercussions is Egypt. Of countries primarily concerned with Syrian situation, [the] US and Egypt have greatest interest in ensuring that country [has] a stable anti-communist government. Their co-operation [is] therefore necessary.

The Ambassador's comments on the message reflected to a certain degree the convergence of aims between the United States and Nasser. 'It is possible therefore that Egypt, though largely responsible for present chaos in Syria, may now be prepared [to] exert serious effort to pull situation out of fire'.[73] Rountree told Ambassador Hare that the United States would 'welcome action designed [to] impede [the] communist threat [to the] security of Syria and [the] entire ME. While we obviously cannot bind ourselves not to take action re Syria in next three months we wish [to] avoid impeding any Egyptian efforts to bring about change in the region'.[74]

Nasser succeeded completely in his efforts to gain the dominant role in Syrian politics. The Americans had abandoned the fight against Nasser in Syria. They now believed that Nasser was the only Arab leader who could stop communism there. There is no evidence that the views of the British were sought on what was a most momentous change in American policy. It seems that they were able to read the signs and began to seek agreement with the Egyptians with more energy than they had previously. The Cabinet Secretary, Norman Brook, wrote to Macmillan suggesting a rethink in the United Kingdom position towards Arab nationalism. He pointed out that the United Kingdom was aligned with the forces of reaction and that 'we run the risk that by the time they [the nationalists] gain control, we shall by our support of existing authority have driven them into anti-British policies … our future policy should be to harness these movements rather than to struggle against them'.[75] However, Macmillan appeared to be utterly unaware of the American moves towards Nasser. His diary entry of 19 December is at complete variance with the actual situation. He noted that Eisenhower and Dulles 'are now completely converted – too late – and wish devoutly that they had let us go on and finish off Nasser'.[76]

Despite a more positive British attitude, the resumed financial talks came very close to breakdown. The Egyptians' offer at the start of December 1957 seemed to offer some hope. The Chancellor of the Exchequer, Peter Thorneycroft, assessed it on 11 December for the Prime Minister. The main points of the offer were: (a) that the British would release £18 million of blocked sterling; (b) that there would be a resumption of trade; (c) no de-Egyptianisation of United Kingdom assets; (d) compensation for Egyptianised property; (e) £30 million in advance; (f) a broadly neutral arbitration; (g) the desequestration of non-Egyptianised property; (h) no compensation for (g) unless there were irregularities by the sequestrator and no arbitration on that point; (i) no restoration of old United Kingdom rights in taxation etc. The last three points raised the gravest problems for the government but it had to be acknowledged that breakdown in the talks would lead to the permanent seizure of United Kingdom assets. An attached note pointed to the fact that Britain held £70 million in Egyptian sterling while claims against Egypt amounted to £166 million. The conclusion was that an agreement held more advantages than disadvantages for the United Kingdom. The talks broke up on 12 December 1957 to allow for consultations and were due to resume on 20 January 1958.[77] This was not popular with everybody in Whitehall. Sir Freddie Bishop, Macmillan's private secretary, wrote that the No. 10 Private Office 'have always had rather strong doubts in the desirability of concluding the negotiations'.[78] The Foreign Office was now in favour of an agreement on the grounds that it was unwise not to have some means of contact with the most influential Arab country. The position that was adopted was that a partial settlement was to be sought that would leave aside the problems over sequestrated property.[79] That there was even the possibility of an agreement suggested that the cold war between the two countries was slowly thawing. Two issues delayed progress. These were the creation of the United Arab Republic in February 1958 and the continuing subversion of Lebanon and Jordan by both Syria and Egypt.

NOTES

1. *FRUS 1955–57*, Vol. XIII, Doc. 49, 10 Dec. 1956.
2. General British policy in the Middle East was discussed in PRO CAB 134/2338, OME, 57, No. 3, 1 Feb. 1957, and No. 14, 29 Apr. 1957.
3. PRO CAB 128/31, Cabinet Conclusions, 17, 12 Mar. 1957.
4. See the memoirs of C. Johnston, British Ambassador in Amman, for an account of the monarchical coup. *The Brink of Jordan* (London, Hamish Hamilton, 1972), pp. 34–74. Richard H. Sanger, *Where the Jordan Flows* (Washington, DC, Middle East Institute, 1963), pp. 381–7. Dann, *King Hussein*, pp. 52–66.
5. Seale, *Struggle for Syria*, p. 290.
6. Cited in Elie Podeh, 'The Struggle for Arab Hegemony after the Suez Crisis', *Middle Eastern Studies*, 29, 1 (1993), pp. 91–110.
7. Andrew Rathmell, *Secret War in the Middle East: The Covert Struggle for Syria, 1949–61* (London, I.B. Tauris, 1995), p. 132.
8. *FRUS 1955–57*, Vol. XIII, Doc. 62, 14 Mar. 1957.
9. Rashid Khalidid, 'Consequences of the Suez Crisis in the Arab World', in Roger Louis and Owen, *Suez 1956*, p. 384.
10. PRO PREM 11/1786, Baghdad–FO, No. 632, 15 May 1957.
11. PRO CAB 134/2340, OME, 57, 27 (Revise), 12 Apr. 1957.
12. PRO FO 371/125444, J.H.A.Watson minute, 20 May 1957 and FO–Washington, No. 2263,19 May 1957.
13. PRO PREM 11/1796, Brief for Anglo-Egyptian talks in Rome starting on 23 May 1957.
14. Ibid.
15. PRO PREM 11/1786, Rome–FO, No. 348, 30 May 1957.
16. PRO FO 371/127757 VG 1075/37, Trevelyan minute, 17 June 1957.
17. Seale, *Struggle for Syria*, p. 291.
18. Most accounts suggest that they were indeed plotting against the regime. Seale, *Struggle for Syria*, p. 294. Rathmell, *Secret War*, p. 139. D. Little, 'Cold War and Covert Action', *Middle East Journal*, 44, 1 (1990), p. 71. The most conclusive proof perhaps is in the memoirs of the US Ambassador to Syria. Charles Yost, *History and Memory* (New York, Norton, 1980), pp. 236–7.
19. Press Release 462, 14 Aug. 1957, *Dept of State Bulletin*, 2 Sept. 1957, pp. 388–9.
20. Seale, *Struggle for Syria*, pp. 290–3.
21. Note that the Syrians had broken relations with the British during the Suez crisis.
22. Horne, *Macmillan*, Vol. II, p. 42.
23. Those that have been released have only been available since 1995. As an example of how sensitive the files were and still are and the importance

attached to them not leaking, Macmillan wrote to Sandys, Minister of Defence, ordering him not to show them even to the Chiefs of Staff, warning 'everything depends on the greatest discretion'. PRO PREM 11/2521, M 486/57, Macmillan–Sandys.
24. Seale, *Struggle for Syria*, p. 296.
25. *FRUS 1955–57*, Vol. XIII, Doc. 373, Miner–Dulles, 26 Aug. 1957.
26. Ibid.
27. Eisenhower, *Waging Peace*, p. 199.
28. Little, 'Cold War and Covert Action', p. 73.
29. Horne, *Macmillan*, Vol. II, pp. 41–2.
30. Macmillan, *Riding the Storm*, pp. 277–8.
31. PRO CAB 128/31, Cabinet Conclusions, 63, 27 Aug. 1957.
32. Horne, *Macmillan*, Vol. II, p. 42.
33. Caccia–Hoyer-Millar, 10 Sept. 1957, cited in William Roger Louis and R. Robinson, 'The Imperialism of Decolonisation', *Journal of Imperial and Commonwealth History*, XXII (1994), pp. 505–6, Endnote 140.
34. *FRUS 1955–57*, Vol. XIII, Doc. 382, 7 Sept. 1957.
35. PRO CAB 128/140, Cabinet Conclusions, 64, 1, 6 Sept. 1957.
36. *FRUS 1955–57*, Vol. XIII, Doc. 392, 10 Sept. 1957.
37. PRO CAB 128/140, Cabinet Conclusions, 65, 1, 10 Sept. 1957. The British copy is in PRO PREM 11/2119, Top secret Syria memo, 10 Sept. 1957.
38. PRO FO 371/125444, JE 1052/26, William Hayter minute, 19 Sept. 1957.
39. PRO FO 371/125444, William Hayter minute (not dated, JE 1052/26).
40. Macmillan Diary, 24 Sept. 1957, Dep. d. 30 (photocopy sanitised), Macmillan Papers, Bodleian Library.
41. PRO FO 371/125445, JE 1052/26, Lloyd–Ormsby Gore, 21 Sept. 1957.
42. PRO PREM 11/2119, Record of conversation between Secretaries Lloyd and Dulles, 16 Sept. 1957, Top secret.
43. PRO PREM 11/2521, New York–FO, No. 1533, For Prime Minister from Secretary of State, T 402/57, 21 Sept. 1957.
44. Ibid.
45. Ibid.
46. PRO PREM 11/2521, FO–New York, No. 2376, For Secretary of State, 23 Sept. 1957.
47. See L. Johnman, 'Playing the Role of a Cassandra', in Kelly and Gorst (eds), *Whitehall and the Suez Crisis*, pp. 46–62.
48. PRO PREM 11/2521, Washington–FO, No. 1953, 28 Sept. 1957.
49. The copy in the Public Record Office is in PRO PREM 11/2521, PM 514/57. His biographer had access to the Macmillan Papers which are still not available for research. Horne, *Macmillan*, Vol. II, p. 45.
50. PRO PREM 11/1899, Sandys–Macmillan, Note by COS, Possible British action to support Iraq against attack by Egypt, 1 Oct. 1957, Top secret.
51. PRO FO 371/125444, JE 1052/48, Ross minute, 2 Oct. 1957.
52. PRO PREM 11/2119, Wright (Baghdad) to FO, No. 1198, 4 Oct. 1957.
53. Seale, *Struggle for Syria*, pp. 303–4. D.W. Lesch, 'Nasser and an Example of Diplomatic Acumen', *Middle Eastern Studies*, 31, 2 (Apr. 1995), p. 365.
54. Rathmell, *Secret War*, p. 142.
55. PRO PREM 11/2521, FO–Washington, No. 3884, 29 Sept. 1957.
56. PRO PREM 11/2119, Istanbul–FO, No. 201, 26 Sept. 1957.
57. Matthew Elliot, *Independent Iraq* (London, I.B. Tauris, 1996), p. 128.
58. PRO PREM 11/2119, FO–Washington, No. 3956, 4 Oct. 1957.
59. PRO PREM 11/2521, Morris (Washington) to Hood and Hayter, Working papers XVII and XIX, 11 Oct. 1957. Completed drafts of the working group's working

papers were contained in telegrams around this time, PRO PREM 11/2521, Lloyd–Macmillan, No. 2084, 15 Oct. 1957.

60. USNA Memcon, 15 Oct. 1957. Selwyn Lloyd visit. Bureau of Euro Affairs. Office of British Commonwealth and North European Affairs. Alphanumeric files relating to the UK 1949–62, Box 3.
61. Little, 'Cold War and Covert Action', p. 73.
62. See Lesch, 'Nasser and an Example of Diplomatic Acumen', pp. 367–8.
63. *New Statesman*, 19 Oct. 1957.
64. PRO PREM 11/2119, New York–FO, No. 1715, 16 Oct. 1957, reports Fawzi asking Syria not to proceed with the complaint.
65. Macmillan Diary, 15 Oct. 1957, Dep. d. 30 (photocopy sanitised).
66. PRO FO 371/125444, JE 1052/48, CRO–FO, No. 422, 22 Oct. 1957.
67. PRO FO 371/125444, JE 1052/38, Brenchley paper, 24 Oct. 1957.
68. PRO PREM 11/2521, Caccia–FO, No. 2354, 13 Nov. 1957.
69. *FRUS 1955–57*, Vol. XIII, Dulles to London, 26 Nov. 1957, pp. 826–7.
70. *FRUS 1955–57*, Vol. XIII, Doc. 392, 4 Nov. 1957.
71. *FRUS 1955–57*, Vol. XIII, Doc. 398, 13 Nov. 1957.
72. Quoted in Lesch, 'Nasser and an Example of Diplomatic Acumen', p. 373.
73. *FRUS 1955–57*, Vol. XIII, Doc. 420, 11 Dec. 1957.
74. *FRUS 1955–57*, Vol. XIII, Doc. 421, 12 Dec. 1957.
75. PRO PREM 11/2418, Joint Intelligence Committee, Norman Brook–Macmillan, 6 Dec. 1957.
76. Macmillan Diary, 19 Dec. 1957, cited in William Roger Louis, 'Macmillan and Middle East Crisis of 1958', *Proceedings of the British Academy*, 94 (1996), p. 214.
77. PRO PREM 11/2648, Thorneycroft–Macmillan, Financial talks with Egypt, 11 Dec. 1957.
78. PRO PREM 11/2648, Bishop–Butler, 8 Jan. 1958.
79. PRO PREM 11/2648, Egypt financial negotiations, Note by the Treasury, Rome financial talks, Misc. points and PRO FO 371/131344, GEN 627, 1st meeting, J.H.A. Watson minute, 28 Jan. 1958.

7

From the Creation of the United Arab Republic to the Iraqi Revolution, 1958

THE UNITED ARAB REPUBLIC

IN OCTOBER 1957, Macmillan went to Washington to discuss the Syrian crisis and the threat posed by the Soviet ballistic missile programme. Macmillan came away from the conference with a raft of agreements that the apparently shaken Americans had been willing to agree to. These ranged from the sharing of atomic secrets to an agreement to continue joint planning in the Middle East. During the meetings, Selwyn Lloyd pointed out that 'containment plus' 'would be "containment minus" if we could not support the friendly governments of Lebanon, Jordan and Iraq'. The Americans agreed that this potential problem should be urgently studied and 'appropriate assurances given by the two wherever we could feasibly act'.[1] One product of this joint planning was a report entitled 'Measures to Forestall or Counter an Anti-Western *Coup D'état* in Jordan or the Lebanon'.[2] The Lebanon was of vital importance to the West but most especially to the Americans. President Chamoun and Foreign Minister Charles Malik were the strongest Arab supporters of the Eisenhower Doctrine. If the United States could not prevent Lebanon from falling to Nasser and the radical Arab nationalists, there was little prospect of anywhere else in the region being held.

The plan the British and the Americans agreed at the end of December 1957 was primarily a simple statement of military possibilities. It described various options that the allies could use in the event of a Nasserite or Soviet-inspired coup in Lebanon and Jordan. The Americans did not share the British enthusiasm for the joint plan; the Joint Chiefs of Staff feared that it 'would be a military campaign with political overtones comparable in many respects to the United Kingdom–France–Israeli debacle of 1956'.[3] An integrated command structure was never set up and, by April, the chances of the plan being implemented seemed rather remote. Moreover, the Lebanon crisis was overshadowed by the creation of the United Arab Republic and its battle for supremacy in the Middle East with the British-backed Arab Union of Jordan and Iraq.

Since gaining its political independence at the end of the Second World War, Syria had been the cause of much instability in the Middle East. Part of Syria's problems was that the struggle between the pro-Western and reactionary Arab forces on one side, and the radical Arab nationalists on the other, was at its most violent and acute there. Coupled with this, the Syrian people had little loyalty to their own state, which had been artificially created under the Sykes–Picot accord of 1915. Instead they sought to look to the wider Arab community for their hopes. The Ba'ath (Renaissance) party formed after the Second World War was a leading proponent of an ideology of socialism and Arab unity. Their ideas predated Nasser's by many years. The relative numerical insignificance of the party was mitigated by the fact that many of its members occupied key positions in the major offices of state and in the army. Since the summer of 1957 Syria appeared to be facing either a communist takeover, or military action by the West and the Baghdad Pact designed to overthrow the radical government. Both were viewed by the Ba'ath as equally distasteful.[4]

The only alternative, it was felt, was to turn towards Nasser. Hopwood suggests that the Egyptian President was seen by the Ba'ath as a means of facilitating their ambitions, as the 'appeal of Nasser as leader tended to be seen as the solution to all their problems. His popularity was a threat to Arab regimes everywhere. In Syria, the Ba'ath saw him as a foundation for their grand dream of Arab unity and as a support for their own power at home.'[5] They also, as Seale points out, felt exposed by their lack of electoral success.[6] Nasser was a means of ascent to power for the Ba'ath, something that would have been almost impossible for them without him. For Nasser, the involvement in Syria had many complex reasons. It was intimately bound up with his own Arab unity aspirations. The major factor for the Egyptian leader was that Syria could not be allowed to drift into either of the competing Cold War blocs without damaging his prestige and isolating him in the Arab world.[7] Other commentators, even Arab ones, were more cynical. They saw Nasser as merely using the Ba'ath and Syria as stepping-stones to eventual personal hegemony over the entire Arab world.[8] P.J. Vatikiotis, while acknowledging the above as being part of the ambitions of Nasser, points also to his 'personal disposition and apparently genuine sympathy with the Arab cause'.[9] This contradiction is borne out to a large extent by his attitude to the delegation of

Syrian army officers that came to Cairo on 12 January 1958 to negotiate union with Egypt. Nasser was generous in the sense that he was willing to unite Egypt with the economic and political mess that was Syria. His own personal ambitions were demonstrated by the stringent terms that he extracted from the Syrians. These included: a strong central government based in Cairo with Nasser as President; the exclusion of the army from politics; and the abolition of all political parties except his own National Union. The Syrians agreed these terms, sacrificing themselves for the greater good of Arab unity. On 1 February 1958, the United Arab Republic (UAR) was proclaimed. Nasser boldly claimed that 'Today Arab Nationalism is not just a matter of slogans and shouts; it has become an actual reality.'[10] The formation of the UAR was to unleash a chain of events that were to destroy what was left of Britain's power in the Middle East.

The creation of the UAR marked the complete success of the Nasserite project in Syria. Hopes that the British and the Americans might have entertained that Syria could be brought into the Western camp were dashed. Reactions from the West and the other Arab powers were distinctly unfavourable to the new entity. Dulles, Lloyd and the other foreign ministers of the Baghdad Pact were meeting at Ankara when the news of the formation of the UAR broke. At the suggestion of Secretary Dulles, Adnan Menderes, the Turkish Prime Minister, called a special meeting of the heads of the pact delegations. The tone of the meeting was intensely hostile to the Egyptian–Syrian merger. Nuri al-Said, the Iraqi Prime Minister, spoke at considerable length. He said that

> the union idea was being pushed by the Soviet Union and by Nasser. Nasser's object was to obtain domination over the Arab world and union with Syria would certainly be followed by heavy pressure to bring the other countries under his control. The Syrian public was opposed to union since the people knew the Egyptians would take advantage of Syria … It was difficult to know exactly what should be done about Union with Egypt, but certainly it should be opposed.

The other Arab leaders felt similarly about the union. What was surprising perhaps was that the British and the Americans as led by Lloyd and Dulles appeared to write a blank cheque for any forceful action that the Arabs might take. Lloyd 'intervened early in the discussion to say that it was clear that the proposed union was a danger to all our interests'. Lloyd mentioned three courses of action that the pact powers could take:

to co-operate with the proposed union which we all agreed was no good; to oppose it tooth and nail and try to disrupt it immediately; or to accept it but work for its ultimate destruction. *I said that the second course was clearly the best but the question was how and whether we were able to do it successfully; to fail would be a diplomatic victory for the other side.*[11]

Dulles, perhaps, used the strongest rhetoric. While he admitted that his views were necessarily tentative, as a full policy decision was the call not of the Secretary but of the President, he made clear his displeasure at developments in Syria:

> The US agreed that the union was dangerous: there was a strong possibility that it was supported by the Soviet Union; if it was accepted passively it would continue on and create a great danger that Jordan and Lebanon would be absorbed, putting Iraq and Saudi Arabia in great danger. Such an arrangement might appear to be putting the Arab states under the domination of Nasser but actually they might be under the control of Soviet Union.

Dulles feared that it might take as much as a decade to repair the damage from the union. He than went as far as he could in pledging virtually open-ended United States support for any Arab initiative to combat the union:

> If action, apart from statements, was to be taken soon, speed was essential. If steps were not taken soon, and matters were allowed to drift, it was likely that nothing would be done. The general approach of the US was that we were not ourselves directly interested in the area and could not take initiative in the area; that any initiative must come from the Arab states and not non-Arab states; but that we were prepared to support initiative taken by any Arab state. If the Arabs were unwilling to act, he doubted that the US could do anything really effective.[12]

Lloyd said that 'the United Kingdom position was very similar to that of the United States. We would take no initiative ourselves: we had tried that a year ago and it had not worked. But if there were to be an Arab initiative, the United Kingdom would take the same line as the United States and would support it.'[13] However, the only concrete decision taken was that it would be wise to display a restrained public reaction and that any lead should come from the Arab powers.[14]

Nuri, judging by his future actions, went away from the meeting convinced that he had a guarantee of virtually open-ended American and British support. However, it quickly became clear that this was not the case. The creation of the UAR was a huge blow to Iraq, still Britain's key regional ally. Nuri had continued to hope that he could bring Syria into the Iraqi camp. The British reaction was to make no public comment on the matter but privately there was bitter disappointment at the event. Macmillan saw the news as 'a new and threatening move'.[15] The British Cabinet like Nuri was not fully convinced of the finality of the Syrian issue. On 4 February, the Cabinet agreed that the Western allies should foster co-operation between Jordan, Iraq and Saudi Arabia, 'in order to provide an alternative focal point for the people of Syria who were probably concerned at the prospect of Egyptian domination'.[16] On 14 February, Jordan and Iraq proclaimed the Arab Union as a scheme to rival the UAR. It lacked two vital commodities: popular support and – as it turned out – money.

The creation of the UAR also caused problems for the Anglo-Egyptian talks, which the Foreign Office had been hoping might be resolved soon. Prior to the announcement of the UAR, Adam Watson of the Foreign Office pointed out that the agreement seemed fully justified on its merits as well as other reasons such as the Canal being the main conduit for Middle Eastern oil for the foreseeable future. However, Watson did not argue for the pursuit of friendly relations with Nasser. On the contrary, he repeated the refrain that the 'process of limiting Egypt's influence abroad and cutting Nasser down to size should continue'. However, after union, Archibald Ross was a little more concerned that a deal with Nasser might weaken the resolve of Britain's friends: 'Having assured our Arab friends of our support in their efforts to resist the spread of Nasser's influence through the Union, we clearly must not weaken their resistance by seeming to help Nasser, or by appearing to curry favour with him.'[17] William Hayter argued that the union

has made it more than ever necessary that any agreement we conclude with Nasser should be demonstrably to our financial advantage, and that there are at present no political advantages to be gained from a conclusion. Even if we reached an agreement on the financial aspects, I think we ought to be in no hurry now to re-establish diplomatic relations. This is not the moment to give Nasser anything which might look like an addition to his already excessive prestige.[18]

Lloyd described to Caccia some of the tactics that the British were considering using in any campaign against the Union. Lloyd believed that 'overt resistance would be premature in present circumstances and would tend to consolidate the position of the present leaders. However, it seems highly probable that a short experience of union with Egypt will bring disillusion in Syria and will strengthen the opposition.' Iraq, he argued, should not do anything too quickly except making the plebiscite as unconvincing as possible:

> Thereafter, the Arab committee should exploit what I anticipate will be the mounting discontent in Syria, with a view to creating a situation in which a Syrian resistance movement will proclaim its independence of Egypt and appeal, if necessary, for military intervention from Iraq and Jordan. Please suggest to Mr Dulles that the Working Group should consider again the problem of air cover at the stage described in my last paragraph. In the new circumstances we must presumably reckon with Egyptian intervention as a certainty.[19]

However, Dulles' call for action at Ankara had been tempered by wiser counsels when he returned to Washington. The Near Eastern experts and diplomats, who had a more benign opinion of Nasser than Dulles, made their views felt. The American Ambassador in Syria believed that, if Egypt behaved with reasonable circumspection towards the Syrians and combined this with emotional appeals and firm police control, the Union would be consolidated. Therefore, there was no point in encouraging a revolt.[20] Intelligence reports pointed out that the Union had in fact prevented a communist coup. Dulles soon began to regret his impetuosity in Ankara. In a meeting with the National Security Council, he rather lamely claimed that the American delegation had been cut off from solid intelligence in Ankara. This hardly excused the blank cheque he wrote with Lloyd.[21] His argument to the President on 8 February was that the United States was in an impossible position and that recognition was inevitable:

> We believe that if our Arab friends cannot formulate common action which we could feasibly and appropriately support and particularly if one or more of them recognise, we could not justifiably withhold our recognition of the United Arab Republic without renouncing our traditional policy on Arab Unity and without giving offence to the popular appeal of Arab nationalism.[22]

He informed the British of this the next day. He added that it was his particular concern that, whilst they might be able to 'stir up a little trouble for Nasser in preventing a smooth passage for the Union and increasing its economic difficulties, this might only have the effect of driving Nasser to rely wholly on the Russians and might prejudice any chance that the union would not develop as a wholly communist controlled state'.[23]

The reaction of Nuri to the UAR was to have major repercussions for British policy and power in the Middle East. The Arab Union concept, which the British had such initial enthusiasm for, began to lose its sheen when it became clear that Nuri wanted the British protectorate of Kuwait to join it. He argued to Macmillan that the adherence of Kuwait to the Union was of vital import. It would provide the financial muscle to take on Nasser. He also spoke of plans, 'some of them rather dangerously vague – for detaching Syria from Egypt'. Macmillan wanted to head off some of Nuri's 'more impossible or dangerous schemes, which are bound to fail, without … injuring his will to resist Egypt and Syria'.[24] Nuri's plan, which he outlined to Macmillan, was that Syrian exiles and leaders would bombard the United Nations with complaints about the UAR claiming it was really an Egyptian occupation. This would be followed by an uprising and Iraqi intervention.[25] This 'impossible and dangerous scheme' does not sound all that different from what Lloyd was proposing to Caccia a couple of weeks before. However, Nuri appears to have made a serious blunder by claiming that he regarded 'Mr Dulles as having committed himself to support of the Iraqi plan and to the proposition that the American pilots of some squadrons should be ordered to fight as volunteers'.[26] As previously stated, Dulles and Lloyd had made some rather strong statements at Ankara. They were now reaping the rewards for those indiscretions with the 'Arab initiatives' that Nuri was proposing. Dulles accepted that he had promised to support Arab action 'but Nuri had built up an entirely fictitious picture of what he had agreed to do'.[27] The Iraqis quickly realised that Western support was unlikely to be forthcoming and informed Ambassador Wright in Baghdad that it would be some months before a favourable opportunity would arrive to intervene in Syria.[28] The Americans and the British consistently complained about the sloth of their Arab allies but, when one suggested that they might act, the Americans in particular were running for cover.

The Foreign Office was unsure of how much help should be given to Nuri over Kuwait. Advice was torn between the need to support the Arab Union for Britain's strategic position in the region and the fact that pushing the Emir of Kuwait into union could destroy his confidence in the British government 'on which our main interests in Kuwait rest i.e. the availability of Kuwaiti oil on existing terms and for sterling and the investment of the Ruler's surplus revenue in the United

Kingdom'.[29] There were other reasons to display caution: both the British agent in Kuwait and the Ruler were aware that the UAR was a more popular cause domestically than the Arab Union.[30] Despite this, Nuri and King Faisal of Iraq pressed their scheme on Selwyn Lloyd in March. They advised that Kuwait should be declared independent and should accede to the Arab Union. The problem dragged on without much movement until June when the Iraqis demanded that the Kuwaitis hand over offshore islands and portions of territory which it was believed were oil-rich. Nuri argued that he needed these to provide for increased defence expenditure. He based Iraqi rights in the area on the old boundaries of the Ottoman Empire that suggested that Kuwait was part of the southern area of Iraq. Sir Michael Wright in Baghdad argued for supporting the Iraqis. Macmillan and the Americans, worried about the stability (mental, as well as financial) of their key ally, were forced to put together a package to aid the Arab Union.[31] The whole affair served to illustrate that Britain had no easy options in the region. Taking the fight against Nasser and agreeing to Iraqi demands was just as likely to lead to a deterioration in the British position as seeking to compromise with the former. Therefore, it was of little surprise when the British began to move once more towards a settlement with Nasser and to review their policies towards Syria.[32]

The Anglo-Egyptian financial talks had resumed in Rome on 30 January. The head of the Egyptian delegation, Dr Zaki, brought bad news. He was of the opinion that his government was more concerned with the satisfaction of claims for war damage than the release of the sterling balances. Discussion then turned on the British proposal for a partial settlement of claims. The Egyptians were immediately concerned by the clause referring to a mutual waiver of claims, which would have seen the Egyptian war damages claim set against the fixtures and fittings of the Canal base. However, the Egyptians agreed to continue discussions.[33] The main points of contention continued to be the former question and the neutral assessment of Egyptianised property.[34] The Cabinet on 5 March considered the latest proposals for agreement, which would have seen the British release £23 million in blocked sterling in return for the release of British private property. A sum of £10 million would be held as a deposit against claims for damage to sequestrated property by British evacuees, and £6 million would be used to pay for contracts that had been signed before Suez. The remainder of the sterling balances would be released upon the assessment of compensation for property that had been Egyptianised. The issue of war damage and the British base would be left to one side pending a final settlement.[35] The French asked the British to delay their agreement with the Egyptians as their talks were lagging some way behind. The Foreign Office was sceptical of the French request: they have 'little claim on us to postpone the signature, nor do we think that this would benefit them'.[36] The Iraqis also had worries about financially strengthening Nasser. The objections of allies were of only minor import. The problem that eventually ended hopes of a swift agreement was the continued determination on the part of the Egyptians not to accept a waiver on claims for war damage. The talks, by the end of March 1958, were once more on the point of collapse.

Confidence in Egypt was not enhanced when Nasser's ally, the Imam of Yemen, launched a series of border incursions into the Aden protectorate. The Cabinet concluded that the incursions were being orchestrated from Cairo and required consideration, 'since the Yemen was working in association with the United Arab Republic ... against the wider background of the conflict between the rival Arab States in the Middle East'.[37] However, at the same time as these events, the Egyptians began making concessions on the Suez Canal Company issue. This saw them make a very reasonable offer of £28.3 million for the Egyptian assets of the company.[38] The Treasury and the Foreign Office were at one in recommending acceptance of the offer. The Foreign Secretary wrote that 'a quick acceptance might help to improve the atmosphere and bring about a measure of relaxation in the Middle East'.[39] The Egyptians were motivated, to a large extent, in making the offer by the fact that the United States would release the blocked Egyptian balances when the Suez Canal Company issue was disposed of.

The American change of policy towards one of accommodation with Nasser was even more evident. At the end of March, the State Department considered the relaxation of restrictions in the economic and cultural fields. This elicited some hostile comment in Whitehall.[40] When British officials asked questions of the new American policy, they received the reply that they were pursuing exactly the same line as the British, i.e. attempting to improve relations with Egypt but not appeasing Nasser. Adam Watson was informed by the Washington Embassy that 'American official attitudes on this subject are not easy to pin down'.[41] In May, Dulles at a meeting with Lloyd in Copenhagen confirmed that the United States would unblock the Egyptian dollar balances as soon as a deal was struck over the Canal company. However, American policy remained 'correct but not cordial' towards Nasser. Lloyd replied that the British view was that 'our relations with Nasser should be correct but cool. I thought it essential that we should show that vice does not pay ... I still hoped that Nasser had taken on more than he could cope with in the Union with Syria.'[42]

CRISIS IN LEBANON

It was at this point that the Lebanon, after some months of relative calm, erupted into another bout of inter-communal violence. The crisis broke in May 1958, after Camille Chamoun announced his intention to seek re-election to the presidency and an opposition press editor was assassinated. Chamoun had received an assurance the previous November of Anglo-American military support if his regime was threatened by external aggression, i.e. from Nasser. On 14 May Chamoun made his appeal for outside help. Macmillan, in a communication to his New Zealand counterpart, spoke of the possibility of military intervention. He also described his fears that the whole Middle East was once more in danger of falling into Nasser's hands if the Lebanon fell:

> The moral effect throughout the Middle East of such a coup by Nasser would be very great, indicating as it would the extreme lengths to which the UAR are prepared to go in subverting the lawful government of an independent neighbour country ... if the [Chamoun] appeal is made, and the Americans and we do not respond to it, I fear that the situation will slip, that the Lebanon will drift into Nasser's camp and that Nasser's forward march will be unstoppable. On the other hand a rapid response could in itself help greatly to restore the situation by stiffening the determination of the Lebanese to act firmly and by discouraging the opposition.[43]

In response to the deteriorating internal security situation, the Americans and the British on 16 May looked once more at the plans for joint operations in Lebanon code-named 'Blue Bat'. On 18 May, Caccia indicated to Dulles that Selwyn Lloyd agreed with the Iraqi King that 'in the absence of an adequate alternative it was better to support Chamoun for re-election even at the price of a civil war now, rather than having a civil war later under a weaker regime'. At a meeting the following day, the central themes of which were how to find the solution for the internal political problem in the Lebanon and to cool British enthusiasm for military action, Dulles went to the trouble of advising Caccia that 'some of our people, not just in Washington but elsewhere, had the impression that we were being crowded by our British colleagues into intervention in Lebanon'.[44] The United States delegation to the United Nations was most suspicious of the British. Cabot Lodge, the American Ambassador to the United Nations, was convinced by the Canadians that the British were seeking to draw the United States into a Suez-style operation. The Canadian Ambassador to the UN felt that the UK might be encouraging the Lebanese 'as part of UK's desire to get back at Nasser aside from other considerations'.[45] Cabot Lodge believed that the United States should only intervene if the pro-western forces were in 'grave danger':

> Our impression here is that UK would be willing to send troops in circumstances far less compelling, and is seeking [to] build Security Council position with this in mind. I think it would be unfortunate if US became involved in such a joint UK–US venture which might destroy much of the confidence in US created by our behaviour at the time of the Suez crisis.[46]

The American Ambassador in Lebanon sought a negotiated settlement that would leave a Western-backed government in charge in the Lebanon. He recognised that the conflict was as much sectarian as inspired by Nasser.[47] The British Ambassador, Sir George Middleton, shared much the same view. On 26 May, he informed the Foreign Office that he now believed that the situation was 'favourable to a compromise solution'. Moderate opinion saw the country was on the 'verge of the abyss and that common prudence demands a retreat'. He pointed out that 'Chamoun cannot hope to be re-elected but UAR intervention has been checkmated. A purely Lebanese answer to the crisis must now be sought. I see no reason to suppose that it will be unfavourable to western interests.'[48] The United States attempted to solve the situation through negotiation via back channels with Nasser. On 28 May, the American Ambassador in Cairo passed on a message requesting that Nasser use his influence with the Lebanese opposition to forge a peaceful solution. Nasser suggested that the trouble in the Lebanon might be ended with a compromise agreement that would see Chamoun replaced with his army commander, General Chebab, and the rebels halting their activities.[49] On 6 June, apparently strongly encouraged by the British and possibly intended to scupper the above peace moves, Charles Malik, the Lebanese Foreign Minister and a supporter of Western intervention, submitted to the Security Council that the United Arab Republic was actively subverting the independence of Lebanon.

Macmillan, who was visiting Canada in early June, went to Washington for consultations. The Middle East was at the top of the agenda. Besides Lebanon, the questions of dealing with Iraq and with Nasser were discussed. Macmillan was now viewing Iraq as a grave problem. They had formed a union with Jordan, which from an Iraqi point of view was a liability and now they wanted to include Kuwait. Macmillan foresaw 'an acute crisis breaking out'. Nuri also was making large monetary demands on Britain and the United States. Macmillan, however, stated that the break-up of the Union would be a 'terrific blow to our side' and suggested that the UK and the United States should set up a study to assess what aid should be given to save it. However, he noted that 'Nuri had been difficult for some time and was now attempting a Nasser-type operation against Kuwait'. It had been a 'great shock to learn that Nuri had "out and out threatened" Kuwait'. Dulles was unhappy as well and believed that 'Nuri's personality had become a liability in recent times and that he put the most extravagant demands on us when here with the threat of resigning, which may be a kind of blackmail'.[50]

The conversation then turned from Britain's great Arab 'friend' to its great Arab 'enemy': Nasser. Macmillan was still wondering how the West should handle him: continue to treat him coolly and support the West's Arab friends, or attempt to buy him off. Britain, he stated, was not going to add to his prestige through any financial agreement. Eisenhower complained about the calibre of Arab leader that was friends with the West. Allen Dulles, Director of the CIA, said that the 'best solution would be to "wave a wand" and have Nasser disappear completely. Since we have no wand and since Nasser has a very great influence, which we cannot completely ignore, we must find some means to combat it.' Secretary Dulles pointed out the central problem that the West's Arab allies wanted Britain and the United States 'to take the initiative in getting rid of Nasser but we cannot do so unless they are willing to stand up and oppose him'. Allen Dulles stated the importance of avoiding giving Nasser a victory while the President focused on the need for an Arab alternative to Nasser. Eisenhower concluded that the 'only alternatives short of some sort of war are (1) to get rid of Nasser, and (2) take him over in some fashion'. Sir Patrick Dean, the head of the UK's Joint Intelligence Committee, pointed out that Nasser was dependent on 'obtaining some victory every six months and that our task now is to prevent him winning these victories. The Prime Minister declared that we must hold on to Lebanon, maintain the Arab Union and in our negotiations with Nasser see that he does not win a prestige victory (by stalling or other means).'[51]

The discussions on Lebanon were centred on Nasser's seeming willingness to compromise. Macmillan suggested that Nasser 'might feel that the revolt in the Lebanon was being too successful and that he was afraid that Chamoun might call upon the British and the Americans to intervene in accordance with our assurances'. He felt that Nasser might be calculating that he should wait for less dangerous circumstances to start a revolt. Macmillan felt that the United States should tell Nasser to communicate directly with the Lebanese. The

British Prime Minister saw the message as means of getting Nasser 'on a hook' in the sense that, by suggesting that he could bring the disorder to an end, he was making an admission of complicity that could not be withdrawn.[52] Eisenhower agreed that the United States should not be the lackey of Nasser in delivering the message.

On 11 June, after a debate, the Security Council accepted a Swedish resolution that a UN observation group be established 'so as to ensure that there is no illegal infiltration of personnel or supply of arms and material across the Lebanese borders'. During this, what appeared to be the winding-down phase of the crisis, both the Americans and the United Nations Secretariat continued to be extremely suspicious of the British, worried that they might be seeking to bring about a military intervention that would allow Suez to be vindicated.[53] Lloyd attempted to disavow Hammarskjold of this impression in a meeting on 18 June. Lloyd 'sincerely hoped' that the UN action would work but that if it did not the British and the Americans would be faced with a request to intervene. Lloyd acknowledged the dangers that such an interven-tion would entail. The other point of the meeting was Lloyd's effort to assure Hammarskjold that 'any idea which had been current in some American quarters that Britain was longing to go into the Lebanon with the US to prove how right we had been over Suez and how wrong the US had been was nonsense'. The British were well aware that there would be 'serious repercussions' such as the blowing of the Syrian pipelines and the general impetus to extreme Arab nationalists.[54]

A Commonwealth Relations Office telegram to Ottawa pointed out the new realities of the situation:

> We remain convinced that if Lebanon falls to Nasser it will be a resounding defeat for the West. But circumstances have changed since Chamoun first approached us. Rebels have been able to represent position as one of popular revolt, Lebanese authorities have shown lamentable lack of decision and have lost control of large tracts of the country, and the United Nations have become actively engaged with the despatch of observers. Whatever we decide to do must now therefore be clearly presented in a United Nations framework.[55]

The United Nations Observer Group in Lebanon (UNOGIL) proved to be relatively successful at reducing the flow of material across the border from Syria. By the end of June, the chances of an Anglo-American intervention had diminished once more.

Despite the pressure of the Lebanese crisis, the Egyptian conces-sions over the Suez Canal Company had managed to inject some life into the talks in Rome. A visit by Mr Hamiliton of the Bank of England to Cairo in May, to investigate on what basis the talks might be resumed, made a certain amount of progress. The Egyptians were now thinking in terms of a lump sum to be paid by them in final settlement of all claims and counter-claims. In this way they hoped not only to get some satisfaction of their claim for war damage, but also to avoid the need for neutral assessment of the value of Egyptianised property. Norman Brook had learned from Hamilton that the Egyptian lump sum was likely to be £25 million, and estimated 'that to accept it would be the equivalent of paying the Egyptians something of the order of £10–£15 millions for war damage, apart from giving up our claim to compensation for the loss of the base'.[56]

These terms were patently unfavourable but, as an assessment of them said, 'there is a good deal to be said for a more positive move towards the cool and correct relationship with Egypt which we have recently decided to be the appropriate policy'. However, the settlement of claims with Egypt might be misinterpreted among friends and foes alike with Nasser continuing to be 'actively undermining western interests throughout the Middle East'. With regard to the amount of the lump sum, 'we should be implicitly admitting that we accept quite a substantial share of responsibility for the "damage" done by our 1956 intervention'. Whilst agreement was important, Lloyd stressed to the French that: 'It was important it should be so arranged that Nasser could not convincingly claim that he had scored a diplomatic triumph.' Lloyd and Macmillan agreed that negotiations should proceed on the basis of a lump sum offer.[57] The latter informed the Cabinet that an acceptable settlement on the financial issues would be attempted but that it should 'not be regarded as implying any modification of our political attitude towards the Egyptian government'.[58] Even Bishop, so sceptical a few months before about any deal, now suggested that agreement with Egypt might form part of 'a general settlement – so far as can be obtained of the Middle East at a Heads of Government meeting'.[59] On 13 July, the Suez Canal Company question was resolved. The following day the Iraqi government and monarchy were toppled in a coup by a grouping of Iraqi Free Officers.

THE IRAQI REVOLUTION

Because most of the Egyptian–Syrian activity was aimed at Jordan and Lebanon, the British and the Americans had believed that Iraq was a stable and secure ally. Long the dominant figure in Iraqi politics, Nuri al-Said was Anglophile, anti-communist, anti-Nasser and pro-Western.

He was, to the British, the personification of the good Arab. British policy in Iraq and the Middle East was focused around this elderly political fixer whose political ideas had not advanced much since the First World War. Nuri and the Iraqi monarchy were weakened gradually by the successive crises of the Baghdad Pact, Suez and the constant bombardment of Egyptian propaganda. British and American diplomats, whilst being well aware of the undercurrent of support for Nasser on the streets, believed that Iraq was safe from revolution. Professor Roger Louis cites British Ambassador Wright's remarks on the political situation in Iraq in April 1958. Wright claimed that it was 'quite certain that, today a revolutionary situation does not exist' and 'the army ... is likely to go on supporting the regime'. Admittedly, the Levant Department in the Foreign Office expressed 'dissenting astonishment' at the assessment of Wright.[60] Within the army, a Free Officer movement similar to the Egyptian original had been in existence for some time. Owing to strict control by loyal officers the opportunity for a coup had never presented itself. However, in early July, a plot against King Hussein of Jordan was uncovered in Jordan. Nuri reacted by ordering a protégé, Brigadier Qasim, to move an Iraqi infantry brigade to Jordan. Instead, Qasim took the opportunity to overthrow the Iraqi government in the early hours of 14 July. For a couple of days, mobs ruled the streets taking the lives of many innocent people. Nuri, the King and the royal family were all murdered.

Iraq was (and still is) perhaps the Arab country with the most economic potential, combining a substantial population with substantial oil reserves. Therefore, losing Iraq to the revolutionary forces in the Middle East was a devastating blow to the West's cause. It removed the chance that a pro-Western regime might act as a magnet of attraction away from Nasser. It forced Britain, and to a lesser extent the United States, out to the fringes of Arab politics defending last-ditch positions in the Persian Gulf, such as Kuwait. It ended what slim chance Britain had of challenging Nasser through another Arab regime for the time being. In other words it transformed the basis of the Anglo-Egyptian relationship completely, though this did not become immediately apparent to some British ministers.

The news of the revolution must have come as a devastating blow to the Cabinet. Not only had the Iraqi monarchy fallen, but there was also a plea from President Chamoun for the deployment of Anglo-American forces to the Lebanon. To the British, the figure at the centre of all this turmoil was President Nasser. Macmillan warned the Cabinet that the situation must be considered in a wide context and that a temporary intervention in the Lebanon alone would be neither to Britain's advantage nor to its benefit. It would expose British interests to attack and offer 'no prospect of a permanent solution to the political tension which is spreading through the Middle East'. The Lebanese intervention was not caused by an internal situation but was 'a form of covert aggression promoted by the United Arab Republic'. British forces might be kept in reserve 'against possible need to provide assistance to the governments of Iraq and Jordan'. Furthermore, it was to be made clear to the United States that the British government 'should expect them to regard the whole enterprise of restoring political stability in the Middle East, as a joint task which they should share with us'.[61]

However, Britain's ability to restore the situation was limited. It quickly became apparent to the British and American Ambassadors in Baghdad that a move to restore the *status quo* in Iraq would put at risk the large British and American expatriate community there.[62] With the question of using force in Iraq out of the way within 24 hours of the coup, the attention of the allies was turned to securing the Lebanon and Jordan. Within hours of Chamoun's request for the deployment of forces, the United States moved marines into Beirut from the Sixth Fleet in an unopposed operation. This was a unilateral United States action and the British were specifically requested by Eisenhower to keep out, on the grounds that they might be needed for deployment to an area where the administration would not have the constitutional authority to deploy US troops. Others have suggested that the Americans did not want to be too closely associated with the British with Suez still in the Arab mind.[63]

However, Macmillan was determined to do something. It appears that Hussein – with the encouragement of the British – was urged to make an appeal to themselves and the Americans for aid. The focus of the appeal was that a coup orchestrated from the United Arab Republic was about to take place. Some of the documentation suggests that the British hoped that their landings might spark a royalist revival in Iraq. The Americans were wary of deploying their own troops into Jordan so the operation would have to be British alone, immeasurably increasing the risk that if a serious uprising occurred British forces would be placed in deadly peril. Despite these dangers, the Cabinet, on 16 July, decided that British troops would be deployed to Jordan. Macmillan in his summation to the Cabinet pointed out that the danger of Jordan coming under UAR control was greater than the political and military risks.[64]

The attempt to focus the blame for the whole crisis on the United Arab Republic was a major concern of the British government. Macmillan informed the House of Commons that Dag Hammarskjold's 'journey to Cairo and his partial success in Cairo are really a confirmation of the close connection between the situation in the Lebanon and the efforts to ferment revolution springing from a foreign country'.[65] The Commonwealth Secretary, Lord Home, was even more explicit in his denunciation of the United Arab Republic: 'Unless somebody puts a stop to this process which the United Arab Republic is fomenting in this part of the world, then not only shall we see the whole of the Middle East go, but the rot will spread to Africa and beyond.'[66] Ironically, the most pressing opposition to the British landings came not from Nasser but from the Israeli government, which proved to be uncooperative in allowing over-flight rights. It required the intercession of the Americans to persuade the Israelis to relent and allow the completion of the deployment of the British Parachute Brigade. However, the Israelis continued to press for a halt to the flights. Ben-Gurion was willing to make a deal which would see Israel enter a tacit alliance with Britain similar to its alliance with France. The British were – for obvious reasons – unwilling to enter such a compact. The Israeli intransigence, however, complicated an already high-risk operation.[67]

There was now no prospect of Britain and the United States carrying out operations in Iraq. Jordanian forces were sent on a brief foray that was quickly abandoned while the Turks, as they had the previous autumn, talked about invading. Lloyd informed Macmillan of the Turks' intentions on 18 July. The latter replied that the Turkish invasion plans were 'criminal folly'. The rest of the text of the telegram supplies plenty of ammunition for those who point to the machiavellian side of Macmillan's nature. (This telegram was written just 72 hours after a coup which had seen the bloody murder of Nuri and King Faisal, close friends of Macmillan and Lloyd.)

> We must be realists in this affair. I do not at all give up hope that the new Iraqi government may be detached from Nasser and drawn gradually into our own circle, even after a period of indecision. It would be madness now to force them into the other camp … it may well work out that we will do better to try and wean them away from Nasser and bring them over to our side.[68]

Of course, the telegram is also a remarkable testament to the highly trained political antenna of the British Prime Minister, correctly anticipating that the Arab cold war between Baghdad and Cairo would continue, even if the cast of characters had changed. A Cabinet committee within a week of the coup in Iraq was proposing not only that the new Iraqi regime be recognised, but that 'good relations' should be established with it, and that it might be possible to exploit the natural differences in outlook between the Iraqis and the Egyptians. It concluded that 'In brief, coming to terms with the growth of Arab nationalism did not necessarily mean the establishment of a friendly relationship with Colonel Nasser.'[69] This attitude is reinforced by a telegram from Macmillan to Lloyd emphasising that in his speech to the United Nations it was important that he [Lloyd] did not 'assume or imply that the threat to Jordan comes from Iraq … The plot against Jordan was a Nasserite plot running between the two branches of the UAR in Cairo and Damascus, and we must stick to this throughout.'[70] On the same day as they considered a tilt towards Baghdad, Selwyn Lloyd was paying – in the light of the above – a rather hypocritical tribute to absent friends: 'This country has lost three trusted friends, [King Faisal, his uncle and Nuri] and I wish to put on record our profound sense of loss and our deep regret for the manner in which they met their deaths.'[71]

The increasingly erratic behaviour of Nuri since the creation of the UAR might suggest that a change of regime in Iraq may not have been entirely unwelcome in Whitehall. Matthew Elliot in his study of independent Iraq and the British influence has concluded that Britain did not have great confidence in Nuri and he was by no means the 'imperial flunkey' that Nasser made him out to be.[72] Therefore once it became clear that Qasim was not an acolyte of Nasser, he potentially provided Britain with the Arab nationalist champion that they and the United States had been seeking for so long. As it turned out, this was all wishful thinking, but Macmillan – who appears to have been the director of the pro-Qasim lobby – drove along this policy until it became clearly unsustainable in the spring/summer of 1959. Some opinion in the Foreign Office agreed that the new government afforded an opportunity to come to terms with Arab nationalism. However, they doubted that the new regime could be moulded into a weapon to beat Colonel Nasser with. Indeed, they suggested that the new regime might lead to improved relations with Nasser.[73] A top secret meeting of the Middle East Cabinet committee on 30 July to discuss the recognition of Iraq and how the new regime could be used considered using the new Iraqi regime as a 'counterweight' to Nasser.[74]

Nasser, who had been holidaying in Brioni, Yugoslavia when the crisis broke, appears to have been worried that the Anglo-American operations in the Lebanon and Jordan were aimed at toppling the new Iraqi regime or even his own regime. With this fear in his mind, he immediately set off to the Soviet Union to get Russian support in the event of an Anglo-American operation to retake Iraq. Khrushchev, well aware of Soviet inferiority, was, to say the least, reticent about offering support for such a course of action. Nasser, in spite of the disappointment in Moscow, concluded a military pact with the new regime in Baghdad. He need not have worried himself too much. Within days of the interventions, it became clear that the Americans and British were not going to carry out anything more than a holding action and the panic subsided.[75]

Talks on the financial agreement were resumed at the beginning of August in Rome as had been agreed during Mr Hamilton's visit to Egypt in June.[76] The talks were soon deadlocked on the question of how much the Egyptians would pay in respect of the lump sum. The chief British negotiator, Sir Denis Rickett, emphasised that the Egyptians would not go beyond £25 million. The Cabinet had only agreed to resume talks on the basis that it was to be a £35 million lump sum and in the hope that it could be part of a wider attempt to solve the Middle East situation. The British delegation was of the opinion that the Egyptians did not want an agreement and that was why they had pitched their offer at such a low level. However, Roger Makins of the Treasury pointed out that 'We are not in a very strong negotiating position, and if we proceed as proposed we may be forced to choose between the Egyptian terms and nothing, but we are on a wasting asset here.' The Paymaster-General commented that 'I would not be so sure about the politics of it but personally I would take the risk.'[77] The issue was discussed at a meeting of ministers on 11 August in which while there was a desire to close the topic there was a worry that settling for £25 million would lead public opinion to suspect that Britain had paid a substantial sum by way of compensation for war damage.[78]

The Yugoslav Ambassador informed William Hayter that, while on holiday in Yugoslavia, Nasser had spoken with great conviction of his desire to resume good relations with the Western powers. Hayter replied that the British government was likewise of this opinion 'but this did not necessarily mean that we should be able to co-operate with Nasser in view of his expansionist ideas and his designs on our oil interests'.[79] Macmillan was equally sceptical, having being confirmed in his view of Nasser by a conversation with Robert Murphy, the American Deputy Secretary of State. In this meeting Murphy commented on his recent talks with Nasser, in which the latter had said that he did not consider the present an 'opportune time to improve his relations with Great Britain'. At the meeting, it was generally agreed that there was very little basis for any understanding with Nasser. Murphy went so far as to describe him as 'schizophrenic', suffering from a sense of great personal insecurity. However, he also seemed to suggest that some kind of deal with Nasser, while unpalatable, would be necessary at some stage.[80] The British continued to woo the new Iraqi regime. Lloyd met his Iraqi counterpart on 18 August. It was a friendly meeting with Lloyd assuring the Iraqi that Britain had not intrigued and was not 'intriguing against the new regime'. He expressed the hope that both countries could 'learn from the recent history of British relations with Egypt and seek to avoid the situation in which we and the Egyptians now found ourselves'.[81]

A COMPROMISE AT THE UNITED NATIONS

While Nasser was certainly aware that his agents were involved in the subversion of both Lebanon and Jordan, it is unlikely that he had a serious plan to overthrow either government. The risks were almost certainly too grave. Nasser assured the American envoy, Robert Murphy, on 8 August that he did not seek to destroy Lebanon and merely opposed Chamoun. He was happy that General Chebab was due to become President. With regard to Jordan, he did not want to do anything to topple Hussein, as that might provoke Israel to seize the West Bank.[82] In early August, however, the British Ambassador reported another Nasserite plot, involving a mutiny of the Jordanian army. The fear in Whitehall was that the British forces who were without any armour support would be exposed to destruction in the event of fighting. There was a fear that Israel would refuse the over-flight of British air support – forcing Britain to fly over Syria – which could lead to a military clash with the UAR. The Chiefs of Staff were of the opinion that this option was a lesser evil than the unthinkable option of clashing with the Israeli air force or the political consequences of a fighting withdrawal out of Aqaba.[83] Fortunately neither of these scenarios came to pass.

On 18 August, an Arab resolution was passed unanimously by the United Nations General Assembly calling for non-interference in the internal affairs of other Arab states. This allowed a thaw in Anglo-Egyptian relations. In a conversation with Pierson Dixon and Hammarskjold in New York, the Egyptian Foreign Minister Fawzi attempted to come to a *modus vivendi* with the British over Jordan. He agreed that the UAR would cease attempting to topple Hussein. In the light of this, Macmillan suggested to Lloyd that he should tell Fawzi 'that it seems about time that we reached agreement and put our relations on a normal basis'.[84] On 21 August, Lloyd had a two-hour conversation with Fawzi. The conversation mainly concerned the future of Jordan where it turned out there was considerable common ground between Nasser and the British. Fawzi eventually agreed – under pressure from Lloyd and Hammarskjold – that King Hussein ought to be maintained in Jordan for the foreseeable future. Fawzi also agreed that he would stop the propaganda war with Hussein.[85] The conversation turned towards Anglo-Egyptian relations. Lloyd made clear the desire of the British government for an improvement in relations. Fawzi suggested halving the difference in the conflicting values of the Anglo-Egyptian lump sum. Fawzi also suggested that diplomatic relations could be restored.[86]

The United Nations resolution of August gave Secretary-General Hammarskjold the power to set up an office in Jordan from which he planned the calming of the situation and the evacuation of the British force. At the end of September, the British Cabinet agreed that the situation in Jordan had settled down enough to allow the evacuation of British troops to begin on 20 October.[87] This was extremely fortunate, as the situation in Lebanon had resolved much more quickly than Jordan. After the arrival of the American troops, Nasser's June compromise was implemented. This saw the ending of the Chamoun presidency and the election of General Chebab as President with cross-sectarian support (rather bizarrely under the bayonets of the United States Marine Corps) at the end of July. It was a solution that Eisenhower pointed out in his memoirs as not 'wholly unreasonable'.[88] American troops were evacuated at the same time as the British retired from Jordan.

NOTES

1. USNA CF 926, Macmillan visit, Memcons Box 136, 22–25 Oct. 1957.
2. As Nigel Ashton, *Problem of Nasser*, p. 111, points out, this has not yet been released by the UK or the US government. To the best of my knowledge, it has still not been released.
3. Ibid., p. 111.
4. Seale, *Struggle for Syria*, p. 316.
5. D. Hopwood, *Syria: Politics and Society 1945–1990* (London, Allen & Unwin, 1990), p. 39.
6. The Ba'ath failed to win a number of by-elections in late 1957, exposing their electoral Achilles heel. Seale, *Struggle for Syria*, p. 317.
7. Stephens, *Nasser*, p. 272.
8. See Vatikiotis, *Nasser and his Generation*, p. 226.
9. Ibid., p. 227.
10. Hopwood, *Syria*, p. 40.
11. This is quoted from the British account of the meeting, PRO FO 371/134386, VY 10316/10, Lloyd (Ankara, No. 195)–Lord Privy Seal Butler (who was acting Prime Minister as Macmillan was away on a Commonwealth tour), 28 Jan. 1958, which differs slightly but significantly from the American account. The American account of the highlighted comments is different. According to this, Lloyd says that, 'Assuming that we all agreed that union was not a good thing, he nevertheless perceived of no diplomatic offensive which could be taken with any chance of success in preventing it, and military action seemed out of

the question. It seemed more fruitful not to oppose it but try to develop Syrian opposition and, if it should nevertheless materialise, bring about a counter organization as between Jordan, Iraq and Saudi Arabia.' See USNA Memcon Ankara, 28 Jan. 1958. Conference files (CF) 968. Ankara 1/27–30/58 Memcons Box 143.

12. USNA Memcon Ankara, 28 Jan. 1958. CF 968. Ankara 1/27–30/58 Memcons Box 143.
13. Lloyd's comments are not reported in the American account. PRO FO 371/134386, VY 10316/10, Lloyd (Ankara, No. 195)–Lord Privy Seal Butler, 28 Jan. 1958.
14. PRO FO 371/134386, VY 10316/12, Lloyd–FO, No. 223, 30 Jan. 1958.
15. Macmillan, *Riding the Storm*, p. 503.
16. PRO CAB 128/32, Cabinet Conclusions, 8, 22 Jan. 1958.
17. PRO FO 371/131344, JE 1051/6, Adam Watson submission, 28 Jan.1958 and Ross minute, 7 Feb. 1958.
18. PRO FO 371/134888, VY 10316/81, Hayter (Baghdad)–Harold Beeley, 10 Feb. 1958.
19. PRO PREM 11/2520, Lloyd to Caccia (Washington), No. 582, 8 Feb. 1958.
20. *FRUS 1958–60*, Vol. XIII, Doc. 192, 8 Feb. 1958.
21. *FRUS 1958–60*, Vol. XII, Doc. 10, 6 Feb. 1958.
22. *FRUS 1958–60*, Vol. XIII, Doc. 194, 8 Feb. 1958.
23. PRO PREM 11/2520, Caccia–FO, No. 281, 9 Feb. 1958.
24. Macmillan, *Riding the Storm*, p. 504.
25. PRO PREM 11/2520, FO–Washington, No. 821, 17 Feb. 1958.
26. PRO PREM 11/2520, FO–Washington, No. 820, 17 Feb. 1958.
27. PRO PREM 11/2520, Washington–FO, No. 395, 18 Feb. 1958.
28. PRO PREM 11/2520, Baghdad–FO, No. 395, 18 Feb. 1958.
29. Ovendale, *Transfer of Power*, p. 190.
30. When the Parliament of the Arab Union met on 18 February 1958, all possible opposition was silenced. Deputies and speakers with anti-regime groups were not allowed to speak. Lawrence Tal, 'Britain and the Jordan Crisis of 1958', *Middle Eastern Studies*, 1, 1 (1995), p. 45. In the account in Dann, *King Hussein*, pp. 78–85, the whole federation had plenty of problems.
31. PRO PREM 11/2403, FO–Baghdad, No. 492. 22 Feb. 1958, Baghdad–FO, No. 335. Ovendale, *Transfer of Power*, p. 190.
32. PRO PREM 11/2520, FO–Washington, No. 1113, 28 Feb. 1958. In this telegram, the FO agreed that a review of Syrian policy was necessary as 'UAR had meant a temporary setback for communism in Syria. However, it was likely to increase the risk of extreme Arab nationalist subversion in Jordan, Iraq and the Lebanon. Iraq is worried about control of the TAPLINE and they therefore are more likely than at any previous time to take concrete action to bring Syria under their control.'
33. PRO PREM 11/2648, Anglo-Egyptian financial talks, 26 Feb. 1958.
34. See PRO PREM 11/2648, Treasury memo–Harold Macmillan, Financial talks with Egypt, 27 Feb. 1958 and telegrams Rome–FO, Nos 130, 131, 132, 136, 137.
35. PRO CAB 128/32, Cabinet Conclusions, 20, 5 Mar. 1958.
36. PRO PREM 11/2648, DC Symons (FO)–P. de Zulueta, 12 Mar. 1958.
37. PRO CAB 128/32, Cabinet Conclusions, 31, 15 Apr. 1958.
38. Reported in PRO PREM 11/2648, Paris–FO, No. 175, 14 Apr. 1958.
39. PRO PREM 11/2648, Lloyd–Macmillan, 17 Apr. 1958.
40. See the annotated barbs/comments of officials on Report of Dulles press conference, 10 Apr. 1958, cited in Ashton, 'Macmillan and the Middle East'.
41. PRO FO 371/131339, JE 10345/4, Morris (Washington)–Watson, 15 Apr. 1958.

42. PRO FO 371/131339, JE 10345/4, Lloyd (Copenhagen)–FO, No. 18, 4 May 1958.
43. PRO PREM 11/2386, Macmillan PT 174/58 CRO to UKHC New Zealand, No. 481, 14 May 1958.
44. *FRUS 1958–60*, Vol. XI, Doc. 45, 21 May 1958.
45. USNA AmDelUN to State, No. 1326, 16 May 1958. DOSCF 783A/00/5.1658.
46. USNA AmDelUN to State, No. 1354, 21 May 1958. DOSCF 783A/00/5.2058.
47. McClintock, the American Ambassador in the Lebanon, in early June warned that the United States 'should adopt an attitude of caution in our UN presentation unless for other motives, we desire to use Lebanon issue as a means for carrying out a conscious policy of enmity toward Nasser and UAR with a view to splitting off Syria and trying a "neo-Suez" against Nasser. As seen from here British, Turks, Iraqis, and Jordanians would like nothing better than to seize upon current difficulties in Lebanon as an excuse for fighting Nasser. To do so they will have to stretch the case to an extreme in order to fit the procrustean bed of their policy if the issue is to be fought on facts as they are in Lebanon.' *FRUS 1958–60*, Vol. XI, Doc. 56, 2 June 1958.
48. PRO PREM 11/2386, Middleton–FO, No. 616, 26 May 1958.
49. Eisenhower, *Waging Peace*, p. 268.
50. USNA Memcon White House, 9 June 1958, MCT MC/5, CF120, Macmillan Talks Miscellaneous, Box 150.
51. Ibid.
52. PRO PREM 11/2386, Macmillan–FO, T 234/58, Washington to FO, No. 1483, 10 June 1958.
53. Lamb, *Macmillan Years 1957–63*, p. 34.
54. PRO FO 371/134124, VL 1015/378, ROC between SOS Lloyd and UNSG Hammarskjold at London, 18 June 1958.
55. PRO PREM 11/2385, CRO–Ottawa, No. 1011, 20 June 1958.
56. PRO PREM 11/2648, Norman Brook–Prime Minister, 19 June 1958.
57. PRO PREM 11/2648, Note–Prime Minister, 30 June 1958, Record of conversation between Selwyn Lloyd and Couve de Murville at the Quai d'Orsay, 30 June 1958, Lloyd minute–Macmillan, PM 58/54, 4 July 1958.
58. PRO CAB 128/32, Cabinet Conclusions, 50, 4, 26 June 1958.
59. PRO PREM 11/2648, Bishop note–Macmillan, n.d., July 1958.
60. W. Roger Louis, 'The British and the Origins of the Revolution', in Robert A. Fernea and W. Roger Louis, *The Iraqi Revolution of 1958: The Old Social Classes Revisited* (London, I.B. Tauris, 1991), pp. 51–3.
61. PRO CAB 128/32, Cabinet Conclusions, 55, 1, 14 July 1958.
62. *FRUS 1958–60*, Vol. XII, Footnote 1, p. 326.
63. Ashton, *Problem of Nasser*, pp. 169–70 argues along this line.
64. PRO CAB 128/32, Cabinet Conclusions, 58, 1, 16 July 1958.
65. *Hansard*, HOC Debates, 591, Col. 1366, 16 July 1958.
66. *Hansard*, HOL Debates, 210, Col. 1313, 17 July 1958.
67. See Ovendale, *Transfer of Power*, p. 208. It is noticeable that Israeli requests for tanks suddenly started to receive a more favourable hearing in London.
68. PRO PREM 11/2368, Macmillan–Lloyd, PMPT 367/58, FO–Washington, No. 4792, 18 July 1958.
69. PRO CAB 130/153, GEN 658, 1st meeting, 22 July 1958, cited in Ashton, *Problem of Nasser*, p. 179. Ashton points out that, 'In hindsight, the speed with which the British government was to move in trying to establish close relations with Qassem does indeed appear extraordinary.' Ibid., p. 179.
70. PRO FO 371/134220, VG 1051/28/G, Macmillan–Lloyd in FO to Washington, No. 4833, 19 July 1958.
71. *Hansard*, HOC Debates, 592, Col. 230–1, 22 July 1958.

72. Elliot, *Independent Iraq*, p. 166.
73. PRO FO 371/134220, VQ 1051/33, Crawford minute–Rose, Policy toward Iraq, 23 July 1958.
74. PRO CAB 134/2341, OME, 11th meeting, 30 July 1958.
75. Stephens, *Nasser*, pp. 287–90.
76. PRO PREM 11/2648, Norman Brook–Macmillan, 21 July 1958.
77. PRO PREM 11/2648, Rome–FO, No. 413, 2 Aug. 1958, Collier–Bishop, 3 Aug. 1958, Makins–Macmillan, 6 Aug. 1958.
78. PRO PREM 11/2648, Meeting of ministers, 11 Aug. 1958.
79. PRO PREM 11/2953, FO–Belgrade, No. 359, 8 Aug. 1958.
80. PRO PREM 11/4056, Record of conversation between Prime Minister and Robert Murphy, 10 Aug. 1958.
81. PRO PREM 11/2371, Record of conversation between S. Lloyd and the Iraqi Foreign Minister, 18 Aug. 1958.
82. See Murphy, *Diplomat among Warriors*, pp. 498–506.
83. PRO DEFE 4/110, COS, 55, 71st meeting, 11 Aug. 1958. See also Tal, 'Britain and the Jordan Crisis of 1958', p. 45.
84. PRO PREM 11/2648, Macmillan PT 431/58–Lloyd (New York), No. 184, 19 Aug. 1958.
85. PRO PREM 11/2381, Lloyd (New York)–FO, 22 Aug. 1958.
86. PRO PREM 11/2648, New York–FO, No. 944, 21 Aug. 1958. The conversations are summarised for the Middle East committee of the Cabinet in PRO CAB 134/2342, OME 58 (43) meeting, 11 Sept. 1958.
87. PRO CAB 128/32, Pt 2, Cabinet Conclusions, 67, 1, 29 Sept. 1958.
88. Eisenhower, *Waging Peace*, p. 199.

8

Decision for Détente, 1958–59

FUTURE TACTICS

THE PERIOD after the fall of the Iraqi monarchy saw an interregnum in Britain's policy towards Nasser and, more generally, in its broader Middle Eastern strategy. A series of debates took place within the British government about how to approach the completely changed strategic situation. The pursuit of an accommodation with the new Iraqi regime was one favoured option for a time. There was also a wider debate about how to proceed with Anglo-Egyptian relations and as to whether Britain (with American help) should seek a final confrontation with Nasser while Western military superiority over the Soviet Union still existed.

At the height of the 1958 crisis, in July and August, the Chiefs of Staff (COS) produced two papers on the Middle East. The first on 28 July is notable for the hyperbolic tone taken about the effect of a premature withdrawal of the allied forces from Lebanon and Jordan. This paper claimed that withdrawal would lead to the absorption of those countries into the United Arab Republic and the longer-term consequences would not be confined to just those countries:

> We would be compelled to disengage progressively from the whole of the Arabian peninsula since the Rulers in those parts, now friendly to us, would feel that their only course was to come to terms with the United Arab Republic. This, in turn, would probably lead to our eventual withdrawal from North Africa. This may eventually affect our position in Singapore and Malaya, and may have its effect also on the attitude of Nepal, and our ability to recruit Ghurkhas from there.[1]

The paper considered that this might be the last opportunity, while the United States and the United Kingdom were in their present position of strength and with Russia fearful of the consequences of provoking a global war, to secure long-term stability in the Middle East.

The COS felt that a settlement had to be imposed that would satisfy the following requirements: '(a) Egyptian leadership of Arab nationalism, as imposed by Nasser today, must be broken and in particular Syria must be separated from the United Arab Republic. (b) An international authority must secure the unimpeded use of the Suez Canal and a corresponding air corridor above it. (c) The continued supply of oil must be guaranteed.' Until these terms were satisfied, the COS considered that it would be disastrous to withdraw Anglo-American forces from the Lebanon or Jordan, or to reduce to any significant degree those already in the Middle East.[2] The follow-up to this paper, distributed a week later, warned of the dangers of seeking an Austrian-type neutralisation of Lebanon and Jordan. In the opinion of the Chief of the Imperial General Staff, Field Marshal Gerald Templer, three options were open to the West.

Course A was to do a deal with Nasser. This course entailed the acceptance of continued moves towards Arab unity under the Egyptian President's direction coupled with the military disengagement of the West from the Arabian Peninsula, with the effect that East–West strategic communications would be virtually severed in an emergency. In return, Nasser would end his African ambitions, cease his propaganda, abandon his Soviet links and accept Israel. Course B was to issue an ultimatum to Nasser. In this case, he would be made to agree to the above without the West accepting his ambitions. Economic aid should be used as bait but Nasser 'in his present position of political strength must refuse any such ultimatum unless confronted with the clear intentions of the United States and the United Kingdom to use force if necessary'. The COS acknowledged that while force would achieve decisive results it would probably lead to war with Egypt and, in consequence, the closure of the Suez Canal and a temporary loss of Middle Eastern oil to the West. Public opinion would have to be educated before this course could be contemplated. The final course, Course C, was to break Nasser's leadership by less direct methods. This would require the maintenance of military strength in the Middle East through the retention of UK and US forces in the Levant and the publishing of a joint Anglo-American policy for the Middle East. The policy would recognise the rights of the Arab world to self-determination, refuse to recognise Nasser as the leader of the Arab world and require the creation of an economic plan for the region including the solving of the Palestinian refugee problem. Nasser would be combated by the effective jamming of Cairo Radio and the disruption of the UAR 'by the separation of Syria, using economic and subversive means and, if these fail, by military action against her'. The paper concluded that Course A was the riskiest and could not be recommended. Course B 'would be likely to lead to war with Egypt but it is the certain course to achieve quick and decisive results and could be adopted now without danger of global war'. According to Field Marshal Templer, Course C was the minimum course of action required to safeguard the interests of the West.[3]

The Permanent Undersecretary for War, Julian Amery, proposed a scheme along similar lines in September. The plan was as radical and as flawed as the Chiefs of Staff's ideas in August. Nevertheless, Philip de Zulueta deemed it worthy of the Prime Minister's attention. Amery, rejecting any deals, called for the rolling back of Nasser. Britain should maintain sufficient forces in the Middle East to fight a limited war with Nasser. This would allow Britain to provide protection for pro-Western regimes and allow the United Kingdom to seize any 'opportunity which Nasser or third parties might give us for taking military action against the UAR'. The United States would be needed or a massive build-up of British forces would be required. Amery concluded by saying that 'it is probably true to say that if we act together [with the United States], there is no danger, if we act alone, there is no chance; if neither of us act there is no hope'.[4] De Zulueta's minute to Macmillan on the above is quite revealing about his own attitudes: 'If he [Amery] is right, we shall I think have either to bring down Nasser by military means or lose all our favourable positions over oil supplies from the Middle East, to say nothing of our strategic position there ... we are not quite faced with it yet.' However, de Zulueta doubted if 'action [against Nasser] without the United States now has a chance of success'.[5] The voices of reason were now in the ascendancy.

Since the Syrian crisis of late 1957, the United States had been reluctantly forced to conclude that, once Nasser had proved more likely to be a bulwark against rather than a conduit for Soviet penetration of the Middle East, some degree of accommodation had to be achieved with him. The Americans had also come to the conclusion that their intervention in the Lebanon had been rather unnecessary. In the final analysis, Nasser's compromise proposal that General Chebab should succeed to the presidency was implemented with the backing of the United States Marine Corps. On 29 July, a paper prepared by the NSC planning board laid out the pros and cons of seeking an accommodation with radical Arab nationalism and Nasser. On the one hand it was argued that, as Nasser 'is the symbol of radical Arab nationalism, unless and until we are able to work with him we cannot really avoid the onus of appearing to oppose the dominant force in the Arab world'. The opposing view was that 'Pan Arab nationalism under his leadership may be virtually insatiable; it may not stop its march until it has taken over large parts of Africa.'[6] Secretary Dulles at the meeting of the

NSC of 31 July tended to support the latter point of view, comparing Nasser to Hitler – except not as dangerous. He 'relies on the same hero myth, and we must try to deflate that myth'.[7] The majority of the NSC planning board according to the 19 August draft was in favour of the need to 'Accept [and to work with radical] pan-Arab nationalism of which Nasser is the present symbol, where consistent with our bedrock objectives'.[8] On 4 November 1958, the NSC produced a Statement of US Policy toward the Near East which argued that the United States should seek 'to normalise our relations with the United Arab Republic. Recognising that US accommodation with Nasser would contain elements contrary to US interests, deal with Nasser as head of the UAR on specific problems and issues, area-wide as well as local, affecting the UAR's legitimate interests, but not as leader of the Arab world.'[9]

The British Foreign Office, as always, believed that an agreement with Egypt was necessary on both political and financial grounds. However, the resumed financial talks were unsuccessful, with the Egyptians refusing to increase their offer beyond the £25 million that had been on the table at the start of the summer. Ministers rejected the Egyptian terms once more believing that it was likely that Nasser would not move on the issue until Britain announced the date of the evacuation of its forces from Jordan.[10] It also appears that Fawzi had overstepped his authority in his talks with Lloyd in August when he had suggested that the conflicting figures for the lump sum could be split. As a result, on 8 September, the talks were adjourned.[11] However, other factors may have played a part in the reticence of the Egyptians to conclude a deal.

The Egyptians had noted the *rapprochement* between Iraq and Britain with growing alarm. Apparently, they saw the hidden hand of the British behind their own deteriorating relations with Iraq and a series of setbacks throughout the Middle East. The pro-Nasser deputy of Qasim, Arif, had been ousted in Iraq. There was also the problem of increased tension with the Sudan over the Nile waters. A report from the Belgian Embassy in Cairo claimed that the 'Egyptians were in a highly nervous state about what they thought were widespread and cunning British activities in the Middle East directed against Egyptian interests'. Everywhere they looked, they saw themselves being thwarted by the British. The question being asked in Cairo was whether this was pressure for a financial agreement or, 'in fact, the declaration of open war against Nasser'.[12]

Despite this, both sides needed to conclude a deal on the financial issue eventually. There was a strand of opinion in the Foreign Office that even favoured restoring relations without concluding a deal. Even Selwyn Lloyd was not indisposed to resorting to unorthodox diplomacy as a solution to the problem of getting to grips with Egypt. In November, he proposed to Macmillan that he write to the UN Secretary-General, Hammarskjold, with the aim of restarting the talks. Furthermore, he suggested that Macmillan might express a willingness to meet Nasser on neutral ground to hammer out a solution to the financial imbroglio. De Zulueta was cynical, commenting that it was Nasser who should be making the overtures.[13] While Macmillan was wary of an early meeting with Nasser, he did see it as an idea that might emerge eventually. While his feelings about Nasser remained distinctly mixed, Macmillan – more than ever before – was interested in at least compromising with Nasser. His minute provides one of the best commentaries of Macmillan on the Egyptian leader:

> I wonder too if it would not be well to start your letter by pointing out to Hammarskjold that many people both in the Middle East and outside, regard Nasser as a sort of Mussolini, who must expand or collapse: he is quite prepared to keep his people in poverty and to sell the Arab world to the Russians for arms provided he can maintain his own regime. If this analysis is right there is nothing that we can do to avert future trouble which Nasser will inevitably create: all we can do is try to deal with it when it comes. There is however a chance that Nasser, as he himself would claim, is not as mad or as bad as all this, but genuinely interested in the pacification and economic advance of his country and well aware of the danger of Soviet domination. So far we have seen little to encourage us in this more optimistic view but we are ready to make another probing operation.[14]

The decision was taken not to make this particular approach. It was instead decided to use the good offices of Eugene Black of the World Bank.[15] Black settled the question of the Shell oil company's assets in Egypt in November. He agreed to return to Egypt in the New Year to attempt to settle the wider problems.

Towards the turn of the year, the Middle East committee of the British Cabinet was primarily concerned with crafting a new policy towards Nasser and Arab nationalism. It assessed that there were two schools of thought. One was that the West could never come to terms with Nasser and that 'we should therefore seek to contain him in every possible way. The "other" was based on the assumption that he and the Arabs were not implacably hostile, and that Arab nationalism had come to stay: we should therefore confine our defence against it to certain key positions and see could we reach a *modus vivendi* with the Arab world.'[16] Whether Arab nationalism as represented by Nasser could be successfully appeased was the question at the heart of the debate on future British policy in the Middle East. If not, was there an alternative policy of opposing Arab nationalism?

It was in Iraq that the problem for Britain was most acute. Here, the traditional rivalry between Baghdad and Cairo had re-established itself with astonishing haste. The pro-Nasser elements in the Iraqi junta steadily lost ground in the autumn of 1958. Brigadier Qasim, who had become sole leader, relied on the Iraqi Communist party as his closest supporters. The United States and Nasser viewed these links with growing concern. Macmillan's initial plans for co-operation with the new Iraqi government had proved fruitless. However, in early December, Britain received word of a plot led by the old nationalist Rashid Ali to seize power.[17] They decided to tip off Qasim, who crushed the attempt. The Americans in possession of the same information had decided not to pass on the message – on the grounds that Nasser, for all his dangers, was preferable to the creation of a pro-communist regime. British ministers evidently felt the opposite and considered that a communist-controlled Iraq might be easier to deal with than a pro-Nasser regime.[18] William Rountree, the Director of the NEA in the State Department, had undertaken a Middle Eastern tour in mid-December because of 'what he thought was the growing antagonism between Communism and Nasser'. In a meeting with Roger Stevens of the Foreign Office, he had expressed surprise at Britain's recent actions in Iraq, as had President Nasser, who had treated Rountree with great cordiality. Such was the meeting of minds between Nasser and his American visitor that Rountree felt able to claim that a 'distinct community of interest was appearing between Nasser and the west' because of communism. In Baghdad Rountree, who had been met by communist-directed demonstrations and suffered an unproductive meeting with Qasim, was now convinced that Nasser had to be adopted as the West's weapon against communism in the Arab world. Macmillan was almost scornful of the American concerns, annotating that 'Mr R seems easily alarmed'. His private secretary was less sanguine, warning of the danger 'of another disagreement between us and the United States about policy in the Middle East ... if we are not jointly ready to carry out and pursue such a [middle-of-the-road] policy, we may well have to choose between Nasser and communism in the short term; but either would be bad for us in the long term'.[19]

As Macmillan continued to look closely at the Iraqi option, other British ministers and civil servants continued the debate on the creation of a new policy for the Middle East. The Middle East committee first considered that Britain should adopt a creative policy for the Middle East. This might involve a plan for the sharing of oil revenues between the Arab haves and the Arab have-nots. The West might also consider the feasibility of supporting Arab unity in certain circumstances. The Foreign Office was also drafting a paper on Britain's new policy. This was shown to the Americans at the beginning of January.[20] The paper considered that the revolution in Iraq and the growing movement towards Arab unity had 'gravely weakened the basis for a policy of trying to maintain a balance of power in a divided Arab world with the oil bearing States linked individually to the west but entirely separate from one another. It is necessary to consider how our basic requirements in the Middle East can best be secured in the new conditions which are emerging.' Britain's basic requirements were oil (its flow and its earnings for the sterling area) and transit rights (the maintenance of over-flying and shipping rights).

The threat to these interests stemmed from hostile Arab nationalism and the Soviet Union. The Soviet Union was using Arab nationalism as its chief weapon. Therefore the problem for the West was how to handle Arab nationalism in such a way as to thwart Soviet ambition while preserving Britain's basic interests in the Middle East. It was doubtful, the report argued, that a full understanding could be reached with it owing to the 'grave obstacles' of the existence of Israel, the British position in the Persian Gulf and Britain's oil position. However, it was suggested that Britain should confine its defence against Arab nationalism to those positions which Britain had to hold, for strategic or economic reasons.

The key question was the approach to be taken towards Arab unity. The paper argued that such was the dominance of Arab unity as a political and an emotional force that Britain would be unwise to oppose it. British policy should be that 'where greater Arab solidarity is in our interest, we should support it. Where it is not, we should still not oppose it more than is absolutely necessary, for external opposition will make it take a form hostile to the West whereas its absence will allow the fissiparous tendencies in the Arab world to rise to the surface.'[21] The paper argued that, in certain circumstances, Arab unity was desirable and in Britain's interests. Moreover, there were considerable reasons not to oppose Arab unity. The following conclusion could be drawn:

> We have, on balance, a positive interest in greater Arab solidarity provided that it does not establish a political control so widespread and effective that it threatens our oil and strategic interests (whether or not we should even positively welcome and support an extension of the UAR as the only means of preventing an individual Arab state, e.g. Iraq, from coming under Soviet domination, can only be decided in the light of particular situations). The best

way of ensuring that this does not happen too quickly and that it does not take a violently anti-western form is to refrain from opposing and even to welcome Arab solidarity provided that it subsists between equal and independent partners and is not imposed by force or subversion.

As to the question of Nasser's future tactics, it was assumed that Nasser's main ambitions remained the same. However, it was felt that he was revising his tactics. Nasser was unsure what form Arab unity was going to take. He probably would have preferred that the UAR was a 'looser association in which he can have as much power, but less responsibility'. Nasser may have modified his programme by deferring his plans to change the regimes in Jordan and Lebanon by force or subversion. He also probably wished to avoid arousing Iraqi hostility, and was likely to seek the rebuilding of his relationship with the West, so that Egypt was not completely dependent on the Soviet Union. 'The most reliable touchstone of Nasser's desire to improve relations with the West is probably, at the moment, the extent to which he shows himself willing to reach a financial settlement with the United Kingdom.' However, his threat remained, as Nasser 'being an opportunist ... may not hesitate to organise subversive coups if they seemed assured of success. For the reasons given above, he may temporarily abandon such activity in the Levant and turn his attention to targets in Africa – Sudan, Libya and Tunisia – which may seem at once more vulnerable and less dangerous.' Nasser appeared to be using the Arab League as his instrument for organising Arab unity. This could still provide a threat for the West.[22]

How was the West supposed to react to the new developments? It was considered that the West would be wise not to oppose the revival of the Arab League. More importantly, the West should disengage from inter-Arab politics:

> The disappearance of the old Iraqi regime has in one sense freed our hands from inter-Arab disputes. If Jordan can be effectively protected for the time being by the United Nations, it should be possible for us to escape from the position of backing one part of the Arab world against the other and thus appearing to be the cause of division. As suggested ... although it might increase the immediate risk to our oil position, a more united Middle East might in the long term suit us from some points of view.

The big losers from Arab unity, the paper speculated, might indeed be the Soviets, not the West. The paper concluded that Britain should also disengage from the Palestine problem. However, Britain could not disengage from the Persian Gulf. It remained 'essential that we should not give the impression of inability and unwillingness to defend those rulers whom we have the obligation to protect'. However, at the same time,

> we must recognise that even our most loyal Arab friends will feel the need to come to terms to some extent with the new move towards Arab unity. Our best policy may be to allow them to do so in whatever way they think best. They will not want to lose their wealth and identity by assimilation into an Egyptian empire or otherwise coming under Nasser's thumb, and they will be better able to avoid this if they can blunt the edge of local agitation by paying lip service, and even contributing money, to the Pan-Arab movement. If we try to prevent them, we may either force them to abandon their British connexion in order to stay in power or stimulate such powerful opposition that pro-Nasser coups remove them.

Regarding relations with Egypt, it was necessary to restore them as soon as possible and to seek some common ground between British interests and Nasser. The restoration of relations should be taken at the first opportunity whether or not a successful conclusion to the financial details had been worked out. Britain could never be 'reconciled to Nasser's efforts to acquire control of our oil supplies'. However, the paper acknowledged the inequity of the current Middle East. It suggests that one possible means of reducing the urgency of Egyptian expansionism would be some sort of economic co-operation and sharing of wealth between Arab states. Britain should support any suitable arrangements resulting from President Eisenhower's initiative or Mr Hammarskjold's discussions with Arab leaders that would contribute to this end. The above policy did not mean that Britain should abandon the idea of 'containing' Nasser, or that it should recognise the inevitability of his pan-Arab empire:

> In particular, we must continue to do our best to stop him overturning the regimes of Sudan, Libya and Tunisia, and we should not hesitate to give them both private and public support in standing up to Nasser in such ways as are acceptable to them and will not weaken their position by arousing nationalism against them.

Interestingly, the paper concludes that the West should place more reliance on the United Nations on the grounds that if 'Nasser was confronted with the prospect of being hauled before the United Nations whenever he threatened one of its Arab members this might prove to be a useful means of restraining his ambitions'.[23] This marked a considerable reversal of British policy since Suez when the United Nations was a major contributor to Britain's humiliation.

Indeed, this paper is one of the most important documents of post-war British foreign policy as it encapsulates a moment in history when Britain made a decisive change in policy towards the Middle East. After Suez, the aims of British policy remained essentially the same as they had been prior to Suez. After the Iraqi revolution, this policy became unsustainable. This paper marks the recognition of that reality. Macmillan personally voiced support for the views put forward in this paper at a meeting of the Middle East committee on 16 January 1959.[24]

THE PATH TO THE ANGLO-EGYPTIAN DÉTENTE

The change in policy in the Middle East coincided with a breakthrough in the Anglo-Egyptian talks. Once the issue had come down to the value of the lump sum that Egypt was to pay Britain for Egyptianised property, the question became a matter of which side would compromise first on the war damage claim. On 19 December 1958 – thanks to the intervention of Eugene Black – a draft agreement was initialled. On 4 January 1959, a figure of £27.5 million was agreed as the value of the lump sum that Egypt would pay Britain for Egyptianised property. The final nuances of the deal were to be worked out in Cairo. The British also felt that they had got guarantees that the British men (Zarb and Swinburn) imprisoned for espionage would be released. The Egyptians had agreed to increase their offer after the British allowed a drawing on the sterling balances to pay for the instalment due on the purchase price of the Suez Canal Company in January. Black returned to Cairo on 1 January. He made considerable progress and requested that a delegation be sent to Cairo. Macmillan was unhappy about the British having to travel to Cairo. He confided, in his diary, his reticence: 'I do not want our men to go to Cairo unless there is a very fair chance of a settlement. In many respects, I do not like them going to Cairo at all. Discussions in Rome are more dignified.'[25]

The British delegation arrived on 10 January. Besides the financial issue, the British delegation was to seek the release of the two British prisoners and to get diplomatic relations restored at chargé d'affaires level.[26] The agreement was initialled on 22 January. However, disagreements immediately arose over the status of the British diplomatic mission, which was needed to oversee the agreement, and the status of the Smouha estate outside Cairo. The Egyptians claimed the land was agricultural and therefore was to be Egyptianised while the British and Smouha family believed that the land was development land and should be desequestrated. The conflicting interpretations of the value of the land had the potential to upset the deal as, if the British had to pay Smouha compensation for development land, the £27.5 million would be completely inadequate. Macmillan feared that the talks were going to fail. His diary entry though is surprisingly empathetic with Nasser: 'The Egyptian treaty is hanging fire and may go sour altogether … I hope this is a genuine misunderstanding and can be cleared up. But I fear that Nasser may have got "cold feet" and shrinks from rebuilding his bridges with the UK even to get £46 Million. He too, I have no doubt, has his "Suez Group"!' [27]

The Smouha case favoured the Egyptians as it turned out. The greater problem remained the question of diplomatic relations. The British had entered the agreement primarily to get these restored. However, the anti-British element in Cairo had Nasser's ear. Even the subject of diplomatic immunities and secure communications for the British Property Commission led to much stonewalling by the Egyptians. Roger Stevens of the Levant Department described the difficulties as probably 'characteristic of the crab like manner in which our relations with Nasser would progress'. [28] Fawzi eventually agreed that the British representative would have immunities. However, the Smouha land deal proved intractable. The negotiations dragged on into the middle of February. Macmillan was 'very concerned at the delay'. He pondered whether Nasser was 'thinking more of Iraq rather than us'. [29] The wider Middle East picture was casting its influence upon British policy again. Eugene Black was called in to make one more intervention to save the talks and the final difficulties were ironed out on 1 March 1959. The deal that was agreed was probably fair. The Egyptians would have nationalised or regulated most of the companies involved, making it difficult to repatriate profits. The American Embassy assessed that, if that had transpired, 'British private interests are lucky indeed to have picked up 27.5 million pounds sterling for their Egyptian holdings'. [30]

Fred Errol, the Economic Secretary to the Treasury, was despatched to Cairo to sign the agreement. He was briefed by the Middle East committee of the Cabinet to get the essence of the new British Middle East policy across to Nasser, that of non-interference in Arab affairs and that Britain was no longer opposed to Arab unity. [31] Errol did not get to deliver his message in person and his major task was signing the agreement on behalf of the British government. It is unlikely that the message would have had much effect anyway as, within days of the signing of the agreement, the UAR received what they considered evidence of renewed British intrigue and perfidy in Iraq.

The Mosul revolt in early March, just days after the signing of the Anglo-Egyptian agreement, saw the Iraqi President Qasim, strongly backed by the communists, defeat a Nasser-inspired coup. Nasser saw the hand of the British in the continued survival of his new Iraqi foe. Colin Crowe, the British representative in Cairo, spoke in April of the Egyptians being 'hypnotised' into thinking that the British were co-operating with the communists in Iraq.[32] Indeed Macmillan was undecided as to what his attitude should be. Macmillan noted the failure of the 'Nasserite' revolt but wondered whether this would mean that the present regime would go 'more and more communist. We are in a bad position here – between the devil and the sea.'[33] Efforts to turn the British Property Commission into a proper diplomatic mission foundered on Egyptian suspicions over Iraq. Nasser seemed determined to be as uncooperative as possible. The British, feeling that their efforts to accommodate Nasser were being rebuffed on spurious grounds, reconsidered their decision to seek agreement with him. British policy was once more in a state of flux.

In retrospect, the failure of the Mosul revolt might be seen as one of the turning points in the modern history of the Middle East. It was Nasser's greatest setback since he had come to power. It established Qasim as the Iraqi leader firmly for the next four years. It was perhaps the decisive defeat in this the first phase of Nasser's career. Never again would he be as close to dominating the Middle East. Somehow, the combination of diplomatic acumen and luck that had seen him win victory after victory over Britain, the United States and his Arab foes never really occurred again. Hopeful developments in 1963 and 1967 would end in the first case in rapid disappointment about a renewed federation of Arab states and in the second in bitter defeat at the hands of the Israelis. Before 1959, Nasser appeared to have learned his diplomatic skills under the tutelage of Bismarck. After 1959, he appears to have changed tutors to Kaiser Wilhelm II – with the same degree of success as that unlamented German monarch. The growing strength of the Iraqi Communist party limited the freedom Nasser had enjoyed since the 1955 arms deal. He did not want an outright breach with the Soviets but his stinging attacks on Syrian communists in December 1958 were signs of his growing fears that the Soviets were as much of a threat as the West. The abortive Mosul revolt caused Nasser to renew his assault on communism, Qasim and even Khrushchev. The Americans saw this as forcing Nasser westwards in his inclination as his conflict with Arab communism had created a 'limited area of mutual interest between Nasser and the west'.[34]

On 22 March 1959, Macmillan and Lloyd met Eisenhower at Camp David. There was another division of opinion on the subject of Nasser. In the morning meeting of Foreign Office and State officials, Lloyd said that the British, while not being too fond of Nasser, 'wanted to move ahead slowly in improving relations with him. They feared he would turn on them when he could.' Lloyd then asked what was Nasser's attitude towards the United Kingdom. Rountree said that Eugene Black of the World Bank had the impression that

> Nasser wanted to get ahead in settling the issues with the United Kingdom ... A big question in Nasser's mind was what was the UK attitude toward the Qasim–Nasser issue. Friends of the UAR here have pointed out to us the importance to Nasser of assurances that if the Russians cut off all support from Egypt that he would not be stabbed in the back by the West.

Rountree suggested that the United States was willing to make PL-480 food aid available to Egypt. This allowed the purchase of American grain in local currency. Dulles 'believed it was important to give Nasser some indication that the West was not abandoning him'. Sir Frederick Hoyer-Millar, Permanent Undersecretary at the Foreign Office, felt that 'Nasser should get nothing until he performed on his agreement with them'. Lloyd said that he was looking for 'a sign regarding the true nature of Qasim. He supposed the UK position as of the moment was neutrality and to try for an independent Iraq with reasonably good relations with the UAR.' In reply to Rountree's opinion that communist control would be a worse alternative to UAR control of Iraq, Lloyd said that

> the UK had not made up its mind with respect to these alternatives, because their basic thought was that the worst thing would be for the oil of the Middle East to get into the hands of one man. He implied that in the long term it would be less dangerous to have a communist controlled Iraq.

The Americans understandably disagreed. Rountree argued that Iran would not long survive a communist Iraq on its frontier. Lloyd, however, opined that a communist-controlled Iraq would ease Britain's difficulty in Kuwait.[35] At the afternoon meeting, which brought Eisenhower and Macmillan into the discussion, it was confirmed that to the British Nasser remained 'a completely uncertain quantity'. While the Egyptian leader's new-found anti-communism was welcome, Lloyd, in a succinct if clichéd turn of phrase, opined that 'Dining with the devil called for a long spoon.' However, the Americans were now desperately worried that Iraq was about to go communist. Eisenhower commented that Qasim was a 'bad actor' and that, while Nasser was 'not a character we respected', the problem was 'degrees of dis-respect'.[36] The meeting ended with the British again under no illusion but that Nasser was likely to be a continuing source of argument with the Americans. The Camp David summit though marked a watershed. It was to be the last Anglo-American summit that would feature the Middle East so prominently for nearly a decade. The focus of the East–West confrontation switched first to Berlin, then Cuba and Vietnam. The Middle East would not be the focus of real East–West conflict again until 1967.

Some American opinion was now favourable to making a bold and imaginative move towards Nasser. Charles Johnston in Jordan reported that the American Ambassador in Cairo was proposing a new policy, 'which would involve America embracing Nasser and trying to build up an Arab anti-Communist front under his leadership'. This would mean Jordan, which might stand in his way, would be abandoned.[37] Lloyd replied that he was not taking this policy too seriously. At the March discussions at Camp David there was 'no suggestion that the State Department were seriously thinking of adopting such a drastic policy in the near future'. Lloyd went on to comment on some of the wider issues involved:

> First of all, I am all in favour of an Arab anti-communist front. This would be desirable whatever the outcome in Iraq may be. I think, however, that the front will be on a more stable and healthy basis if it grows from within rather than is set up from without: I am not sure that it will work most smoothly and effectively by Nasser having it all his own way … It would seem to be based on the principle that the only way of coming to terms with Nasser is to eliminate potential sources of friction by unilateral action and con-cessions from the Western side. If this policy were to be followed through to its logical conclusion it would have implications in the Persian Gulf and the Arabian peninsula (including Saudi Arabia) which neither of us could accept. If this is the price that is to be paid for getting Nasser to lead an anti communist front in the Arab world, then so far as I am concerned I would be bound to oppose it. This is not to say that I am opposed to trying to work out a rapprochement with Nasser. I regard this as a highly desirable aim … Events are not only pushing Nasser towards an anti-Communist position but have also set a considerable curb on his expansionist ambitions and activities. This suggests that the possibility of a new

relationship with Nasser on a live and live basis may be worth exploring. He needs western financial assistance, he is alarmed at the growth of communism and perturbed at the success of a new form of nationalism in Iraq: at the same time the moral support of the rest of the Arab world, provided he does not try to dominate it too directly, can give him self confidence and a sense of independence that he has hitherto lacked. Against this background the possibility of a real community of interest with the west may well emerge, given good will (a doubtful factor) and always providing that we pursue the substance of co-operation without too much regard for the appearance of it, which he will always seek to avoid.[38]

This was a noticeable change in approach by Lloyd. It recognised, at last, the metamorphosis in the strategic picture in the Middle East.

The willingness to move towards Nasser but also the need to keep the Iraqi option open was evident when the question of the supply of arms to Iraq came up for discussion at the Cabinet meeting on 20 April. While most countries had raised no objection, the more important problem was the effect that it might have on Egypt. Nasser was intensifying his anti-British propaganda and appeared to be delaying the fulfilment of his obligations under the Anglo-Egyptian financial agreement. He would certainly resent a British offer of arms to Iraq, but it seemed unlikely that he would on that account repudiate the financial agreement. On the other hand, it seemed unlikely that, if Britain refrained from making the offer, he would on that account be more co-operative in fulfilling the agreement. The discussion that followed supported the view that arms should be supplied. The Cabinet felt that they 'had little prospect of establishing cordial relations with Egypt, and it is of no disadvantage to us that the traditional antagonism between Iraq and Egypt should continue'. However, it was decided that forewarning should be given to Nasser before the news broke publicly.[39] The pessimists were proved right about relations with Egypt. Crowe was informed on 26 April that the Egyptians would not establish diplomatic relations and only a small mission with five members to deal with the desequestration issue would be allowed. They also continued their refusal to release Zarb and Swinburn, the two British nationals convicted of espionage. Iraq was the primary reason. In London, Hoyer-Millar commented on how 'exasperating and in ways rather humiliating' all this was. However, with the Iraq arms deal announcement imminent, it had to be acceded to.[40]

Crowe, the British representative, was tasked with giving the information about the arms deal. However, Dr Fawzi was away and the Egyptian Vice-President, Zulcifer Sabri, one of the most anti-British of

Nasser's ministers, refused to see Crowe. On the morning of 1 May, however, the Canadian Ambassador was able to deliver the message to Nasser. The Foreign Secretary reported that 'Nasser's initial reaction was far more favourable than we could reasonably have hoped. He appeared to understand and respect our decision, acknowledging that in the situation which had now been reached it might well on balance prove sound.' British policy, he said, 'was a gamble, but in all circumstances Qasim and the Iraqi army might be the only hope left of preserving the country from communism'. However, some of the benefit from this disclosure was marred when John Profumo told the House of Commons that Nasser had been informed in advance. Nasser responded with some indignation to this disclosure but the Canadian Ambassador felt that no lasting damage was likely to accrue. The Canadian Ambassador and Nasser then had a more wide-ranging discussion about Anglo-Egyptian relations, which the Foreign Office noted was 'of considerable interest'. Nasser seemed ready to recognise that the lack of channels for direct consultation between Cairo and London was 'a real weakness', but the President seemed to be 'unduly influenced by what he read in the United Kingdom and Arab press about the "real policy" of the United Kingdom, which he found hostile'. Nasser agreed that he needed more reliable channels of communication with London. 'But he went on to ask "what do you want me to do? Do you expect me to welcome the British in Cairo after all that they have done, not only in November 1956 but subsequently?" This seemed to be not merely a debating point but a genuine question of perplexity.'[41]

Lloyd seems to have been convinced by this meeting that the time to make a more serious overture to Nasser was at hand. Another influencing factor might have been the situation in Iraq, which appeared to be swinging even further to the left. On 14 May, Macmillan wrote to Eisenhower that the situation there 'was giving much cause for anxiety'.[42] Lloyd wrote to Macmillan on 25 May that it 'seems as though Colonel Nasser and his colleagues are prepared to think again about their relationship with this country. Although I still fundamentally distrust him, I think it is wholly to our advantage to procure a détente in our relations.' Lloyd, as we have seen from his message to Washington at the end of April, had believed that it was possible to do a deal with Nasser. The conversation between the Canadian Ambassador and Nasser had merely confirmed this. However, this time Lloyd wished to approach the matter in a bolder manner and emphasise that now 'We do not oppose, in fact welcome, movements towards Arab unity by evolution.' This was too much for Macmillan and de Zulueta who while agreeing with the general approach urged this part to be dropped. This, of course, contradicted the 'Points for a Middle East

Policy' agreed in January, which had argued for just such an approach. Lloyd sent his message to Nasser with the necessary deletions made.[43] The approach made little headway. Editorials in the Cairo press remained full of accusations against the UK. *Gumhuriya*, a Cairo daily, declared on 11 June that relations would not be restored 'till [the UK] has abandoned all hope of resisting our growing Arab nationalism'.[44]

Some opinion in the Foreign Office was still worried in June 1959 that Britain might be left to face Nasser on its own without support from the United States. This fear was expressed in an early version of a paper on the future of Anglo-American relations in June 1959: 'If Nasser's quarrel with the Russians becomes irreconcilable and the Americans convince themselves that he is basically anti-Russian, they will not necessarily be restrained by respect for oil and communications interests from supporting his ambitions for a Middle East Empire.' The calming of the situation in the Middle East by the end of July and a growing confidence that the Americans would not pull the plug on the British probably explains the deletion of the above from the final version of the document.[45]

In a long despatch at the end of June from Cairo, Crowe reviewed Anglo-Egyptian relations since the beginning of the year. He believed that Mosul dashed all hopes of diplomatic relations. Crowe was despondent about any early resumption of diplomatic relations: 'Fundamentally, I think it is due to general feeling of inferiority towards the UK and to the fear that we still intend to overthrow the regime.' Other reasons were that the Egyptians feared that the mission would be used for spying and that the old Embassy with its former role as *de facto* government house was still a source of anger to the Egyptians.[46]

This despondency was further confirmed by Crowe's meeting on 9 July with Ali Sabri, an Egyptian Vice-President. Sabri claimed Egypt desired good relations 'but that the actions of Her Majesty's Government in various spheres made them feel that our policy had not changed'. In Iraq, the 'UAR could not understand our policy there at all, but as far as they could see, we seemed to have followed a policy of preferring Communism to Arab nationalism out of hatred for Nasser'. Furthermore, King Hussein's hostility had been supported in the UK press and radio. Macmillan had reiterated support for the Suez operation. Crowe argued that all this was untrue. The UK had urged Hussein and the Sudanese to mend fences with the UAR. In Iraq, military supplies were sent to show support for Qasim. 'Indeed in our view, it was pressure from the UAR which had tended to force Qasim into the hands of the communists.' This new tide of allegations was a cause of deep concern in London. Crowe, while on leave in the middle of July, met with Macmillan and other senior officials and it was decided to give a point-by-point rebuttal of the allegations direct from Macmillan himself. Crowe was instructed to say that Macmillan was 'distressed to see in Ali Sabri's allegations evidence of a complete misunderstanding of Her Majesty's Government's position and indeed of the facts'.[47] As a result of this prime ministerial intervention, Crowe's next meeting with Ali Sabri was friendlier.[48] Indeed there seemed to be a more general warming in relations as the tensions of the spring receded. In early October, Emil Bustani, the Lebanese financier, friend of Nasser and a contact for the British, informed Crowe that Nasser 'no longer needed persuading' to resume relations with the United Kingdom. According to Bustani, 'Nasser's chief and almost sole preoccupation now was the fight against communism: he was convinced that communists were trying to undermine him in Syria and destroy him in Egypt. He would like to be able to reach a quiet understanding with us, but he still mistrusted us, particularly in relation to Iraq.'[49] He was waiting to see the results of the British general election before restoring relations, presumably as he did not want to confer any benefit on the Conservatives. Even though, one might have thought that it would have reopened Suez wounds at an inopportune moment for them.

Since the establishment of the British Property Commission, the most important contact that Colin Crowe made was with the editor of *Al-Ahram*, Mohammad Hassinein Heikal.[50] To call Heikal a journalist would be an understatement. Quite simply, he was the best-connected man in the Arab world. It is believed that he ghosted Nasser's *Philosophy of the Revolution*. He was also a close adviser on diplomatic matters to Nasser. Because Crowe was strictly speaking only a representative of the British Property Commission, he had very limited diplomatic standing. Therefore, he had to work through informal contacts like Heikal. On 14 October, Heikal told Crowe that the UAR would move to full consular and economic relations within two months. Crowe objected that this would not give any benefits and wanted chargé d'affaires-level representation. Heikal suggested that the British write a letter discussing their requirements. This was rejected in London as it would breach protocol. Instead it was decided to ask Hammarskjold to tell the UAR and UK's Ambassadors to the UN that it was time to restore relations.[51] The Egyptians continued to complain about British aid to Iraq. Qasim, they claimed rather disingenuously, would not last 24 hours if the British abandoned their support for him. Meanwhile, Macmillan was triumphantly re-elected. Finally, on 23 November, Heikal told Crowe that relations would be restored on 1 December.[52] Chargé d'affaires status was at last granted to Crowe. Perhaps the Shadow Foreign Secretary, Aneurin Bevan, deserves the last word. His House of Commons response to Lloyd's announcement of the restoration of relations strikes the right note, with his declaration of 'appreciation of the fact that after a long and unnecessary journey the Right Honourable and Learned Gentleman has now returned us to the point of departure'.[53]

NOTES

1. PRO DEFE 5/84, COS, 183, 28 July 1958, 'Position in the Middle East'.
2. Ibid.
3. PRO DEFE 5/84, COS, 189, 5 Aug. 1958, Note by the CIGS – Position in the Middle East.
4. PRO PREM 11/2397, Amery to Macmillan, 8 Sept. 1958.
5. PRO PREM 11/2397, de Zulueta to Macmillan, 10 Sept. 1958.
6. *FRUS 1958–60*, Volume XII, Doc. 35, 29 July 1958.
7. *FRUS 1958–60*, Volume XII, Doc. 36, 31 July 1958.
8. *FRUS 1958–60*, Volume XII, Doc. 42, 19 Aug. 1958.
9. *FRUS 1958–60*, Volume XII, Doc. 51, NSC Report, 4 Nov. 1958.
10. PRO PREM 11/2648, Rome–FO, No. 617, 6 Sept. 1958, FO–Rome, No. 1234, 7 Sept. 1958.
11. Crowe Papers, St Antony's College, p. 33.
12. PRO FO 371/133970, Report from the Belgian Embassy, Cairo, 6 Oct. 1958.
13. PRO PREM 11/2398, Draft letter from Selwyn Lloyd to UNSG, 16 Oct. 1958.
14. PRO PREM 11/2398, Macmillan to Lloyd, M 330/58, 21 Oct. 1958.
15. PRO CAB 128/32, Pt II, Cabinet Conclusions, 77, 22 Oct. 1958.
16. PRO CAB 134/2341, OME, 13, 1, 26 Nov. 1958.
17. Rashid Ali had attempted a coup with the support of Germany in 1941, which had led to the intervention of British forces. Perhaps Rashid Ali's past 'form' might have encouraged the British to tell Qasim.
18. Meeting of ministers, 21 Dec. 1958, cited in Ashton, *Problem of Nasser*, p. 199.
19. PRO PREM 11/2396, Roger Stevens meeting with Rountree, London Airport, 20 Dec. 1958, Philip de Zulueta–Macmillan, 29 Dec. 1958. It is important to note that Macmillan was unlikely to have seen this account until after the meeting cited in the note above. This file is often cited. See Ashton, *Problem of Nasser*, p. 198, and Lamb, *Macmillan Years 1957–63*, p. 44.
20. At the time of writing, this UK paper, 'Points for a Middle East Policy' (revised version), was subject to closure in the PRO for 50 years even though the essence of the paper is contained in Cabinet meetings and policy documents. There was a final version which appears to be a summary in PRO CAB 134/2342, Points for a Middle East Policy (final), OME, 56, 15 Dec. 1958. This copy was in the Conference Files of the State Department at the National Archives, College Park, which were bulk-declassified in 1997. See USNA, Attachment 2, 'Points for a Middle East Policy' (revised version), CF 1210, Briefing Papers, Macmillan Talks, Washington, Box 167, RG 59. The second part of the paper, which dealt with future policy in the Middle East in the event that there was a major crisis, is not anywhere to be found and does not appear to have been shown to the Americans.
21. Ibid., Part A, 'Introduction'.
22. Ibid., Part B, 'Nasser's Future Tactics'.
23. Ibid., Part C, 'Points for a Western Policy'.

24. PRO CAB 134/2230, ME(M) 59, 1st meeting, 16 Jan. 1959.
25. Macmillan Diary, Typescript, 5 Jan. 1959.
26. PRO FO 371/141920, VG 1051/4, Crowe minute, 7 Jan. 1959.
27. Macmillan Diary, Typescript, 22 Jan. 1959.
28. PRO FO 371/141920, VG 1051/20, Record of conversation between Roger Stevens and Mr Elath, the Israeli Ambassador, 22 Jan. 1959.
29. PRO PREM 11/2649, PM 70/59, 14 Feb.1959.
30. USNA AmEmbCairo to State, Desp. 774, DOSCF 641.86B92/3-2359, 23 Mar. 1958.
31. PRO FO 371/141921, VG 1051/34, OME 3, Revised brief for Mr Errol, Mar. 1959.
32. PRO FO 371/141922, VG 1051/58, UKRep Cairo to FO, No. 176, 8 Apr. 1959.
33. Macmillan Diary, Typescript, 11 Mar. 1959.
34. USNA, UAR Developments, Macmillan talks, March 1959, Briefing paper, CF 1210, Box 167.
35. USNA, Memcon Morning, 22 Mar. 1959, Macmillan talks, Memcons, CF 1214, Box 167.
36. USNA, Memcon Afternoon, 22 Mar. 1959, and Ashton, *Problem of Nasser*, p. 201.
37. PRO PREM 11/3028, Amman to FO, No. 301, 7 Apr. 1959.
38. PRO PREM 11/3028, FO to Washington, No. 1939, 14 Apr. 1959.
39. PRO CAB 128/33, Cabinet Conclusions, 24, 1, 20 Apr. 1959.
40. PRO FO 371/141923, VG 1051/67, Cairo to FO, No. 205, 26 Apr. 1959, Hoyer-Millar, annotated comments on Beith minute, 27 Apr. 1959.
41. PRO FO 371/141924, VG 1051/95, FO to Baghdad, No. 237, 22 May 1959.
42. PRO PREM 11/3427, T 255/59, Macmillan to Eisenhower, Telegram No. 2312, 14 May 1959.
43. PRO PREM 11/3266, Lloyd to Harold Macmillan, PM/59/60, 25 May 1959, Philip de Zulueta–ACI Acland (FO), 26 May 1959. In the message that was sent through the Canadians, Lloyd was particularly interested to hear that the government of Egypt was conducting a review of its policy towards the UK and 'feels it is important to dispel misunderstandings on the part of Cairo'. PRO PREM 11/3266, CRO to Ottawa, No. 107, 1 June 1959. Nigel Ashton seems to suggest that the move towards Cairo came out of the blue. Ashton, *Problem of Nasser*, pp. 203–4.
44. *Gumhuriya*, 11 June 1959, in PRO FO 371/141925, VG 1051/104, Cairo to FO, No. 272, 11 June 1959.
45. PRO FO 371/143672, ZPI/26, Permanent Undersecretary steering committee, The Future of Anglo-American Relations, 12 June 1959. It was removed from the revised version of 10 July 1959.
46. PRO FO 371/141925, VG 1051/111, Crowe despatch to Lloyd, 26 June 1959.
47. PRO FO 371/141926, VG 1051/117, Cairo to FO, No. 300, 9 July 1959, Meeting 10 Downing St, 13 July 1959, FO to Cairo, No. 137, 27 July 1959. See also PRO PREM 11/3266 for the correspondence.
48. PRO FO 371/141925, VG 1051/126, Cairo to FO, No. 330, 5 Aug. 1959.
49. PRO PREM 11/3266, Cairo to FO, No. 414, 6 Oct. 1959.
50. Crowe Papers, p. 99.
51. PRO PREM 11/3266, Cairo to FO, No. 421, 14 Oct. 1959, de Zulueta to Macmillan, 15 Oct. 1959.
52. PRO PREM 11/3266, Cairo to FO, No. 435, 26 Oct. 1959, Cairo to FO, No. 486, 23 Nov. 1959.
53. *Hansard*, HOC Debates, 601, Col. 1011–12, 1 Dec. 1959.

9

The Difficulties of the
Anglo-Egyptian Détente, 1960–62

THE QUESTION OF Egyptian consulates in British-administered territories remained a source of serious contention between the British and the Egyptians for the rest of the year. Consequently, an exchange of ambassadors did not take place until January 1961. In 1960, the question of consulates for Britain encompassed not just Liverpool and Glasgow but a large chunk of Africa, the Persian Gulf and a number of colonies in Asia. The British Colonial Office, particularly in East Africa, had serious security reservations about letting the Egyptians have diplomatic representation. Cairo Radio continued to pour out a steady stream of invective and propaganda against British colonial rule. The Egyptians, in retaliation for what they felt was stalling on the part of the British, refused to open consulates for the British in Damascus and Suez, or to allow the exchange of ambassadors. Macmillan shared the concerns and suspicions of the Colonial Office, fearing that Egyptian consuls would do 'much mischief'.[1]

Progress in relations remained very slow. In a conversation with Arnold Smith, the Canadian Ambassador to Egypt, in January 1960, Lloyd complained that the Egyptians were failing to fulfil their part of the bargain by not carrying out the financial agreement and by refusing to release Zarb and Swinburn. Smith replied that Nasser wanted a deal with the UK but did not want this to be seen as weakness. Lloyd replied that 'Nasser ought to realise that the UK wished to disengage so far as possible from the Middle East. We had certain commitments in the Persian Gulf and Southern Arabia which were burdensome but could not be shrugged off.' He went on to say that the Middle East was of lessening importance to the UK since the new oil discoveries in North Africa and West Africa. 'We are much more relaxed about the Middle East than people seem to think', and, with regard to the UAR, 'we do not care one way or the other'.[2] It was part of a general trend of declining British interest in the Middle East. The Middle East committee noted the success of the British policy since the adoption of 'Points for a Middle East Policy' in a review of the political situation in December 1959. It also noted that the oil situation, which had looked so ominous only a few months previously, had improved. The committee noted that the 'resources of North Africa were being rapidly developed and in a few years time this area might be one of the major oil producers. In consequence, the tanker surplus would be exacerbated and the demand for either Venezuelan or Middle Eastern oil would be reduced.'[3]

Macmillan had initiated in July 1959 a wide-ranging review of British strategy in the Future British Policy exercise. By the time it came to Cabinet, its basic premise was gloomy – Britain's relative economic power was likely to decline further and British interests would have to be subordinated to the general interests of the West. The committee that discussed the matter split between those who wished to make a dramatic retrenchment of Britain's east-of-Suez role and those who wished to continue the burden. The final draft of the report concluded that war in Europe was unlikely and that Britain should maintain a capability to fight small-scale, brush-fire wars in the Middle East and the Far East.[4] The recommendations of the report were never specifically endorsed by the Cabinet, which suggests that the previous policy of maintenance of the east-of-Suez role remained a cornerstone of British policy.

While the Middle East had entered a period of calm, tensions were never far from the surface. In February 1960, after a number of incidents on the Israeli–Syrian frontier, reports circulated of an Egyptian mobilisation in the Sinai desert. The crisis known as 'Rotem' soon passed without an outbreak of fighting even though it did cause a few jitters in London. The Egyptians continued to question the British bona fides of protestations of friendship while the British toyed with, but rejected, the idea of sending a message to Nasser from Macmillan.[5] British arms sales to Israel meant that relations remained cool for the first half of the year.[6] What was most notable about 1960 was that it was without doubt the quietest year in the Middle East since 1945. The world's and Britain's attention was switched on Europe and the Paris summit.

In June, Sir Roger Stevens, Deputy Undersecretary at the Foreign Office, requested that Crowe push for an improvement in relations. Stevens wished to find out if a real improvement in relations was possible on a *status quo* basis. Stevens had already made a number of gestures with the aim of securing better relations. He had made 'representations to the *Daily Telegraph* to tone down its coverage of Egypt'. He hoped that, as well as making the financial agreement work, better relations might have some slight restraining effect upon the tone of Cairo propaganda, 'which again is always liable to be used at this end by Nasser's critics as a (quite justifiable) stick with which to beat him, and for that matter any British government trying to secure better relations with him'.[7] Crowe was of the opinion that a *rapprochement* on the basis of the *status quo* was unlikely – every Arab nationalist wanted Britain out of the Middle East. Nasser's policies were only likely to change if an Arab state went communist and there was nothing that he wanted that the UK could give.[8]

Crowe, because of his lowly diplomatic status, was unable to secure a meeting with Nasser. Relations remained stagnant. In September, Mahmoud Riad, a senior official in the UAR Foreign Ministry, told a British official that, while there had been high hopes for an improvement in relations at the start of the year, they were now 'slightly worse'. Why?

> Britain was still working against Arab nationalism and against the UAR ... The British press, the BBC, Sir Anthony Eden's memoirs, and many other phenomena, indicated that the mentality which had gone to the making of the Suez episode was still dominant in England, not only in the Conservative party, but in the Foreign Office too.[9]

An unexpected chance of a meeting between Macmillan and Nasser arose with the extraordinary General Assembly of the UN on the Congo in late September and early October. Nasser was fêted at the session as one of the big three of the non-aligned movement along with Nehru and Tito. Stevens warned that it would be bad for relations if Macmillan did not meet Nasser, as everyone else would. Macmillan, he suggested, needed to improve Nasser's psychological perception of Britain and get across to him that 'we do not regard him as a moral outcast ... [and that] we are not trying to undermine him'. Dr Fawzi and the new British Foreign Secretary, Lord Home, met first on 26 October. They agreed to come to some arrangement about consulates and that de-sequestration had to be hurried along. A meeting was arranged between Macmillan and Nasser for 3 October. The meeting of Macmillan, who had not so long ago viewed Nasser as an 'Asiatic Mussolini', and Nasser, who was apparently convinced that Britain was still conspiring against him, was cordial. It was agreed that ambassadors should be exchanged. The bulk of the meeting concentrated on global issues. The only disagreement was over attitudes to Israel. Macmillan wrote in his diary that the 'talk was rather formal but friendly. Nasser, of course, denies any responsibility for the worsening position in the Middle East. But he seemed to want our relations to return to normal.'[10] Nasser was much more enthusiastic. He informed the Speaker of the Canadian House of Commons of the importance which he now attaches to personal contact between the Heads of Government. By way of illustration, he referred to his discussions with the Prime Minister in cordial terms. He said that he had found Mr Macmillan a much warmer personality and much easier to get on with than he would have expected from his conventional views of a British Minister who had been in power in 1956. As a result, he had been able to agree with the Prime Minister that the two countries could work together towards normal relations.[11]

Despite the meeting, the issue of consulates continued to act as a drag to full normalisation of relations. The colonial governors in Aden and East Africa remained opposed to the UAR having representation because of the impending political developments that were due to take place in them in the near future. By January 1961 the issue had not yet been resolved. However, the British expressed a willingness to let the UAR have a consulate in Kuwait, which hindsight was to prove a fortunate decision, as within months Iraq was threatening the emirate.[12] This was to be the key concession to the Egyptians. Finally, they agreed to exchange ambassadors on 14 January.[13] The Levant Department described the agreement as 'an unexpectedly satisfactory result'.[14] Soon after this the Israelis, according to Crowe, made a drama about a British arms shipment to disrupt relations. Crowe suggested that it allowed the Egyptian opponents of Britain to say 'There you are, you cannot trust the British' and to suggest that 'we merely waited until the exchange of Ambassadors was in the bag before carrying on in our old way'.[15] Crowe, who was coming to the end of a difficult stint in Cairo, wrote in one of his valedictory despatches of growing economic problems in Egypt, which were particularly affecting the middle classes. He advised Lord Home not to read too much into it. This was because of the stable nature of domestic society, which made the Egyptians supremely confident:

> They seem to be utterly convinced that they are in the right and on the winning side whatever the battle. Their enemies – Sir Anthony Eden, Guy Mollet, Nuri Said, Camille Chamoun, Adnan Menderes and soon (they hope) the Shah of Iran – fall by the wayside and they continue their 'sacred march'. It is sometimes hard to resist the conclusion that the internal affairs of Egypt have little significance in relation to the external conduct of President Nasser and the government of the UAR.[16]

On his last evening in Cairo, Crowe was given a present by Heikal of a cheque with the word 'Zarb' written upon it, indicating that the convicted spy would be released imminently.[17]

Harold Beeley, an experienced Arabist, was designated the new British Ambassador. His directive stated that 'the principal object of your mission ... must be to establish a good and business-like relationship between HMG and the UAR government so far as possible'. He was to emphasise that Britain did not oppose the Union with Syria and that it did not take sides in the Arab–Israeli dispute.[18] Beeley noted in his early despatches the friendly reception that he was receiving. A meeting with Fawzi, the Minister for Foreign Affairs, was cordial. The Egyptian said that there were 'no doubt some real obstacles to the improvement in relations, but he thought that a frank inquiry into these would also reveal the existence of a number of "mirages"'. The new British Ambassador had the impression that, in making this statement, 'he was not exclusively referring to our attitude to the UAR, but was admitting the reality of some of the suspicions of British policy prevalent here'.[19] Beeley, as a fully accredited ambassador, had a major advantage over Crowe in that he had access to Nasser. Their meeting, on the presentation of Beeley's credentials, showed Nasser in conciliatory form:

> Now we are making a fresh start. The Egyptians were 'good people' and had no feelings of bitterness. It was no good expecting miracles. There were some subjects on which we clearly should not be able to reach agreement. The building up of a new and better relationship would require great patience, but he believed it could be done.[20]

The calm in the Middle East since the summer of 1959 had given Anglo-Egyptian relations a breathing space in which to develop. The financial agreement and the Egyptian refusal to hurry it along remained the main British concern but was more an irritant than a real crisis. Then in the summer of 1961, the first major crisis since 1959 broke in the Middle East. The primary concern of British policy-makers for the Middle East remained the defence of Kuwait from external attack or an internal coup. In the spring of 1961, the Ruler of Kuwait requested the abrogation of the 1899 agreement, which made Kuwait a British protectorate, and its replacement by a treaty reaffirming friendship and support. On 19 June 1961, letters were exchanged between the British Political Resident in the Gulf, Sir William Luce, and the Ruler of Kuwait, which essentially fulfilled the Ruler's request.[21]

Qasim, the Iraqi leader, reacted with some menace to the news. On 25 June, he proclaimed Iraqi sovereignty over Kuwait, setting off deep concern in London that the Iraqis might invade the emirate. The British Ambassador in Iraq urged that Britain should try to get other Arab states which had supported the Kuwaitis to take the lead in defending Kuwait. However, the Iraqi military threat seemed to grow ever more threatening and the Ruler was advised by the British political agent to request British support. The danger of inserting British troops was, of course, that it could lead Nasser and other Arab leaders to side with Iraq and blame Britain for the crisis.[22]

British forces with their mobility and reaction times vastly improved since Suez were quickly deployed. An Iraqi invasion now became unlikely. In the UN Security Council, the UAR delegate remained conspicuously neutral. 'No Arab [i.e. Qasim] he said was justified in opening a way for British imperialism.'[23] It was clearly not in the interest of the UAR to have Qasim in control of Kuwait. Undoubtedly, as Malcolm Kerr points out, the whole Kuwait affair was deeply embarrassing to the Egyptians:

> What was embarrassing was the spectacle of British troops camped on Arab soil, defending an interest which the UAR had declared as its own, at the invitation of the Kuwaiti government. When British forces had gone to Jordan in 1958, at least the UAR could feel free to denounce the operation without reserve, even while indirectly benefiting from it.[24]

Therefore, on 5 July, the UAR delegate to the United Nations suggested that the Kuwait problem could be solved by the Arabs themselves and insisted on the withdrawal of UK forces. He tabled a resolution to that effect on 6 June. It and a British resolution failed on 7 June. The British were a little concerned that any Arab League involvement would lead to demands from them, for a share of the oil revenues. However, the UAR continued to be co-operative and pronounced a willingness to support a Kuwaiti application to join the United Nations, something which the British Ambassador in Baghdad suggested might be a way of getting international acceptance of Kuwait.[25]

On 10 July Kuwait informed the Arab states that it would ask the British force to withdraw when Kuwait was admitted to the UN and if an Arab League force would replace it.[26] The UAR representative to the Arab League, Dr Mohammed Zayyat, said that the UAR would meet the Kuwaiti request for troops. Subsequently, the League debated the issue of Kuwaiti membership.[27] At the meeting of the Arab League on 20 July, Kuwaiti membership was agreed, provoking an Iraqi walkout.[28] The British had a slight fear that the UAR might dominate the Arab League force. This proved to be wrong. The UAR Ambassador to Britain was confident that the crisis was over, explaining that the 'UAR took a perfectly sensible and realistic line about Kuwait'. He continued 'inter alia that he did not think that Qasim would try to attack Kuwait now or once an Arab force was installed because he knew that the whole of the Arab World would intervene against him'.[29] On 12 August the Ruler of Kuwait requested the withdrawal of British forces upon arrival of the Arab League contingent, which were due on 10 September, thereby ending the crisis.[30]

THE FALL OF THE UAR AND ITS AFTERMATH

The Kuwait crisis was the first time that Britain and Nasser's Egypt had co-operated over a major international crisis. Political and strategic necessities had brought about a convergence of interests. Neither nation wished to see their main Middle Eastern enemy, Qasim's Iraq, seize the oil-rich emirate. The resolution of the crisis demonstrated a willingness on the part of the British government to co-operate with the Arab League. This allowed the successful withdrawal of the British military force and the achievement of its political objective – the securing of Kuwaiti independence with the aid of the UAR. Unfortunately, the convergence of interest this produced was temporary. Anglo-Egyptian relations remained on too fragile a basis to survive a major crisis. Therefore, it came as little surprise when the relationship broke down once more over the Yemen civil war, where both sides had seriously divergent interests.

Prior to that crisis the fragile state of Anglo-Egyptian relations had been exposed when the United Arab Republic disintegrated with the secession of Syria in September 1961.[31] Neither Britain nor the other Western powers contributed to the collapse of the UAR.[32] Nonetheless, they found their relationship with the Nasser regime suffering in the fallout from the crisis. Perhaps Nasser required the West and the reactionary monarchies of the Middle East as an excuse for the mortal blow to his dream of Arab unity, inflicted upon him by the collapse of the UAR.

With the exception of the Six Day War, the fall of the UAR was undoubtedly the greatest political setback of Nasser's political career. It was to have a malign influence on his future foreign policy, being a key factor in his decision to intervene in the Yemen civil war and part of the reason for his aggressive policies in the build-up to the Six Day War. The failure in Syria was not caused by the intrigues of Nasser's foreign enemies; it was primarily the fault of his consistently disastrous domestic and economic policies in Egypt and Syria that failed to lift living standards. The economic policy of Nasser was based on the Soviet model of long-range state planning. Unfortunately, this bred corruption and inefficiency on a vast scale and, while Nasser personally was honest, many of the lower echelons in his regime were not. This, combined with the failure to improve the living standards in Syria and curb some of the endemic corruption, was among the primary causes of the growing restiveness of that country by 1961. Nasser not only failed economically, but he also singularly failed to deliver on his promises of a better life for all. The Syrians were treated almost as a conquered people.[33] Lacouture accuses Nasser of having a colonial/imperialist attitude to Syria, which is ironic to say the least.[34]

Even the Ba'ath, initially the most fervent supporters of the Union and of Nasser personally, had rapidly cooled their ardour towards it, disappointed with the manifest failures of the Union and their own marginalisation from the centre of power in Cairo. They were further disappointed with the westward inclination of Nasser's foreign policy from the end of 1958. The co-operation with Jordan and Britain over the deployment of the Arab League force to foil Qasim in Kuwait served to 'alienate many of the remaining pro-Nasserists in Syria who had been willing to accept Egyptian domination in return for the opportunity of sharing in the glories of a radical foreign policy'.[35] Thus, by the middle of 1961, Nasser had managed to alienate both the left and the right in Syria. He also seemed to be unwilling or unable to recognise the discontent, as he forced further unpopular nationalisation measures on the Syrians in July 1961 without any consultation.[36] His only concession to Syrian opinion, bringing Sarraj, the heavy-handed, native security chief, to Cairo as interior minister, merely had the effect of removing the eyes and ears of the police state.[37] Podeh identifies four major errors: the removal of the Syrian personalities, particularly the Ba'ath, who had helped forge the union; the abolition of political activity except Nasser's National Union; overweening Egyptian involvement in the internal affairs of Syria; and the security state established by the Egyptians that had not really been there previously.[38] Right-wing Syrian army officers seized the opportunity provided by the paralysing of the police apparatus to stage a *coup d'état* on the night of 28 September 1961. The British Foreign Office received the first reports from Beirut the same night.[39] The unpopularity of Nasser and the UAR may be gauged from the lack of resistance that greeted the coup.

The Foreign Office expressed concern when the news was confirmed. They believed that the coup could only act against the interest of the British by destabilising Syria and the entire region. To their surprise, Nasser had been a benign influence on Syria. Syria was no longer the centre for intrigue and subversion against Britain and its regional allies that it once had been. The Foreign Office declared that it was 'important that we should continue to be seen to be adhering to our policy of non-involvement in Arab affairs. It may take some time for Arab opinion to crystallise on the dispute and meanwhile it is important that we should not appear to be rejoicing at what can be represented as a setback for Arab unity.' [40]

The United States displayed even greater concern at the news.[41] President Kennedy, since he had come into office, had been conducting a warm and friendly correspondence with Nasser.[42] The American Ambassador, John Badeau, rushed to assure Nasser that the United States or the CIA had played no part in the coup. In Washington, there were mixed reactions to the coup. Robert Komer, at the National Security Council (NSC), recognised the danger of instability in the aftermath of the coup but also saw that there was a possibility that the affair might make Nasser more 'tractable'. Komer's advice was that the United States should have a 'public posture of hands off, discreet, indirect encouragement of new regime, and nice noises to Nasser'.[43]

There were certain complications when Britain's closest regional allies, the Jordanians, proved to be the most enthusiastic supporters of the coup. King Hussein had remained the bitterest opponent of Nasser. He urged the British to move towards swift recognition of the Syrian regime. Concerned that Hussein might intervene in the event of Nasser attempting to re-establish his power, the British Ambassador in Amman left him in no doubt that Britain would strongly disassociate itself from any such Jordanian action, and, if necessary, leave it to its fate.[44] The Cabinet, despite their still generally hostile view of Nasser, were as reticent as the Foreign Office and the Americans on the question of recognising the new Syrian regime. They agreed that it would be in Britain's best interest not to recognise the regime for a considerable period of time.[45]

This was combined with a major diplomatic effort by the British to make it clear to Nasser that the British had nothing to do with the coup. Roger Stevens went so far as to tell the UAR Ambassador that the British government viewed the secession of Syria with 'regret'.[46] Even Macmillan was not greatly interested or moved by this blow to Nasser, perhaps illustrating his growing detachment from Middle Eastern affairs.[47] If the break-up of the UAR had occurred a couple of years previously, Macmillan would have been delighted at such a setback to Nasser but events had conspired to create an unlikely convergence of opinion between Britain and the United Arab Republic on the need for stability in the Middle East. The Foreign Secretary made this clear to his colleagues:

There does not seem to be much hope of stability in the long run. Syria has always been deeply divided and in its thirteen years of existence there has been numerous military coups. Although in 1958 the country as a whole favoured union with Egypt, there has been much discontent recently as a result of the displacement of Syrians by Egyptians and of President Nasser's measures of nationalisation and centralisation.[48]

The Foreign Secretary could only foresee problems ahead as Nasser might well be tempted to retrieve his prestige by subversion in Jordan, Libya or Saudi Arabia. He predicted accurately that 'we may be in for a new period of unrest in the Middle East after some three years of relative calm'.[49] The Cabinet, at its next meeting, discussing the tricky problem of recognition of Syria, were aware that under Foreign Office practice Britain generally recognised a regime that was in *de facto* control over a country. The fear on the British part was that Nasser might break off diplomatic relations with any country that recognised Syria. He had already broken relations with Turkey and Jordan for this reason. Nobody in Whitehall wished to repeat the tortuous process that it had taken to restore relations in 1959–60, so Britain had to tread very warily. A wait-and-see attitude had to be adopted. Stevens prepared the ground, telling the UAR ambassador that the United Kingdom viewed the matter of recognition 'cold bloodedly'. Recognition would have to be granted if the present regime in Syria remained in control.[50]

This turned out to be the case. Nasser did despatch some paratroops to Syria but, when they failed to attract support and were captured, he decided not to pursue an attempt to coerce Syria.[51] The Americans discreetly made it clear to Nasser that, while they viewed the collapse of the UAR with disappointment, they did not want to see it restored by force.[52] In fact, he displayed considerable magnanimity when he recognised in a speech on 5 October 1961 that the Union was over. He announced that he would not oppose Syrian entry to the United Nations or the Arab League.[53] (Of course, he was soon plotting the destruction of this new regime with his usual methods of propaganda and subversion.) This cleared the way for British recognition. The Foreign Office noted that 'in view of Nasser's change of attitude there seems to be no objection to our recognising after the Americans'. The decision to recognise was received with more resignation than anger by the Egyptians on 12 October.[54] The Foreign Office continued to attempt to reassure the Egyptians about British attitudes and policy. Lord Home and Dr Fawzi were due to meet on 17 October. A Foreign Office brief suggested that Home might take the opportunity 'to indicate to Doctor Fawzi that we took no satisfaction in the separation of Syria from Egypt, since the period of union of the two countries was one of relative stability in the Middle East, and it is stability that we regard as the most important objective'.[55]

To the Foreign Office, Nasser and the United Arab Republic seem to have become new members of the *status quo* in the Middle East. Keeping them that way was a vital policy objective for both the British and the Americans. Within Whitehall, there was also some concern as to what effect the secession would have on Nasser's future policy towards Kuwait. These concerns were heightened when reports circulated of an Egyptian withdrawal from the Arab League force in Kuwait, as this might have

> sinister implications, especially if it represents a change of policy resulting from the breakdown of the United Arab Republic. The possibility we have in mind is that the drawing together of Jordan and Syria might have encouraged Nasser and Qasim to co-operate in some way, e.g. by Qasim furthering Nasser's ambitions in Syria and Jordan in return for Nasser leaving Qasim a free hand in Kuwait.[56]

These fears of a new Qasim/Nasser axis proved groundless. Even so, the whole Syrian affair did provoke renewed strains in the Anglo-Egyptian relationship.

The secession provoked the gravest crisis that Nasser had faced internally since he had deposed Neguib in 1954. His once unassailable position looked a lot less secure at the end of 1961. The economy was in serious trouble. The middle classes were suffering under the weight of 'economic reforms' that were designed to redistribute wealth. Nasser's reaction to the crisis was to swing sharply to the left. He began with a purge of his perceived domestic enemies on the right. A new wave of sequestrations of private property and businesses began. Substantial numbers of the richest Egyptians had their wealth confiscated. Nasser also convened a conference of 'popular forces' to reinvigorate the moribund revolution.[57]

In the field of foreign policy, Nasser began a minor *rapprochement* with the Soviets. He also began a rather bizarre confrontation with the French. A number of members of their property mission were arrested on charges of espionage at the end of the year. The British diplomatic mission noted the intense and security-laden atmosphere in Cairo at this time. British attempts to raise the subject of the French prisoners were greeted with disdain and some annoyance by the Egyptians. *Al-Ahram* trumpeted that Cairo would not 'accept British intervention for the release of the spies'.[58]

These ominous signs in Nasser's dealings with the West may have been related to the French support for the Israelis and to show solidarity with the National Liberation Front (FLN) in Algeria as the Evian negotiations began.[59] Nasser, though, seemed intent on alienating the entire West, which he saw as standing behind his Arab enemies, the Jordanians and the Saudis. As a consequence, *Al-Ahram* and the state-controlled media launched a series of blistering attacks on British policy from the middle of October. The press campaign reached its peak of intensity in the last week in December. Accusations were made about British plotting in Beirut and naval movements that threatened Egypt. In Lebanon, the Chebab government had nearly fallen after a coup attempt that the Arab press claimed was Jordanian- and British-backed. Since Chebab was popular with just about everybody, this claim was bizarre, to say the least. At the same time, British intelligence had detected what it believed was a renewed Iraqi threat to Kuwait. The British made a big show of moving naval vessels to the Gulf. This drew massive criticism in the Arab press and serious anger in Cairo. The Americans were also annoyed by what they saw as unnecessary British sabre rattling in the Middle East. As a result of the British action, there were unconfirmed rumours in the Cairo press that the Egyptians and the Iraqis were having secret consultations about Kuwait.[60] Ambassador Beeley expressed concern about the 'undoubted deterioration' in Anglo-United Arab Republic relations since September 1961. He spoke of a myth going around ruling circles in Egypt about external plotting against Nasser and the UAR: 'King Hussein and King Saud were the immediate instigators of this plot with Britain, Turkey and of course, Israel in the background.'

> The Syrian fiasco, in other words, has brought out in Nasser the paranoiac tendency which seems to be present in so many dictators. In his case it is natural, in the light of the whole history of Anglo-Egyptian relations since 1882 and in particular the events of 1956, that his suspicions should circle round Her Majesty's Government. I was not at all surprised to learn from my Danish colleague that, when he made representations to Zulcifar Sabri [UAR Deputy Foreign Minister] about the French arrests, Zulcifar referred to his parallel conversation with me and said that when he saw the British Ambassador he could never forget that the Ministers who had been in the British Government at the time of Suez were still in office.[61]

The tendency in the Foreign Office was at first to dismiss the Egyptian hostility as designed to win favour with the Russians as negotiations about aid and loans for the Aswan Dam project were due to start in Cairo soon. However, Beeley's meeting with Riad confirmed that, while the Egyptian claims may well have been fantasy, they were strongly held. It would appear that the Egyptians were convinced that the British press, especially *The Times*, was state-controlled.[62] Riad attacked the press in Britain for rejoicing over Syria and stated that Britain had 'interfered over French official' and that 'when they heard of British naval movements in the area their thoughts went back to 1956'. Egypt had 'hoped for a new relationship after the resumption of diplomatic relations, and they had certainly had "fair words" from the Prime Minister, from your self [Lord Home] and more recently from me. But we had not followed these up with any action calculated to convince them of our sincerity.'

Sir Harold replied with a restatement of the British policy in the Middle East, which he claimed was now designed to seek better relations with the United Arab Republic:

> I then said that I thought the authorities here had failed to appreciate the evolution of Her Majesty's Government's policy since 1958. They were not backing any one Arab Government against any one other. It was an objective of their policy to encourage the resistance of the Arab countries to communism, but they believed that the best weapons for this purpose were economic growth and social reform. They consequently viewed with sincere sympathy the efforts which President Nasser was making along these lines in the UAR. Thus, the foundations existed for a better relationship; but it would be difficult to build on them if the present atmosphere of suspicion persisted.[63]

When a Foreign Office official, Geoffrey Arthur, attempted to disabuse two Egyptian officials of British intentions, he was informed that the main concern was the British support for Hussein. Arthur commented that it is clear 'that Jordan is the central problem in United Arab Republic thinking about British policy in the Middle East'.[64] In the light of these interviews and other evidence probably provided by the Americans the Foreign Office agreed that 'Nasser probably genuinely suspects that there has been some conspiracy on foot led by Her Majesty's Government and designed to isolate the United Arab Republic'. Britain would have to get rid of these suspicions, he concluded.[65]

The Egyptians, at last, seemed to realise that Britain was genuinely looking for *rapprochement*. Thus, Beeley was granted an interview with Nasser on 24 February. Despite the poor state of Anglo-Egyptian relations, Nasser was in conciliatory mood. Beeley noted, in a rather paternalistic manner, that he 'was clearly anxious (as I was) not to say anything too provocative and this in itself is probably a good indication'. Nasser's suspicions, he warned, 'are likely to plague us for some time to come, but I do not think he has a closed mind and it is probable that he will respond to any signs of confidence we can show in him'.[66]

Nasser had his reasons for this change in attitude to Britain. On one level, he was impressed by the seeming desire of the British to allay his fears. Secondly, the United States launched its most ambitious attempt to win over Nasser yet. In late January 1962, the President agreed to propose a $500 million food aid package to the United Arab Republic over three years in an effort to put relations with Nasser on a more long-term basis. Previously, this food aid package had been renewed every six months, which gave the Egyptians the impression that they were on probation until the next tranche of aid had been approved. The question of a new policy toward Nasser had been a matter of some debate within the Kennedy administration. In early December 1961, Robert Komer of the NSC proposed that a long-term food aid package should be offered to Egypt. His rationale for the new policy was that it would 'give Nasser the impression we're opening a new chapter, using as bait the very substantial aid we're probably going to give him anyway'. Komer, though, remained under no illusions about Nasser. There remained too many issues of difference between the two sides to have anything other than what he described as a 'limited marriage of convenience'.[67] Komer was quite correct. There were too many issues that divided the West from Nasser. A food aid package might improve the atmosphere between the West and Egypt but it would not seriously alter the contentious relationship. However, as it turned out, the package almost certainly had a positive influence on the Anglo-Egyptian relationship.

There was also another factor. The UAR was suffering serious economic problems as a result of the worst cotton crop failure in years. This caused a serious balance of payments crisis in the middle of the year, which necessitated the calling in of the IMF and other international assistance. This gave the British the required leverage with the Egyptians to settle some of the outstanding issues that were left over from the 1959 agreement. The Egyptians had been intimating for some time that they were willing to negotiate the clearing up of any remaining conflicts over the interpretation of the 1959 document. Fawzi, when he met Lord Home in Geneva in March, agreed that things were not going fast enough.[68] Nasser, himself, expressed surprise that so many issues of interpretation were left outstanding from the financial agreement at a meeting with Beeley and Sir Roger Stevens. At this meeting,

Stevens explained to Nasser that the United Kingdom's primary concern in the Middle East was its oil interests. Nasser was at his most disarming and conciliatory and claimed 'that he would never do anything against our oil interests. The Arabs in the oil producing countries benefited from our presence there; they got 50% of the profits and this was fair. They could not drink the oil, and if they drove us out it would be useless to them.' Nasser concluded the meeting by asking for a British minister to visit Cairo.[69] The Foreign Office assessment of Nasser's new direction was positive. Nasser was in the mood for détente and appeared to be moving from foreign adventurism to domestic economic problems. Home was less sure, commenting that 'I must confess that I will believe all this when I see some concrete evidence.'[70] For once, there actually was 'some concrete evidence' that Anglo-Egyptian relations were at last moving in a friendlier, more constructive direction. Negotiations on clearing up the problems left over from the 1959 financial agreement began in April and were completed in July. Two agreements were signed in August 1962. These essentially consisted of the Egyptians agreeing that the process of desequestrating British property would be completed in three years. Conflicting interpretations of the 1959 agreement were resolved. In return for these concessions, Britain agreed to take part in the rescue plan for the Egyptian economy and provide a loan for £10 million.[71] The Cabinet discussed the matter in June and was in general amenable to the idea of helping the Egyptians. Some in the Cabinet raised objections on the grounds that no loan should be granted without the settling of all outstanding claims.[72] These doubts were brushed aside. The summer of 1962 was a time of real hope in Western capitals that Nasser could be turned into a genuine friend of the West.

In Egyptian domestic politics the spring and early summer were taken up with the drafting of the National Charter, which was a complete reconstruction of Egypt's political system. The Charter, which was inaugurated, was a mixture of capitalism, corporatism and centralised planning. It did little to change the new ruling oligarchy in Egypt and power very much remained in the hands of Nasser and his closest associates. The Charter was also a reaction to the Syrian secession, as it seemed to presage a new move against the forces of reaction in the Arab world. Nasser made it explicit that he wanted the removal of all Arab monarchies and their replacement with republican and socialist models. The commitment to pan-Arabism was by no means dead. In its first paragraph, the Charter proclaimed the continuing commitment of Egypt not only to the Arab world but to liberation movements throughout the world.[73] The problem for Nasser was that he was convinced that he needed foreign adventurism to ensure his regime's popularity. Domestically his regime had presided over the transfer of power from the forces of capital and reaction to the ruling cadres of his own National Union without having significantly altered the power structure of the nation in favour of the masses. Nasser was unable either satisfactorily to delegate authority to his colleagues or to increase democratisation.[74] The Egyptian masses could only be kept on the side of the government (and Nasser) by success in the Arab world. Nasser may have had his weaknesses but one of his major strengths was his ability to rouse the masses to support foreign projects that gave Egypt self-respect. However, in 1962, success in foreign policy seemed about as likely as success in curing Egypt's economic ills. The summer of 1962 had climaxed with a fractious meeting of the Arab League called to debate Syrian accusations of Egyptian subversion. In an extraordinary move, the meeting was not held in the League's headquarters in Egypt but in the Lebanon. The meeting climaxed with the walkout of the Egyptian delegation.[75] Nasser's influence among the Arab governments was at its lowest since prior to Suez.

NOTES

1. PRO PREM 11/2651, de Zulueta to Wilfors, 7 Dec. 1959, Lloyd to Macmillan, 12 Dec. 1959.
2. PRO FO 371/150923, VG 1051/9, Record of conversation between A. Smith and Lloyd, 6 Jan. 1960.
3. PRO CAB 134/2343, OME, 4th meeting, 18 Nov. 1959.
4. Pickering, *Britain's Withdrawal from East of Suez*, pp. 112–14.
5. PRO FO 371/150926, VG 1051/40, Rothnie minute, 6 Mar. 1960.
6. USNA, AmEmbassy Cairo to State, No. 2939, DOSCF 611.86B/3-2360, 23 Mar. 1960.
7. PRO FO 371/150927, VG 1051/60G, Stevens despatch to Crowe, 13 June 1960.
8. PRO FO 371/150928, VG 1051/68G, Crowe to Stevens, 27 June 1964.
9. PRO FO 371/150932, VG 1051/101, Record of conversation between Geoffrey Arthur and Mahmoud Riad,12 Sept. 1959.
10. Macmillan Diary, Dep. c 21/1, 2 Oct. 1960.
11. PRO FO 371/150933, VG 1051/116, Cairo to FO, No. 783, 13 Oct. 1960.
12. PRO FO 371/155804, VG 1051/7, Cairo to FO, No. 24, 7 Jan. 1961.
13. PRO FO 371/155805, VG 1051/40, Cairo to FO, No. 51, 14 Jan. 1961.
14. PRO FO 371/155805, VG 1051/40, Levant Dept brief on UAR relations, 16 Jan. 1961.
15. PRO FO 371/158807, VG 1041/61, Crowe to Crawford, 3 Feb. 1961.
16. PRO FO 371/158786, VG 1016/8, Crowe to Home, 9 Feb.1961.
17. Crowe Paper, p. 226.
18. PRO FO 371/158809, VG 1051/115, Directive for Harold Beeley, 24 Mar. 1961.
19. PRO FO 371/158809, VG 1051/114, Beeley to Beith, 21 Mar. 1961.
20. PRO FO 371/158809, VG 1051/118, Beeley to FO, No. 411, 29 Mar. 1961.
21. The general background is outlined in Ovendale, *Transfer of Power*, pp. 227–8.
22. Ovendale, *Transfer of Power*, pp. 228–30. See also Simon C. Smith, *Kuwait, 1950–*

65, *Britain, the Al-Sabah and Oil* (London: British Academy/Oxford University Press, 1999), pp. 115–25 for the crisis.

23. PRO PREM 11/3428, UKDELUN to FO, No. 1076, 2 July 1961.
24. Kerr, *Arab Cold War*, p. 27.
25. PRO PREM 11/3429, Baghdad to FO, No. 849, 7 July 1961.
26. PRO PREM 11/3429, Kuwait to FO, No. 436, 10 July 1961.
27. PRO PREM 11/3429, Cairo to FO, No. 713, 13 July 1961.
28. PRO PREM 11/3429, Cairo to FO, No. 747, 21 July 1961.
29. PRO FO 371/158813, VG 1051/176, Meeting between Sir Roger Stevens and Ambassador El Kony, 2 Aug. 1961.
30. Ovendale, *Transfer of Power*, p. 234.
31. A massively under-researched topic. E. Podeh, *The Decline of Arab Unity* (Brighton, Sussex Academic Press, 1999) is one of the few up-to-date accounts of the fall of the UAR.
32. Indeed the British diplomatic representation in Damascus had only recently been restored.
33. Hasou, *Struggle for the Arab World*, p. 114.
34. J. Lacouture, *Nasser* (London, Secker & Warburg, 1975), p. 196.
35. Rathmell, *Secret War*, p. 159.
36. Hasou, *Struggle for the Arab World*, p. 115.
37. Stephens, *Nasser*, pp. 338–9.
38. Podeh, *Decline of Arab Unity*, pp. 179–80.
39. PRO FO 371/158787, VG 1016/45, Beirut–FO, No. 829, 28 Sept. 1961.
40. PRO FO 371/158787, VG 1016/48, FO–Amman, No. 1047, 29 Sept. 1961.
41. PRO FO 371/158787, VG 1016/59, Washington–FO, No. 2584, 28 Sept. 1961.
42. D. Little, 'The New Frontier on the Nile: JFK, Nasser and Arab Nationalism', *Journal of American History*, 75 (1988), p. 504.
43. *FRUS 1961–63*, Vol. XVII, Doc. 115, 30 Sept. 1961.
44. PRO PREM 11/4510, Mr Henniker-Major (Amman)–FO, No. 814, 2 Oct. 1961.
45. PRO FO 371/158788, VG 1016/82, Amman–FO, No. 808, 30 Sept. 1961 and PRO CAB 128/31, Cabinet Conclusions, 52, 28 Sept. 1961.
46. PRO FO 371/158789, VG 1016/119, R. Stevens minute, 29 Sept. 1961.
47. Macmillan Diary entry, 1 Oct. 1961, in *Pointing the Way*, p. 386.
48. PRO CAB 129/107, C. 152, Note by the SOSFA–Syria and Kuwait, 6 Oct. 1961.
49. Ibid.
50. PRO FO 371/158789, VG 1016/142, FO–Cairo, No. 1471, 4 Oct. 1961.
51. M. Be'eiri, *Army Officers in Arab Politics and Society* (London, Praeger, 1970), p. 144.
52. Podeh, *Decline of Arab Unity*, p. 157.
53. It would have been beyond the logistical capability of the Egyptians anyway. See Stephens, *Nasser*, pp. 340–3.
54. PRO FO 371/157829, EY 1023/53, Miller submission, 9 Oct. 1961 and EY 1023/43, Cairo–FO, No. 1000, 12 Oct. 1961.
55. PRO FO 371/158814, VG 1052/11, Blaker brief for SOSFA lunch with Dr Fawzi, 17 Oct. 1961.
56. Ibid.
57. In a speech on 16 October 1961, he criticised himself for not doing enough to crush the forces of reaction: 'We directed our blows against pacts and bases, while the enemy was hiding all the while in the palaces and safes of the millionaires.' Lacouture, *Nasser*, p. 203.
58. See the following correspondence in PRO FO 371/158796, VG 1016/290, Cairo–FO, No. 1203, 11 Dec. 1961 and No. 1213, 14 Dec. 1961.
59. Nasser disliked the French for the military support that they provided Israel.

Relations had not yet been fully restored. The rumours about the French-supplied nuclear reactor at Dimona that was to develop the Israeli bomb were just appearing at this time. The Israeli bomb and the West's (particularly France and the United States) connivance in its creation is comprehensively explored in Seymour Hersh, *The Samson Option* (London, Sceptre, 1991). The link to Algeria would seem to have more basis in fact, with the sudden collapse of the trial of the French spies two weeks after the Evian accords in March 1962. Nutting, *Nasser*, p. 313.

60. *FRUS 1961–63*, Vol. XVII, Doc. 155, 29 Dec. 1961.
61. PRO FO 371/165360, VG 1041/61, Beeley to Stevens, 28 Dec. 1961.
62. PRO FO 371/165360, VG 10451/1, Stevens to Beeley, 12 Jan. 1962.
63. PRO FO 371/165360, Beeley to FO, No. 10, 4 Jan. 1962.
64. PRO FO 371/165361, VG 1051/30, Arthur record of meeting with Sidqi and El Misri, 19 Jan. 1962. 'The Americans in December said that Nasser accused Hussein of being involved in both Syrian separation and Lebanon coup. Much of this he blames on British as power behind Jordanian foreign policy.' *FRUS 1961–63*, Vol. XVII, Doc. 161, 11 Jan. 1962.
65. PRO FO 371/165361, VG 1051/11, FO to Cairo, No. 91, 25 Jan. 1962.
66. PRO FO 371/165361, VG 1051/39, Beeley to FO, No. 18, 26 Feb. 1962.
67. *FRUS 1961–63*, Vol. XVII, Doc. 149, Attachment, 8 Dec. 1961.
68. PRO FO 371/165362, VG 1051/53, Record of conversation SOSFA and Dr Fawzi at Geneva, 21 Mar. 1962.
69. PRO FO 371/165362, VG 1051/56, Beeley–FO, Saving telegram, No. 38, 17 Apr. 1962.
70. PRO FO 371/165362, VG 1051/60, Beith submission, 19 Apr. 1962.
71. PRO FO 371/172857, VG 1011/1 H, Beeley–Lord Home, Annual Review for 1962, 24 Jan. 1963.
72. PRO CAB 128/36, Cabinet Conclusions, 41, 4, 22 June 1962.
73. Stephens, *Nasser*, p. 349.
74. In favour of this argument you have Fred Halliday, *Arabia without Sultans* (London, Penguin, 1974), pp. 65ff. Also see Nutting, *Nasser*, p. 301.
75. See Hasou, *Struggle for the Arab World*, pp. 118–24.

10

Aden, Yemen and the Decline of the Anglo-Egyptian Détente, 1962–63

THE OPPORTUNITY for Nasser to regain the initiative in the Arab world returned in September 1962 when pro-Nasser elements in the Yemen armed forces overthrew the Imam Badr in September 1962. The Yemen, even by the standards of the pre-oil boom Arabian Peninsula, was a particularly backward, quasi-feudal country.[1] The Imams, the religious and political rulers of the country, had attempted to avoid progress and revolution by allying themselves with Nasser in the Union of Arab States in 1958. Nasser abandoned this arrangement in 1961 and relations between Yemen and Egypt deteriorated. Therefore, while the Egyptian leader played no direct part in the revolution of 27 September 1962, he welcomed it.[2]

The British government most certainly did not welcome the revolution for it brought a regime of Nasser-influenced republicans to the borders of their South Arabian protectorates at a most inopportune time. The British government had just engineered – after bitter debate in the Aden legislature – the merger of their Aden Crown Colony with the hinterland protectorates (Federation of South West Arabia since 1959). Aden port had been a Crown Colony for over a century, while the hinterland consisted of emirates under British protection. Aden's military and strategic value had been minor until the 1950s, when the forced withdrawal of British forces from bases in Egypt, Kenya, Iraq, Sri Lanka and Jordan left it as the only significant British base in the Indian Ocean and the Middle East. It was thus the key base for intervention in the Gulf and as a staging post covering the route to Britain's defence responsibilities in the Far East. Aden was designated a fortress colony in the late 1950s and it was made clear that it was a long way from independence.[3]

Thus any potential Egyptian threat to Aden caused deep concern in British circles. In 1958, one of the sultans who 'enjoyed' British protection was toppled after he was found to be in treasonable communication with Cairo.[4] This set off disturbances in Aden that necessitated the maintenance of a state of emergency for 12 months. There was also the growth of a powerful trade union movement that demanded British withdrawal and proper measures of democratisation. There was but one check on the radicalism of the Adenis, which was that, while British rule was unpalatable, it was preferable to the Imam's tyrannical rule in North Yemen. The governor, William Luce, feared that if a progressive regime came to power in the Imamate the British position and base would be untenable.[5] By 1962 the Aden base had become, along with the United Kingdom and Singapore, one of the key links in the British global defence strategy. To solidify the British position, it was decided to merge Aden with the Federation of South Arabia. The Colonial Office evidently hoped that this would see the conservative sultans of the interior outweigh the radical Adenis. The day after the merger of 26 September 1962, pro-Nasser army officers toppled the Imam Badr.

Unfortunately for the republicans the coup had failed in its main objective – the assassination of the Imam. He was able to flee to the mountains and rally tribal support. The Saudi Arabian monarchy – understandably distressed at the thought of a progressive regime in the Arabian Peninsula – supported the Imam's attempt to overturn the coup. In response, the president of the newly proclaimed Yemen Arab Republic (YAR), Brigadier Sallal, appealed to Cairo for military aid. Nasser, presented with a 'golden opportunity to break out of his isolation' as well as the opportunity to come to grips with the Saudis who had supported the Syrian secession, deployed substantial numbers of Egyptian troops to the YAR.[6] By mid-November, some 8,000 Egyptian troops were deployed to Yemen. Nasser was prepared to pay the wages of pan-Arabism in the currency of Egyptian blood.[7]

The initial British reaction to the coup was cautious but decidedly fearful of the consequences of a Nasserite satellite in the Arabian Peninsula. Prince Hassan, the Imam's uncle and Yemen's representative at the United Nations, was given safe conduct to the Yemen border via Aden. The Governor of Aden, Sir Charles Johnston, wanted Hassan to be given a chance to establish himself before the British decided to recognise the new regime.[8] David Ormsby-Gore, the British Ambassador in Washington, informed the Americans that the British government was going to provide help to the royalists. The State Department were unhappy, fearing that it could increase the level of Egyptian support and that the 'ultimate result would be the weakening of the very position in that area the British seek to preserve by their support of Hassan'.[9] Macmillan first registered concern when the news of

Egyptian troop deployments became known, in a minute to Peter Thorneycroft, the Minister of Defence:

> I am worried about the Yemen since I believe it is a most serious situation. If things go wrong, we may be faced with the loss of Aden and therefore of the Gulf ... It would seem from the newspapers that Nasser might be intervening openly. I should be most grateful if you could arrange for the Chiefs of Staff to consider our military resources should we be driven to adopt an overt policy.[10]

The Americans had invested a great deal of time and effort in bilateral relations with Egypt. They had no wish to see this thrown away over such a marginal interest as the government of the Yemen. Their problem was that America's key regional allies, Saudi Arabia, Britain, Israel and Jordan, saw the Yemen intervention as a revival of Nasser's pan-Arab ambitions and a threat to their regimes and interests. Robert Komer argued that 'a compromise would be most worthwhile from US standpoint if it protected our investment in Nasser and at the same time preserved the vital interests of our friends'.[11] The British wanted to avoid the question of recognition and were deeply suspicious of American desires to open negotiations on a compromise with Nasser as well as the assurances that they had already received in Cairo. The Foreign Office suspected that Nasser had calculated 'that for the present at any rate, it is not in his interest to embarrass us too severely over Aden', and he was trying to 'at least partly stave off assistance to Hassan, while the United Arab Republic itself exerts itself to pour still more assistance into the Yemen to aid the Republican regime'. Harold Beeley was told to inform the Egyptians that Britain would not be recognising the new regime in the Yemen for a considerable period of time, as there was 'genuine perplexity' over who controlled the country.[12] The Foreign Office, however, was resigned to having to recognise the new regime sooner or later. Indeed Mr Gandy, the British Consul in Taiz, was instructed to see if he could extract a pledge from the republican government to respect frontiers and to abstain from subversion in South Arabia.[13] However, these first steps towards recognition were derailed by Egyptian air attacks on the British-protected state of Beihan. It was targeted because the Egyptians believed correctly that it was being used as a conduit for supplies to royalists. The Americans had come up with a proposal to resolve the Yemen crisis consisting of an end to Jordanian and Saudi support for the royalists in return for the phased withdrawal of Egyptian forces. Consequently, Lord Home now advised Macmillan that the time to recognise had come.[14] This was even accepted in the Prime Minister's office. Eventual recognition of the Yemen would have been the likeliest outcome if it were not for the arrival on the scene of the maverick Conservative MP, Lieutenant-Colonel Neil McClean. McClean, a right-winger with a distinguished war record, had hawkish views on the Middle East and on President Nasser. On a tour of the Middle East in the autumn of 1962, he was granted an audience with King Saud of Saudi Arabia in October 1962. The King warned McClean that the intervention in the Yemen was part of a wider plot by Nasser in which the Russians were involved. Therefore, Saud requested that the British withhold recognition and provide air support to the royalists. He also expressed a wish to restore diplomatic relations, which had been broken at the time of Suez.[15] Philip de Zulueta, Macmillan's private secretary, was particularly impressed by this communication. He pointed out to Macmillan that the minus of losing relations with Yemen would be more than made up for by restoration of ties with the Saudis.[16] In Cabinet on 6 November Macmillan decided to delay recognition until after the House of Commons debate on the merger of Yemen and the Federation on 16 November.

This week's delay proved fatal to the cause of recognition. The Colonial Office under Duncan Sandys was implacably opposed to recognition partly because South Arabia was the last major British colony of which the Colonial Office still retained a major input into the day-to-day running. After the Yemen leader, Brigadier Sallal, was reported making anti-British statements, Sandys asked Macmillan to 'indefinitely postpone the question of recognition by Britain'.[17] The Americans, however, remained resolute in seeking some sort of compromise despite UAR bombing attacks on Saudi towns, which were aimed at dissuading them from supplying the royalists. They became convinced of Nasser's good faith after he informed Ambassador Badeau that he was ready for a disengagement agreement.[18] Macmillan pleaded with Kennedy not to recognise. It was to no avail. Nasser accepted the United States plan for a mutual disengagement of forces on 21 November 1962. Egypt would withdraw its forces in return for the termination of Saudi/Jordanian and British support. Governor Johnston in Aden was not placated by the plan, which was 'too obviously slanted in Egypt's favour'. He urged pressure to be put on Washington 'to stop the Americans from making what looks like a major blunder in their own interests and in our own'.[19] The Americans were convinced that the deal that had been hammered out was 'acceptable to the United Kingdom'. Macmillan wanted more concessions, particularly a firm commitment from the Yemen to recognise South Arabia's frontiers. 'In present circumstances that's the least that they can do!' he told Home on 4 December.[20] Sallal, in a conversation with the American

Ambassador, refused to make any reference to Aden but agreed to respect the 1934 Treaty of S'ana, which had established the present frontier.[21]

By now opinion in the British government was running strongly against recognition. The Colonial Office warned that 'Recognition may seem to have been forced on Her Majesty's Government by the Americans and may discourage the rulers and the sheikhs in the protectorate, Saudi Arabia and the gulf, who (like all Arabs) will be tempted to join the stronger side.' It would also make it more difficult 'to give countenance to still more assistance to Royalist attempts to overthrow Sallal'.[22] The Americans went ahead and recognised on 19 December 1962. Britain was now the only Western power not to have recognised the Yemen Arab Republic. The Foreign Office experts on the Arab world were certain that the issue would have an eventual catastrophic effect on Britain's relations with the Arab world. Harold Beeley, in Cairo, warned of the folly of 'disclosing a preference for a Royalist victory at the moment when this seemed ever more unlikely'.[23] The Egyptians, who had been displaying uncustomary patience over the British decision on recognition, were now convinced that the British were once again supporting the conservative forces in the Middle East. Mohammad Heikal, the editor of *Al-Ahram* and a close adviser and confidant to President Nasser, warned Beeley that 'nothing would be easier than to undertake sabotage in Aden'. Heikal circumscribed his remarks by claiming that 'the last thing that Nasser wanted was our departure from the gulf. This would only result in chaos, of which the UAR would be an impotent spectator.'[24] Beeley was disturbed by the growing tension in Anglo-Egyptian relations. He was discomforted, in particular, by the forthcoming resumption of relations of Saudi Arabia without a reciprocal recognition of the YAR, as this would be seen in Cairo 'as a demonstration of support for the Saudis, of solidarity with the Royalists in the Yemen, and above all of hostility towards the United Arab Republic'.[25] The political officer for the Middle East forces was contemptuous of the Foreign Office which was 'too ready to turn the other cheek and keep quiet'.[26] Ambassador Ormsby-Gore in Washington was of the opinion that 'the Americans would allow Nasser to get away with a great deal before taking action against the UAR which would seriously impair their relationship with him'.[27] Despite this, the non-recognition party remained in the ascendant in Whitehall as was demonstrated by the paper that the Cabinet considered on 10 January 1963. The pro-recognition part of the paper warned of the danger of confronting Nasser. The anti-recognition paper (Tom Bower claims it was drafted by Colonel McClean) warned that recognition would be of an 'Egyptian puppet' and a 'humiliation for us'. As a result 'the Arab mentality would see recognition as a devastating blow to our prestige and authority'. The paper called for a repudiation of the American policy of appeasing Nasser:

> The same [Arab] elements, though bitterly critical of United States recognition, have accepted it as logical in terms of a United States policy aimed at building up President Nasser. They know that this is not the policy of Her Majesty's Government, and would see no logic in early United Kingdom recognition. We should thus risk losing our own identity in their eyes and they would feel that the independent United Kingdom policy in Arabia had been swallowed up in the Pax Americana.[28]

This part of the paper essentially repudiated British policy since 1958. While the Cabinet was probably not as extreme in its thinking as this, nonetheless it rejected recognition once more.[29] Gandy, the British representative in Taiz, was recalled and succeeded in persuading Lord Home that there was a reasonable chance of a relationship. The Colonial Office envisaged a different scenario. Governor Johnston wrote to Sandys in February: 'Seen from here, we and the Americans have the same objective. We both want to get Nasser out of Yemen.' The United States, as far as Johnston was concerned, wanted to achieve this by giving Nasser complete victory. Johnston implied that Britain should follow an alternative strategy of non-recognition of the YAR and help for the royalists:

> On the contrary, I believe that, if he finds that victory is unobtainable and the only possibilities are indefinite stalemate or defeat, all he needs to do is to invent a new Israeli threat to enable him to withdraw with honour apparently safe, on the basis of prior duty of defending Arabism against the Jews.[30]

The Americans took a diametrically opposing view warning that the consequences of non-recognition would likely see the YAR abandon its 'policy [of] restraint and [the] initiation [of] aggressive policy against Aden'. President Kennedy had already appealed directly to Macmillan to recognize the YAR as it would damage British relations with both the YAR and the UAR, 'without at the same time enhancing the prospect that the Royalists will win out'.[31] Macmillan finally came down on the side of non-recognition, a decision that was endorsed by the Cabinet on 14 February. The British mission was closed a few days later. Macmillan wrote in his diary that 'I think it's the best thing in the short term … in the long run it may bring us trouble.'[32]

A NEW BRITISH POLICY

There was a wide divergence in opinion in Whitehall about British policy towards Nasser. The 'Arabists' in the Foreign Office and the Cairo Embassy were deeply concerned at any anti-Nasser tilt. Beeley believed that Nasser was not the danger that some believed and 'would not mount a major offensive against our positions in the Arab world unless his interests urgently require it'. One who begged to differ was Harold Macmillan who annotated the above document with the comment, 'For Nasser put Hitler and it all rings familiar.'[33] Sir William Luce, the British Resident in the Gulf and a former Governor of Aden, was urging a rethink in British Middle Eastern policy. A Shell oil executive, Luce noted, had recently stated that world oil demand would double in the next 15 years. If such a scenario was true, Luce warned that the 'relative importance of Middle Eastern oil to Britain and the west will have increased very considerably by 1977'. He saw Nasserism as the main threat to the British position in the Gulf, 'though not in the military sense but as a subversive and revolutionary force which aims at undermining the stability of existing regimes and seeks to replace them with Nasserite regimes hostile to British or any other western influence in the area'. Therefore, he argued that

> We must follow a robust policy to maintain our own position and to contain 'Nasserism' by first, building up a position of moderately progressive anti-Nasser states in the Arabian peninsula, based for the most part on the principle of constitutional monarchy, and secondly, by reducing the undoubted attraction of President Nasser for the educated class in the Arab world by a program of social and economic evolution.[34]

Luce's argument did not find immediate favour with the Foreign Office, notably with Roger Stevens, the Deputy Undersecretary supervising the Foreign Office departments dealing with the Near East, who was still in favour of détente with Nasser, primarily because of his recent track record as a bulwark against communism. However, there were signs that the relative British disinterest in the Middle East was coming to an end. A circular telegram was issued to British missions warning them to emphasise that the United Kingdom did not have a policy of 'non-involvement' in the Middle East: 'There is therefore no question of Her Majesty's Government contracting out of the affairs of the Middle East, which continues to be an area of the highest economic importance.'[35] This was certainly a change in the tone, if not the substance, of British policy in the Middle East.

A combination of factors had led to the renewed British interest.

One was that it had to be made clear to Nasser that Britain would not be removed from its remaining positions in the Middle East. Another was the success of the Kuwait operation. The operation, if not exactly wiping the slate clean *vis-à-vis* Suez, had demonstrated that British military power was still a major factor in the Middle East. Furthermore, the Macmillan government had reoriented its foreign policy eastwards, with more emphasis on the global role from the later part of 1962. The realisation that Western strategic superiority had greatly diminished the Soviet threat in Europe had led many British government analysts to conclude that the major areas of instability were likely to be in Africa, East Asia and the Middle East. Phillip Darby notes that the 'events of the following three years strongly confirmed the government's strategic assessment. East of Suez one crisis succeeded another. British forces saw action in Malaya, in Arabia, and in Africa.'[36] The eastward orientation was only further confirmed by the rejection of the British application to join the EEC by General de Gaulle in January 1963. East of Suez or the global role was perhaps the foreign policy role that Britain, according to Dean Acheson's hurtful remarks (that Britain had lost an empire but not yet found a role), was searching for.

In spite of the new policy and the failure to recognise the Yemen, Anglo-Egyptian relations did not deteriorate as quickly as might have been expected. Instead it was the Americans and their carefully cultivated relationship with Nasser that ran into difficulties. Their first disengagement plan failed utterly. The stream of supplies to the royalists from Saudi Arabia continued while Egypt poured in more troops to save the republican cause. Nasser responded to the Saudi supplies with air attacks on Saudi border towns. In March 1963 the United States agreed to send an air force squadron to Saudi Arabia. In return they demanded an assurance that Saudi aid for the royalist cause would cease.[37] A more concrete disengagement agreement was hammered out on 29 April 1963. The deal was notably one-sided in favour of Nasser. He only had to make a token withdrawal of forces while the Saudis had to cease all supplies to the royalists. The British Cabinet expressed deep scepticism about the agreement.

The 'Nasserite' cause was on the march throughout the spring of 1963. On 8 February the increasingly erratic Qasim regime in Iraq was toppled by pro-Nasser elements of the Ba'ath party. There are some second-hand allegations of British and American covert involvement. This was followed by the overthrow of the Syrian regime in March. Both new governments were Ba'athist rather than pro-Nasser but both pledged to work for Arab unity with the Egyptian leader. In less than a year since the diplomatic isolation of the Arab League summit in Shtoura, Nasser, mainly by chance, had restored his position at the centre of the Arab world. The balance of power in the Middle East that had come about in 1959 had been swept away. The major losers in this transformation were the conservative powers in the Middle East: Saudi Arabia, Jordan and Britain. Macmillan was deeply concerned with the turn of events, as he made clear in his diary.[38]

Senior British and American officials met to discuss the Middle East situation in late April. The Americans held to their benign view of Nasser. The Foreign Office officials were also relatively cautious. The main division of opinion was over Arab unity, which the British officials saw as a danger to the supply of oil on the present reasonable terms. Furthermore, they were of the view that the 'present divided nature of the several oil producing countries of the Gulf constitutes the best safeguard to preclude "indecent behaviour" by any one of them in respect of the West's oil requirements'.[39]

These talks were followed by renewed crisis in the Middle East when a series of anti-government riots on the West Bank of Jordan threatened the stability of the Hussein government. A combination of factors created the gravest threat to King Hussein's rule since 1958. Nasser cranked up the 'Voice of the Arabs' once more and poured vitriol and propaganda against Hussein in revenge for this support for the royalist cause in Yemen. The upheaval in Iraq and Syria added to the problems for Hussein. As Zaki Shalom notes: 'By the beginning of March 1963 it was evident that Jordan was surrounded with a new, quite threatening, strategic environment.'[40] The signature of the Tripartite Agreement between Egypt, Iraq and Syria provided the spark in the middle of April. The crisis raised doubts in President Kennedy's mind about his pro-Nasser policy for the first time, leaving him wondering whether it was 'helping him pursue expansionist policies'. Some American officials wanted British troops to be used to save Hussein should this be necessary. The British Cabinet did not even consider the idea as was made clear to the Americans.[41] Jordan was now peripheral in British considerations in the region in comparison to the Persian Gulf. The crisis in the Middle East that spring blew over quickly. The unity agreement between Egypt, Iraq and Syria, which was announced with considerable fanfare in May, proved to be unworkable. King Hussein, not for the first time or the last, saw off the threat to his regime. With the Yemen disengagement plan in operation the Middle East appeared to be heading for a period of calm. This was a mirage.

In June 1963 a National Liberation Front (NLF), committed to the liberation of South Arabia, was established in S'ana in North Yemen under Egyptian patronage. With Egyptian and Yemeni aid, it began to plan a guerrilla war against Britain. The same month a group of British servicemen were held hostage by Yemen troops after accidentally straying over the border. They were only released after the payment of a ransom. At the same time it became clear that the Egyptian/Saudi disengagement agreement was not worth the paper it was written on. The British Cabinet, noting this on 27 June, agreed that there was no question of recognising the YAR in such circumstances. Then on 8 July, the *Daily Telegraph* reported a circumstantial report that Egyptian aircraft were dropping gas bombs against the Yemeni royalists. Immediately, Conservative backbenchers – many former members of the Suez Group not noted for their humanitarian concerns for the oppressed peoples of the third world – began raising the matter in the House of Commons. Macmillan was equally indignant and bemoaned the fact that, if Britain indulged in a twentieth of what Nasser was doing in the Yemen, in Aden, there would be Afro-Asian resolutions and condemnations in the United Nations. It was, therefore, of little surprise that the British government drew the attention of the United Nations to the claims. The War Office analysed some bomb fragments from an alleged Egyptian chemical device. The Foreign Office was unimpressed by the affair, noting that 'it was undesirable for HMG to become involved in polemics on the gas issue. We do not wish to wage, much less appear to wage, an anti Egyptian campaign and no specifically British interest is concerned.'[42] It would be easy to overstate the centrality of the Yemen crisis and the deterioration in Anglo-Egyptian relations in 1963. During the Kennedy–Macmillan summit in June 1963, 'the subject [of Yemen] was barely discussed'.[43] The test-ban treaty and most of all the Profumo scandal dominated the agenda in Britain that summer.

Anglo-American talks in July on the supply of oil from the Middle East revealed that William Luce's fears about oil supplies had been accepted. The British used the talks as a forum to 're-emphasise repeatedly that whereas Near Eastern oil was of substantial interest to the United States, for the UK it was a matter of overwhelming importance'. The British desired stronger language in the joint conclusions, which the United States opposed, as it 'would have drawn [the USA] into a position of appearing to oppose Arab unity irrespective of how conceived'.[44] While some opinion in the Foreign Office, notably Frank Brenchley, Head of the Arabian Department, favoured a move towards recognition of the Yemen, Lord Home, influenced by the failure of the disengagement agreement and the evidence of increasing Egyptian troops in Yemen, was now a leading opponent of recognition.[45]

The Americans were hardening their pro-Nasser position. Robert Komer, special assistant at the US National Security Council, had now moved to a firmly pro-Nasser policy. Frank Brenchley warned in November 1963 that the Kennedy administration 'was almost as committed as Nasser to the preservation of a republican form of government in the Yemen, regardless of whether or not that is the will of the inhabitants'.[46] Hopes that the poison gas allegations would embarrass Nasser were dashed when the War Office investigation of bomb fragments proved nothing. This incident merely irritated the Egyptians. What concerned them far more was the steady stream of supplies to the royalists through Beihan. Some of this had come from Saudi Arabia to avoid UN monitoring but much of it was being sourced from Aden with the co-operation of the new High Commissioner, Kennedy Trevakis. He believed that a Nasserite victory in Yemen would endanger the base facilities at Aden. Contrary opinion, he argued, overlooked the 'human instinct to exploit success, and the compelling attraction which Aden would have to both the Egyptians and the Republicans'.[47]

Trevakis appears to have pursued with the full acquiescence of his boss, Duncan Sandys, an independent foreign policy, without the knowledge of the Foreign Office, which included covert support for and arming of the royalists.[48] The most authentic source is the memoirs of Sir Peter de la Billière, the British Commander during the Gulf War, which describe his modest role in the procurement of British mercenaries and arms for the Yemeni royalist cause. The arms supply was masterminded by Trevakis's adjutant, Flight Lieutenant Anthony Boyle, with the co-operation of a motley crew of ex-SAS servicemen, organised by war heroes such as David Stirling. It began sometime in early 1963. The mercenaries – never afraid to exaggerate their own achievements, but who never numbered more than a couple of dozen – were convinced that their actions broke the back of the Egyptian army in Yemen and/or contributed to the defeat of Nasser in the Six Day War.[49] Adam Curtis in his television series *The Mayfair Set* describes the actions of Stirling and the others as the first example of the 'privatisation' of British foreign policy as its worldwide role wound down in the mid-1960s.[50] My initial supposition was that the operation was done with only low-level involvement of the British government but it would seem that the operation had the tacit acquiescence of virtually the entire British Cabinet. Nigel Fisher, Parliamentary Undersecretary of State for the Colonies, recalls Macmillan authorising 'very substantial help to the Royalists'.[51] McClean, who appears to have been the linkman with the mercenaries, was closely associated with the Minister for Aviation, Julian Amery. Amery, as Macmillan's son-in-law, was hardly likely to have been operating without some sort of approval from the top.[52] In the PRO files, there are hints about what is going on but no great revelations.

In the late autumn and early winter of 1963, Nasser watched as an old adversary, Macmillan, and a recent friend, Kennedy, both left the world stage. In London, Macmillan, after the black year of the Profumo scandal and the Skybolt/EEC disasters, had by October made a political recovery of sorts. He decided that he would continue in office and fight the next election. However, fate took a hand again and the Prime Minister was stricken with what appeared to be a life-threatening prostate condition. In fact he recovered quickly and lived another 23 years. He resigned as Prime Minister on 9 October. In a rather surprising choice, he was replaced by the Foreign Secretary, Lord Home, who resigned his peerage and became 'plain' Sir Alec Douglas-Home. The end of the Macmillan era was followed just over a month later (22 November) by the brutal assassination of President Kennedy in Dallas. An era in Western politics was at an end. As D.R. Thorpe notes, the 'golden days of Mac and Jack were over and a more uncertain period began. Lyndon Baines Johnson, the political operator from Texas, and Alec Douglas-Home, the border aristocrat were temperamentally poles apart.'[53] More importantly, the death of Kennedy removed the West's greatest suitor for the loyalties of nationalists such as Nasser.

NOTES

1. See Fred Halliday, *Arabia without Sultans*, pp. 90–104.
2. The background is in Edgar O'Ballance, *The War in the Yemen* (London, Faber, 1971), pp. 10–35.
3. See Lord Lloyd's statement to the Aden Legislative Council in 1956, cited in Phillip Darby, *British Defence Policy East of Suez*, p. 211. Also Colonial Secretary Lennox-Boyd's 1958 comments on Aden's importance to Commonwealth defence in A.N. Porter and A. Stockwell (eds), *British Imperial Policy and Decolonisation, 1938–64*, Vol. II, *1951–64* (London, Macmillan, 1989), pp. 495–6.
4. PRO CAB 128/32, Cabinet Conclusions, 53.2, 10 July 1958.
5. Barbour-Paul, *Britain's Relinquishment of Power*, p. 73.
6. Hasou, *Struggle for the Arab World*, p. 139.
7. O'Ballance, *War in the Yemen*, p. 85.
8. PRO PREM 11/3877, New York to FO, No. 1431, 27 Sept. 1962, Johnston (Aden)–Colonial Office (CO), 3 Oct. 1962.
9. *FRUS 1961–63*, Vol. XVIII, Doc. 76, 9 Oct. 1962.
10. PREM 11/3877, PM M 271/62, Macmillan to Thorneycroft, 6 Oct. 1962.
11. *FRUS 1961–63*, Vol. XVIII, Doc. 79, 12 Oct. 1962.
12. PRO PREM 11/3877, FO to Cairo, 15 Oct. 1962.
13. PRO PREM 11/3877, FO to Taiz, 17 Oct. 1962.
14. PRO PREM 11/3877, PM 62/139, Home to Macmillan, 25 Oct. 1962.
15. PRO PREM 11/3878, Aden No. 934 to SOS Colonies, Sandys, 26 Oct. 1962 and Parkes (Amman) to FO, No. 1206, 1 Nov. 1962.
16. PRO PREM 11/3878, de Zulueta to Macmillan, 7 Nov. 1962.
17. PRO PREM 11/3878, Sandys to Macmillan, 38/62, 10 Nov. 1962.
18. *FRUS 1961–63*, Vol. XVIII, Doc. 96, 12 Nov. 1962.
19. PRO PREM 11/3878, Johnston to SOS Colonies, No. 1076, 13 Nov. 1962.
20. PRO PREM 11/4356, M 327/62, Macmillan to Home, 4 Dec. 1962.
21. PRO PREM 11/4356, Washington to FO, No. 3114, 11 Dec. 1962.

22. PRO PREM 11/4356, Prime Minister's Note, Top secret, 12 Dec. 1962.
23. PRO PREM 11/4356, Beeley to FO, 17 Dec. 1962.
24. PRO PREM 11/4356, Cairo–FO, No. 11, 6 Jan. 1963.
25. PRO PREM 11/4356, Beeley (Cairo)–FO, No. 16, 8 Jan. 1963.
26. PRO FO 371/168625, POMEF to Bushell (FO), 27 Dec. 1962.
27. PRO FO 371/172869, VG 103145/1, Ormsby-Gore to Home, 8 Jan. 1963.
28. PRO CAB 139/112, 3, Memo by the SOSFA, 10 Jan. 1963.
29. PRO CAB 128/38, Cabinet Conclusions, 10 Jan. 1963.
30. PRO PREM 11/4357, Johnson to Sandys, No. 155, 8 Feb. 1963.
31. *FRUS 1961–63*, Vol. XVIII, Doc. 156, and Note 3, p. 347.
32. Diary entry, 17 Feb. 1963, in Macmillan, *Pointing the Way*, pp. 275–6.
33. PRO PREM 11/4173, VG 1051/6, Beeley to Home, 25 Feb. 1963, with Macmillan's annotations.
34. PRO CO 1055/61, B 1052/3/G, Luce (Bahrain) to Roger Stevens, 17 Jan. 1963.
35. PRO CO 1055/61, Stevens to Luce, 8 Feb. 1963. PRO FO 371/172872, VG 1051/7, Beith addressed to Chancery, 6 Mar. 1963.
36. Darby, *British Defence Policy East of Suez*, p. 215.
37. See Little, 'New Frontier on the Nile', pp. 521–4.
38. Macmillan Diary, D 48, Second series, Vol. 21, 11 Mar. 1963.
39. The talks are in the following airgram: USNA, State to London, No. 2119, Pol UK–US 1963, Box 4081.
40. Z. Shalom, *The Superpowers, Israel and the Future of Jordan 1960–63* (Brighton, Sussex Academic Press, 1999), p. 48, and Dann, *King Hussein*, pp. 129–34, for the rest of the crisis.
41. *FRUS 1961–63*, Vol. XVIII, Doc. 222, p. 484. *FRUS 1961–63*, Vol. XVIII, Note 1, p. 487. PRO CAB 128/38, Cabinet Conclusions, 29, 3, 2 May 1963.
42. PRO CAB 128/38, Cabinet Conclusions, 43, 27 June 1963. The *Daily Telegraph* weighed in with a suitably outraged editorial in the paper. The issue was raised in Cabinet twice but the minutes are not very discursive. PRO CAB 128/38, Cabinet Conclusions, 46, 11 July 1963 and Cabinet Conclusions, 47, 18 July 1963. Diary entry for 16 Aug. 1963 in Macmillan, *At the End of the Day*, p. 277. See PRO FO 371/168804, BM 1015/363, FO guidance telegram, No. 478, 16 Aug. 1963, PRO FO 371/168804, BM 1015/365, FO to Bamarko, No. 111, 9 Aug. 1963.
43. USNA, Conference Files, 2275, Box 318, Memcon Birch Grove, 30 June 1963 and Memcon, 28 June 1963.
44. *FRUS 1961–63*, Vol. XVIII, Doc. 291, 5 July 1963.
45. PRO FO 371/168804, BM 1051/376, Brenchley minute, 23 Aug. 1963 and Home annotations.
46. *FRUS 1961–63*, Vol. XVIII, Doc. 329, Komer paper, 20 Sept. 1963. PRO CO 1055/2, Brenchley paper, 19 Nov. 1963.
47. PRO FO 371/168816, BM 1024/1/G, Trevakis (Aden) to CO, No. 19, Extracts, 14 Oct. 1963.
48. See Bloch and Fitzgerald, *British Intelligence and Covert Action*, pp. 128–30 and Tom Bower, *The Perfect English Spy* (London, Mandarin, 1995), pp. 251–4.
49. Sir Peter de la Billière, *Looking for Trouble* (London, Harper Collins, 1994), pp. 202–11.
50. *The Mayfair Set,* Episode 1, Broadcast BBC2, 16 July 1999.
51. See the Nigel Fisher Interview Transcript, MSS Brit Empire S.452(3) 46, Rhodes House Library, Oxford, cited in S.C. Smith, 'Revolution and Reaction: South Arabia in the Aftermath of Yemeni Revolution', in K. Federowich and M. Thomas (eds), *Diplomacy and Colonial Retreat* (London, Frank Cass, 2000), p. 201.
52. Bower, *Perfect English Spy*, pp. 251–4.
53. Thorpe, *Alec Douglas-Home*, p. 340.

—11—

Confrontation with Nasser, 1964

THE SUDDEN and dramatic changes in leadership in Britain and the United States in the later part of 1963 caused a major change in the West's relationship with Nasser. Alec Douglas-Home had been Foreign Secretary for just over three years before attaining the premiership. He was a cold warrior suspicious of the Russians and Nasser alike. As Commonwealth Secretary, he was in the 'inner councils' during Suez from the opening of the crisis to the fall of Eden and remained a firm supporter of the operation.[1] A virtual stranger to domestic and economic matters, he put forward, as his main political virtue, a willingness to protect Britain's interests abroad. During his time as Foreign Secretary, Anglo-Egyptian relations had for the most part been cool if in the main correct. Home was, as we have seen, suspicious of some of the initiatives put forward by his civil servants to improve Anglo-Egyptian relations. Initially during the Yemen War, he had counselled moderation in British policy but his minutes and comments on Foreign Office memorandums suggest that his position was hardening against Nasser as 1963 wore on.

The new Foreign Secretary, R.A. Butler, was a liberal Tory. He was the ideas man who more than anyone else had presided over the rebirth of the Conservative party after the 1945 election debacle. He had a reputation for indecisiveness and as an appeaser. This reputation was initially garnered as Lord Halifax's deputy at the Foreign Office at the height of appeasement but confirmed during his time at the Treasury and his vacillation during Suez. Macmillan was determined that he would never make the top job and set up the leadership for Home in order to thwart Butler. Butler was to find himself aligned against the Prime Minister, the Defence Secretary and the Colonial Office in the next few months over policy towards Nasser. In the United States, the failure to achieve an Egyptian withdrawal from the Yemen or any meaningful arms control measures had damaged US–UAR relations. Moreover, the assassination of President Kennedy had removed a vital channel of personal messages to Nasser. This was a major setback. President Johnson was noticeably less indulgent of the

Egyptian leader. A politician to the fingertips, he was by electoral considerations and by personal friendship pro-Israeli. However, this did
not mean that he actively sought confrontation with Nasser. Indeed he
and many in his administration were more disturbed by the behaviour
of the British than of the Egyptians during the 1964 crisis.

Upon acceding to the premiership, Douglas-Home ordered a review
of British policy towards the Yemen. The Foreign and Colonial Office
were, for once, in agreement that the present stalemate in the Yemen
suited British interests. The only question for discussion was, as Oliver
Wright the Prime Minister's private secretary pointed out, 'whether we
need to do any more at the moment to keep the situation on the boil'.[2]
What was most worrying to the British government was the increasing
signs that an Egyptian-backed campaign against British rule in South
Arabia was taking shape. In the last months of 1963, there was increasing guerrilla activity in the Radfan region of the Federation, as well as
numerous politically motivated strikes in Aden. Trevakis wanted
increased development in the Federation to combat growing radicalism. Sandys, indeed, wanted to go further and cede independence to
the Federation in return for satisfactory assurances about the retention
of the base. Trevakis was leaving for a conference in London to discuss
this plan on 10 December 1963 when an assassination attempt with a
grenade injured 50 bystanders and killed Sir George Henderson, one
of his chief advisers. This led to the immediate imposition of a state of
emergency and the abandonment of the conference.[3]

The British strongly suspected Yemeni and Egyptian involvement.
Moreover, it was the signal for the beginning of an urban guerrilla war
aimed at driving the British out of the Federation. Sandys, in the House
of Commons, rebuffed the pro-Nasser Conservative MP, William Yates,
claiming that he 'would be happy to see Aden swallowed up by the
Yemen and ruled from Cairo'.[4] To Cairo, this comment seemed to be a
return of old British attitudes. It led Nasser to use his strongest anti-
British rhetoric since the 1950s at his Evacuation Day speech on 22
December. He began to gear up for a major anti-British offensive in the
New Year strengthened by a successful Arab summit in Cairo.

CONFRONTATION 1964

The British began to worry. Frank Brenchley informed the American
Embassy of 'accumulating evidence' that the YAR/UAR was about to
step up subversion in the South Arabian Federation (SAF). There was
a 'long list of intelligence reports submitted from Aden indicating
YAR/UAR [were] arming more Radfan tribesmen and ... also reports

that Yemeni terrorists plan [to] infiltrate into Aden, ostensibly as refugees from Yemen, with mission of eliminating Aden VIPs'. There were further alarming reports of increased movements of UAR troops to the southern part of Yemen 'which could mean direct Brit–UAR military confrontation in that area'.[5] However, it was off-the-cuff comments by Douglas-Home in Canada on 10 February 1964, expressing his regret that the Americans, in 1956, had not 'allowed us to deal with the Egyptians as we'd wanted to', that were to spark the most serious Anglo-Egyptian crisis since the Iraqi revolution. Nasser, according to the British Embassy in Cairo, 'was deeply hurt by what the PM had said' and had 'conceded that those who have argued that Britain (or the present British Government at any rate) is implacably hostile to him are right'.[6] Hurt or not, Nasser used the opportunity, in his Merger Day speech on 22 February, to launch a major attack on British Middle Eastern policy. After declaring Britain responsible 'morally and historically' for the creation of Israel, Nasser claimed that Douglas-Home's comments on Suez had opened 'Arab eyes to the dangers threatening them from British bases by which they were surrounded'. He claimed that the renewal of the Libyan base lease 'would expose the Arab nation and particularly the UAR to further imperialist dangers … Therefore, their bases in the Middle East must be liquidated.'[7]

The effects of Nasser's speech were quickly felt; the Libyan government requested the immediate review of their defence pact with Britain and made it clear that they sought the closure of the base. Foreign Secretary Rab Butler warned the Cabinet of the need to preserve over-flight and other transit rights in Libya. The Cabinet noted that 'the Egyptian Government were intensifying their measures to compel us to evacuate our bases in the Mediterranean and the Middle East. If they succeed in securing our eviction from the Libyan base our position would be seriously weakened.'[8] American co-operation was to be sought on how to oppose this new threat from Nasser. Unfortunately, the Americans considered the British the authors of their own misfortune. Secretary of State Rusk called in British Ambassador Harlech and urged a rethink in British policy, noting that the impression was being created that 'HMG was actively supporting restoration [of the] Imamate, inducing YAR/UAR [to] "go after" HMG in South Arabia'. Harlech admitted that some supplies were going through the Federation to the royalists but he 'emphasised that Her Majesty's Government's policy was to discourage this private enterprise which was a very amateur operation, because they realised that infiltration from the Federation led to retaliation'.[9]

Within Whitehall there was mounting frustration with Nasser. The UAR air force carried out increasing numbers of over-flights of the

Federation. On 13 March, a YAR air attack on South Arabian territory brought an outcry from Federal rulers that the British were not protecting them. Both Trevakis and the GOC Aden, General Harrington, strongly urged retaliation. This was initially rejected in Whitehall. However, Harrington was in London on 25 March when the issue arose again. Thereupon, with Butler alone opposing, UK ministers decided in principle that retaliation should take place when and if YAR aircraft again took hostile action in SAF territory. Within two days Harrington requested permission to launch a retaliatory air strike on Yemen territory after a UAR helicopter strafed a South Arabian village. Permission was granted and an attack was made on the fort at Harib near the international frontier.[10]

The fort was badly damaged and considerable casualties were inflicted. The Arab League swiftly condemned the attack and member states were urged to 'reconsider their relations with [the UK]' and 'that they should press for the liquidation of British bases in the Arab area'. Butler suggested to Home that the time had come to press for constructive measures to ease tensions on the border. However, the imposition of UN monitors could not be contemplated 'unless we had taken a firm decision that Federal territory was not to be used for aid to the Royalists'. However, a British refusal 'would be taken by all concerned as proof that it is we rather than the Yemenis who have something to hide'.[11]

The Americans were intensely annoyed by the British action. The American Ambassador to the Yemen described the attack as 'anachronistic at this juncture of history in [the] Middle East'. The actions of Trevakis made it very difficult for the United States to continue to represent British interests in the Yemen as his ability to influence the UAR to exercise restraint was 'practically nil as result of gradual escalation [of] British covert actions in Yemen'. The Egyptians moved swiftly to secure United Nations condemnation of the air attack. Adlai Stevenson, the American UN Ambassador, was in favour of voting for the resolution. It was only the intervention of Secretary Rusk that prevented this. President Johnson informed Douglas-Home that he had made the decision reluctantly on the grounds of Western solidarity. He 'had no illusions about Nasser or the mischievous game he is playing but I quite frankly doubt that at this point in time abrupt challenges to the Arabs are useful to our joint interests'. Robert Komer, the architect of the American pro-Nasser policy, was distinctly unhappy, suspecting that the 'Tories think that LBJ team an easier mark than New Frontier. I think they're wrong.'[12] Oliver Wright, Douglas-Home's private secretary, wrote a thoughtful minute on the Harib incident. While he agreed that the strike was right, he warned of the dangers of falling out with the United States and of exaggerating the danger from Nasser.[13]

The resolution on the Harib incident passed at the UN as Britain joined the Americans in abstaining rather than vetoing it. It did nothing to lessen the growing confrontation in Southern Arabia between Britain and Egypt. There was mounting evidence of YAR/UAR-backed subversion in the Federation. Trevaskis, on 16 April, reported 'reliable information' that the Egyptian Commander-in-Chief in the Yemen was endeavouring to organise a campaign of terrorism and sabotage in Aden. The British informed the American Embassy that they had captured some official YAR documents which 'considerably aroused UK Ministers'. One document was purportedly written by the YAR Chief of Staff and concerned the smuggling of 12 high-explosive bombs for use against senior Federation and Aden officials.[14] Douglas-Home wanted to respond. The objective of British policy in the Yemen should be to secure the withdrawal of the UAR influence from the Yemen, or, 'if we cannot achieve a victory of this kind, at least tie down as many UAR troops as possible in the Yemen while maintaining the morale of our friends in Southern Arabia and their ability to hit back on a scale which will prevent Nasser from winning outright'. The Prime Minister was not sure that Britain had 'exhausted all the possibilities open to us as regards both attributable and unattributable action'. He suggested that Britain's options 'should be set down, preferably in ascending order of "intensity" – so that we can take definite decisions on how far we are prepared to go'.[15]

According to one account, that of the Foreign Office Deputy Under-secretary, Stewart Crawford, to American Ambassador David Bruce, there were serious splits in the Cabinet over the issue: 'Sandys, Thorneycroft and Prime Minister believe situation sufficiently serious to require more vigorous responses. Latter school also strongly influenced by Tory Backbench pressures.'[16] Butler, for all his moderation, was willing to press for a cut in American aid to Nasser and even limited counter-subversive measures across the frontier. Thorneycroft, the Minister of Defence, proposed much bolder measures to deal with the cross-border threat:

It is important to tackle these activities at their source. To this purpose I recommend the following action.

a) Tribal revolts should be covertly organised in those areas adjacent to the Federation from which subversive activities are being launched.

b) Deniable action should be taken to sabotage intelligence centres and kill personnel engaged in anti-British activities (including the Egyptian intelligence HQ at Taiz).

c) Covert anti Egyptian propaganda in the Yemen should be intensified.[17]

President Nasser was equally prepared to escalate. On 23 April, he made his first visit to Yemen and attacked British policy and bases once more. This further increased the determination of Britain to strike back. Butler went to Washington tasked with the mission of converting the United States to an anti-Nasser crusade. He informed Rusk that the events of the last few months had convinced him that 'there was now no doubt that Nasser was a major enemy of the United Kingdom and I believed of the United States also'. Butler wanted to formulate a joint anti-Nasser policy with the United States. His position was that Britain 'was not proposing to take part overtly in the Yemen war. Nevertheless, we were quite unwilling to allow the UAR to get away with the present situation, and we would not wish to see the Royalist cause go under.'[18] Butler also pointed out that his presentation would have been more radical if he were 'in the hands of the extremists in the Cabinet'.[19]

Secretary Rusk was becoming more sympathetic to the British point of view but, in the place that mattered, the NSC, Robert Komer considered the British were 'grossly over reacting'. He was strongly against any British covert attack on Nasser on the grounds that 'they can't win':

> In sum the Brits can't have thought through their proposals. They'd stand to gain nothing but trouble. And this to bail out a lame duck cabinet whose policy might get reversed come October. What to do? Unless we turn the UK off hard, I'm afraid we'll get whipsawed … So the best defence may be strong attack.[20]

Butler's encounter with President Johnson had an element of farce about it. Butler was hardly able to get a word in about Britain's *bête noire*, Nasser, owing to the fact that the President was too busy haranguing the Foreign Secretary for British trading links with America's public enemy number one, Fidel Castro. Butler was not completely despondent about his trip. He was especially encouraged by the attitude of Secretary Rusk and the State Department who had told him privately that they were 'squaring up to an assessment of their position *vis-à-vis* Nasser'.[21] The State Department may have been influenced by their suspicion that the Soviets were behind the anti-British offensive. A State Department intelligence memorandum assessed that the British position in the Near and Middle East, specifically the base at Aden and the South Arabian Federation, 'appears to have become the principal target of Soviet policy in the region'. They were using propaganda as well as advising their Arab friends to concentrate on Britain rather than Israel or the reactionary regimes.[22]

The American Ambassador in Cairo, John Badeau, recognised a distinct strategy behind Nasser's anti-British offensive. He assessed that it had three main objectives, in the following order of importance:

(1) bring about Saudi recognition of the YAR, thereby permanently securing Yemen's northern border, by converting Yemen conflict into anti-imperialist crusade; (2) put momentum behind efforts to consolidate republic by giving it new dimension, i.e. liberation Arab south; (3) punish British sufficiently hard to get them to shut off supplies from Beihan and at same time show them that they cannot make punitive raids against Yemeni territory without paying political consequences.

Badeau was gravely concerned that the British would overreact to the Egyptian President's challenge as 'Nasser has shown in past he will not hesitate risk creation [of] conflagration rather than be placed in position of appearing to back down to bigger power'. Badeau urged that the British should be told to exercise restraint. He also deplored using the threat of withdrawal of food aid against Nasser, as it was the basis of American influence in Cairo.[23] Rusk agreed with the analysis offered from Cairo but he insisted that Badeau had to make representations on behalf of the British. Rusk hoped that 'a combination of US diplomacy, British restraint and acceleration of process of Adeni "constitutional advance" (which British officials here last week hinted at) will check current trend toward erosion of British position'.[24] The American Ambassador Badeau held two meetings soon after with Nasser and the new Egyptian Foreign Minister, Mahmoud Riad, in an effort to ameliorate the situation. In the first Nasser made it clear that his verbal attack in Yemen on the British position in the region was motivated by the fact that the UAR had 'completely reliable and convincing evidence' of British arms, money and military support to Yemeni dissidents flowing across the southern border. President Nasser added: 'Because of this our men are being killed and I cannot accept this, hence my attack on the British.' Nasser was in 'lessons of the past' territory as well.

In general, the present UK Government under Lord Home seems to have reverted to the Eden outlook. Macmillan honestly tried to make a fresh start, letting bygones be bygones. Ever since Ottawa speech it has been clear to UAR that Home's Government has turned its back on conciliatory Macmillan policy and is now acting in Eden mood.[25]

In the second meeting Badeau made it clear that the United States had an interest in the maintenance of the British position in Aden and the Gulf on the grounds that they were a source of stability in the area. Foreign Minister Riad rejected the argument that the British were a source of stability, claiming that, while the British position might have served a useful purpose up to ten years ago, this was no longer the case. Britain, he strongly argued, had taken 'no real steps to announce principle of self determination and independence, little economic progress had taken place, and essentially the area from Muscat to Aden is no different than it had been two hundred years ago when British power first appeared'. The central problem that Riad saw was that Britain was basically hostile to the UAR. The steps that Riad considered necessary to allow the UAR and the UK to 'sit down, talk things over, and plan process of adjustment and restoration of good relations' were a British statement of intent that they planned to withdraw and elections in the South Arabian Federation. He saw a time scale of six months to independence rather than the slower one foreseen in London.[26]

The American refusal to support any vigorous counter-measures caused a rethink in London. The Colonial Office and MOD line, which had been in the ascendant over the more moderate line of the Foreign Office, lost ground. The Prime Minister contemplated getting rid of the increasingly troublesome Trevakis. Douglas-Home noted that, 'whether we like it or not, we have to face the fact that the escalation of the Aden–Yemen trouble always rebounds to Nasser's advantage and not to ours, since it always rallies to him popular support, not least in Aden itself'.[27] Consequently, the Defence and Overseas Policy Committee decided to defer a decision on the supply of arms to the royalist cause on 8 May.[28] Emotions in Britain were heightened by rumours of the beheading of two British soldiers in the Radfan and that they were on display in a Yemen town. This prevented the Labour Opposition from being too critical of Douglas-Home. This was rather fortunate as the top-secret support for the royalists was exposed when correspondence belonging to Boyle, aide-de-camp to Trevakis, was captured by the Egyptians and published on 1 May in *Al-Ahram*. It was subsequently published in the *Sunday Times* in July leading to questions in the House of Commons to Douglas-Home and unconvincing denials.[29] The revelations may have further undermined the Prime Minister's confidence in covert means of getting at Nasser.

However, coming to terms with Nasser was easier said than done. The Radfan, the most troublesome area of South Arabia, exploded into rebellion in early May. It was estimated that 200 Egyptian-trained guerrillas were leading some 500 NLF rebels. The guerrillas, according to Frank Brenchley, were equipped, uniformed and led by obviously trained officers on a scale not before encountered. Harold Beeley was instructed to seek an appointment with Nasser and to tell Nasser that 'HMG is well informed of degree of UAR involvement in encouraging dissidence in SAF'. Nevertheless, Britain, according to Brenchley, 'remained ready to reduce tensions on the basis of Security Council resolution. It favours demilitarised zone or delimitation, but this is of no value unless Nasser calls off subversion. Failing this, UK will be compelled to defend itself.' Brenchley concluded by describing the various counter-subversive measures that the British had planned.[30] Harold Beeley did not anticipate any positive results from a meeting with Nasser. 'It might indeed be thoroughly unpleasant', he cautioned.[31] Indeed Beeley had to settle for an unpleasant and unproductive meeting with Foreign Minister Riad, which featured the traditional stream of accusations and counter-accusations. Riad informed the Americans that the UAR required independence within six months and elections in South Arabia to call off the anti-British campaign.[32]

Meanwhile, the Colonial Secretary authorised the supply of certain quantities of both arms and money to royalists on 28 May. It is not clear whether this was a government or a departmental decision as the only evidence is a short note in the Defence Secretary's private office files from July.[33] This was combined with a major deployment of British troops to crush the revolt in the Radfan – an effort that succeeded to a considerable extent. However, the crushing of the revolt required the deployment to Radfan for the rest of the year of much of the British force in Aden. By tying down the Aden force and preventing it from being deployed elsewhere the NLF and the Egyptian intelligence service removed a good deal of the *raison d'etre* for the base with the Radfan rebellion.[34]

The strain between the Colonial Office and the Foreign Office was on full display in an extraordinary meeting between Sandys, Butler and George Ball, American Undersecretary of State, on 8 June. In what David Bruce described as a 'strong but somewhat rambling presentation', Sandys demanded reassurance that Britain still had American support in Arabia. Sandys

> complained that HMG has at times felt a bit unhappy at what he described as our detached attitude. He sought to equate [the] British position in Aden with US concern over Cuba. HMG, he continued, is facing a difficult situation. Arms and mines are being smuggled into SAF. HMG and the SAF are being attacked on Radios

Cairo and S'ana. Image is being projected that US friendship with Nasser and support of YAR is more substantial than what US is doing for SAF. He hoped US might be sympathetic re Aden, not only in private, but also in public. US position re Aden should be 'a little more robust'. He hoped USG would not merely take impartial position between [the] two sides.

Sandys then attacked the United Nations, which 'freely criticises HMG, but does nothing to stop UAR subversive activities'. He 'thought that we ought to consider trying to get a Security Council resolution condemning the UAR even if we get voted down in the process'. After Sandys had left, an annoyed Butler apologised, declaring that the Colonial Secretary 'had spoken inappropriately in thus criticising US position re Aden'.[35]

It was singularly unfortunate that the Anglo-Egyptian crisis should have coincided with the departure to a new posting of Sir Harold Beeley. Beeley had probably made a greater contribution to Anglo-Egyptian relations than any other person. He held a final meeting with Nasser on 16 June. It was inevitably dominated by the crisis in Anglo-Egyptian relations. Nasser listed his grievances against Britain. The raid on Harib, he declared, was a major turning point: 'Aden had not been on his agenda before these events, but a small power like the UAR would not permit attacks to be made on it without retaliating.' The Egyptian President did not deny his responsibility for the turmoil in the Radfan. He said that 'it had always been within his capacity to harm us in Aden, and that after Harib there was no reason why he should not do so'. He refused to countenance demilitarisation of the frontier as the YAR did not recognise it. The meeting concluded with Nasser saying: 'Sometimes … I feel that the West hates us.' However, he did agree to continue discussions, and a dialogue of sorts was maintained throughout the summer, but it did not make very much progress.[36] The same day as that meeting, the foreign affairs debate in the House of Commons devoted considerable time to the subject of Nasser and the Middle East. Harold Wilson raised the question of British support for the royalists. He warned that peace and stability in the Middle East could only come when 'we shall have come to terms with the facts of Middle Eastern life, which include President Nasser'.[37]

The beginning of July saw a considerable change in the attitude of the Egyptians. After an announcement from Sandys that Britain would, subject to assurances about the base, grant independence to South Arabia by 1968, Nasser told the diplomatic correspondent of the *Observer*, Robert Stephens, that he would be willing to accept a British staging post at Aden. While the Foreign Office saw nothing new in the offer, the Cairo Embassy believed it marked somewhat of a new departure for Nasser.[38] Whitehall remained split over what to do. The Defence Secretary, Peter Thorneycroft, was in no mood for compromise. He assessed that in 'the foreseeable future the only threat to our control [of South Arabia] will come from President Nasser'. Strict logic decreed that there could be 'no half measures in dealing with him and we must either seek a thoroughgoing accommodation with him, or we must oppose him without inhibition, doing whatever is necessary to protect our interests'. While acknowledging that 'strict logic' could be 'a dangerous guide for political action', Thorneycroft urged that negotiating with Nasser could not take place until Britain had strengthened its own position and weakened his. To achieve this he recommended 'a sharp increase in deniable support in terms of both arms and money for the Royalists'.[39] The Foreign Office was severely critical of the Thorneycroft paper. Frank Brenchley felt that there were slightly better prospects in the alternative course of keeping up in Cairo the private dialogue started at the farewell interview of H. Beeley and Nasser and since continued at lower levels by the chargés d'affaires. Brenchley noted that it could not 'hope to lance the Yemen/South Arabian abscess but may prevent or delay the poison spreading'. This should be coupled, he suggested, with pressure in the UN for observers, demilitarisation and demarcation on the frontier.[40] It was Oliver Wright who came up with the most devastating critique of the Colonial Office and Defence Department. He urged the Prime Minister to 'think very carefully' before taking their advice: 'We are on collision courses [UK and Egypt]; would it not be worthwhile seeing if we could not reverse the engines a bit before we actually collide.' The only solution was political. Wright considered that it was 'a fundamental mistake' not to have recognised the YAR and that the government had been acting on 'consistently bad advice' from Aden: 'Practically, everything suggested from Aden has been self-defeating: for the simple reason that the Colonial Office never look beyond Aden.' Arming the royalists was only superficially attractive. He concluded by identifying the prime failure of British policy in the Middle East since World War Two. Britain, he said,

> should recognise that Nasser has been able to capture most of the dynamic and modern forces in the area while we have been left, by our own choice, backing the forces, which are not merely reactionary (that would not matter so much), but shifty, unreliable and treacherous.[41]

Unfortunately, a change in British policy was not going to be easy as Nasser was determined to end the Yemen War and strengthen his hand against the Saudi leader, Faisal, before the second Arab summit, scheduled for September. (By this stage King Saud had been displaced for his all-round uselessness.) To this end, the summer of 1964 saw the largest UAR offensive yet. Colonel McClean reported to Kenneth Strong, the Director-General of Intelligence at the Ministry of Defence, of the fading power of the royalists. He also carried a threat from Prince Faisal that 'he could not go alone indefinitely with the Yemeni problem … If we do not help Faisal to provide the Royalists with enough aid to enable them to continue the struggle, he will almost certainly decide to come to terms with Nasser before the Royalists collapse.' An American oil executive, Harry Kohn, urged the British to help the Saudis or Britain would not only lose Yemen but would also have no friends in the region. Strong's assessment of this information was that 'if we take these two statements together a fair summing up might be that Royalist morale has fallen and war weariness increases. Both statements indicate that covert British assistance should be given to the Royalists.'[42]

The Americans were increasingly concerned that the Saudis were going to start rearming the royalists. They sought British aid in restraining them. Frank Brenchley gave the Americans some discomforting news: the Saudis had been supplying the royalists all along despite the disengagement agreements, albeit perhaps on a reduced level. Brenchley gave the impression that much of this aid had been channelled through British-protected territory, namely the state of Beihan, which was out of sight of the UN observer mission. Brenchley denied that the British had ever urged the Saudis to halt supplies and they would not do so now. While Britain had not supplied the royalists with arms, Brenchley 'did not think that British Ministers were prepared [to] jettison their policy decision of not letting Yemeni Royalists go down the drain. If so and it was decided to implement such policy, he personally wondered if any British aid that might be given to the Yemeni Royalists ought to be channelled through Saudi Arabia rather than directly.'[43] All of this was strongly contrary to American policy. Brenchley, however, continued that ministers did not want the Saudis to be without assets at the Arab summit, i.e. a still-functioning royalist force. David Bruce believed that there was a marginal possibility that a 'quiet one time shot in arm aid increment, given through Saudi Arabia cannot be entirely ruled out once Parliament rises later this month. Tory Backbenchers will press HMG to do so arguing that HMG has nothing to lose by such an action.'[44] The American worries were to be proved correct. The British Ambassador in Jedda, Colin Crowe, was instructed to tell Faisal that it was a British objective, 'as they believe it his, that the Royalists should not be overwhelmed by outside intervention by Egypt' and that, should a deal be made with Nasser in Cairo or at any other time, 'he may have sufficient assets in his hands and will not accept a sell out to Egypt'. To this end, the British government 'warmly welcomed the efforts which Faisal has made to maintain the balance in the Yemen'. If Faisal requested money or arms, that would be considered, but Crowe was to attempt to uncover why they needed such assistance. Even then the Saudis were hardly short of cash. The main purpose of the conversation was to assure Faisal that 'we sympathise with his general objectives as we understand them; that we would deprecate any deal with Nasser which did not secure the complete and early withdrawal of the Egyptian troops; and that his efforts have our support'.[45]

The British were once more moving away from compromise. The acting Head of the North and East African Department of the Foreign Office, Peter Laurence, explained that the Egyptians had implied a willingness to trade the end of subversion in the Federation in return for recognition of the YAR. Laurence was of the opinion that 'there is no present disposition on the part of HMG to go along with it'. The reasons he cited were 'domestic pressures on HMG by Tory back-benchers' and that 'a very real doubt exists whether UAR can be relied upon to honour any such arrangement'.[46] The new Ambassador to Egypt, George Middleton, met Nasser in September. The meeting was cordial. Nasser claimed to be interested in good relations but was waiting for the imminent British general election, which appeared certain to return a Labour government, before making any new initiative.[47]

The gulf between the British and Americans over Nasser remained equally evident. Harlech complained to Rusk in September that Butler was 'very unhappy about the American attitude to Nasser … and that [he] had the impression that the American administration were taking a too relaxed attitude to Nasser's highly subversive activities'.[48] A meeting of senior British and American officials was equally fruitless. The Americans refused to prepare a written statement of joint policies on the talks.[49] A British official commented that they 'were not very fruitful in the sense of moving the US Administration's views or of formulating joint ideas on tactics to deal with him [Nasser]'.[50]

The day after these comments were made, the Labour party won a narrow victory in the general election. This gave hope that Anglo-Egyptian relations could be improved. However, with Labour committed to virtually the same Middle Eastern policy as the Conservatives, these hopes were to prove forlorn.

NOTES

1. If the Security Council plans failed, Home wrote to Eden, 'we have no option but to go through with it. I need not say more but I am convinced that we are finished if the Middle East goes & Russia & India & China rule from Africa to the Pacific.' Thorpe, *Alec Douglas-Home*, pp. 176, 182.
2. PRO PREM 11/4929, Wright to PM, Meeting with the Foreign Secretary, Colonial Secretary and MOD, 22 Nov. 1963.
3. See Barbour-Paul, *Britain's Relinquishment of Power*, p. 80, and Pieragostini, *Britain, Aden and South Arabia*, p. 60.
4. *Hansard* (Commons), Vol. 686, Col. 1448, 19 Dec. 1963.
5. USNA, AmEmbassy London to State, 3903, 12 Feb. 1964, Pol UK–US Box 2785, DOSCF.
6. See PRO FO 371/178594, VG 1051/15, Transcript of Canadian Broadcasting Company broadcast, 11 Feb. 1964. PRO FO 371/178594, VG 1051/14, Maitland (Cairo) to R.S. Scrivener, 27 Feb. 1964.
7. This is the text that was reported to the Foreign Office. PRO FO 371/178581, VG 1022/2, Cairo–FO, No. 136, 23 Feb. 1964.
8. PRO CAB 128/38, Cabinet minutes, 20, No. 3, 24 Mar. 1964.
9. USNA, State to AmEmbassy London, 5977, 17 Mar. 1964, Pol 32-1, Aden–Yemen dispute, Box 1866, DOSCF. PRO PREM 11/4928, FO to Washington, No. 1058, 18 Mar. 1964.
10. This account was given to United States Ambassador Bruce by Frank Brenchley of the Foreign Office, reported in Lydon Baines Johnson Library (LBJL), AmEmbassy London to State, No. 4815, 1 Apr. 1964, Yemen cables, Vol. I, National Security Files (NSF) Country File, Yemen Box 161. The various orders are given in the following correspondence: CINC Aden–MOD MIDCOS, 103, 27 Mar. 1964, Acting Chief of the Defence Staff to CINC Aden, COSMID, 106, 27 Mar. 1964. The authorisation was contained in Sandys to Trevakis, No. 191, 27 Mar. 1964. All in PRO PREM 11/4679.
11. PRO PREM 11/4679, Butler to Home, PM 64/38, 4 Apr. 1964.
12. USNA, Taiz to State, No. 549, 29 Mar. 1964, Pol 32-1, Aden–Yemen dispute, Box 1866, DOSCF. LBJL, Rusk telcon with Johnson, Citation No. 2931, WH 6404.05, Johnson tapes. Johnson's message is in PRO PREM 11/4679, FO to Washington, No. 5115, 15 Apr. 1964. LBJL, Komer to McGeorge Bundy, 2 Apr. 1964, NSF Country File, Yemen memos, Vol. I, Box 161.
13. PRO PREM 11/4679, Wright to Home, 8 Apr. 1964.
14. PRO DEFE 13/569, Trevakis to CO, No. 355, 16 Apr. 1964. USNA AmEmbassy London to State, No. 5239, 23 Apr. 1964, DOSCF, Pol 32-1, Aden–Yemen dispute, Box 1866.
15. PRO DEFE 13/569, Home to Butler, M 39/64, 23 Apr. 1964.
16. USNA, AmEmbassy London to State, No. 5267, 24 Apr. 1964, DOSCF, Pol 32-1, Aden–Yemen dispute, Box 1866.
17. PRO DEFE 13/569, Thorneycroft to Douglas-Home, 22 Apr. 1964.
18. PRO FO 371/178583, VG 1023/5/G, Following from Butler, Washington to FO, No. 1587, 28 Apr. 1964.
19. This line is in the American version of the above meeting. LBJL, Memcon, 27 Apr. 1964, UK meetings with Butler, NSF Country File, Box 213.
20. LBJL, Komer to McGeorge Bundy, 28 Apr. 1964, UK meetings with Butler, Sanitised copy, NSF Country File, UK Box 213.
21. LBJL, Memcon between President and Foreign Secretary Butler, 29 Apr. 1964, UK meetings with Butler, NSF Country File, UK Box 213. PRO PREM 11/4980, Butler to Home, PMPT T 122A/64, 29 Apr. 1964.

22. *FRUS 1964–68*, Vol. XXI, Doc. 53, 13 Apr. 1964.
23. LBJL, Cairo to State, No. 2585, 3 May 1964, Section 1 and 2 of 2, United Arab Republic, Vol. I cables, NSF Country Files, Box 158.
24. LBJL, State Circular to London, No. 2064, 5 May 1964, United Arab Republic, Vol. I cables, NSF Country Files, Box 158.
25. *FRUS 1964–1968*, Vol. XXI, Doc. 341, 8 May 1964.
26. LBJL, Cairo to State, No. 2660, 10 May 1964, United Arab Republic, Vol. Cables, NSF Country Files, Box 158.
27. PRO DEFE 13/569, Home to Butler, M 49/64, 5 May 1964.
28. I could find no reference to this discussion in the minutes of the DOPC on that date. It is mentioned in Note for Secretary of State for Defence, 20 July 1964, PRO DEFE 13/570.
29. S. Dorril, *MI6: Fifty Years of Special Operations* (London, Fourth Estate, 2000), pp. 692–3.
30. LBJL, AmEmbassy London to State, No. 5522, 6 May 1964, NSF Country File, Box 161.
31. PRO CO 1055/246, Cairo to FO, No. 342, 1 May 1964.
32. PRO DEFE 13/569, Beeley to FO, No. 37, 7 May 1964. LBJL, Cairo to State, No. 2660, 10 May 1964, United Arab Republic, Vol. Cables, NSF Country Files, Box 158.
33. PRO DEFE 13/570, Note for SOS Defence, 20 July 1964. This states that 'On 8 May, the OPD deferred a decision on whether we should supply arms, and we cannot trace that any such decision was taken in committee, but on 29 May the Colonial Secretary authorised the supply of certain quantities of both money and arms.'
34. R.J. Gavin, *Aden under British Rule 1839–1967* (London, Hurst, 1976), p. 346.
35. LBJL, London to State, No. 6112, 9 June 1964, Yemen Cables, Vol. 2, NSF Country File, Box 161.
36. PRO FO 371/178594, VG 1051/10, Beeley to FO, No. 462, 16 June 1964.
37. House of Commons Debates, Vol. 696, Col. 1407, 19 June 1964.
38. *Observer*, 5 July 1964, and PRO FO 371/178594, VG 1051/41, Fyjis-Walker (Cairo) to Laurence, 17 July 1964.
39. PRO DEFE 13/570, 'Maintaining our Position in South Arabia', Memo by Peter Thorneycroft, 13 July 1964.
40. PRO PREM 11/4929, Brenchley brief, 16 July 1964.
41. PRO PREM 11/4929, Wright to Douglas-Home, 18 July 1964.
42. PRO DEFE 13/570, Strong note of discussion with Col. McClean, 20 July 1964.
43. LBJL, London to State, No. 435, 27 July 1964, Section 1, Yemen Cables, NSF Country File, Box 161.
44. Ibid., Section 2.
45. PRO PREM 11/4929, FO to Jedda, No. 718, 24 July 1964.
46. USNA, London to State, No. 451, 28 July 1964, DOSCF, Pol UAR–UK, Box 2667.
47. PRO FO 371/175895, VG 1051/41, Middleton to Butler, 10 Sept. 1964.
48. PRO FO 371/178582, VG 1022/26, Harlech to FO, No. 3176, 11 Sept. 1964.
49. The talks are in USNA, Memcon, 17/18 Sept. 1964, US/UK discussion of UAR and the Middle East, DOSCF, Pol UK–US Box 2785. The less detailed British account is in PRO FO 371/175582, VG 1022/30, Lord Harlech to FO, No. 3170, 20 Sept. 1964.
50. PRO FO 371/178584, VG 1023/33, Sir George Harrison to Harlech, 14 Oct. 1964.

—12—

The Labour Government and Nasser, Part I: 1964–66

LABOUR AT ODDS WITH THE UAR

THE LABOUR GOVERNMENT entered office with the declared intention of improving relations with the Nasser regime. In June 1964, the shadow Colonial Affairs spokesman, Arthur Bottomley, commented on the Anglo-Egyptian crisis and suggested that it was in reality a Conservative party–Nasser clash:

> The fact is that the Tory Government has had no Middle Eastern policy since its disastrous Suez adventure. Whether we like it or not, Colonel Nasser is the dominating Arab leader and it is futile to ignore him … We must recognise that the Arabs are not anti-British but anti Home, Lloyd, Butler and the other 'guilty men of Suez'.[1]

There was a degree of truth in Bottomley's statement. The personal antipathy between Nasser and the Tory party has been well documented here and elsewhere. However, the personality or party factor was only a symptom, not the cause, of the Anglo-Egyptian cold war. The Labour party in opposition and in government were as committed as the Conservatives to policies that were bound to lead it into difficulties with Nasser. Peter Laurence, then acting Head of the North and East African Department of the Foreign Office, made this point to the Americans in July 1964, arguing that,

> even if and when a Labour government comes in, this is not likely to assist greatly in improving relations with [the] UAR unless UAR adopts [a] more positive attitude. In latter event, improved relations would be possible now or at any time. Apart from UAR suspicions that Labour is heavily influenced by [the] Israelis, Laurence thought a Labour government will be as committed to defending British interests as is present Tory government, though

its methods might vary. Labour will most likely find itself having to defend such British interests in Aden, Libya and elsewhere. In consequence, it too will soon be at odds with UAR.[2]

Laurence, in the above quote, identified the problems that the Labour party would face in its bilateral relations with Egypt. While Labour did not have the legacy of Suez to deal with, it had the problem that many in the party hierarchy were passionate supporters of Israel. Labour had strong links with the Jewish intellectual tradition. Prominent Labour ministers such as Richard Crossman and Anthony Greenwood were happy to classify themselves as Zionists. Perhaps the strongest Zionist of all was the new Labour Prime Minister, Harold Wilson. No British Prime Minister has been as pro-Israeli as Wilson. Few international leaders have used part of their retirement to write a book eulogising Israel.[3] His aversion to the views of the passionately pro-Arab Labour MP, Christopher Mayhew, prevented the latter being named as a junior minster at the Foreign Office.[4]

The other problem identified by Laurence was that Labour was committed to the implementation of the same policies in the Middle East as the previous government and the defence of British interests. In May 1964, Wilson had issued a statement supporting the British position in the Middle East. According to the American Embassy, this was 'in response to Labour recognition of deep seated public dissatisfaction (even outside Tory ranks) with what is widely regarded here, as Nasser's role in killing "our boys" in Aden'.[5] On assuming office, Wilson made clear that his government was going to continue the east-of-Suez role. Indeed, Wilson on numerous occasions made great play of wanting to expand the role. In March 1964 Wilson told Robert McNamara, the US Defence Secretary, that he planned to build up British conventional forces in the area as a fire brigade force to keep the peace.[6] The Labour front bench had been especially impressed by the January 1964 interventions in East Africa by British army and naval forces, which had foiled coups against the Kenyan and Tanzanian governments. This, combined with the Indonesian and Chinese threats, had convinced them that the British role in the Indian Ocean was a force for good. Wilson used old-style conservative and imperialist language to describe his worldwide conception. His much derided claim that Britain's 'frontiers were on the Himalayas' was rooted in this thinking. Moreover, as Denis Healey, the Defence Secretary, has pointed out, Britain had commitments that it could not just abandon; treaties with Kuwait, Malaysia and Australia required bases and forces east of Suez.[7] In many ways there was a considerable continuity in British foreign policy under Labour. Labour did not face up to the need

for massive overseas defence cutbacks until its third year in government. Indeed, it would have preferred to have diminished its commitment to the Rhine Army and persisted with a global role until the
necessity to turn towards Europe became evident, as Macmillan had
discovered.[8] Thus, the cause of the most recent Anglo-Egyptian crisis,
British bases in the Middle East, was to remain a barrier to improved
relations as long as Labour remained committed to the global role.

However, with regard to Aden and the Federation of South Arabia,
the Labour party was in favour of a much more progressive solution than the Conservatives. In November 1962 the Labour party had
formally declared itself against the merger of progressive Aden
with the 'feudal' Federation.[9] Anthony Greenwood, the new Colonial
Secretary, was a left-winger and not noted as a great supporter of
sheikhs and sultans. Furthermore Anglo-Egyptian relations looked
likely to be mitigated somewhat by signs that the Saudis and the
Egyptians might be able to broker a deal over the Yemen. At the second
Arab summit held in Alexandria in September 1964, Nasser conferred
with Faisal and both agreed to press their protégés in the Yemen to
compromise.[10]

Patrick Gordon Walker, from the Gaitskell wing of the Labour
party,[11] was made Foreign Secretary by Wilson. While he was by nature
a conservative Foreign Secretary, he had, within a week of taking over
the reins at the Foreign Office, despatched a message to Cairo, expressing a desire for improvement in relations.[12] However, his circular
telegram on the initiative made clear that, in spite of the conciliatory
message to Nasser, 'there will be no basic new departure in British
policy'.[13] One of the fringe benefits of making 'slight overtures' to
Nasser was that it garnered Britain commendation in Washington,
which was a vital component of Wilson's foreign policy. The Egyptian
leader and his policies were discussed at considerable length at the first
meeting between the new British Foreign Secretary and Dean Rusk in
October. When questioned by Rusk about attitudes to Nasser, Gordon
Walker replied that the 'views of the new British government on Nasser
and the UAR were a little closer to the US views than had been those
of the previous British government'. However, what was striking was
the essential continuity in policy between Labour and the Conservatives. Gordon Walker pointed out that Britain had unique problems
with Nasser that the United States did not have: 'First, there was Aden.
Second, there was the danger that if the British appeared too eager;
Nasser would put up the price. Finally there were certain things the
Egyptians would have to do for the British before the British would go
too far in effecting a rapprochement.' Britain, however, no longer
wanted the Americans to use their food aid as a weapon, as it did not

carry that much leverage, and 'it would be bad to throw the UAR completely into the hands of the other side'.[14]

On Yemen, Britain would not recognise the republicans 'as long as Egyptian troops remained in the country and the British position in Aden was under attack'. No coming to terms with Nasser and Arab nationalism would be done 'at the expense of Israel'. Continuing, Gordon Walker said 'that HMG would like to work out with us an absolute guarantee for Saudi Arabia'.[15] Closer military and political links between Britain and Saudi Arabia were to be a key element in British policy in the Middle East over the next three years. The Foreign Office had little confidence that any permanent *rapprochement* with Nasser was possible, as he would not abandon his regional ambitions. The key aim of the dialogue, therefore, according to R.T. Higgins, who was in charge of the UAR desk, was the 'exploitation of Nasser's pragmatic approach so as to moderate his timing and tactics. We seek at most to buy time. To this end we need to reduce the temperature of what has arguably become a cold war between the west, and particularly Britain, and those many Arab nationalists who have taken Nasser as their leader.'[16]

The Egyptians welcomed the British initiative. Nasser informed Middleton that he 'shared the desire for closer contact and understanding', and that it was a mistake to suppose that the UAR was Britain's 'public enemy number one in the Middle East'.[17] The Egyptians pressed for a ministerial meeting to move relations along. However, Gordon Walker wanted to establish a dialogue first rather than go straight to high-level meetings.[18] The Egyptians reluctantly agreed. Nasser made a speech to the National Assembly on 13 November in which he argued that whilst the British remained imperialists and still had bases that were irritants this 'however, does not prevent us from being by all means ready to establish sound and good relations with Britain, for it is not our task to fight the British and create disputes with them'.[19] On 12 November the Foreign Secretary informed the Cabinet that there were increasing signs that the Saudis and Egyptians were close to an agreement that would ensure a cessation of hostilities in the Yemen. If so, Britain would have 'to face the question of whether we should thereafter recognise the regime in the Yemen'.[20] This question was never posed as the agreement broke down like all previous agreements aimed at resolving the conflict. The renewed peace effort started promisingly, as all sides including the Saudis, Nasser and the various Yemeni factions showed a willingness to compromise. At a conference in Erkwit in the Sudan the royalists and republicans were able to compromise their respective differences but the Saudis afterwards refused to accept the designation 'Republic' for the future state of Yemen. Quarrels between the Egyptians and the Yemeni republicans further added to the difficulties. A follow-up conference did not take place and the reasonably well-observed cease-fire had broken down by the beginning of 1965.[21]

The Foreign Secretary held three meetings with the UAR Ambassador, Mr Ismail, on 29 November, 2 and 29 December as part of the 'dialogue'. The objective of the dialogue was to follow up Nasser's stated willingness to improve relations, to contribute to a general reduction of tension in the Middle East and to prepare the ground for a visit to Cairo by a British minister. Gordon Walker told the UAR that an improvement in relations had to be two-sided. Britain, he argued, had serious cause for complaint about propaganda aimed at the Federation and wanted to see a diminution in it. He also explained why Britain required retention of the Aden base. The UAR Ambassador's main complaints were about the base and the increased emphasis that the British government was putting on the east-of-Suez role. He stated that the 'retention of the base was the main obstacle in Anglo-UAR relations and that a radical solution was required'. R.S. Scrivener, who was Head of the Near Eastern Department, commented that, as this is the condition of improved relations, 'no early improvement can be looked for. At the same time, I see some marginal advantage in continuing the dialogue, mainly in order to remove the misunderstandings. Conversely, to discontinue it could produce a fairly strong reaction.'[22]

There was a further Anglo-American consultation in early December. Sir Geoffrey Harrison, a Deputy Undersecretary in the Foreign Office, noted that the Egyptians seemed to expect more from the talks than the British, and were expecting a ministerial visit to lead to agreements being signed.[23] While the talks could hardly be described as a success, they at least opened a channel of communication between the nations. However, by the end of January, a considerable change had occurred in the attitude of the United States towards Nasser. Nasser's offensive against the British in the spring had disturbed Washington. Secondly, Lucius Battle, the new American Ambassador, reckoned there had been 'slippage to the East' since Khrushchev's visit in May. The American Ambassador urged the implementation of a new multi-year food aid agreement to end the stagnation in the US–UAR relationship. His advice was rendered irrelevant by a series of unexpected developments.

These were the increasing American involvement in the Congo, and the accidental shooting down of an aircraft with a friend of President Johnson on board by UAR air defences. Egypt had been a keen advocate of the liberation of the Congo since 1960. The assassinated Congo President Patrick Lumumba was a hero to neutralists the world over, not just to Nasser. Congo, since independence in 1960, had been a battleground, torn apart by civil strife. The United States had connived in the assassination of the left-leaning Lumumba in 1961. By 1964 Moshe Tshombe, who had led the rebel Katanga province, had become President of Congo with the help of the Americans. Former supporters of Lumumba attempted to topple him and had seized the eastern portion of the country. Belgian paratroopers were dropped by the United States air force to crush the rebellion and rescue hundreds of Western hostages. In Egypt, riots, mainly by Congolese exiles, it should be said, greeted the news and the American Embassy library was burned down. Because of these events, coupled with the unfortunate shooting down of the American plane, the new US Ambassador, Lucius Battle – enjoying a baptism of fire – warned Nasser to moderate his policies or face the cutting of aid.[24]

On 23 December, Nasser responded with one of his most memorable and, in retrospect, most ill-judged speeches. After reiterating his support for liberation movements in the Congo and elsewhere, he attacked the United States in the strongest terms:

> If the Americans think that by giving us some aid they can dominate our policy, I hereby tell them sorry, no. The UAR could reduce its consumption of tea, coffee and other commodities to maintain its independence. The Americans gave the UAR about £E50 million worth of goods annually. If necessary this amount could be saved from the £E400 or £E500 million spent on the development plan. The United States Ambassador had the day before told the deputy Prime Minister for supply that he could not discuss consumer goods supplied under the agricultural surplus law because Egyptian money was no good to the Americans. I hereby tell anybody not liking our money to go and drink out of the Mediterranean. The UAR could not sell its independence for £E50 million. Whoever addresses the slightest reproach to us, we'll cut his tongue out.[25]

The CIA commented that the attack was Nasser's 'bitterest on the US since 1956'. McGeorge Bundy advised Johnson not to overreact, as there was no gain in pushing him still further into a public frenzy: 'The history of Aswan and Suez is clear in everyone's mind. On the other hand, no one is particularly interested in ostentatious feeding of the hand that bites.'[26] Nasser never seemed to realise that it was in the gift of the American Congress whether to grant Egypt aid or not, not the American President. Congressmen from Idaho and Iowa did not want to see their surplus grain sustaining the regime of a man seemingly

bent on destroying American influence in the Middle East. Lucius
Battle, the American Ambassador, suggests that Nasser had 'total lack
of understanding of the nature of [US] society' with its system of checks
and balances that were easily upset by an Arab dictator's verbal
assaults.[27] The result of the speech was an immediate reappraisal by the
State Department and the National Security Council of America's
relations with Nasser.

For the British the only light in the speech was the lack of mention
of themselves. However, on the ground in Aden, the violence that had
been unleashed the previous spring was increasing in intensity in spite
of the British government's olive branch to Nasser, and a more progressive policy in Aden. Solving the South Arabian problem was
not proving to be easy. The Colonial Secretary, Anthony Greenwood,
wished to get agreement between the more radical parties, namely the
People's Socialist Party (PSP) – which was led by Al-Asnag – and the
conservative sultans. However, he would not deal with the Marxist-
inclined NLF who greeted his November 1964 visit with an upsurge in
urban terror. Trevakis, the High Commissioner, who wanted to make
a deal with the sultans only, was replaced by Richard Turnbull, a high-
ranking colonial official and a veteran of the successful defeat of
the Mau Mau insurgency in Kenya. Greenwood initially made some
progress. However, the security situation was constantly deteriorating.
British government ministers, officials, the Undersecretary of State for
the Colonies and the head of the Aden Special Branch all made public
statements that the Egyptian government was aiding and abetting the
NLF.[28]

Stewart Crawford, Assistant Undersecretary at the Foreign Office,
assessed that this was caused by the determination on the part of the
Egyptian Intelligence Service that their 'policy of subversion has not
failed and that they can make the Aden base too hot for us to hold'.
Crawford, however, argued against the traditional British remedy for
Egyptian-backed terrorism, which was to advocate increased British
support for the royalists:

> The Foreign Office has never believed that this was a useful
> reaction and we believe this all the more strongly today. The
> situation in the Yemen is unsatisfactory for the Egyptians in that
> the Yemen Government has virtually collapsed and the Royalist
> military position is being perfectly well sustained with Saudi help.
> The political and military stalemate there has no effect at all on the
> capacity of the EIS to promote trouble for us and the stimulation of
> more Royalist activity would do nothing to reduce our problems.

Crawford advised that the remedies were to hit back across the Yemeni frontier and carry out firm anti-terrorist action, build up alternative politicians in Aden and hammer into Nasser that his activities only set back independence.[29]

Scrivener, who in his capacity as Head of the Near Eastern Department was the Foreign Secretary's chief adviser on Anglo-UAR relations, considered at the end of January whether the UK should change its policy towards Egypt now that the United States was reconsidering its policy, and the conviction of King Faisal that Nasser was 'finished'. He noted that a joint US/UK Embassy paper of 1 January recommended that 'we should (a) deny Nasser any excuse to blame West for his misfortunes (b) keep the door open and (c) let the UAR's situation deteriorate a little further with a view in the longer term to a carefully timed Western rescue operation'. George Middleton, the British Ambassador, had further argued that no minister should visit Cairo and that the British 'warn the Egyptians that no visit to Cairo is possible whilst UAR policy is so actively hostile to Britain'.[30] However, at the beginning of February, the new Foreign Secretary Michael Stewart had a cordial meeting with the UAR Ambassador.[31] There were tentative signs that Easter would be a suitable time for the visit of a British minister to Cairo.

However, the 'dialogue' and prospects for a visit were dealt a near-fatal blow in February when Nasser came into conflict with the West German government. West Germany (FRG) had established a good, if primarily trade relationship with Egypt and the Arab world since the termination of the Allied occupation in 1955. Since 1955, under the 'Halstein Doctrine', the FRG refused to enter into diplomatic relations with any country that recognised East Germany (GDR). Consequently, the FRG felt unable to recognise Israel for fear that the Arab world and the neutralist bloc would recognise the GDR and destroy the 'Halstein Doctrine'. To balance this, and because of the unique debt that Germany owed the Jewish people because of the Holocaust, it paid reparations to Israel from 1955. President Kennedy – not wanting to be seen supplying arms to Israel – persuaded Germany to supply NATO surplus equipment to Israel from 1962. This tangle of relationships was further complicated by the fact that German scientists, many with rather dubious Nazi pasts, were working on the Egyptian ballistic missile programme. News of the arms supplies to Israel leaked and led the Germans to cancel the arrangement in February 1965. However, the Germans decided to establish diplomatic relations with Israel. Nasser responded by attacking the FRG government for supplying Israel with weapons for free and by receiving the East German leader, Walter Ulbricht, in Cairo. In his Merger Day speech on 22 February,

Nasser attacked the British government, claiming that it was attempting to give South Arabia 'incomplete independence'. When Germany did recognise Israel, Nasser persuaded most of the Arab League to break relations with the Federal Republic. The Foreign Secretary informed the Cabinet that these 'developments were unfortunate in so far as they were liable to intensify antagonism between the West and the Arab world'. The consequences for the dialogue were that in 'these circumstances, while we should not abandon our attempt to promote more cordial relations with the UAR government, we must clearly moderate our initiative: and it would now be undesirable to pursue the earlier suggestion that a United Kingdom Minister should pay a visit to Cairo at Easter'.[32] Another reason for British reticence was the fuss that the British had made over Nasser's proposed visit to Germany the previous May. German newspapers were pointing to this as the origin of the crisis.[33]

The Egyptians, it was decided, were to be informed that the postponement was because of Egyptian support for terrorist activity in Aden rather than the FRG dispute. When Stewart informed the UAR Ambassador of this, he emphasised that he wished to continue the dialogue. The latter expressed little surprise as the UK had been delaying matters and commented that part of the reason was British support for the FRG. He continued the line that the UAR supported all independence movements.[34] Stewart circulated a memo for the Cabinet on 24 March 1965 on the subject of relations with the UAR. Its assessment was troubling:

> Nasser had as an objective to eliminate the Western influence in the Middle East based on our positions in the area, with our own as his first target, and that as an immediate aim he wished to expel us from Southern Arabia and thus render untenable our position in the Persian Gulf. His aim in South Arabia is made clear by the campaign of intimidation and subversion which is being directed against the South Arabian federation and against the Colonial Secretary's programme for bringing a new South Arabian state to independence by 1968.

However, the Foreign Secretary concluded: 'I thought it important to keep our lines open to him, in order to see whether we could not at least take some of the tension out of our relationship and if possible to persuade him to give South Arabia a chance.'[35]

The Labour government's Middle Eastern policy was in tatters by the end of March 1965. Greenwood's attempts to hold a further constitutional conference in March 1965 foundered and a fact-finding commission to Aden was thwarted by radical nationalist opposition. A July 1965 conference in London of representatives of all Adeni and Federation political elements collapsed owing to PSP demands that Britain withdraw from the base and end the security crackdown. The British rejected both demands. The British had made concessions. Turnbull agreed to appoint the PSP sympathiser, Abd al-Makkawi, to the post of Chief Minister. His first act was to join with the PSP in demanding that the British implement the December 1963 UN resolution, which had called for immediate independence.[36]

All the while the violence continued, even if at a low level. Richard Turnbull requested in April that he be given the right to order retaliation for YAR air attacks on Aden. However, the government was not yet ready to become involved in a repeat of the Harib debacle. Indeed the Harib fort fell into royalist hands in early March 1965. The first half of 1965 was a disaster for the YAR and Egypt as the royalists regained control of nearly half of the country. However, this did not help matters in Aden where the deteriorating political and security situation led Scrivener to advise Middleton that, as the increasing violence was likely to lead to increasing pressure upon Britain's relations with the UAR, 'There might be an advantage in presenting to the UAR at regular and fairly frequent intervals "Chapter and Verse" about incidents of violence in South Arabia for which we have reason to believe that they may bear responsibility.'[37] The Egyptians showed considerable annoyance when challenged. The Minister for Foreign Affairs, Riad, in a meeting with Middleton in May, did not deny that the Egyptians were helping the liberation movement but retorted that the British had 'both actively and tacitly given aid to the Royalist forces in the Yemen'. He wondered whether there was any point in continuing the dialogue against this background.[38] Philip Talbot, the United States Assistant Secretary of State for Near Eastern Affairs, tried to appeal to Nasser to halt his campaign against the South Arabian Federation. The latter reiterated that the British had brought all the trouble there upon themselves with the Harib raid and the arming of the royalists:

> Now British asking UAR to tell them to stop. The British must negotiate with the National groups. Once you agree to support people, it is difficult [to] withdraw support. The question not matter of UAR interests but was response to British intervention in the Yemen. It is not in our capacity to stop aiding or to stop actions. We can however invite talks with the British toward solution [of] problem. He referred [to] fact [that] British had made cessation this activity [a] condition precedent to visit of British Minister to Cairo.[39]

Nasser's suggestion that it was not in his capacity to stop aiding or to stop actions of the NLF was not without truth. He may well have feared that he would lose any influence he had with the increasingly Marxist-inclined NLF forces. However, this is not to say that he was an innocent party. An American intelligence estimate in June 1965 put the blame for terrorism firmly at the door of the Egyptian Intelligence Service. The terrorist 'campaign is the work of a relatively small group of trained men, who are directed by Egyptian intelligence experts and who use Yemen as a safe-haven. So far, the attacks have been aimed mainly at British forces and Aden government officials, especially the Special Branch of the Aden Police, which is concerned with subversive activities.'[40] The prospects for Anglo-Egyptian relations were increasingly bleak. They were further undermined by the 'Sergeant Allen affair' when a Ministry of Defence employee supplied the UAR Embassy with secret allied contingency war plans for the Middle East, which aroused great excitement and suspicion, according to Anthony Nutting, in the Egyptian President. Heikal published the papers in *Al-Ahram*.[41]

The only hopeful signs were the continued number of high-level contacts between British and UAR officials. George Thomson, the Minister of State at the Foreign Office, had a constructive meeting with the UAR Ambassador at the end of May 1965.[42] A delegation of UAR parliamentarians visited London and met with Wilson in the later part of June. The conversation was dominated by the twin problems of Aden and Yemen. On the latter question, Wilson rebuffed calls for recognition on the grounds that it was not a matter of liking or disliking the regime but whether it controlled the country or not. The leader of the Egyptian delegation asked whether a 'package deal' could be done over the problem of the YAR and South Arabia. Wilson 'replied that was tied up with the situation in Aden. So long as bombs were being thrown, it was difficult to improve relations with the Yemen and the United Arab Republic.'[43] Most significantly, Mohammed Heikal, the editor of the leading Egyptian newspaper, *Al-Ahram*, and Nasser's *éminence grise*, on a medical visit to London, held meetings with the Prime Minister, the Colonial Secretary and Thomson, which showed him blowing hot and cold on the subject of Anglo-Egyptian relations. In a meeting with the Foreign Secretary, he asserted that the 'British had not come to terms with Arab nationalism'.[44] Heikal commented to Thomson that the meeting had improved relations. He added that the 'new ideas of the Labour Government had not yet been felt in the Arab World'. To continue the process, he suggested that a minister visit at the end of September.[45] His meeting with the Prime Minister was a robust exchange of views. Wilson asserted that he did not intend to change basic British policies, such as towards the Arab–Israeli dispute. Wilson asked Heikal to tell Nasser to end the 'problem of violence [in Aden] fermented from outside'. Heikal blamed the violence on the allegations that the previous government through certain 'officers on a year's leave and other mercenaries had started to help the Royalists through Beihan, then Egypt had been forced to counter attack'. Wilson said that he could assure Mr Heikal 'that nothing of the sort was being done under the present administration. There was not British involvement from Beihan now.'[46]

One factor that might have salved Anglo-Egyptian relations was the growing acceptance particularly in the Ministry of Defence of the need for major economies east of Suez – including the Gulf. The growing tide of violence was making the Aden base an attractive candidate for abandonment. The Prime Minister informed Secretary Rusk in May 1965 that the UK 'could not count on the indefinite retention of the Aden base though it is a vital staging point for Singapore'.[47] This was coupled with a growing disillusionment about commitments in the Gulf. The Minister for Defence, Denis Healey, was amazed to discover that the British were not allowed to station troops in Kuwait as it would cause domestic riots, and that the Kuwaitis were providing funds to the Free Bahrain movement where British troops were based so that they could intervene to protect Kuwait.[48] It was also discovered that other staging posts could be just as easily maintained without the attendant security problems of Aden. While the 1965 Defence Review had explicitly mentioned that the Aden base was to be maintained, the 1966 Defence Review, which was in preparation, was looking closely at the massive foreign exchange costs of overseas bases. Within Whitehall, there was a growing acceptance that it was not possible to maintain a British presence in the Middle East on a long-term basis. However, the British did not want to see their influence replaced by Nasser's. William Luce, the British Representative in the Gulf, assessed that, of the candidates likely to dominate the Gulf after the British departed, 'the UAR is the one which would sooner or later cause the greatest damage to British, Western and local interests ... it follows that, in my opinion, it must be HMG's policy to prevent it happening'.[49]

Despite the friendly meetings in London, there was no immediate toning down in the rhetoric from Cairo. Nasser blasted the Wilson government's Middle Eastern policy in a speech on 22 July:

> As regards Britain, when the Labour government was formed we said we were willing to open a new page with them but the Labour adopted the same policy as the Conservative Government. What has happened since the Labour Government took over? Aggression

against us in the Yemen has continued. They say we kill the British in the South. But we tell them: Alright, but you also kill Arabs in the Yemen by conspiring against the Yemen. Then there is the conspiracy in the Gulf, and the attempt to keep Arab territories under imperialism.[50]

However, there were some more hopeful signs. Al-Asnag of the pro-Nasser Aden party, the PSP, informed the British that the Cairo press and radio campaign against the South Arabian constitutional talks would be dropped. However, he said that 'Cairo had indicated to him that they wanted to withdraw from Yemen, if they could do so without suffering humiliation. If they were driven into a corner, however, they would turn ugly and engage in further acts of destructiveness.'[51] Further to this they wished the UK to help them withdraw without too much loss of face. Heikal, however, in an article in *Al-Ahram*, launched another bitter attack on the British. Claiming that the UK had not really wound down its Middle Eastern position, he said that a 'deal between the UAR and Britain is out of the question. The reason is that the UAR has no goods to deliver: internally, she will not renounce any of the rights won by her people and externally the UAR does not possess rights that she could renounce.' Heikal did not deny that Egypt was supporting the terror campaign in South Arabia. He justified this with the routine claims that the British were allowing British officers to form 'gangs against the Yemeni revolution'[52] and he saw the 'British hand in all the efforts in our part of the world hostile to the UAR and its ideology'.[53]

Despite these contradictory signs and statements emerging from Cairo, preparations for the first visit of a British minister continued. George Thomson was to visit on 24–27 September 1965. The atmosphere improved with the signing of a cease-fire in Jedda between the republicans and royalists on 25 August. The Foreign Secretary, Michael Stewart, set out for Wilson the objectives of the Thomson visit. The 'agreement reached over the Yemen in the recent talks between President Nasser and King Faisal might, if carried out – and the prospects of this cannot yet be assessed – give us a better opportunity of reaching some measure of understanding with the UAR without letting down those to whom we are responsible in Southern Arabia'.

Stewart saw the talks as being 'largely exploratory' and that it was 'inevitable that progress will be slow and uncertain'. There were simply too many differences between Britain and Egypt:

We are in no position to influence developments in the Yemen one way or another. We cannot do anything to alleviate the UAR's economic difficulties. Moreover, there is no sign that Nasser is prepared to relax his pressure on us in South Arabia, whatever concessions we might feel able to make short of outright abandonment of our responsibilities there. At present, therefore, the ingredients for any far reaching agreement with Nasser do not exist. Nevertheless, our interest lies in reducing the tension that exists between us, particularly as a result of events in Aden, and in working towards the more limited aim of relatively peaceful co-existence.[54]

Britain, in seeking this, could not prejudice its objective of maintaining good relations with the Arab world generally and other governments such as Israel and Iran 'whose governments are both profoundly suspicious of Nasser and hostile to his more aggressive policies'. However, Thomson could make clear that 'we are not inciting them against him' and that Britain wanted to be on good terms with the UAR:

I hope that the Minister of State will be able to remove Egyptian misconceptions about our own policies in the Middle East, and obtain clarification of how Nasser's mind is working. The Minister will seek to dispel some of the suspicions of Britain's motives which are a legacy from the past etc., convince Nasser that having promoted independence for 700 million people all over the world since 1945, it is inconceivable that we should wish to cling to a colonial role in the Middle East. He can point out that we too believe that there must be changes in the Middle East and that the difference between us seems to lie solely in method – subversion, violence and incitement to revolution on the one hand, or on the other, peaceful change without violence and with safeguards for individual freedom. He will, in particular, put to Nasser the sterility of his policy in South Arabia and, on the understanding that he too wishes South Arabia to achieve independence without delay, the advantage in abandoning it.

Thomson's main theme to pursue with Nasser was that, 'whether wilfully or out of ignorance, he misunderstands us'. Thomson would have to get across that our 'objectives are not really dissimilar and we can hope to get on reasonably well with each other'.[55]

It was the deteriorating situation in South Arabia that was to destroy all possibility of progress. Violence was reaching new heights in the autumn of 1965. The Speaker of the Legislative Council, Sir Arthur Charles, was assassinated in early September just prior to the Thomson visit. The Aden Chief Minister, Makkawi, refused to condemn the assassination. On 20 September the High Commissioner, Turnbull, requested permission from the Colonial Secretary to sack Makkawi and introduce direct rule. On 23 September Greenwood gave his assent.[56] According to the account given to the American Embassy, while ministers were aware that the statement might prejudice the Thomson mission, the 'need to act was deemed so urgent as to permit no further delay'. The British official added that 'no one could predict what Nasser's reaction might be'.[57] It was felt that no forewarning could be given to Nasser as the Egyptians would have passed on the message to the Aden government, giving them the opportunity to organise against the suspension of the constitution.[58] Thomson arrived in Cairo on 24 September. The visit began in a favourable atmosphere. Thomson had meetings with Riad, the Foreign Minister. Even when the announcement of the suspension of the Yemen constitution came in over the wires, there did not seem to be an imminent crisis. Nasser, however, refused to see Thomson. According to Anthony Nutting, this was the Egyptian President's reaction:

> Unable to believe that such extraordinary timing could be accidental, he was convinced that Thomson's visit was no more than a perfidious cover plan and that, as at the time of the Suez crisis, Britain's real intentions were to provoke a showdown with him as the principal Arab adversary of British imperialism. The suspicions aroused when he first learned of Britain's contingency planning in the Middle East now seemed to be fully borne out.[59]

These suspicions appear to have been fuelled by a piece in the *Sunday Times* by the veteran political journalist, James Morchach. It suggested that

> British authorities in Aden are satisfied that acts of subversion and terror have been financed and organised from outside by agents and sympathisers of President Nasser ... This gave a particularly sharp edge to yesterday's announcement, since it came at the moment Mr George Thomson, the British Minister of State, was due to call on President Nasser in Cairo. This conjunction of events was not accidental. The British government considered that the Aden announcement should be made while Thomson was having direct talks with President Nasser to show the government's determination to restore order.[60]

Ambassador Middleton's prognosis on the future for Anglo-Egyptian relations was gloomy: 'At best we are likely to be in for a more or less prolonged period of chilly uncooperativeness. If the situation in Yemen deteriorates and we are obliged to take firm action there, the result may well be a more violent reaction here.' The British Ambassador feared the casualties could include British over-flight rights.[61] Nasser, however, was wary of blocking the Canal to British naval ships; he did not attempt to block the despatch of the aircraft carrier *Eagle* to Aden, which was allowed to sail through the Suez Canal unmolested.[62] The Arab League did launch a concerted campaign in the United Nations about the suspension of the Aden constitution that culminated in the passing of a General Assembly resolution 'harshly critical' of British actions in Aden in November.[63]

Perhaps surprisingly, the Foreign Office received private reports from two British businessmen that the UAR wished to continue the dialogue. However, the Foreign Office was reticent about replying to these probes. It was also considered that the dialogue might be better served if resumed after UAR intentions in Yemen and British decisions about South Arabia were finalised.[64] The UAR appeared to want to press the matter. A UAR presidential adviser 'stressed' to a State Department official on 17 November that the UAR was interested in 'backing away from confrontation over South Arabia and improving relations with UK'.[65] Denis Speares, who was now Head of the North African Department, explained to an American official that 'UK tactics *vis-à-vis* UAR are now in process being analysed by UK Embassy Cairo and Foreign Office. Tentative conclusion seems to be that for time being there is little that UK can discuss with UAR.' The American official urged that the matter should be pursued. Speares pointed out that the 'British had nothing to make a gesture with, while the UAR, on the other hand, could prove its desire to back away from confrontation over South Arabia by revising intervention there'. Furthermore, Speares had asked Middleton to make inquiries to the Egyptians to see if there was any initiative from them that needed a reply. The Egyptians had replied 'no'.[66]

The American initiative came to nothing. Their renewed enthusiasm for Britain to make an extra effort sprang from the sudden warmth introduced into US–UAR relations by the Haradh conference that suggested that the Yemen imbroglio might be at an end, and the appointment of the pro-American Zacharia Mohieddin as Egyptian Prime Minister, which convinced the Americans to restore the PL-480 food aid for six months.[67] Lucius Battle, the American Ambassador in Cairo, pressed the Aden problem in a meeting with Nasser on 24 November. He appealed to Nasser to help stop the drift to chaos by using his influence with the liberation movement. The latter was not helpful. 'Next move is up to the British', he declared.[68]

Another British colonial problem now impinged on Anglo-Egyptian relations. The break-up of the Central African Federation in 1963 had seen Zambia and Malawi achieve independence the following year. However, Southern Rhodesia with a sizeable white minority was a special case. The white settlers had no intention of being ruled by the black majority whom they looked upon as their inferiors. In May 1965 the white supremacist Rhodesia Front under the leadership of Ian Smith won the whites-only election. On 11 November 1965, Smith unilaterally declared independence. Wilson immediately announced that Britain was not going to use force to crush the rebellion. The Organisation of African Unity (OAU) at a foreign ministers' meeting on 3 December announced that, unless Britain crushed the rebellion by 15 December, the members should break relations with it.[69] On 17 December, Egypt broke relations with Britain along with many other African nations. Both sides agreed to maintain consular relations. The difference between the swift despatch of the troublesome Aden government in September and the sloth shown towards getting to grips with the Smith regime was presumably not lost on Nasser. (In fairness, there was a considerable problem of logistics.) It was, to radical third world opinion, yet another example of the double standards of imperialists – one rule for the Arabs, blacks, etc., another for the white man. Moreover, the Rhodesian debacle demonstrated that the British base at Aden was not much use for peacekeeping in Central Africa, which was allegedly one of the reasons for its maintenance. However, even without the Rhodesian problem, the American Embassy in Cairo saw little scope for improvement in UK–UAR relations as long as the confrontation over Aden continued. It assessed that 'British interests in the Persian Gulf are probably the next target once Aden is out of the way, if not before. Enmity towards Britain is cheap and popular here. As long as the UAR has little to lose and something to gain from a confrontation, the UAR is likely to be on bad terms with the British.'[70]

The Egyptian President was also becoming increasingly concerned with the British relationship with Saudi Arabia. In it, Britain appeared to have discovered a new Arab proxy to fight Nasserism. Within a week of the severing of relations, Britain agreed to supply the Saudis with an air defence network worth £125 million to defend against Egyptian air incursions.[71]

NOTES

1. *Guardian*, 3 June 1964.
2. USNA, AmEmbassy London to State, No. 451, 28 July 1964, DOSCF, Pol UAR–UK–UAR–US, Box 2767.
3. Harold Wilson, *The Chariot of Israel* (London, Weidenfeld & Nicolson, 1981).

4. Zeigler, *Wilson*, pp. 340–1. Mayhew wrote a book with the disaffected *Guardian* journalist Michael Adams lamenting *The Middle East Cover Up* (London, Longman, 1975). Objective it is not.
5. LBJL, AmEmbassy London to State, No. 5814, 22 May 1964, UK Cables, Vol. 1, 11/63-10/64, NSF Country File United Kingdom, Box 206.
6. Zeigler, *Wilson*, p. 210.
7. Healey, *Time of my Life*, pp. 278–9.
8. P. Catterall, 'Foreign and Commonwealth Policy in Opposition', in Kaiser and Staerck, *British Foreign Policy 1955–64*, p. 104.
9. Gavin, *Aden under British Rule 1839–1967*, p. 343.
10. Stephens, *Nasser*, p. 414.
11. Walker, who had been Commonwealth Secretary during the Attlee government, had the problem that he did not have a parliamentary seat, having lost it rather unexpectedly in the general election to a racist campaign by his Conservative opponent. Wilson still made him Foreign Secretary and another MP was raised to the peerage to make a seat for him. However, Gordon Walker lost this by-election and was replaced by Michael Stewart in January 1965. Zeigler, *Wilson*, p. 173.
12. PRO FO 371/178596, VG 1051/48, FO to Cairo, No. 1721, 23 Oct. 1964.
13. PRO FO 371/178596, VG 1051/48, FO Guidance, No. 576, 23 Oct. 1964.
14. USNA, Memcon, 26 Oct. 1964, Morning, Conference Files 1964–66, CF 2440, Box 359, Lot File 66D 110. The Egyptian leader was only briefly referred to in the afternoon session. Memcon, 26 Oct. 1964, Afternoon, Conference Files 1964–66, CF 2440, Box 359, Lot File 66D 110.
15. Ibid.
16. PRO FO 371/178597, VG 1051/67, Higgins submission, 2 Nov. 1964.
17. PRO FO 371/178596, VG 1051/53, Middleton to FO, No. 969, 30 Oct. 1964.
18. PRO FO 371/178597, VG 1051/67, Harrison to Middleton, 12 Nov. 1964.
19. PRO FO 371/178597, VG 1051/68, Cairo to FO, No. 1038, 13 Nov. 1964.
20. PRO CAB 128/39, Cabinet Conclusions, No. 8, Item 2, 12 Nov. 1964.
21. *FRUS 1964–68*, Vol. XXI, Doc. 360, Special memorandum prepared in the Central Intelligence Agency, 18 Feb. 1965.
22. PRO FO 371/183887, VG 1022/17, FO submission, Mr Scrivener, 'Summary of Present UK–UAR Relations', 31 Jan. 1965.
23. USNA, Memcon, Assistant Secretary Talbot's meeting with Sir Geoffrey Harrison, Pol UK–US, 10 Dec. 1964.
24. The December crisis US–UAR is further developed in Lucius Battle's Oral History, LBJL, pp. 17–20.
25. As reported in PRO FO 371/178582, Cairo to FO, No. 187, 24 Dec. 1964.
26. LBJL, CIA Memo, 24 Dec. 1964, UAR, Vol. II, Cables and McGeorge Bundy to President, 24 Dec. 1964, UAR, Vol. III, Memos, NSF Country File, UAR Box 159.
27. LBJL, Battle, Oral History, p. 21.
28. See Pieragostini, *Britain, Aden and South Arabia*, pp. 101–5.
29. PRO FO 371/179861, BM 1041/6, Crawford submission, 1 Jan. 1965.
30. See PRO FO 371/183907, VG 1051/14, Scrivener submission, 'Anglo-UAR Relations', 31 Jan. 1965. This was a review of the talks written some time after.
31. PRO FO 371/183907, VG 1051/19, FO to Cairo, No. 222, 5 Feb. 1965.
32. PRO CAB 128/39, Pt 1, Cabinet Conclusions, No. 17, Item 2, 18 Mar. 1965.
33. PRO PREM 13/2308, Bonn to FO, No. 293, 13 Mar. 1965.
34. PRO FO 371/183908, VG 1051/41, FO to Cairo, No. 521, 19 Mar. 1965.
35. PRO CAB 129/120, Pt 2, Memo by the Secretary of State for Foreign Affairs, 'UK Relations with the UAR', C 65, 24 Mar. 1965.
36. Barbour-Paul, *Britain's Relinquishment of Power*, pp. 83–4.

37. PRO FO 371/183908, VG 1051/50, Scrivener to Middleton, 6 Apr. 1965.
38. PRO FO 371/183908, VG 1051/50, Middleton to Scrivener, 12 May 1965.
39. LBJL, AmEmb Cairo, 18 Apr. 1965, NSF Country File, UAR, Vol. III, Cables, Box 159.
40. *FRUS 1964–68*, Vol. XXI, Doc. 61, 9 June 1965.
41. Nutting, *Nasser*, p. 370. The papers were certainly interesting. A Mr Figg of the Foreign Office commented that two of them, 'British Strategy in the 1960s' and the DMI Conference, contained comments on governments and personalities which could be embarrassing. PRO FO 371/183974, VG 1691/24, Submission by L.C.W. Figg, 30 Apr. 1965.
42. PRO FO 371/183908, VG 1051/59, P.H. Laurence to Middleton, 3 June 1965.
43. PRO PREM 13/1923, Record of conversation between the Prime Minister and the UAR parliamentary reps at Downing Street, 28 June 1965.
44. USNA, AmEmbassy London to State, No. 188, 14 July 1965, DOSCF Pol UAR–UK–UAR–US, Box 2767.
45. PRO FO 371/183913, VG 1053/10, Record of conversation between Heikal and MOSFA Thomson, 16 July 1965.
46. PRO PREM 13/292, Record of conversation Prime Minister and M.H. Heikal (PM Room, House of Commons), 17 July 1965.
47. LBJL, Memcon between Secretary and the Prime Minister, 1 May 1965, UK, Vol. 4, Memos, NSF Country File, Box 207.
48. Healey, *Time of My Life*, p. 280.
49. PRO FO 371/183709, VG 1051/75, Luce to Brenchley, 8 July 1965.
50. PRO FO 371/179743, B 103116/8, Middleton to FO, No. 590, 23 July 1965.
51. PRO FO 371/179743, B 103116/10, Record of conversation Al-Asnag and MOSFA Thomson, 2 Aug. 1965.
52. Prime Minister Wilson was concerned by this claim and asked for a report. The censored message that replies denies the allegation. PRO PREM 11/1923, Top secret, Peduzie to Cheminant, 31 Aug. 1965.
53. *Al-Ahram*, reported in PRO PREM 13/1923, Middleton to FO, No. 652, 13 Aug. 1965.
54. PRO PREM 13/1923, PM 65/135, Stewart to Wilson, 15 Sept. 1965.
55. Ibid.
56. PRO PREM 13/113, Turnbull (Aden) to SOS Col., No. 1018, 20 Sept. 1965, and Greenwood to Turnbull, No. 838, 23 Sept. 1965.
57. LBJL, AmEmbassy London to State, No. 1325, 25 Sept. 1965, UK Cables, Vol. VI, NSF Country File, Box 208.
58. PRO FO 371/183912, VG 1052/26, FO Guidance, No. 397, 1 Oct. 1965. Thomson gives a longer account of the visit in PRO PREM 13/2208, Cairo to FO, No. 781, 26 Sept. 1965.
59. Nutting, *Nasser*, pp. 371–2.
60. *Sunday Times*, 26 Sept. 1965.
61. PRO FO 371/183912, VG 1052/25, Middleton to Stewart, 4 Oct. 1965.
62. Pieragostini, *Britain, Aden and South Arabia*, p. 161.
63. Ibid.
64. USNA, AmEmbassy London to State, No. 2026, 3 Nov. 1965, DOSCF, 1964–66, Pol UAR–UK, Box 2657.
65. USNA, State to AmEmbassy London, No. 2848, 19 Nov. 1965, DOSCF 1964–66, Pol UAR–UK, Box 2657.
66. USNA, AmEmbassy London to State, No. 2344, 22 Nov. 1965, DOSCF, 1964–66, Pol UAR–UK, Box 2657.
67. It had been stopped at the end of the three-year agreement in June 1965. The reason was a combination of Nasser's confrontational behaviour, a poor

American harvest and the greater need in India, also a recipient of PL-480 aid.

68. LBJL, AmEmbassy Cairo to State, No. 1311, 24 Nov. 1965, UAR Cables, Vol. IV, NSF Country File, Box 159.
69. D.B. Miller, *Survey of Commonwealth Affairs: Problems of Attrition and Expansion, 1953–69* (Oxford, Oxford University Press, 1974), pp. 214–15.
70. USNA, AmEmbassy Cairo to State, 11 Dec. 1965, DOSCF 1964–66, Pol UAR–UK–UAR–US, Box 2767.
71. John Stonehouse, a Labour Trade Minister, had a key role in the negotiation. PRO PREM 13/2362, Jenkins to Wilson, 24 Nov. 1965. Earlier in the year, Faisal had 'gone lukewarm' on having an air force. PRO PREM 13/2362. See Wright to PM, 5 Aug. 1965.

13

The Labour Government and Nasser, Part II: 1966–67

NO RELATIONS

THE FINAL CONSULTATIONS on the British 1966 Defence Review were taking place in the last weeks of 1965. Along with the future of Britain's aircraft carrier force, and the TSR bomber, the continued British retention of the Aden base was the subject of considerable debate in the Defence and Overseas Policy Committee of the British Cabinet. On 20 December, the subcommittee on Southern Arabia considered a JIC paper on 'The Effects in the Middle East and Africa of an Early Announcement of a British Withdrawal from South Arabia in 1967 or 1968'. It concluded that, however presented, it would look like an apparent weakening of the British position:

> The UAR will certainly make every effort to represent it as a defeat for British policy. Their ability to represent it as a victory for the UAR will however, depend to some extent on the progress of Egyptian withdrawal from the Yemen at the time. If the Egyptian presence in the Yemen is substantially unaltered it would be more readily accepted throughout the Middle East that the British had been forced out by the Egyptian subversive campaign and incline Arab states to give greater weight to UAR pretensions in the area.

On the other hand, the paper considered that the British withdrawal might allow the UAR to end their presence in Yemen with greater ease.[1] Events were to bear out the fears of the first conclusion. Meanwhile the British were preparing the ground for retreat from Aden. The Americans were warned that Britain would cut back sharply on its east-of-Suez role once the Indonesian threat to Malaysia was over. The Americans, who had long complained about British colonialism damaging the cause of the free world, were distressed at the prospect of being the only Western power engaged in combat in the third world. The Americans made clear that support for sterling was dependent on the willingness of the British to maintain their global role.[2] However, the Americans were a little more sanguine about the Persian Gulf and Aden. The British made clear that they were committed to maintaining facilities in the Gulf. They now believed that facilities that were being developed on Diego Garcia in the Indian Ocean offered the prospect of a more secure staging post than Aden. On 23 January, the OPD committee of the British Cabinet agreed to make an early announcement about withdrawal from Aden. This was against the advice of the Foreign Secretary, Michael Stewart, who suggested waiting until May or June: 'By then, there should have been some withdrawal of Egyptian troops from the Yemen and our intention to leave Aden would look less like a victory for Colonel Nasser.'[3] Another unnamed minister is quoted as saying that the decision was not a victory for Nasser – 'it was really a victory for British commonsense'.[4] Terrorism and Egyptian support for it were likely to continue, was the opinion of the Foreign Office, despite the withdrawal announcement. R.T. Higgins at the UAR desk warned that even the

> announcement of the British withdrawal is unlikely to end UAR support for terrorists. Sir George Middleton is inclined to the view that he [Nasser] has not [ended support for terrorism]. Nasser is being driven month by month by a single minded, revolutionary urge simply to get the British driven out in a situation of maximum chaos and that he has not considered the kind of independent South Arabia likely to emerge after our departure or his real interests regarding it.

Furthermore Higgins feared that Nasser might decide 'that it suited him best, insofar as he could, to direct the full force of his dissident potential against the British but to avoid further antagonising the moderate South Arabians'.[5] The Foreign Office had little confidence that the Aden withdrawal would be helpful in getting Nasser out of Yemen. They hoped that the United States would be 'prepared to make a much more explicit link than heretofore between UAR withdrawal from Yemen and our willingness [to] provide PL480 food to Egypt'.[6] The American Position Paper on the Defence Review was relatively sanguine on the withdrawal from Aden once Britain built up its forces in the Persian Gulf and in the British Indian Ocean Territory (BIOT). It was considered that, if 'played shrewdly with Cairo, the decision to evacuate the base could be useful as a quid pro quo for the stopping of Egyptian support to the terrorists'.[7] Sir Roger Stevens in talks with the Americans said that the British had evidence that Nasser was training some 300 terrorists in Taiz and he feared that with the announcement of British military withdrawal 'it is expected Nasser will increase these activities in order to hasten the departure and multiply its disorder. The announcement may well encourage him to stay in Yemen.'[8] Unhappily for Anglo-Egyptian relations, the pessimists' view turned out to be the correct one. Nasser was already reneging on the terms of the Jedda agreement of August. During the late autumn/winter of 1965, the Egyptians had withdrawn substantial numbers of troops from the Yemen. They had also abandoned large areas of territory to the royalists. However, January 1966 saw renewed heavy fighting putting the cease-fire agreement in some doubt. On 22 February 1966, Denis Healey introduced the Defence Review to the House of Commons containing the news that Britain was abandoning the Aden base by 1968 and was not extending a defence agreement to the Federation of South Arabia.[9] Prior to the announcement, the British did request that the American Ambassador might 'take the more positive line of asking Nasser to adopt a more constructive attitude towards the problems of South Arabia now that the announcement about the base has removed his main objection to our policies there'.[10] This was rebuffed by Riad, the Foreign Minister, who insisted to Battle that the base was not the issue but independence and that the British had to talk to Nasser's new front organisation, the Front for the Liberation of South Yemen (FLOSY).[11]

The announcement of the Defence Review led to exactly the reaction from Nasser that the pessimists feared. The prospect of moving into South Arabia no longer protected by British troops was too much temptation for Nasser. At worst, he would be able to claim a share of credit for another act of Arab liberation.[12] On 22 March, he announced that 'Britain had decided to grant [Aden] independence in 1968. We will stay there [Yemen] till after 1968.'[13] Nasser decided to pursue a military policy in the Yemen, which he called the 'Long Breath'. Nasser concentrated his forces in the southern triangle of Yemeni towns of S'ana, Hodieda and Taiz. According to Edgar O'Ballance, 'Nasser now looked southwards rather than northwards, and increased the facilities for arming and training dissidents at Taiz for the purpose of raids into the Federation of South Arabia'.[14]

In January 1966 Egypt had engineered the amalgamation of the NLF with the more moderate OLOS, which was made up of the formerly moderate PSP, into FLOSY. This proved to be an unstable alliance with the Marxist-influenced NLF unhappy under Egyptian domination. By November 1966, the NLF had declared independence from FLOSY.[15] However, in February 1966, it seemed to be another sign of Egypt's determination to support the independence movement in South Arabia and to continue confrontation with Britain. The breaking of relations meant that Britain's one outlet of protest about Egyptian support for terror was removed. Indeed, the American Embassy in Cairo was worried that the British had written off UK–UAR relations as early as 23 February. The head of the British consular mission in Cairo, John Wilton, was appointed Deputy High Commissioner in Aden. Battle, the American Ambassador, was convinced that it was

> very much in overall western interest that UK–UAR break be minimized and that UK retain here strongest possible political representation. This was provided by Wilton who [is] senior, experienced Arabist and particularly able Foreign Service Officer. (For your information only: (R.A.) Daniell [his replacement] is [a] political lightweight with widely held reputation in Cairo as having strong anti-UAR bias which both he and wife frequently proclaim loudly and publicly.)[16]

After Nasser's 'Long Breath' speech and the rebuff to the American approach, the Foreign Office in London began to take a much firmer anti-UAR line. There was a growing disinterest in seeking to come to terms with Nasser. Instead Britain made moves to strengthen its relations with the anti-Nasser bloc in the Persian Gulf. The most visible sign of this policy was the massive defence contract with the Saudis. They began to ask for more than mere arms. After the collapse of the cease-fire in the Yemen in early 1966, they asked for RAF support in event of the renewal of war with Egypt.[17] The Trade Minister, John Stonehouse, had in selling the deal to the Saudis told them that HMG would 'consider carefully a request from their Saudi friends for help in an emergency'. Michael Stewart acknowledged that this was close to an obligation and recommended that the British either send an RAF squadron on a goodwill training mission to Saudi Arabia or agree to provide civilian pilots to man the Saudi air force. He warned of the potentially grave political risks that might be involved:

> We might find ourselves engaged in war between Saudi Arabia and Egypt and be under pressure to come to Saudi help on an even bigger scale. The powerful Cairo propaganda machine would represent our action as imperialist intervention in Arab affairs and this could affect our oil interests in Iraq and even perhaps in Kuwait, where oil negotiations are delicately poised.[18]

A Foreign Office official informed the American Embassy that British ministers were 'extremely agitated because of possible effect a Saudi cancellation of Lightning deal might have on British Election since this was only proof at hand that US had taken action to help offset costs of F111A'.[19] The Saudis later withdrew the request for RAF support and the situation stabilised once more.

The Foreign Office also made a pre-emptive objection after they learned of rumours that Secretary Rusk might visit Cairo while at a Central Treaty Organisation meeting in Ankara. According to the report,

> there was widespread feeling within [the] Foreign Office that [a] visit by Secretary to Cairo at this time would be widely misinterpreted in [the] area and would strengthen Nasser's prestige making more difficult a negotiated Egyptian withdrawal from Yemen. They believe it also might complicate British efforts to bring about a political settlement in South Arabia prior to their withdrawal.[20]

Rusk decided to cancel the visit on his own initiative. For most of the rest of 1966, Anglo-Egyptian relations remained in limbo. There was some suggestion in April after Sudan resumed diplomatic relations with Britain that the Egyptians would attempt to do likewise. However, there was no evidence of this despite some statements from Egyptian sources that they were unhappy with the breach, which they blamed on the OAU. R.T. Higgins suggested that the 'UAR will not feel entirely happy about not being on speaking terms. It may be such considerations as these which have inhibited the Egyptians from putting our relations to further strain.'[21] In Aden, the violence continued unabated. The number of terrorist/guerrilla incidents in Aden doubled to over 500 in 1966.[22] Of course, the UAR only had a certain degree of influence over the independence movement. It certainly could not be turned off like a tap. The British and the Americans appear to have completely overestimated Nasser's influence over the NLF faction. An American intelligence report in November 1965 was almost certainly erroneous when it described the movement as Nasser's 'puppet'.[23]

Mohammed Heikal, whom the British believed was one of the 'few foreign affairs advisers President Nasser listens to', told the British press attaché and political officer in Cairo, Harry Fletcher, in May that the differences between the UAR and the UK in the Middle East 'are irreconcilable. There is no hope of any improvement in relations over the next two years and no point in trying to re-establish diplomatic relations.' Heikal could not understand

> why the British always support the reactionary hereditary rulers in the Middle East. British policy will work well for the YAR because 'in two years there will be no more King of Saudi Arabia' and Britain's support of other reactionary governments in the Middle

East will suffer the same fate. Similarly, the British supported Faisal in an attempt to damage the UAR through the Yemen war. One result of this, however, is that Faisal has been forced to begin the building of a modern army and it is this modern army which will be the instrument of his overthrow.[24]

The Americans were toughening up their policies towards Nasser. They decided that they would not negotiate a new PL-480 agreement when the present one ended in June. Walt Rostow who had replaced McGeorge Bundy as National Security Adviser recommended this policy 'with some regret':

> We still think it is worth trying to get closer to Nasser and to avoid splitting the Middle East into US and Soviet camps. But Nasser has left us little choice. He has almost dared us publicly not to renew our agreement. He has lambasted us on Vietnam. He continues to stir things up in Yemen and South Arabia. In general, he has not picked you up on the suggestion you made to Sadat last winter to discuss our differences quietly and build a more constructive relationship.[25]

Nasser saw the loss of the food aid as a sign that the United States was attempting to use aid to mould his policies. He was not willing to put up with this and he formally withdrew all requests for American aid from that moment.[26] In July, the UAR Ambassador to the United States (Mustafa Kamel) intimated to the State Department that Egypt was unhappy at the breaking of relations with Britain. The British mission in Cairo did not see any such sign. In an interview with Alastair Hetherington, the editor of the *Guardian*, Nasser had said as much, referring to the problem of Aden and the Yemen as the key differences between the countries. The British First Secretary in Washington, Christopher Everett, explained the scepticism that existed about making any initiative to the UAR:

> London has three reservations about such an initiative: First, do Ambassador Kamel's remarks reflect official UAR opinion? Second, the economic difficulties of the UAR may not be irrelevant to the Egyptian desire to improve relations with the UK, and third, there is no evidence of any let up in the terrorist activities in South Arabia. It is well known that the Egyptians have a hand in these activities. For these reasons London sees no basis for a British initiative and prefers that the UAR take the initiative. If the UAR takes the initiative, London is willing to listen.

Everett added that 'it is easy to see what the UAR would get out of the resumption of relations but it was not easy to see what the UK would get out of it'.[27] The uncompromising line was evident in a submission on policy towards the UAR, which was being drafted during July by the Permanent Undersecretary's Steering Committee. The submission concluded that the UK should follow a policy of opposition to Egypt as a move to restore relations with Nasser could cause Britain to lose its influence with those nations that opposed him. To this end, Britain should be as economically unhelpful as possible to Nasser and should encourage the United States to withhold food aid from him. The Foreign Office view was 'that if the Americans were firm enough Nasser would be forced to face realities and moderate his policies; and moreover, we would not agree that Western interests would suffer if he were to fall'. Consequently, 'as opportunity offers we should take action to frustrate Nasser's aggressive policies against ourselves and third countries, although without unnecessarily engaging in public altercation with the UAR'.[28] This document was never submitted because Michael Stewart – who was by now in favour of a tough approach to Nasser – was replaced by the much less orthodox George Brown who was known to hold pro-Arab views and was well disposed towards Nasser.

GEORGE BROWN'S PRO-NASSER POLICY

Brown, who was Deputy Prime Minister, would have been appointed Wilson's Foreign Secretary at the start of his term, except for a notorious 'tired and emotional performance' on British television after President Kennedy was assassinated. Fearing that Brown would be an unpredictable Foreign Secretary, Wilson had appointed him as Secretary of State at the Department of Economic Affairs. However, the National Plan, which he was supposed to use as the basis for the economic modernisation of Britain, was abandoned as the British economy and more particularly sterling came under pressure in the summer of 1966. Wilson was forced to compensate Brown with the Foreign Affairs brief. Brown was a protégé of Ernest Bevin and, consequently, shared the late Foreign Secretary's views on the Middle East. Brown had got to know Nasser as early as 1952 and, as he explains in his memoirs,

We had kept in close touch and I had met him many times subsequently. It also happened that I knew those around him. And so I turned my mind and that of the Office towards ways in which v might properly bring about the restoration of relations. Altho·

this aroused some horror on the part of those who saw Nasser in quite a different light from that in which I saw him, I persevered.[29]

The problems of the Anglo-Egyptian relationship were evident when UAR planes launched an air attack on Beihan which was on the verge of joining the Federation of South Arabia. Denis Healey, the Defence Secretary, believed that 'everything points to this being deliberate'. He wanted the right of hot pursuit of infringing aircraft restored and that a list of retaliatory targets should be drawn up. However, Brown and Wilson decided to keep these rights in London.[30] George Thomson, who had been retained as Minister of State, warned Brown in early September that there 'are real and objective conflicts between British interests as the present government has seen them and the Egyptian and Arab interests as President Nasser has seen them'. He believed that the best that could be hoped for was that Nasser would turn towards internal reform.[31]

Brown was willing to use unorthodox diplomacy to move the UK–UAR relationship along when the opportunity arose. In November 1966, while on a visit to the Soviet Union, his aircraft and that of Field Marshal Amer, Nasser's deputy, were both diverted to Leningrad. Brown made contact with Amer. In an informal meeting, Brown expressed a willingness on the part of the British government to improve relations. He made clear that no progress could be made as long as the UAR supported terrorism.[32] Amer passed on the message to Nasser who immediately replied via his Ambassador in Moscow. In it, Nasser affirmed that the UAR had no aggressive intentions against the SAF but he felt that Britain was working with the reactionary forces in the Middle East, and in particular Saudi Arabia, 'which more or less amounted to military alliance.'[33] Brown replied with a message through the Canadians, asking Nasser to cease his violent propaganda on the 'Voice of the Arabs'. Britain's relationship with Saudi Arabia, he explained, was not a military alliance but was based on 'mutual friendship'.[34] The exchange of messages continued throughout December. On 12 December, Nasser replied, claiming to have 'a genuine desire to explore a path leading to mutual understanding together with our hope that circumstances in the near future would afford a suitable opportunity for the restoration of relations between our two countries. I feel that when this occurs, it should be on the firmest basis.'[35] Brown was pleased that Nasser wished to restore relations but he raised the question of Egyptian-backed subversion in South Arabia in his message of 22 December. Despite this continuing problem, Brown's initiative seemed to presage a breakthrough in bilateral relations that was unthinkable a couple of months previously.[36]

The reaction of Britain's allies to Brown's new policy was mixed. The State Department told Brown that they were 'very much in favour of [his] initiative and agreed that relations are most needed when differences are greatest'.[37] Turnbull, the High Commissioner in Aden, warned that, 'unless the Egyptian propaganda and subversive campaign can be first brought to an end, Federal Government will react with utmost bitterness to any proposals to re-establish relations'.[38] King Faisal of Saudi Arabia was almost contemptuous of the British olive branch towards Nasser. He remarked that 'in view of Nasser's known support and encouragement of terrorism and his desire to set himself up as a world leader, he would not have "run after him" in the manner in which we appeared to be doing since this could only play into Nasser's hands and strengthen his position'.[39]

Faisal need not have worried as the momentum towards *rapprochement* soon slowed. The senior British diplomat in Cairo, Mr Tesh, reported on 9 February that contacts appeared to have been halted.[40] The Egyptians also banned the over-flight of British military aircraft *en route* east of Suez. This led one Foreign Office minute to conclude that 'the UAR is not interested in pursuing the correspondence with the Secretary of State to attain a genuine improvement in UK/UAR relations'.[41] The Egyptians made no further moves until early April. Then a visiting British parliamentary delegation met Dr Fawzi, a senior Egyptian Foreign Office official, who informed them that relations would soon be restored. Nasser was waiting for a meeting of African states before an announcement could be made.[42] Brown, however, was coming under increasing pressure from some Conservative MPs for chasing Nasser. Therefore, it was some relief when Heikal called on the British Consulate on 11 April to say that the five African countries that had recently met in Cairo had decided to resume relations with Britain on 1 July.[43] The Cairo consulate was suspicious of the timing of the message:

> The passing of the message may now be simply spoiling tactics by the UAR at a moment of known Parliamentary difficulty for Her Majesty's Government. On the other hand, if President Nasser feels that he has gone too far recently in antagonising the west he may also feel the need for rapprochement of some kind with one of the influential western powers in this region. He could hardly choose the United States.[44]

Brown welcomed the message but wanted relations restored sooner. The reason was South Arabia where the independence movement's terrorist campaign had continued to intensify. The British were aware that revolutionary nationalism was winning. The problem was that the Federal leaders, the sheikhs, for all their manifest inadequacies, were British friends and charges of betrayal were being levelled by the Conservatives. The Labour government did not want to betray them. The demands of the militants, which brooked no compromise with the sheikhs or the British unless they first recognised FLOSY as the sole representative of the South Arabian people, remained unacceptable. The British compromise was a promise of air cover for the Federal government for six months after independence to protect against external, i.e. Egyptian, aggression. Nasser's problem was that FLOSY had come late to the revolutionary game. Al-Asnag, its leader, while strongly anti-British, had held out against violence until recently. The NLF, which had borne the brunt of the violent campaign, was the most powerful revolutionary group in South Arabia, and had become by the end of 1966 increasingly estranged from Nasser. FLOSY's only chance of victory would have been an Egyptian-backed invasion after independence. This was made very risky with the British promise of air support. It would appear that the British overestimated – probably due to Cairo Radio's attribution of all terrorist acts to FLOSY and their own lack of intelligence – the strength of FLOSY and Egyptian influence. The Arab League recognised FLOSY as the legitimate government in March, further adding to the illusion of their importance.[45]

The Head of the Arabian Department, Denis Speares, suspected that the Egyptian motivation for restoring relations was because they wanted for genuine or tactical reasons to be able to make possible diplomatic exchanges with the UK over South Arabia. Egypt, he argued, could not lose from a resumption of relations because, if Britain talked to FLOSY about the setting up of a caretaker government, it would be a defeat for Saudi Arabia and the conservative monarchies. On the other hand, if Britain supported the Federal government in a deteriorating security situation, the UAR would be able to argue that by 'our imperialist opposition to Arab nationalist aspirations in Aden, we have made it impossible for them to resume relations, since to do so would be to condone our actions'. Speares, however, suggested that a ministerial visit to Cairo might be possible to test the water.[46] George Thomson, undoubtedly remembering his own unhappy trip, was against the idea fearing 'that if a country which breaks off relations purely as a political gesture is seen to suffer no ill consequences, such will become even more frequent than they now are'.[47]

Field Marshal Montgomery visited Nasser in the middle of May. The octogenarian victor of El Alamein had assumed the role of self-appointed roving ambassador for Britain. South Arabia had been a major topic of conversation with the Egyptian President:

President Nasser had then said, and he plugged this over and over again (the plugging faithfully reproduced by the Field Marshal) that if we wanted a solution in Aden we had to get the present Federal Government out. If we did this terrorism would cease and a negotiation could be held. Otherwise there would be Civil war, whether before or after independence (and the Field Marshal added, the implication was that the Egyptians would promote it).

George Brown replied that this was not possible.[48] British policy, according to a note from Anthony Parsons of the Foreign Office, was that, while Britain would not conclude a defence agreement, 'we shall do our best short of that, to see that South Arabia does not fall under Nasser's control'.[49] The British Cabinet on 11 May agreed to provide air and naval support for South Arabia for six months after independence. Independence was to be granted in January 1968. The Cabinet also noted that there were indications that preparations were being made in the Yemen by the UAR for the further use of poison gas and, in view of the risk that it might eventually be used in South Arabia, Britain should consider issuing a warning to the UAR on the issue.[50] The Saudi King, Faisal, was received in London with elaborate pomp and ceremony on 17 May. Faisal appealed to Wilson not to abandon South Arabia to Nasser. Wilson pointed to the latest arrangements. Abruptly, Faisal's anti-Nasser policy was abandoned when the crisis over the Straits of Tiran broke suddenly in the last ten days of May 1967. Arab solidarity was more important than Arab rivalry when it came to the question of Israel.[51] Anglo-Egyptian relations were plunged into one last crisis.

NOTES

1. PRO CAB 148/49, OPD subcommittee on South Arabia, JIC 105465, 20 Dec. 1965.
2. I would draw attention to a meeting between Undersecretary Ball and Prime Minister Wilson on 9 September 1965. After Wilson rejected any linkage between the support of sterling and the global role, Ball and David Bruce made it clear that 'it would be a great mistake if the UK Government failed to understand that the American effort to relieve Sterling was inextricably related to the commitment of the UK to maintain its commitments around the world'. LBJL, AmEmbassy London (Ball) to Sec State, Secun 5, 9 Sept. 1965, UK Cables, Vol. VI, NSF Country File, Box 208.
3. PRO CAB 148/25, OPD, 8th meeting, 23 Jan. 1966.
4. Bruce Reed and Geoffrey Williams, *Denis Healey and the Politics of Power* (London, Sidgwick & Jackson, 1971), p. 208.
5. PRO FO 371/185170, B 103116/2, R.T. Higgins submission, 'Nasser's Objectives and Capabilities in South Arabia', 26 Jan. 1966.
6. LBJL, AmEmbassy London to State, No. 3507, 25 Jan. 1966, UK Cables, Vol. VII,

NSF Country File, Box 209.
7. LBJL, American Position Paper on UK position in Aden and the Persian Gulf, 27 Jan. 1966, UK Defence Review, NSF Country File, Box 215.
8. *FRUS 1964–68*, Volume XXI, Doc. 68, 4 Feb. 1966.
9. This led to a storm. The Conservatives promised that they would sign a new defence agreement with the Federation of South Arabia if elected at the forthcoming election. The electorate did not share in the concern of, in this case, Enoch Powell, as Labour was returned with a massively increased majority. Pieragostini, *Britain, Aden and South Arabia*, pp. 178–9.
10. PRO DEFE 13/571, FO to Washington, No. 1703, 14 Feb. 1966.
11. PRO DEFE 13/571, Washinton to FO, No. 821, 9 Mar. 1966.
12. Stephens, *Nasser*, p. 425.
13. Hasou, *Struggle for the Arab World*, p. 152.
14. O'Ballance, *War in the Yemen*, p. 156.
15. Halliday, *Arabia without Sultans*, pp. 211–14.
16. USNA, AmEmbassy Cairo to AmEmbassy London, No. 186, 23 Feb. 1966, Pol UK–UAR, Box 2769.
17. PRO PREM 13/2362, FO to Jedda, No. 183, 19 Feb. 1966.
18. PRO PREM 13/2362, Stewart to PM, 66/25, 4 Mar. 1966.
19. This was reported to the American Embassy. LBJL, AmEmbassy London to State, No. 4324, 14 Mar. 1966, UK Cables, Vol. VIII, NS Country File, Box 209.
20. LBJL, AmEmbassy London to State, No. 4708, 6 Apr. 1966, UK Cables, Vol. VIII, NSF Country File, Box 209.
21. PRO FO 371/190208, VG 1051/33, Higgins minute, 26 Apr. 1966.
22. Julian Paget, *Last Post: Aden 1964–67* (London, Faber, 1969), p. 264.
23. *FRUS 1964–68*, Volume XXI, Doc. 67, 5 Nov. 1965.
24. USNA, Battle (Cairo) to State, No. A-960, 21 May 1966, DOSCF, Pol UAR–UK, Box 2767.
25. LBJL, Memo for the President from Rostow, 18 June 1966, UAR, Vol. IV, Memos, NSF Country File, Box 159.
26. Nutting, *Nasser*, p. 375.
27. USNA, Memcon Everett (UK), Bergus and Bovis (NEA), 19 July 1966, DOSCF, Pol UAR–UK, Box 2767.
28. PRO FO 371/190211, VG 1053/11/G, FO submission C.G. Brown, 2 Aug. 1966, Planning Committee PC (66) 39.
29. Brown, *In My Way*, p. 137.
30. PRO PREM 13/1923, Healey to PM, 3/7/1, 3 Aug. 1966 and Brown to Healey, FS 66/85.
31. PRO FO 371/190211, VG 1053/17, Thomson to Brown, 9 Sept. 1966.
32. PRO FO 371/190209, VG 1051/56, Moscow to FO, No. 2130, 23 Nov. 1966.
33. PRO FO 371/190209, VG 1051/56, Moscow to FO, No. 2133, 24 Nov. 1966.
34. PRO FO 371/190209, VG 1051/61, CRO to Ottawa, No. 2358, 2 Dec. 1966.
35. PRO FO 371/190209, VG 1051/60, Canadian Embassy Cairo to Ottawa, No. 948, 12 Dec. 1966.
36. PRO FO 371/190209, VG 1051/71, CRO to Ottawa, No. 3012, 22 Dec. 1966.
37. PRO FCO 39/253, VK 3/1, Washinton to FO, No. 23, 4 Jan. 1967. The Foreign and Commonwealth Office amalgamated their filing system on 1 January 1967. The old FO 371 series ended and the new FCO with various numbers for each geographical department took its place. The separate jackets for files were also abandoned, so VK 3/1 refers to the whole file and not an individual jacket. Files are open and are more like the PREM files than the old FO 371. This, of course, makes a document more difficult to locate.
38. PRO FCO 39/253, VK 3/1, Turnbull No. 11 to FO, 3 Jan. 1967.

39. PRO FCO 39/253, VK 3/1, Jedda to FO, No. 19, 9 Jan. 1967.
40. PRO FCO 39/257, VK 3/8, Tesh to Speares, 9 Feb. 1967.
41. PRO FCO 39/257, VK 3/8, Unwin minute, 15 Feb. 1967.
42. PRO FCO 39/257, VK 3/8, Cairo to FO, No. 1, 4 Apr. 1967.
43. PRO FCO 39/266, VK 3/16, Cairo to FO, No. 261, 11 Apr. 1967.
44. PRO FCO 39/266, VK 3/16, Cairo to FO, No. 261, 11 Apr. 1967.
45. These points are developed further in Barbour-Paul, *Britain's Relinquishment of Power*, pp. 86–9.
46. PRO FCO 39/266, VK 3/16, Speares to Rose, 20 Apr. 1967.
47. PRO FCO 39/266, VK 3/16, Speares to Brenchley, 1 May 1967 and Brenchley annotations, 9 May 1967.
48. PRO FCO 39/266, VK 3/16, George Brown's discussion with Field Marshal Montgomery, 18 May 1967.
49. PRO PREM 13/1775, Parsons to Palliser, Wilson's private secretary, 11 May 1967.
50. PRO CAB 128/42, Cabinet Conclusions, 30, 9, 11 May 1967.
51. Barbour-Paul, *Britain's Relinquishment of Power*, p. 88.

14

Britain, Nasser and the Six Day War, 1967

BRITAIN AND THE ARAB–ISRAELI CONFLICT

THE SUEZ CRISIS greatly reduced the possibility of British entanglement in the Arab–Israeli conflict, as it ensured that British peacemaking efforts would receive indifference, or even scorn, in the Middle East. Thus Britain played little part in the Arab–Israeli conflict in the decade after Suez. Its role was reduced to applauding American efforts to broker solutions to the River Jordan water rights conflict and the problem of weapons of mass destruction in the 1960s. Britain's principal concern was looking after its own interests in the region – Aden and the Persian Gulf. Robert Komer and McGeorge Bundy, commenting on British myopia in the Middle East, pointed out to President Johnson in 1964 that when the British 'say Mideast they mean Aden and Yemen'.[1]

However, Britain still retained some obligations in the Arab–Israeli conflict. Specifically, these were the Tripartite Declaration of 1950, in which Britain, France and the United States guaranteed the borders of the Middle Eastern states, and the pledges that had been made in the early part of 1957 by both Harold Macmillan in the House of Commons, and Commander Noble in the United Nations on the status of free passage for Israeli ships through the Straits of Tiran.[2] The Suez affair had destroyed the Tripartite Declaration's credibility but technically the document and its obligations remained in existence. In 1960, Macmillan was concerned about British obligations under the declaration during the so-called 'Rotem crisis', when Egyptian troop movements in the Sinai desert caused a minor war scare. They were provoked by Israeli retaliatory raids against the Syrian part of the UAR. The crisis ended fairly quickly.[3] He demanded assurance from the Foreign Office that the Tripartite Declaration was 'a declaration of intention by the three powers and was not a pledge guaranteed by treaty such as the [1939] pledge to Poland'.[4]

However, both Prime Ministers Macmillan and Wilson refused to refute explicitly the pledges in the document when given the opportunity to do so in answers to the House of Commons in 1963 and 1965. They did, however, make it clear that they considered the document had been to a large extent superseded by events. On the earlier occasion, Macmillan endorsed comments by President Kennedy, which specifically reiterated the 1950 declaration. However, the Macmillan answer gave plenty of room for interpretation and, in fact, committed the British Government to very little:

> Her Majesty's Government are deeply interested in peace and stability in this area and are opposed to the use of force or the threat of force there as elsewhere in the world ... I cannot say in advance what action we would take in a crisis, since it is difficult to foresee the exact circumstances which might arise. We regard the United Nations as primarily responsible for the maintenance of peace in the area [the Middle East].[5]

Harold Wilson reiterated this policy in April 1965, specifically adding that the Tripartite Declaration had not been 'retracted'. He did add the caveat that the 'original declaration ... was signed at a time when the signatories could regard themselves as virtually the arbiters of Middle East policy. This is no longer the position today.'[6] Britain and the United States had – for the most part – stuck to the terms of the declaration's stipulations on the limiting of arms to the region. These were completely negated by the pouring of arms into the region by the Soviets to the Arabs, and the French to the Israelis. The United States had begun to supply some advanced weaponry to Israel – namely the Skyhawk jet-fighter – and President Kennedy had given much more explicit promises to protect Israel in the event of an Arab attack. Britain was content to remain on the periphery, balancing supplies of Centurion tanks to Iraq and Jordan with similar quantities to Israel. Britain's main arms commitment lay with the massive contract that had been negotiated with Saudi Arabia in 1966.

Britain's private attitude to the Arab–Israeli conflict 'stripped of diplomatic politeness' was outlined by the then Labour Foreign Secretary, Michael Stewart, in 1966. These documents show that British policy whilst ostensibly neutral understandably had little sympathy with the Arab cause, which proclaimed as its ultimate aim the destruction of Israel. To the Israelis, British policy was as follows:

> We see no prospect that the Arabs will be willing to make peace on terms which you can accept in the foreseeable future, or any means

of compelling them to. You must be realistic about the strength of
Arab feeling on this. You must also recognise that it is important to
western interests – which are extremely important to your own
survival – for us to maintain tolerable relations and some influence
with the Arabs. You must not, therefore, expect us to take sides, or
to appear to take sides, with you against the Arabs. For our part, we
will see that you are able to acquire weapons for your defence; and,
as you know, the Arabs are well aware that they cannot attempt to
destroy Israel without taking on the United States Sixth Fleet. In
return, we expect you to co-operate in preventing the dispute
coming to the boil, by acting with restraint, and by maintaining a
reasonable relationship with the United Nations, so that, if you
have to be helped it can be done under United Nations cover. We
understand the difficulties of your position, but by the law of
possession, the preservation of the status quo works markedly in
your favour.

For the Arabs was this 'grimmer message':

You have lost a diplomatic war, took to arms, lost a military war,
and have been losing a cold war ever since. Some day you will have
to come to terms with reality and face the consequences of this,
instead of wasting your substance and energies in this fruitless
pursuit of what you might have got twenty years ago. There is no
prospect that Israel will make any substantial concessions now or
in the future, and there is no prospect of your being able to force
them to; sooner or later you must swallow your pride and settle for
the status quo with (American) compensation for the refugees.
Meanwhile, you are your own masters. We shall not compel you to
make peace and we shall oppose any attempt by either side to upset
the status quo by the use of force.[7]

British policy was based around the preservation of the *status quo*.
It was extremely desirable that change in the Arab world was ordered
and gradual. When Stewart was writing this despatch, there seemed
to be little prospect of war breaking out in the Middle East between
Israel and the Arabs. Inter-Arab squabbles – as exemplified by the war
in the Yemen – made the possibility seem remote and no Arab state
would dare confront Israel on its own. Nasser, in the 1950s, prior to
Suez, had been a relative moderate on the subject of Israel. He had
briefly considered a peace deal with Israel, but had rejected the
American- and British-backed ALPHA plans for a settlement (as had
the Israelis). Whatever chance of peace there was ended with the Suez

operation. However, even in the aftermath of that war, the Egyptian leader placed Israel low on his list of priorities. He refused to agree with the calls of the more radical leaders for an immediate confrontation with Israel. On the issue of water rights in the region, which threatened war in the early 1960s, he counselled a solution short of war on the grounds of disunity in the Arab camp.[8] This relative moderation on the question of war with Israel was not matched by a desire, on his part, to make peace with or to recognise Israel. It was clear from his statements that he believed a military confrontation with Israel was inevitable at some stage in the future and that he could never recognise an Israeli state.[9] For Nasser, Israel provided both an obstacle and an aid to his ambitions for Arab leadership. Israel, as any map shows, physically blocks land links between Egypt and the Arab world. However, the only matter that Arab opinion has ever been united on was a hatred of Israel. Therefore, while Nasser was probably aware that he could not destroy Israel, he may well have believed that a confrontation that ended in a political victory over the Israelis would massively enhance his prestige.

Reversing the post-Suez truce settlement was perhaps the most obvious target for an attack. This settlement had greatly benefited Israel. It had achieved access to the previously closed Gulf of Aqaba and the interposing of the UNEF on the Egyptian side of the frontier and at Sharm-el-Sheikh. This shielded Israel from guerrilla attacks and the threat of attack from Egypt. Furthermore, Britain, France and the United States had made explicit public statements supporting Israel's right of passage in the Gulf.[10] Most importantly, the settlement had severely limited Nasser's room for manoeuvre *vis-à-vis* Israel. It meant that he was not capable of seriously threatening retaliation against Israeli targets with the UNEF in place, nor was he able to blockade the Straits of Tiran. There was some justice in the claim that the UNEF exposed the other front-line Arab states, Syria and particularly Jordan, to severe Israeli retaliation for guerrilla attacks launched from their soil without any prospect of support from the strongest Arab state, Egypt. This was not a major problem until 1966 when the rate of guerrilla attacks on Israel increased after the coming to power of a radical regime in Syria and the emergence of the Fatah faction as the leading Palestinian guerrilla group. Israel responded to terrorist raids with heavy retaliations in late 1966 and early 1967 against its Arab neighbours. The most serious were the attack on Samu, Jordan in November 1966 and the air battle over Syria on 7 April 1967, both of which saw Israel inflict heavy military and civilian casualties on both countries, apparently with impunity. Jordan Radio bitterly criticised Nasser for hiding behind the UNEF. Raymond Cohen has commented that 'to the Arab leader the fraternal Arab states are what the family is to the individual: the source of his identity and reputation. The revelation of Nasser's impotence in full view of his peers was an excruciating humiliation which could not go unavenged.'[11]

Also, as stated above, a successful victory, political or military, over Israel would immeasurably strengthen Nasser's hand in the Arab world against foes like King Hussein of Jordan and the Saudi monarchy. Both nations were Britain and the United States' key regional allies. The division in the Arab world between the reactionary royal regimes and the radicals like Nasser suited the West most of the time, but as the *New Statesman* pointed out it was 'precisely this division in the Arab world which produces competitive bids against Israel and leads even a cautious campaigner like Nasser to move further towards the brink than either his own political interests, or his military resources justify'.[12] Thus when, in the middle of May, Egypt received reports[13] – from Soviet sources – that Israel had moved 11 brigades to its northern border with the intention of overthrowing the Syrian regime, Nasser felt bound to respond both to deter Israel and as William B. Quandt says 'to restore his somewhat tarnished image in the Arab world'.[14] Nasser's response to the perceived Israeli threat was to demand, through his military commander, the immediate removal of the UNEF from their observation points along the border with Israel on 18 May. The Secretary-General of the United Nations, U Thant, believed that UNEF was only stationed in Egypt with the consent of the Egyptian government. He agreed to comply with the request.[15] In his memoirs, George Brown, the British Foreign Secretary, is very critical about this decision.[16]

The consequences of the UNEF withdrawal were that, for the first time in a decade, Egyptian and Israeli forces confronted each other directly. Cairo Radio heightened the tension with inflammatory broadcasts declaring the destruction of Israel was at hand. The removal of the UNEF did not make war inevitable but Nasser's next move escalated the crisis out of control. The other vital tenet of the 1957 settlement was free passage for Israeli shipping in the Gulf of Aqaba. On the morning of 23 May, Cairo Radio broadcast a speech by Nasser, which had been made the previous day. He announced that 'under no circumstances will we allow the Israeli flag to pass through the Gulf of Aqaba'.[17] He used as his justification the right of a nation to exercise belligerent rights when a state of war existed. Not only was Nasser challenging Israel, but he was challenging those Western powers, including Britain, that had pledged to defend the right of free passage in the Straits. Britain was drawn into one last confrontation with Nasser.

THE COST OF KEEPING THE PEACE

An emergency meeting of the British Cabinet was called for the afternoon of 23 May to decide the British response to the crisis. Prior to the meeting, the Prime Minister Harold Wilson, Foreign Secretary George Brown and Defence Secretary Denis Healey met to consider what policy should be put to the Cabinet. Brown was dubious of American calls to activate the Tripartite Declaration and informed them of his objections.[18] He was, however, for strong action on the question of free passage in the Gulf and wished to inform Secretary Rusk immediately that the United Kingdom was prepared to join with the United States and any other maritime powers in organising an international naval force to keep the Straits of Tiran open to shipping. This would have to be set up independently of the United Nations if action could not be organised in that forum. He added that they 'must take account of the likelihood of Egyptian retaliation against shipping in the Suez Canal if such a force were set up. But its establishment might help to restrain Nasser from excesses.' In the discussion that followed it was pointed out that action over the straits could have serious implications for 'Arab policy as a whole ... especially on the likely attitude of FLOSY if we take really drastic action against Nasser'.[19] However, the tone of the meeting was one of determination to take some action against Nasser's coup.[20] It was odd that Brown, normally the most pro-Nasser member of the Labour government, was now arguing for the strongest measures against him, considering that he had already braved strong criticism for his willingness to mend fences with Egypt. Richard Crossman, another senior Minister, perhaps a little uncharitably suggested that his hard line derived from the fact that his 'entire pro-Nasser policy, on which he's been spending weeks and months, [had] collapsed overnight'.[21]

Brown's recommendation to the Cabinet for action to enforce free passage in the Straits was greeted with considerable dissension. The minutes of the Cabinet meeting are quite uninformative.[22] The account in the diary of Barbara Castle, then Minister of Transport, is far more gripping and dynamic, exposing the inadequacy of Cabinet records particularly in the recording of disagreements.[23] In her account Brown claimed that the only hope of restraining the Israelis was an immediate and unequivocal statement from the maritime powers that they were determined to enforce the right of innocent passage through the Gulf by force if necessary. He wanted the backing of the Cabinet before going to Moscow to urge the Soviets to restrain Nasser. Castle described the reaction of most of the Cabinet 'as one of utter dismay'. She herself thought: 'This is no better than 1956.' Chancellor Jim Callaghan was the most vocal in his criticism of the proposal, warning of the danger to Britain's fragile economic recovery: 'we could say good-bye to our own economic activity'. However, it was the intervention of Defence Secretary Healey which was to prove decisive. He, having consulted with the Chiefs of Staff since the morning meeting, now came down strongly against action to assert free passage:

> The ships we needed were in the Mediterranean (as were the Americans'). If an immediate statement were made, Nasser would promptly close the Suez Canal. In any case, it would take them days to get to the Gulf. And once there how could they deploy? It would be folly to concentrate big ships in the Gulf without first 'taking out' Sharm el Sheikh and Nasser's supporting airfields. Otherwise the ships would be a sitting target. The only way to be sure we could 'assert' our rights would be by pre-emptive action, which would be internationally intolerable.[24]

According to Castle, Wilson then intervened, warning that there were dangers but that there were dangers if the government did nothing:

> The United States would certainly intervene massively, and if we didn't back her she would 'write us off'. The Chancellor then intervened, 'Some of us won't have this policy'. To which Wilson 'snarled', 'Some of us won't have this constant obstruction.'

The overwhelming view of the Cabinet was against the proposal and Wilson and Brown were forced to tone down their more ambitious schemes. The eventual Cabinet decision was that George Thomson, the Minister of State for Foreign Affairs, would go to Washington to ascertain the views of the Americans. All discussions would be *ad referendum* to the Cabinet. Castle and Crossman's diaries present the meeting as a complete defeat for Wilson and Brown but they appear to have got at least part of what they wanted. Wilson saw it as an opportunity to take a leading role in the crisis. The Cabinet, however, had stopped any plans for immediate naval action and the possibility of an armed clash with Egypt.[25]

However, the news from Washington was already casting serious doubts on the viability of the Cabinet's conclusions. The United States Deputy Undersecretary of State, Eugene Rostow, informed the British Ambassador, Sir Patrick Dean, that the United States would fulfil its obligations and co-operate with the British plan for a declaration by the maritime powers but the United States hoped that Britain would take the lead. They preferred a 'British–American initiative to an

American–British initiative'.[26] This was what the Cabinet had explicitly ruled out. It was clear that the United States – preoccupied with Vietnam – was just as wary as the British Cabinet about getting involved in a Middle Eastern war zone. They were only willing to discuss military planning on a contingency basis.[27]

On the military front, realities and logistics were adding to Wilson's political problems. After the Cabinet meeting, Wilson, Thomson and naval advisers met. The advice proffered was that no sensible naval operation could be carried out in the Gulf of Aqaba: 'It would be preferable [the Admiral suggested] to deploy naval forces in the Eastern Mediterranean and thereby offer a generalised deterrent to Egyptian military action, with the threat of taking out Egyptian air force bases.' Wilson pointed out that this type of deployment would be in contradiction of what the Cabinet had agreed earlier in the day. The Admiral agreed that it might be possible to arrange an escort in to the Gulf: 'But clearly this might provoke an Egyptian reaction and thereby involve the need to deploy the deterrent forces from the Eastern Mediterranean into action against Egypt.' Wilson concluded the meeting by suggesting that the force in the Gulf could be linked to the one in the Mediterranean as it would have more credibility.[28] Despite these setbacks, Wilson, to his credit, continued to be the firmest advocate of international action to open the Straits. In a speech in Margate on 24 May, he publicly announced the policy that the British were to pursue for the next 12 days – that Britain recognised the Straits as an international waterway. Furthermore, 'Her Majesty's Government will assert this right on behalf of all British shipping and is prepared to join with others to secure a general recognition of this right'.[29]

The Cabinet's other objective, to operate through the United Nations, was equally unlikely to succeed. The French made it clear that they saw no use in working through that body and opposed even a meeting of the Security Council. De Gaulle, spotting an opportunity to bestride the world stage, proposed that the United States, the Soviet Union, Britain and France should meet and attempt to resolve the problem of the Middle East. This was readily accepted by Wilson whose ardour for robust action had cooled. France's traditional support for Israel had also been abandoned in favour of strict neutrality.[30]

The Israelis had intended to strike out against Nasser on 23 May but had been persuaded not to by the American Ambassador, Waldorf Barbour. He warned that to do so would forfeit any prospect of Western support. Barbour floated the British idea of a multinational force as an alternative to war or an Israeli surrender.[31] American officials were wondering what Nasser wanted. Was it a propaganda victory or something more? At the National Security Council meeting on 24 May,

Lucius Battle, the recently recalled American Ambassador in Cairo, wondered aloud whether 'Nasser either had more Soviet support than we know about, or had gone slightly insane'. He noted that 'it is most uncharacteristic for Nasser not to leave a door open behind him, and that is what he appears to have done in this case'.[32] The Israeli Foreign Minister, Abba Eban, was despatched on a mission to Paris, London and Washington to drum up support for Israel among the international community. Eban was given a very cold reception in Paris.[33] In London, Wilson was rather more encouraging. He promised that, while Britain wished to seek a solution in the United Nations, other avenues such as naval action would be explored if that approach failed. According to Eban, he also warned that the Cabinet was much more reticent about the risks than he was.[34]

Minister of State Thomson's talks in Washington had come up with a tentative plan. Britain and the United States would press for effective action through the United Nations to guarantee free passage through the Straits. They would also canvass for a multilateral declaration to assert freedom of passage through the Gulf. Finally, a mechanism was set up for talks on planning for a military contingency should all other means fail. The talks were based on a British military plan. This proposed:

> (a) a small UK–US probing force to escort merchant vessels in the Straits of Tiran; (b) a covering force consisting of British Carrier HMS *Hermes* and its escorts; and (c) a deterrent force in the Eastern Mediterranean consisting of the 6 fleet, the British attack carrier *Victorious* and the British bombing force on Cyprus. The British contemplated that these forces to be under US command.

The United States Joint Chiefs of Staff preferred that the force be designed as protective presence – not for escort duty – and be capable of defending itself. It was also clear that there was as yet 'no meeting of minds between the military on the design of the force'. That was something that had to be left to the governments.[35] The British and the Americans had substantial disagreements about what to do. Both wanted the other to take the lead. In Britain, Defence Secretary Healey reiterated to Wilson on the same day that 'it was militarily unacceptable to operate an aircraft carrier in such confined waters [as the Straits] without first destroying the enemy airforces'. In other words the United Kingdom would find it very hard to break the blockade without first taking military measures, that is, a pre-emptive strike, to ensure the safety of United Kingdom ships.[36]

The Cabinet meeting on 25 May was a much more restrained affair, with Brown in Moscow and Wilson now having swung against any swift response to Nasser's blockade. The Prime Minister backed de Gaulle's plan for the Four Power meeting and had decided to send Fred Mulley to Paris to put a more concrete proposal together. There was uniform disquiet in the Cabinet about the American preference for a British lead in any military operation in the Straits. The Cabinet Conclusions stress that the United Kingdom did not wish to be seen taking the lead in a military adventure to reopen the Straits:

> As regards military action (should this become necessary) to enforce the freedom of passage for the ships to the Gulf of Aqaba, the initial proposals of the United States which rested heavily on the use of British naval forces, in the Red sea, including the aircraft carrier HMS *Hermes*, were unacceptable to us politically and were militarily misconceived.[37]

Castle gleefully reported in her diary that the Cabinet had saved Wilson 'from his own impetuosity – or George's!'[38]

Wilson seemed to take a slightly different view. He informed Brown in Moscow that the Cabinet seemed much happier to accept planning for contingencies: 'But some Ministerial feet are still a little chilly and the support for the Four Power proposal derives in part from the hope that this puts off the evil day of having to opt for something more robust.' Wilson, despite the fact that the Americans had talked the Israelis out of an immediate recourse to war, was pessimistic that Israel would be able to avoid war: 'Obstinate and critical problems and decisions therefore still lie not very far ahead.' However, Wilson was unwilling to speed up plans for action until de Gaulle's Four Power proposal was given a 'fair run' as this had been the price of the Cabinet giving him some leeway.[39]

Brown had gone to Moscow in an effort to get the Soviets to restrain their Arab clients. His mission was hampered by the fact that the British and the Americans had not yet decided what their strategy was going to be. In Moscow, the Soviets showed little interest in the de Gaulle Four Power plan.[40] While they professed not to want war, the events since 15 May had drastically altered the balance of power in the Middle East in favour of Nasser and the Soviet Union. They had no reason to change the new *status quo*. On 25 May, the Foreign Office issued a guidance telegram to British diplomatic missions which complained about the mendacity of the Egyptians and Russians.[41] It stated that it was British policy to 'avoid taking sides in the dispute or passing judgement. Unlike the Russians, who have for many years been openly partisan, we are equally interested in peace and security for all countries in the area.' However, it was acknowledged that

> All Arab governments are likely to support the United Arab Repub-
> lic government's view that they are entitled to close the Straits of
> Tiran to Israeli shipping and they will accuse those who object of
> supporting Israel ... The [Western] Objection is in fact based on the
> principles of international law and the wider interest of all mari-
> time nations in assuring the right of passage through international
> waters even when they are within territorial waters.[42]

The pressure for Western action was growing with reports from Tel Aviv that an Israeli strike was imminent. There were also rumours that the Eshkol government would fall and be replaced by a right-wing or even a military government. Israel seemed to go through a couple of days of self-doubt unable or unwilling to take action. President Johnson urged Eban not to go to war and promised that he was work-ing on getting international action. He reiterated the phrase of Rusk, that 'Israel will not be alone unless it decides to go alone'.[43] However, political realities were piling up that would prevent any bold Western action in the Straits of Tiran. In the United Nations, the threat of a Russian veto and the refusal of the French to co-operate in even putting forward a resolution had led Lord Caradon, Britain's permanent repre-sentative, to assess that there was no chance of getting a holding resolution through, or to get Security Council authorisation for the UNEF to be reconstituted as a naval force.[44]

In the Arab world, there was a growing sense of unease and anger at what seemed to be pro-Israeli partisanship on the part of the British and the Americans. Nasser was fuelling these concerns with his propaganda machine directed as much at Britain and the United States as at Israel. In a speech on 26 May he made a strong attack on the West:

> Today every Arab knows foes and friends. If we do not learn who
> our enemies and our friends are, Israel will always be able to benefit
> from this behaviour. It is clear that the United States is an enemy
> of the Arab because it is completely biased in favour of Israel. It is
> also clear that Britain is an enemy of the Arab because she, too, is
> completely biased in favour of Israel. On this basis we must treat
> our enemies and those who side with our enemies as our actual
> enemies.[45]

The effect of both Britain's attitude in the crisis and successful propaganda deployed by Nasser was that British Middle Eastern interests were soon being threatened by usually friendly Arab states. The British Representative in the Gulf, Sir Stewart Crawford, warned that British support for Israel would jeopardise British facilities on the island of Bahrain.[46] The Kuwaiti Foreign Minister told the British Ambassador that hostile acts by Britain would lead to the cutting of oil supplies. He clarified that 'an enforced passage [through the Straits] would amount to a hostile act within the meaning of this communication'.[47]

The Permanent Head of the Foreign Office, Sir Paul Gore-Booth, was extremely pessimistic, considering that the crisis had altered the whole Middle Eastern situation against the West. He wrote to Brown in Moscow that it might well be better to take no action in the crisis but hope that the Israelis could sort out the problem themselves by resorting to military action. This sentiment was to gather momentum as the crisis wore on. Interestingly, he identified that the Straits issue's importance was not as a matter of the freedom of the seas, but for the change it had caused in the Middle Eastern balance of power.[48] Gore-Booth's suppositions appeared to be borne out by the uncooperative attitude of the Soviets from whom Brown had returned without any help being proffered.

President Johnson now wanted to canvass immediately for a maritime declaration and then prepare for naval planning on a contingency basis. Wilson already knew that de Gaulle would not be in favour of any joint action with Britain and France. Brown and Wilson decided that 'If the Israelis sent an ultimatum demanding action the Prime Minister and the Foreign Secretary would try to canvass as many nations as possible for a maritime declaration.' In a letter to Johnson, Wilson spoke of the danger of war: 'I have in mind particularly the need to avoid a situation in which it could seem to the world and, even more important the Soviet Union would be enabled to claim that the United States and Britain were taking sides militarily in the Arab–Israel conflict.'[49]

It was feared in Washington and Whitehall that the Israeli Cabinet meeting the following day, 27 May, was to decide for peace or war. However, the promises of United States and British support forestalled an Israeli strike.[50] The Americans, now that the Israelis had given pause to await Western support and the maritime plan, wished to press ahead with military planning as 'It was now essential to fulfil our part of the bargain.' One can only assume that Eban was able to persuade the Israeli Cabinet that the assurances he had received from Johnson were concrete enough. However, these promises were far from binding and did not go beyond anything said in public. Johnson was so disappointed by the inadequacy of his pledges to Eban that he commented to his advisers at the conclusion of their meeting, 'I've failed. They'll go.' However, this appears to contradict what Eugene Rostow said to Dean where Eban did not threaten a first strike.[51] Perhaps Eban was able to give sufficient weight to the constant American refrain, 'Israel will not be alone unless it decides to go alone.' Johnson also sent a strongly worded letter to Eshkol warning him not to strike first. In a conversation with the British Ambassador, Michael Hadow, on 28 May, the Israeli Minister for Labour, Yigal Allon, expressed the conviction that Eban had received explicit assurances of naval action from President Johnson but could not publicly announce them. This had stalled the war party in Israel for a few days more. Allon demanded that Britain and the United States show more haste in bringing together the naval force. He also made a request for 'firm declarations by Britain and the United States that any aggression against Israel would be considered an aggression against the United States and the United Kingdom themselves'. Hadow replied that this was 'asking for the moon'.[52]

Wilson asked Brown to submit a paper to him by 29 May on the crisis and assess the options open to Britain, in response to Brown's inquiry as to whether Britain should be prepared to go alone in the event of no one else being willing to commit themselves to a naval operation. Wilson said that it should be known in the next few days as to what were the prospects for some kind of United Nations naval force or for a concerted approach by a group of maritime powers. He was now firmly on the side of caution:

> As things were at present, in the light both of the likely views of the Cabinet and of his own approach, he did not think that we should look beyond that point and certainly not envisage action by the United Kingdom alone. Indeed, he himself would be concerned if there were to be any question of action by Britain and the United States alone.[53]

The Foreign Secretary's paper pointed out that Israel would only be deterred from war if it felt sure that its oil supplies would be allowed through the Straits. He identified three main possibilities developing from the situation: a) war started by Israeli action; b) a settlement restoring free passage; c) a settlement seeing continuation of the blockade. If the first scenario developed, Britain should stay out but would risk being identified with the Israelis in the Arab mind and would also risk parting company with the United States. The second scenario was the best as it would force Nasser to give up his gains and the damage to British interests would be short-term. The gravest difficulties would be caused by the final scenario which would see Nasser and his Soviet backers being appeased. If this occurred,

> the longer term consequences are likely to include the following: the Jordanian regime will be toppled. The South Arabian settlement will be impossible except on Nasser's terms. Other regimes where our interests are concentrated (e.g. in the Persian Gulf) will be open to Nasserist/Soviet penetration. A war to destroy Israel will become inevitable. There are great risks whatever we do (and in doing nothing) but I conclude that it will be wisest to persist with the course on which we are already set. This means pursuing our efforts at the United Nations for a suitable Security Council resolution and at the same time go ahead with the planning of practical multilateral means of keeping the Straits of Tiran open.[54]

The crisis paper that the Foreign Office had drawn up was equally stark in its assessment of the situation and the dangers of appeasement. In many ways, it is a document very reminiscent of Suez 1956, with its allusions to Munich and appeasement and its casting of Nasser and the Soviets as the villains of the piece.[55] While acknowledging that Nasser was unlikely to attack first, the Egyptians, the Foreign Office believed, 'will for the time being adopt the role of peace loving guardians of the new situation whilst perhaps offering some "concessions of no substance"'. The paper assessed that British interests in the Middle East required orderly change:

> We thus stand to be major losers if President Nasser's present cheap victories are acquiesced in. His enhanced prestige will enable him to intensify with greatly increased chances of success his campaign against 'Arab reactionaries and western imperialists', probably with increased Soviet support ... The consolidation of the UAR victory could lead to the rapid undermining of the Arab states where our economic interests are concentrated and expanding.

The problem that had to be addressed was that any action taken to restore freedom of passage was likely to be interpreted as anti-Arab and was likely to incur the risk of the following consequences: (a) the closure of the Suez Canal; (b) interference with oil supplies, an Arab boycott and the withdrawal of the sterling balances. There would also be strategic problems such as the loss of over-flight rights in the Middle East. What tactics to employ was an even bigger problem. Doing nothing or appeasement was equally unappealing. The paper argued that the lesson of 1938 is that, 'if a power pursues aggressive and predatory policies amid widespread criticism and gets away with it, that power will tend to go further and that its ambitions may well grow *pari passu* with its successes'.

The attendant risks with military action, particularly unilateral British action, were very grave. The scenario the Foreign Office envisaged would involve the British government informing the United Arab Republic of their intention to maintain right of passage. Other nations might then be called on to follow the British lead. The operation would have public support and would open the Straits. Unfortunately, the likelihood was that

> President Nasser would probably accept the challenge and stop the passage of our ships unless we had a credible deterrent available. The escorting vessels which would take time to assemble, would not themselves be able to force a passage if resisted, and we should have to assemble forces likely to deter the UAR and accept that a consequence could be full scale war with the UAR.

International action, the paper's authors suggested, was the only realistic way of proceeding. This meant the continued pursuit of international action in the United Nations, the seeking of a joint declaration by interested parties asserting the freedom of passage in the Straits and the assembly of deterrent forces in the Eastern Mediterranean.[56] The annex on the practical aspects of an escort operation described the sheer logistical difficulties involved in gathering a force. The earliest an escort force could be assembled would be 7 June and the overwhelming component of it would be British.[57] The Foreign Secretary and the Foreign Office were strongly for international action to foil Nasser.

The effect of these strongly pro-active arguments was, to a large extent, negated by a case study made of the economic consequences of an Arab oil boycott of Britain which demonstrated what was at stake. Assistant Undersecretary at the Foreign Office Frank Brenchley explained to the Americans the consequences that were to be expected. If three or four Arab suppliers denied Britain oil, the

> effect would be 'disastrous', with a run on sterling, devaluation, severe crippling of production. [A] massive injection of US assistance would soften [the] blow. Foreign Office considers that Iraq and Kuwait certainly, Libya and Saudi Arabia probably, would deny oil to UK if so requested by UAR. Foreign Office fears UAR would so request if British engaged in forceful 'pro-Israel' test of the straits.

Coupled with this Wilson was also 'concerned about effect on UK's Common Market bid of primarily Anglo-American Gunboat Diplomacy'.[58]

What is clear is that the crisis had developed far from the question of freedom of passage in the Straits of Tiran. What was at stake now was the wider question of control of the Middle East. Michael Hadow in conversation with senior Israeli military commanders informed London that they were all in favour of war. The issue was not the Straits but the question of the general position in the Middle East if Nasser was not discredited.[59] Eugene Rostow said more or less the same thing to Dean on 30 May believing that 'Nasser's fundamental objective was not to destroy Israel, which he no doubt recognised as impossible but to take over the Arab world'. In the same meeting, Rostow continued to place the onus on the British to lead allied forces in the Red Sea in any operation in the Straits.[60] The British Foreign Office began to let it be known to the Americans that they had begun to move toward a position which favoured a quick Israeli victory as the solution to all problems. In a conversation with David Bruce, the American Ambassador to Britain, Willie Morris, the Head of the North and East African Department of the Foreign Office, confided that he (and some other Foreign Office pros, he implied) 'believe only the Israelis, acting unilaterally, can take the edge off Nasser's present victory. The Foreign Office recognises that in view of US and UK commitments, that option is out, provided the Israelis play game according to our rules.' Morris then described how Israel would have to compromise on access in the Straits. He speculated that the inclusion of the right-wing parties in the new Israel government was good news, for without them Israel could not compromise and, on the other hand, with them, the government of Israel 'might well decide to go it alone, thus restoring US and UK manoeuvrability'. He also explained that the

> Cabinet [was] in state of considerable shock about the likelihood that the whole fabric of power relationships in Middle East will be destroyed if rush towards polarisation not reversed soon … HMG Ministers also quote shocked unquote by realisation that UK, after two years of trying to detach itself from most Middle East responsibilities, now finds itself apparently locked into a potentially operational role. As Morris puts it, if present trends continue, question is not whether UK involved or not, but whether British interests in area are quote drawn, hanged or quartered. One by-product of the situation is that quote scales have fallen from some Ministerial eyes and Ministers now very pessimistic about possibility of doing business with Nasser.[61]

Morris had identified the key issue. The only means of restraining Israel was for the British and the Americans to take risks in the Straits. On the contrary, a quick Israeli victory would end the problem of the Straits and would damage Nasser. It was no wonder that the West began to lose enthusiasm for bold plans in the Straits of Tiran. An American State Department official, Kohler, thought that 'Nasser (and Russia) are bound to win a major political and prestige victory unless Israel attacks (when in his view, she would beat the Arabs). But US policy is directed to preventing this – and therefore to winning a victory for the USSR and Nasser.' This was obviously illogical. Michael Palliser, Wilson's Private Secretary for Foreign Affairs, commented that the US diplomat seemed unclear as to the conclusions to be drawn from this:

> But it seems to me – and this is purely personal speculation based on that most unreliable of touchstones, 48 hours in a foreign Capital – that the logic of the US position could be before long, either to be less determined in the exercise of restraint on Israel: or, alternatively (and this is the line one senses as not unwelcome in the Pentagon) to press Israel to make concessions – such as recognising that no Israeli ships can be allowed through the Tiran straits but only those of non-belligerents – which Israel will not accept without war: and then to use the war to force sense (and therefore concessions also) out of the Russians and the Arabs. This is certainly not a conscious US policy, but there is a lack of conviction in what is being tried at present that seems likely before long to lead to a search for (or an acceptance of) something more drastic.[62]

The British Cabinet meeting on 31 May was again split on the question of what to do. Brown began the meeting by stressing the continued gravity of the situation. In his opinion, the key to the situation lay in convincing Israel that the great powers were seeking a solution to the crisis which would enable shipping to have the right of innocent passage to Eilat. Four Power or United Nations action seemed unlikely. Britain would canvass for an international declaration in favour of the rights of innocent passage through the Straits and continue with contingency plans to enforce this if all else failed. There was considerable dissension in the discussion which ensued. Most of the Cabinet was firmly against military action. It was argued

> that the changes which had taken place in the military disposition by the Arab countries and particularly the United Arab Republic represented a permanent change in the balance of power in the

Middle East, to the disadvantage of Israel which both she and the Western powers would have to accept, although we must seek to ensure that this change did not lead to a further series of Arab victories which would endanger Israel's existence. We should not take the lead in even organising a declaration as whatever our pro-Israeli sympathies, our economic interests lay with the Arabs.

Furthermore, the legal position of navigation rights was unclear. Supporters of more vigorous action in the Cabinet pointed out that in the broadest view, i.e. freedom of the seas, it was a United Kingdom interest to maintain the freedom of navigation in the Straits:

> Moreover, although there could be no question of our seeking the overthrow of President Nasser, which could be contrary to our interests in South Arabia and in the Persian Gulf, our wider interest in the Middle East would suffer further damage if it were seen that the President had been wholly successful in his recent moves and had thereby put at risk the continued existence of Israel.[63]

Others argued that Britain had to do something to prevent war and the collapse of the West's Middle East position. The Prime Minister summed up by saying that Britain would continue to seek a negotiated settlement and that the Foreign Secretary should be authorised to canvass for a maritime declaration and planning should continue with the aim of establishing an international force.[64] According to Crossman's account, Wilson again tried to foist a more radical policy on the Cabinet, which was rejected. The Cabinet wished to make it clear that, 'until it was certain there was an effective force, we would not be committed to any international action and that if it turned out to be a merely Anglo-American force, Britain should not take part'.[65] Wilson's pro-Zionist inclination seems the most likely reasoning behind his continued advocacy of a major British role in the crisis, though he did say to Barbara Castle in July that he might have seen the international crisis as an excuse for devaluation: 'The Middle East might have given us the opportunity if the Arab nations had withdrawn all their reserves. I can just imagine how I should have gone on TV. These Arabs, Nasser and all that, trying to dictate our foreign policy.'[66] It certainly would have been a more stylish, going-down-all-guns-blazing speech than the 'pound in your pocket' phrase that Wilson used in November after the devaluation. Crossman on the other hand was convinced by a meeting with Leskov, the previous Israeli Chief of Staff, that Israel could deal with the situation on its own.[67]

Serious Anglo-American efforts to impose a Western solution to the crisis ended at this Cabinet meeting. The new British policy was reflected in the diminishing enthusiasm in the Foreign Office for canvassing for the maritime declaration – something that drew some barbed comments from the Americans. The Foreign Office backtracked so far that by 2 June it was conveying acute unhappiness about the Americans' attempt through the press to project a 'strong image of UK being out in front on exclusively UK/US maritime declaration initiative'.[68]

With the caveats that had been attached by the Cabinet, it seemed unlikely that Britain, even with the United States, could take any meaningful action to break the blockade and prevent war. Further-more, as previously stated, the Straits issue was receding in impor-tance. This was emphasised by the signing of an Egypt–Jordan military alliance on 30 May. Even King Hussein – who a week previously believed Nasser was 'behaving like a madman'[69] – could not remain aloof from the clamour for Arab unity against Israel. This setting up of a joint Arab command led to hard-liners such as Moshe Dayan and Menachem Begin joining the Israeli Cabinet virtually assuring that war was inevitable.[70] The fact that the signals from Washington and Whitehall were now saying to Israel that it would have to accept a compromise on Israeli rights in the Straits of Tiran confirmed the Israeli determination to go to war. There were signs that Egypt was seeking to cut a deal with the West which would allow non-Israeli-flagged ships to use the Straits or that only strategic goods such as oil would be blockaded. Israel felt that war was a minor danger in comparison to the damage that would be caused by a retreat over the Straits.[71]

The fact that Britain couldn't or wouldn't do anything was further underlined by the remarkably restrained and bland House of Com-mons debate on the Middle East on 31 May. Brown went out of his way to put forward a moderate line, specifically warning of the danger of seeking a confrontation with Egypt. He did admonish Nasser gently but his comments suggest someone who knows that the day when Britain could take action was past:

> We must not fall into the trap of regarding, or allowing others to regard, our Middle Eastern policy as a struggle to the death between ourselves and President Nasser … At the same time I am not blind to his errors … I believe that in the last two weeks he rashly adopted a policy in the Middle East which could endanger, not only himself and his country, but the peace of the whole world. We are not setting out – to use the colloquialism – to 'topple Nasser', as hon. members opposite once foolishly attempted to do. But neither are we prepared to accept that he has the right to topple

another Middle Eastern nation at the risk of plunging us all into war.

Brown's room for action was limited severely by the previous day's Cabinet so he did not go beyond promising to canvass other nations for a maritime declaration.[72] It seems likely Prime Minister Wilson's speech would have been tougher but the Cabinet, as Crossman commented, had 'taken the guts out of the speech Harold Wilson had hoped to make'. It instead ended up being nothing but a string of platitudes.[73]

On 2 June, Wilson left for North America to confer with President Johnson. The lethargic moves towards planning an international maritime force suggest that both countries were not that serious any more about taking the risks necessary to prevent war. Johnson said that he 'felt that a military initiative in the Middle East, which he expected would be an Israeli one would overtake us'. Wilson felt that the American President was 'clearly concerned about the risk that the Israelis will go it alone in the next day or two or that, even if they don't, we shall very quickly reach the point at which everything will be seen to turn on whether the subscribers to the International Declaration are prepared to put teeth into it'. The timetable Wilson reported to Brown envisaged 'that we will allow up to Tuesday [6 June] or Wednesday to let it be seen that nothing is going to come out of the United Nations: that thereafter we will publish the maritime declaration: and that it may not therefore be until the end of the week that the question of enforcing it will arise.'[74] Neither Johnson nor Wilson had the political capital to put teeth into the declaration. Wilson could not get his Cabinet to give him the authority and Johnson, likewise, faced the same problem with Congress. There is considerable evidence that the President, if not actually in favour of an Israeli strike, was moving towards a position of neutrality on the subject. He had already made a number of statements through intermediaries to the Israelis that the United States while not supporting an attack would not oppose one either. Israel was worried about signals from the State Department that a compromise solution was being sought that would not restore the pre-crisis *status quo*. Meir Amit, the Head of Mossad, got the impression from Defence Secretary Robert McNamara that the United States would not mind if Israel settled the crisis militarily.[75] Eban received a message from Israel's Ambassador to the United Nations that Justice Abe Fortas, a close Johnson friend and intermediary with the Israelis, had said that the President had remarked that he welcomed the Israeli pause to 'explore options other than Israeli force. If they had not done so, it would have been difficult to secure the President's sympathy.'

These two pieces of evidence convinced the Israelis that war could be fought with tacit United States blessing.[76] Arthur Goldberg, America's UN Ambassador, told Eban that because Johnson had promised action subject to US constitutional provisions he had actually committed to nothing since the constitutional provisions referred to were a joint resolution of Congress before coming to Israel's aid 'and the President can't get such a resolution because of the Vietnam war'.[77] Johnson was also probably influenced by the signals from Cairo which suggested that Nasser would neither compromise on the Straits nor let the blockade be challenged. The British, and especially the Ambassador, Michael Hadow, appear not to have given the Israelis any such intimation and seem to have been completely in the dark about the Israeli attack. Hadow, on 4 June, noted that Israel had relaxed its posture and was not likely to strike for the time being. The lethargic preparations for the maritime declaration and the naval force suggest that both Britain and the United States no longer saw the ideas as having much use. Contingency talks were not even due to begin until 7 June.[78] This delay must raise doubts about the seriousness of this planning. Wilson arrived back in London late on 4 June. When he awoke on 5 June, news was coming in of the massive Israeli pre-emptive air strike on Egyptian airfields. Within three hours the Egyptian air force was wiped out on the ground, leaving the Egyptian ground forces in the Sinai without air cover. It was a blow from which the Arabs would not recover.[79]

NOTES

1. LBJL, Bundy/Komer memo for the President, 29 Apr. 1964, NSF Country File UK, Box 213.
2. See Chapter 5.
3. For an account of the Rotem crisis, see Uri Bar-Joseph, 'Rotem: The Forgotten Crisis on the Road to the 1967 War', *Journal of Contemporary History* (1996), pp. 547–66.
4. PRO PREM 11/4358, de Zulueta–ACI Samuel, 26 Feb. 1960.
5. *Hansard*, 710, Commons Oral Answers, Col. 142, 14 May 1963.
6. *Hansard*, 710, Commons Oral Answers, Col. 1153–6, 13 Apr. 1965.
7. PRO PREM 13/1617, E 1051/13, Stewart–Hadow (Tel Aviv), 29 Mar. 1966.
8. For instance, 17 Dec. 1963, Cairo Radio broadcast: 'The UAR will not let itself be pressured into the adventure of a war against Israel as long as all the Arab states are not unified.' Lacouture, *Nasser*, p. 291.
9. Nasser justified many of his actions as having the ultimate aim of destroying Israel. For instance, in 1962, it is reported that he said 'The liberation of Yemen is a step towards getting rid of Zionism', cited in David Pryce Jones, *The Closed Circle* (London, Weidenfeld & Nicolson, 1986), p. 253.
10. See Chapter 5.

11. Cited in Ben D. Mor, 'Nasser's Decision Making in the 1967 Middle East Crisis: A Rational-Choice Explanation', *Journal of Peace Research*, 28, 4 (1991), pp. 359–75.

12. *New Statesman*, 26 May 1967.

13. While it seems Israel would very much like to have seen the fall of the Syrian regime, there is a fair degree of evidence from UN observers that Israel *had not* concentrated troops on its northern frontier and certainly not on the scale suggested by the Soviets. Walther Laqueur points out that the Soviets were claiming Israeli troop concentrations on the Syrian frontier for many months prior to May. Laqueur, *The Road to War* (London, Penguin, 1968), pp. 74–5. What is certain is that Nasser believed or chose to believe the Soviet claims in May. An American NSC official opined that the 'Soviet advice to the Syrians that the Israelis were planning an attack was not far off, although they seem to have exaggerated the magnitude. The Israelis were planning an attack – but not an invasion.' LBJL, Saunders memo to M. Bundy, No date but drafted sometime before 19 June 1967, Middle East crisis, Vol. 1, National Security File, NSC History, Box 17.

14. William B. Quandt, *Peace Process* (Washington, DC, Brookings, 2001), p. 24.

15. U Thant, Report on the withdrawal of the UNEF, 27 June 1967, in Laqueur, *Road to War*, App. 1.

16. Brown, *In My Way*, p. 136.

17. Laqueur, *Road to War*, p. 90.

18. In a meeting with Undersecretary Eugene Rostow on 21 May, Ambassador Dean conveyed the British government's wariness of having to invoke the Tripartite Declaration, which they regarded as out of date. USNA, State–AmEmbassy London, 21 May 1967, ME Crisis Files, Misc. Doc. Box 14.

19. PRO PREM 13/1617, Meeting between Prime Minister, Defence Secretary and Foreign Secretary, 23 May 1967.

20. Brown, before the Cabinet meeting, informed the Washington Embassy that he was recommending to the Cabinet that Britain should 'join with the United States and such other powers as can be persuaded to take part in concerting naval action to assert the right of free passage through the Straits of Tiran'. PRO PREM 13/1617, Brown–Washington, No. 5617, 23 May 1967.

21. Crossman, *Diaries of a Cabinet Minister*, Vol. II, p. 355.

22. CAB 128/42, Pt 2, Cabinet Conclusions, 31, 23 May 1967.

23. Cabinet minutes were informative until 1940. The vividness of the disagreements between the Cabinet during the Battle of France led to the minutes being made far drier and with the excising of much of the argument. As regards the veracity of Castle's account, she was a trained shorthand secretary and would have been able to take notes as quickly as the Cabinet stenographer. Richard Crossman, who was on holiday in Cyprus, relied on memory to transcribe his recollection usually on the evening of the event. Interestingly, upon his return from holiday, he read the Cabinet minutes and compared them to the accounts he heard from Roy Jenkins and Barbara Castle and this made him 'realize once again how misleading the official record can be … The discussion was passionate and extremely stirring yet when it had been boiled down and dehydrated by the Cabinet Secretariat very little of it remained. In fact the account which they circulated was trimmed down to suit the conclusions the PM wanted to have recorded.' Crossman, *Diaries of a Cabinet Minister*, Vol. 2, 29 May 1967, p. 356.

24. Castle, *Castle Diaries, 1964–70*, p. 258.

25. Ibid.

26. USNA, State to AmEmbassy London, No. 9751, 23 May 1967, Middle East crisis

chronological, 21–23 May, Middle East crisis files, Box 7.

27. PRO PREM 13/1617, Dean–FO, No. 1729, 23 May 1967 and also Dean–FO, No. 1746, 24 May 1967.
28. PRO PREM 13/1617, Note of meeting between Prime Minister and MOSFA George Thomson, 23 May 1967.
29. *Times*, 25 May 1967.
30. This support had been diminishing since the early part of the decade. The French no longer needed Israeli help for their own nuclear project. The end of the Algerian war had seen France's relationship with the Arab world improve dramatically. Israel had also lessened its dependence on French arms with much of its military equipment sourced from the United States and Britain. The collapse of the Franco-Israeli alliance is outlined in the classic work by Sylvia K. Crosbie, *A Tacit Alliance: France and Israel from Suez to the Six Day War* (Princeton, NJ, Princeton University Press, 1974), pp. 170–214.
31. See Quandt, *Peace Process*, p. 28.
32. LBJL, Record of NSC meeting, 24 May 1967, Middle East crisis, NSF, NSC History, Box 17.
33. De Gaulle evidently believed that Eban was seeking French military support for a pre-emptive attack on the Arabs and warned that France would take no risks for Israel. He explicitly warned against Israel firing the first shot. It was a disastrous and depressing meeting for the Israelis. Their key Western ally had deserted them. Crosbie, *Tacit Alliance*, pp. 190–1.
34. PRO PREM 13/1618, Record of conversation between Prime Minister and Foreign Minister Eban, 24 May 1967.
35. USNA, State to AmEmbassy London, No. 203624, 26 May 1967, Middle East crisis chron., 26–28 May, Middle East crisis files, Box 7.
36. PRO PREM 13/1618, Healey–Wilson, 24 May 1967.
37. CAB 138/42, Pt 2, Cabinet Conclusions, 31, 25 May 1967.
38. Castle, *Castle Diaries*, p. 259.
39. PRO PREM 13/1618, PM PT 134/67, Wilson–Brown (Moscow), No. 1346, 25 May 1967.
40. PRO PREM 13/1618, Record of meeting with President Progeny, 25 May 1967.
41. PRO PREM 13/1618, FO guidance telegram, No. 116, 25 May 1967, 'Middle East Situation'.
42. PRO PREM, FO guidance, No. 116, 25 May 1967.
43. Quandt, *Peace Process*, p. 35.
44. See the following correspondence: PRO PREM 13/1618, Caradon (New York)–FO, Nos 1106, 1107 and 1108, all 26 May 1967.
45. Nasser's speech of 26 May 1967 to Arab trade unionists, reprinted in Appendix 4 of Laqueur, *Road to War*, pp. 294–7.
46. PRO PREM 13/1618, Crawford (Bahrain)–FO, No. 356, 26 May 1967.
47. PRO PREM 13/1618, Arthur (Kuwait) to FO, No. 197, 27 May 1967.
48. PRO PREM 13/1618, Gore-Booth–Brown, 26 May 1967, 'Middle East Crisis – Balance of Power'.
49. USNA, Wilson to Johnson, AmEmbassy London to State, No. 203986, 28 May 1967, Secret Middle East crisis chron., 26–28 May, Middle East crisis files, Box 7.
50. Quandt, *Peace Process*, p. 36.
51. PRO PREM 13/1618, Dean–FO, No. 1804, 27 May 1967.
52. See the following correspondence: PRO PREM 13/1618, Hadow–FO, No. 402, 28 May 1967, PRO PREM 13/1618, Dean–FO, No. 1811, 28 May 1967.
53. PRO PREM 13/1618, Note of meeting between SOSFA and PM in the Cabinet Room, 28 May 1967.

54. CAB 129/130, C 88, Memo by the Foreign Secretary, 29 May 1967.
55. Crossman felt the same way about the paper. 'The most striking feature of the FO document was its passionately anti-Russian and anti-Nasserite tone ... The line was broadly to do a Suez but without the mistakes involved in the actual Suez campaign.' Crossman, *Diaries of a Cabinet Minister*, Vol. 2, p. 357.
56. PRO CAB 129/130, C 88, Middle East crisis paper by Foreign Office officials, 29 May 1967.
57. PRO CAB 129/130, C 88, Annex B, 'Practical Aspects of International Action', 29 May 1967. The Chiefs of the Defence Staff had already worked out a plan which described in greater detail the military options that could be taken in event of military force being needed. It had already been decided that 'Risks to escort force will be accepted and the onus of initiating hostile action will be placed on the UAR.' The paper goes on through the various military scenarios likely. PRO DEFE 4/218, COS, 42nd meeting, DP 49/67, Min. 2. Other material relating to this is contained in PRO DEFE 5/174, COS, 58/67.
58. USNA, Bruce (London)–State, No. 9932, 30 May 1967, Situation reports, 29–31 May, Middle East crisis files, Box 14.
59. PRO PREM 13/1618, Hadow–FO, No. 390, 27 May 1967.
60. PRO PREM 13/1618, Hadow–FO, No. 390, 27 May 1967. PRO PREM 13/1619, Dean–FO, No. 1840, 30 May 1967.
61. USNA, AmEmbassy London to State, No. 9931, 30 May 1967, Middle East crisis chronological, 29–31 May, Middle East crisis files, Box 7.
62. PRO PREM 13/1906, Palliser to Wilson, 1 June 1967.
63. Egypt, even though economically a virtual basket case, could still damage Britain by closing the Canal. The Foreign Office thought: 'It would be risky to assume that the UAR government will not (repeat not) in any circumstances close the canal to some or all British and American shipping. In addition the UAR would of course lose some canal revenues by instigating interference with Middle East Oil supplies, but we doubt if this would deter them if they judged it politically necessary.' PRO PREM 13/1619, FO–Washington, No. 5889, 30 May 1967.
64. PRO CAB 128/42, Pt 2, Cabinet Conclusions, 33, 30 May 1967.
65. The Cabinet according to the Crossman account was overwhelmingly against any ambitions operations. Only the Commonwealth Secretary, Herbert Bowden, and the Minister for Labour, Ray Gunter, favoured unilateral action. Crossman, *Diaries of a Cabinet Minister*, Vol. 2, p. 358.
66. Castle, *Castle Diaries*, p. 282.
67. Crossman, *Diaries of a Cabinet Minister*, 31 May 1967, p. 359.
68. USNA, London–State, 10100, 2 June 1967, Secret/Nodis Chron., 1–3 June, Middle East crisis files, Box 7.
69. PRO PREM 13/1617, Amman–FO, No. 417, 23 May 1967.
70. R. Ovendale, *The Origins of the Arab–Israeli Wars*, 2nd edn (London, Longman, 1991), pp. 202–3.
71. Ibid.
72. *Hansard*, 747, HOC Debates, Col. 110, 31 May 1967.
73. Wilson ended his speech as follows: 'I feel that it is right to interpret this debate as a mandate to Her Majesty's Government by every means in her power to continue working with all who are working with us in the search for peace, as we are working with them, but in a wider sense, to use this opportunity been given, having peered into the abyss as we have, to turn the threat of military war into the reality of total war in the Middle East against man's most ancient enemies of poverty, hunger and disease.' *Hansard*, 747, HOC, Col. 212, 31 May 1967. Crossman, *Diaries*, p. 361.

74. PRO PREM 13/1619, PM PT 150/67, Wilson–Brown, UKMISNY–FO, 1202, 3 June 1967.
75. Ahron Bergman and Jihan El-Tahri, *The Fifty Years War* (London, Penguin, 1998), pp. 84–5.
76. Quandt, *Peace Process*, pp. 38–9.
77. LBJL, Arthur Goldberg Oral History, p. 22.
78. Rostow informed Dean of this. PRO PREM 13/1619, Dean–FO, No. 1898, 3 June 1967.
79. Stephens, *Nasser*, p. 493.

15

The Six Day War and its Aftermath

PRESIDENT NASSER was not informed of the extent of the damage caused by the Israeli air strike until late on the afternoon of 5 June. Confronted by military catastrophe Nasser decided to accuse the British and the Americans of helping the Israeli attack. The skill with which the attack had been executed, the fact that the Israelis flew in over the longer Mediterranean route and the apparent massive strength of the attack may well have convinced Nasser that the attack was carried out in concert with the Americans and the British. The seeming determination of Johnson and Wilson in the days before the war to aid Israel only increased the feeling of collusion in Arab circles. Memories of Suez were never far from the mind of the Egyptian President. King Hussein, who had joined the attack on Israel under the mistaken assumption that Egypt still had an air force, was contacted to back up the Egyptian claim. The conversation was intercepted by the Israelis and demonstrates that Nasser had no real proof of any collusion.[1] Despite this, he decided to broadcast the claims over Cairo Radio and break relations with the United States.

The accusations led much of the Arab world to sever relations with Britain and the United States. Oil-producing Arab states denied oil supplies to Britain.[2] The Suez Canal was closed as it became apparent that the rapid Israeli advance was threatening the Canal. The British immediately denied the allegations in the United Nations and in the House of Commons where Wilson also attacked the closure of the Canal in the strongest terms: 'we are not at war with Egypt as the tendentious propaganda suggests ... Clearly, in these circumstances, the Egyptians have no right to close the Canal to us and to others because of the trumped up statements of the kind that have been made.'[3] In the United Nations, the Syrian delegate made further damaging claims of British involvement with claims that a captured Israeli pilot had admitted that British forces were based in Israel.[4] Rusk contemptuously described the Egyptian charges as a gigantic alibi. They quickly received the title of the 'Big Lie'.[5] How to nail the 'Big Lie' was a pressing problem for the allies. Chet Cooper of the State Department suggested that the Prime Minister and the President should request a UN investigation, perhaps to be handled by three members of the Security Council. Brown asked Caradon to request 'an immediate, impartial investigation of the charges by the United Nations'.[6] El Kony, the UAR's Ambassador, said that it had been proved beyond doubt that Britain and the United States had participated in air strikes against Arab lands, and provided an air umbrella over Israel since 5 June. Despite this continued barrage of false allegations, Caradon remained on reasonable terms with the Arab ambassadors including El Kony: 'When I told him today that we must keep our lines open he warmly thanked me.' The British Ambassador reiterated, 'We must start rebuilding bridges with them.'[7]

By the late evening of 6 June 1967, it was clear that further fighting on the Egyptian and Jordanian fronts would only lead to increased loss of territory and troops on the Arab side. The Soviets now pressed for a resolution calling for the ending of hostilities on the basis of the current front line. A more strongly worded resolution calling for an immediate cease-fire was passed on the evening of 7 June when the first call failed to elicit an affirmative response from the combatants. This second resolution was accepted by Jordan and Israel immediately. Egypt did not accept until 8 June, by which time the Israeli army was on the east bank of the Suez Canal. What was noticeable was that the British and equally the French played little part in the cease-fire agreement. It was the Soviets and the Americans who now were the only powers with influence in the region. Britain's lack of influence was plain for all to see.

Brown sent a memorandum outlining how British interests in the Middle East could be best secured in the light of the massive Israeli victory. It was almost a blueprint for reordering the region in favour of the West. Britain had to secure the immediate reopening of the Canal and the resumption of oil supplies. He feared that if Britain did not

> secure them at the onset of what promises to be a long period of bargaining for a Middle Eastern settlement, we shall find that the Russians and Egyptians, probably with the reluctant support of the oil producing countries, try to insist in a bargain whereby the *quid pro quo* for the resumption of oil supplies and the opening of the Canal is a total Israeli withdrawal. This is something we might not be able to deliver and moreover might not want to deliver.[8]

The Russian/Egyptian tactic might in the end break down because the oil-producing states would eventually need to sell the oil. 'But in the meantime it might cause us serious material damage while at the same time it would greatly complicate, if not destroy, the prospects of securing a sensible long term Arab–Israel settlement.' Britain should not agree to any Security Council resolutions condemning Israel or calling for a withdrawal until British interests were secured. Furthermore Britain should consider making the following demands: the withdrawal of the Egyptian army from the Yemen and the resumption of diplomatic relations with those Arab states that have broken them off. A resumption of ties with the Egyptians would have the advantage of discrediting the 'Big Lie'.[9]

Brown also articulated plans for a Middle Eastern settlement to Pat Dean that called essentially for land for peace. Britain would seek to guide behind the scenes rather than attempt to take the lead in any search for a settlement. Brown evidently saw that the West's bargaining power was at its height. He acknowledged that, if 'Nasser survives, relations with him will be very difficult but we should concentrate on efforts on improving relations with the Arab countries where our interests lie'.[10] Brown's proposals for a peace settlement were questioned by the British Ambassador in Amman who believed the war provided the opportunity for Britain to make a final disengagement from the Middle East:

> Furthermore, we should frankly recognise (and this has been clearly brought out during the recent Arab–Israel conflict) that we no longer have the material power or the influence on our own to enforce a policy of our own choosing in the Middle East. We should, therefore eschew any invitations to take the lead in controversial disputes between the two parties as e.g. over the Straits of Tiran.

In fact, to take a lead in the peacemaking would only allow the radical Arabs to present any deal as a great power *fait accompli* like those of the past. As for Nasser, Britain 'should not be a party to nor encourage others to the economic support of Nasser who has done more in the last week to damage Western interests in the Middle East than any other Arab'.[11] On 9 June, the Egyptian President had appeared on Egyptian television announcing his resignation. Public reaction forced Nasser to reconsider and he withdrew his resignation the following day. Brown on hearing the news wrote to Wilson suggesting that Britain should use every 'opening available to us to support the view that Nasser had let down all his friends and had failed on every ground'. Wilson commented that Britain should not 'be seen to be trying to topple Nasser who, if he remains – George argues – his words – will be a dead duck'. However, British diplomats and politicians rather understandably were even more hostile to Nasser than usual. This hostility was strongly reflected in the British press. The normally pro-Arab *Economist* commented that Nasser was a 'would be Bismarck who handled the preliminaries like a Master – the Ems telegram, the assembly of the armies and all only to get swiped for six at Sedan'. The *Daily Telegraph,* which always viewed Nasser with a jaundiced eye, was even more forthright. The 'West must be profoundly grateful to Israel for doing, against its earnest advice, what it shrank from doing itself'. And for the moment, the West was.[12]

Primarily, this was because Egypt continued its baseless allegations of Anglo-American collusion, citing both countries' solid support for Israel in the build-up to the crisis as conclusive evidence of 'treacherous complicity'. Gore-Booth warned that Britain had to conduct its affairs 'on the worst possible assessment, namely, that the UAR leadership is committed to doing its best to get western influence and interests out of the Middle East. This has been said at intervals and is implicit in the actions not only of the UAR but also of e.g. Syria and Algeria.' He also warned that any attempt to move towards the Arabs like the French had done was likely to lead to severe criticism from public opinion. Brown's initial enthusiasm for getting involved in the peace process was dimming. Advice in the Foreign Office ran counter to his plans. E.M. Rose, the Head of the Eastern Department's 'own feeling [was] that the best way of recovering our interests in the Middle East is to let ourselves drift with the Arab tide, keeping in with those states which are still prepared to be friendly and as far as possible avoiding attacks on the others'.[13] Brown agreed with this, as he had by 14 June modified his own plans to more realistic levels. He briefly summarised post-war British policy as having the following aims:

> Our immediate objective is defence of our direct national interests in the short term. Our broader aim is a reasonable eventual settlement, or modus vivendi, between the Arabs and the Israelis as the basis of a more stable Middle East in which our interests can be secure. Our strategy must be to avoid offering fresh targets for Soviet/Egyptian attacks, to weaken Nasser's leadership in the Arab world and to concentrate on improving our position in the Arab countries where our material interests mainly lie. Our tactics must be flexible, and realistic, and our arguments adopted to particular audiences.[14]

RENEWED TROUBLE IN SOUTH ARABIA

Egypt was viewed in Cabinet and the Foreign Office as a major threat to British interests until the beginning of August. The South Arabian problem still had the potential to cause a military clash between Britain and Egypt. The plan to station a naval force off Aden to prevent UAR/YAR aggression against South Arabia for six months after independence had been expanded to include the stationing of Vulcan bombers on Masriah Island. Brown, in a memorandum to Cabinet of 8 June, explained the reasoning behind the decision. He described the Vulcans' role as 'essentially deterrent. That is to say that their presence would be made known and potential aggressors would have to be warned that these airforces would be employed in active support of South Arabia if clearly organised military aggression conducted across the frontier were organised by UAR or Yemeni republican forces.' [15]

On the day that Brown publicly announced the decision to provide air and naval backing for the Federation, the NLF went on the offensive. They seized the Dhala emirate as British troops began to withdraw from the hinterland. Elements of the Federal army mutinied and occupied the Crater district in Aden. The British army suffered dozens of casualties in a somewhat bizarre battle with formerly allied troops. The British reoccupied the Crater area in July but, fearing a 'little Vietnam', refused to use their military power to save the hinterland states, which succumbed one after the other to the NLF between August and October.[16] The disintegration of the Federation was complete by November. The British maintained their position in Aden under constant guerrilla attack until November but the hopes of handing it over to a moderate government were forlorn. Sir Humphrey Trevelyan, who had been sent as the last High Commissioner in May to salvage some semblance of order before independence, was unable to get face-to-face talks with the radical organisations or reconstitute an effective Federal government.[17]

The Soviets had decided to move the debate on the Arab–Israeli conflict to the General Assembly with the intention of forcing the United States and Britain into voting against a resolution that called for an Israeli withdrawal behind the pre-conflict lines. This would further alienate the Arab states from the Western powers. Brown was aware of the danger. To split the moderate Arab states away from Nasser and the other radicals was the objective of his speech to the extraordinary session of the General Assembly. His speech was pitched squarely at moderate Arab opinion. After reiterating his denials about the 'Big Lie', he insisted that gains could not be made from war, thus appearing to rule out any territorial gain by Israel. He made a plea for the safety and security of the refugees. He also called for a special representative to be appointed by the United Nations to go to the Middle East to work for peace on the Secretary-General's departure.[18] The new British strategy was the subject of some serious doubt in Whitehall. In Cabinet, Zionists such as Crossman, who had forced the Prime Minister and Foreign Secretary to back down from their proactive plans a few weeks previously, were aghast that Brown expected Israel to hand back everything to the Arabs.[19] Brown's strategy was undoubtedly correct since it did Israel no harm and it did assuage the Saudis, the Kuwaitis and the Jordanians. King Faisal was still bitterly opposed to Nasser blaming him for the Arabs' defeat. He told the British Ambassador that he remained 'deeply mistrustful of the man he considers to be an arch intriguer and his inveterate enemy'.[20] The Soviets attempted to get a two-thirds majority in the General Assembly for a resolution which would condemn Israel. Brown warned the Cabinet that this would bring the issue back to the Security Council and would force the United States and Britain to veto it.[21] Fortunately this measure, despite a massive Soviet and Arab effort, could not get the requisite votes.

In early July, the Cabinet considered a paper by the Foreign Secretary on 'Arab attitudes and British economic interests'. Egypt and Nasser were still seen as the main threats to Britain. The paper claimed that in 'both 1956 and 1967 our national interests, political and economic, would have been endangered if Israel had been defeated and Nasser's hegemony in the Arab world established'. It was felt that 'hopes of economic easement depend basically on the non revolutionary governments and the extent to which they are able to act independently of the UAR government':

> As time passes, we can expect disenchantment with Nasser and recriminations between the Arab governments about responsibility for defeat to weaken Arab solidarity and the will to maintain a state of affairs which hurts them as much as it hurts the target of their hostility ... A key element will be the position of President Nasser. If he disappeared, then there would almost certainly be a strong trend towards a less heroic and less cavalier attitude to the Arabs' own economic interests. At present his disappearance does not seem likely to happen; but it is not impossible, and short of it, the trend of his prestige and influence seems likely to be downward, unless he can produce some new political success.[22]

In the Cabinet discussion that followed, it was agreed that British interests would be facilitated by a decline in the prestige of Nasser, but in terms of the Arab–Israeli dispute the United Kingdom should remain neutral.[23] The oil embargo had proved ineffective. What was damaging to Britain was the closure of the Suez Canal and even that was not as catastrophic as it might have been.[24] It was the United States and the Soviet Union that made the running on Arab–Israeli peace. In July, the Soviet Foreign Minister, Andrei Gromyko, and the American Ambassador to the United Nations, Arthur Goldberg, came close to an agreement on a Security Council resolution. However, Israel, after initially seeming to be willing to trade land for peace, was not ready to agree a deal yet which called for withdrawal.

RAPPROCHEMENT WITH NASSER

President Nasser, by mid-July, was beginning to recant his anti-Western attacks. He let it be known through King Hussein of Jordan that he 'now regretted having cut his links so completely with the west'. Nasser claimed that he had resigned, albeit briefly, in favour of Zacharia Mohieddin to rebuild Egyptian relations with the West.[25] This gave the British hope that a *modus vivendi* with Nasser might be possible. The primary British reason to rebuild relations was economic self-interest. While the Arab oil blockade had been completely ineffective, the closure of the Suez Canal had severely damaged the slight signs of a British trade balance recovery. It was adding some £12–14 million a month to the UK balance of payments.[26] Sterling, which had recovered some of its health in the early part of the year, was now under renewed pressure. Wilson foresaw the Canal being closed for at least a year. He opined that the 'Egyptians' intention is evidently to keep the Canal closed so long as the presence of Israeli troops gives them the excuse for doing so; they evidently think that the Canal is the strongest card that they have to play in recovering from their recent defeat'.[27] Brown told Ambassador Dean in Washington that in public, at least, 'we must continue to show "a stiff upper lip" and conceal our real concern at the canal situation'. Thus, he argued, their 'immediate aim must therefore be a Security Council resolution which at best will secure the reopening or, at worst, will bring it appreciably nearer'. Brown acknowledged the difficulty of the proposition, which was made 'no easier by the fact that our urgent need for the canal is not shared in anything like the same degree by the other members of the Security Council, especially not by the USA'. He concluded that Britain must make the running for a resolution in private, '(but, at any rate at present, not in public) and in particular we must try to get the Americans to give full weight to our interests'.[28] Dean raised these points at a dinner at the British Embassy on 28 July. The Americans had now moved into an anti-Nasser position not seen since the OMEGA planning of 1956. Eugene Rostow said that the State Department was considering recommending to Johnson a 'policy of maintaining a firm position in Libya, jointly with the United Kingdom, to deter any attempt at take-over by Nasser, through subversion or more visible means'.[29] There were major US–UK talks on the Middle East at the United Nations on 9–10 August. It was agreed that the Soviets were likely to back Nasser in the short term:

> Nasser remains Soviets' best instrument in context of UAR domestic situation and as means to assert influence on rest of Arab world ... British expressed opinion that economic difficulties of UAR would within one year reach point where, taken together with general political dissatisfaction and tendency of the army to blame politicians for UAR defeat, they would produce good chance of Nasser's overthrow. US view, expressed by Assistant Secretary Battle, was that overthrow of Nasser has often been predicted before, but Nasser has proved long-lived, in manner reminiscent of Mossadegh. However, a defeat in Yemen would increase public dissatisfaction for this and other reasons, it is therefore unlikely that UAR will get out of Yemen.

Recent peace feelers from Nasser and Heikal which indicated UAR interest in resuming diplomatic relations with America were likely to have an 'unacceptable price tag attached'. Battle said that the US would require a retraction of the 'Big Lie'. These conversations confirmed that the British urgency over the Canal was not shared by the Americans.[30] The British and the Americans did develop a draft resolution that called for the appointment of a United Nations representative, whose task it would be to make contact with the parties and provide assistance to them. This was linked to the Goldberg–Gromyko agreement of July to link the withdrawal of Israeli forces with an Arab acknowledgement of Israel's right to exist. Ambassador Goldberg tried out the UK–US formulation on the Israelis and received a negative response.[31] The apparent British conversion to a more pro-Arab agenda irritated Israeli Foreign Minister Eban. Opening the Canal was not just a question for the Egyptians, he warned, since the Israeli army was entrenched on the eastern bank and was therefore in the position to claim Israel's own rights with regard to the Canal.[32]

At the beginning of September the Arab leaders gathered in Khartoum for a summit to discuss policy towards Israel. The summit was considered by some opinion in the West as a triumph for the moderates. While the end communiqué of 'No peace, no negotiations and no recognition' seemed to suggest that nothing had changed, spokesmen for Nasser and Hussein claimed that they were still willing to enter negotiations through a third party, agree a state of peace if not a formal treaty and *de facto* if not *de jure* recognition of Israel.[33] As a concession to the West it was agreed to lift the oil embargo against Britain, the United States and West Germany. Also King Faisal was able to force Nasser to quit Yemen by December 1967 – in return for a subvention to keep the Egyptian economy afloat. Brown informed the Cabinet that his impression was that the Arab states appeared to be taking a more realistic view of the Middle East. Furthermore, they also seemed to realise that they had been mistaken in branding the United Kingdom as an aggressor and seemed to wish to restore relations with it. Nasser had let it be known that he would be willing to resume talks with the UK.[34] The Khartoum summit persuaded Brown to join with the United States to push a resolution that would recognise Israel, but would not receive a Soviet veto. Johnson, also encouraged by the relative moderation of Khartoum, agreed with Brown. In the first week of October, Lord Caradon and Goldberg agreed that the whole Middle East question needed to be dealt with in the Security Council. It was felt that the best chance for success lay in pursuing the line agreed by Gromyko and Goldberg in July.[35]

The Egyptian move towards *rapprochement* with Britain was confirmed when Heikal, in an article in the *Sunday Times,* urged talks as equals between Egypt and Britain. In a lengthy historical analysis of the Anglo-Egyptian cold war, he claimed that there had never been a 'genuine dialogue between our two countries':

> I would suggest that it is time for this dialogue to begin. We must admit that Britain has legitimate interests in the Middle East. As has been often said, we Arabs cannot drink our oil so we must sell it. On your side you must recognise the existence of Arab nationalism and Egypt as the biggest power in it if only because of the size of its population. You will then understand what is in our minds.[36]

Brown wished to grasp these peace feelers as quickly as possible. He sent a message to Nasser suggesting relations might be restored by October. The British representative in Cairo, Mr Tesh, urged caution. He warned that the general Arab view, as seen from Cairo, seemed to be that Khartoum was a return to a 'practical policy of diplomatic means backed up by economic pressure from the closure of the Canal – not (repeat not) any change of heart over Israel, nor much readiness to face major concessions or loss of face'. He supported the move to restore relations with some reservations:

As I see it, it has always been in our interest to have some kind of dialogue with the Middle East's most populous state and it is possible that the moment is now propitious because Egypt is in need of friends and apparently loosening up its policy and pre-pared to disengage, for some time at least from external adventures. The question is what do we talk about? Not (repeat not) aid, since we have none to give. Nor perhaps Palestine ... (We should, how-ever, begin to restate our points of sympathy with the Arabs). On South Arabia, however, subject to the views of the experts, we should have a common interest in clearing up a situation, which embarrasses both.[37]

Egyptian publication of the private correspondence between Brown and Nasser again delayed matters as it had in the spring. The Foreign Office files were full of correspondence from the public expressing anger at the government for running after Nasser.[38] Brown met the Egyptian Foreign Minister, Mohammed Riad, at the United Nations on 24 September. Riad said that Nasser very much appreciated the Foreign Secretary's message and that after consultations with other Arab and African states thought there were reasonable prospects for a favourable reply in a couple of weeks. Riad also asked that a British representative be sent to Cairo in a couple of weeks to sort out the matter.[39]

Harold Beeley was chosen as the British representative to Cairo. The Egyptians had great respect for him from his previous tenure as Ambassador where his personal relations had held up much better than his country's. Paul Gore-Booth commenting on his brief sug-gested that 'the tone of the brief is a little too innocent. What we are in fact trying to do is to take advantage of the first moment of real weak-ness in Egypt for more than ten years to get Anglo-UAR relations on to a sensible mutual basis.' He warned that Britain must be careful that it did not fall into the idea that Nasser did not harbour some old ambitions:

Finally, and perhaps a little contrary to the line of this whole argu-ment but not inconsistent with it, could not the 'Gloria' be some-what to the effect that Egypt, like Ireland, is one of those countries with whom we have never for long got our relations quite right? Could not the sobering effects of recent events provide a starting point for a new and permanent look leading to the possibility of a new and permanent friendship?[40]

Beeley met with Nasser on the morning of 24 October. The former, speaking under instructions, wished to bring the date of the resumption of relations back to London. Nasser replied that he had to have consultations with Syria and Algeria before he could resume relations. When Beeley asked whether, if they objected, this would prevent a resumption of relations, Nasser replied that it would make no difference to his decision but he must have the opportunity of conditioning them to it. He then agreed to exchange ambassadors in the first half of December but that this was to be kept secret until he had told the Syrians and Algerians. Nasser also promised to press the NLF and FLOSY leaders to see Sir Humphrey Trevelyan about the transfer of power in South Arabia. With most of the Egyptian army withdrawn from Yemen, Nasser commented that he 'did not want to have to think about Yemen again in the next five years'. The extent of Nasser's willingness to seek *rapprochement* and his weakness were evident in his apology for the 'Big Lie':

> He said that he wanted to convey a message to you about the accusation that British aircraft had participated in the fighting on 5 June. I said this had indeed shocked you, had created public indignation, and had created unnecessary difficulty for the friends of the Arabs in Britain. He said that on the morning of 5 June Amer had suggested that this statement should be made. His own first reaction was to insist that he should be shown a British or American aircraft or pilot as evidence before any accusation was made. Then had come Hussein's telephone call, which appeared conclusive. He hoped that allowance would be made for the state of excitement in which they were living at the time.[41]

It is noticeable that he blames Amer, his former best friend who had 'committed suicide' after being implicated in a coup in August. The Israelis, who were now determined to topple Nasser, were annoyed at what they felt was the increasingly pro-Arab direction of British policy. They were particularly angry that Britain was attempting to help the Arabs find face-saving ways out of having to face up to the question of recognition.[42] One Israeli newspaper attributed the British policy to a revival of 'Bevinism' at the Foreign Office. Brown stoutly defended what he was doing to the Israeli Ambassador pointing out that 'it was to Israel's interest as well as ours that we should have diplomatic relations with the UAR: we would be better able to influence them'.[43]

Tension in the Middle East was escalating once more. An Israeli destroyer, the *Eilat*, was sunk by an Egyptian anti-ship missile. The Israelis retaliated with a bombardment of the oil refinery at Suez, destroying most of Egypt's oil stocks. Brown noted these developments and the imminent resumption of relations with Egypt in Cabinet on 23 October. Some in Cabinet voiced dissent against the move. The view was expressed that a resumption of relations between the UK and the UAR might be misunderstood by opinion in the UK and elsewhere, and, 'especially if it took place when tension was rising, might be regarded as taking sides in the dispute between Israel and the Arab states. The UAR had been responsible for breaking relations with us. But now we were taking the initiative in seeking their resumption.' Others pointed out that Rhodesia had been the reason for the breach and that the Israeli Foreign Minister had not reacted unfavourably to the move to resume relations. Furthermore, 'it was a British interest that we should be able to exert influence in the United Arab Republic and thus help towards the reopening of the Suez Canal and a Middle East settlement'. The Prime Minister, summing up, said that the matter would have to be brought back to Cabinet before a decision was taken.[44]

One aspect of the Anglo-Egyptian relationship that was no longer going to cause tensions was Yemen and South Arabia. Brown informed the Cabinet that, since the external threat to South Arabia had diminished with the withdrawal of the UAR army from Yemen, the British army could speed up the evacuation of its own forces now concentrated in Aden.[45] South Arabia was to be given independence at the end of November rather than January 1968. The long struggle in South Arabia ended in humiliation for the British. The Federal government collapsed. A civil war broke out between the Marxist NLF and the Nasser-backed FLOSY for control. The South Arabian army was asked to back one or the other faction by its British commanding officer so that the British might have somebody to hand over power to. The army chose the NLF, which soon finished off FLOSY. The British after cursory negotiations in Geneva handed over power to the NLF unconditionally on 29 November.[46] The great fear of the Americans that the constant British opposition to Nasser would lead to communist penetration of the Middle East had come through, but perhaps not in the way that they or the British expected.

The Cabinet considered the Foreign Secretary's paper on 'Resumption of Diplomatic Relations with the UAR' on 2 November. Brown was in favour of going ahead with the resumption, arguing that, whether 'we like it or not, the UAR is still the most influential Arab state. It is certain to remain so.' Other countries that had broken relations would probably agree to the restoration of ties once the UAR had done so. Brown argued that the UK should not 'ignore our capacity to influence for good events inside the UAR ... Our resuming relations with them would do something to move them back in the direction of non-alignment and would give encouragement to those Egyptians who wish to resist the increasing penetration of Egypt by communist influence to which Harold Beeley has drawn my intention.' The memo also pointed out that progress had been made before the June war to restore relations. There were also the feelers put out by Nasser and Heikal in September and Nasser taking in the moderate policy agreed at Khartoum. Brown decided that 'it would not be right to ignore these indications or to miss any chance of influencing President Nasser to maintain a moderate course, which may become increasingly difficult for him'. This was why he had pursued the peace feelers from Nasser. Brown continued by describing Beeley's meeting with Nasser and emphasised that Nasser had made no attempt to extract concessions and in effect had apologised for the lie about British collusion with the Israelis. Nasser was also fit and well and not likely to fall from power. Most importantly, the Yemen/South Arabia problem would no longer mar relations. He concluded by attacking those critics who said that 'by making friends with Nasser now we are building him up and encouraging him to be intransigent. Alternatively, they say that he will not last long and we should be in no hurry to commit ourselves to him rather than his successors whoever they may be. I believe such criticisms to be misguided.'[47] The Cabinet approved the Foreign Secretary's paper and the policy of engagement with Nasser.[48]

Britain's new-found acceptance from Nasser and other Arab states allowed it to play the role of 'honest broker' in the drafting of Security Council resolution 242 on 22 November. The resolution was again based on the Goldberg–Gromyko formula of July. The deteriorating situation in the Middle East referred to above increased the need for some framework for peace. The Latin American countries, the United States and India all produced resolutions, which were to varying degrees unacceptable to either the Israelis or the Arabs. Caradon came up with a compromise resolution. The Israelis demanded changes in the draft that circumscribed the power of the United Nations representative who was to broker peace. On 22 November 1967, the resolution was agreed by the Security Council.[49] Brown was suitably pleased with the result, describing the passing of the resolution as 'the first effective British initiative on a contentious issue for a long time' and 'a triumph for the United Kingdom Representative of the United Nations. It was too early to say whether it would turn out to be the first step towards a settlement.'[50] It certainly was.

The success in the United Nations must have provided a small measure of relief for the Wilson government, which was forced to devalue sterling on 16 November, ending three years of fruitless struggle to preserve its parity. The Labour government, which had been forced into severe economic retrenchment in August 1966, seemed to have recovered some of its self-confidence by September 1967.

However, the October 1967 trade figures revealed a huge trade gap. Sterling came under savage pressure in the foreign exchange markets. The Wilson government never really recovered from the disaster. As previously stated, he blamed the June war for the devaluation, and certainly it was a contributory factor, if not as important as Wilson claims. The consequences of devaluation were far-reaching, particularly in the sphere of overseas defence expenditure. The new Chancellor, the very pro-European Roy Jenkins, demanded that Britain abandon the worldwide role once and for all. That this was a huge policy reversal was demonstrated by the publication of the 1967 Defence Review as early as July 1967. It envisaged a scaling down but not an abandonment of the east-of-Suez role. Singapore was to be abandoned as a base by 1975. Interestingly, there was no mention of leaving the Middle East and the Persian Gulf in the White Paper. Devaluation changed all that. The subsequent reshuffle, with Jenkins becoming Chancellor, upset what Jeffrey Pickering describes as the 'Bevinite' consensus in the Cabinet – that is the coalition in favour of maintaining a continued global role.[51] In a series of tense meetings of ministers and the Cabinet in early January 1968, the decision was taken to leave British bases in the Gulf and south-east Asia by the end of 1971 and abrogate the defence treaties that required British intervention. It was all very humiliating, as Britain had pledged as late as October that its presence in the Gulf would be maintained. Economic realities now struck home. Britain would no longer intervene east of Suez. It would no longer be a major power in the Middle East.[52]

NOTES

1. The conversation went as follows: *Nasser*: 'Shall we include also the United States do you know of this, shall we announce that the United States is co-operating with Israel? …' *Nasser*: 'Hello, will we say the United States and England or just the United States?' *Hussein*: 'the United States and England.' *Nasser*: 'does Britain have aircraft carriers?' *Hussein*: answer unintelligible. *Nasser*: 'good …' *Nasser*: 'by God, I say that I will make an announcement and you will make an announcement and we will see to it that Syrians will make an announcement that American and British airplanes are taking part against us from aircraft carriers. We will issue an announcement, we will stress the matter and we will drive the point home.' This transcript was issued by the Israelis on 8 June and was carried in the British and international press the following day. *Times*, 9 June 1967.
2. See D. Yergin, *The Prize* (New York, Simon & Schuster, 1991), p. 555.
3. PRO PREM 13/1620, Caradon–FCO, No. 1240, 6 June 1967, and HOC Debates, 747, Col. 800, 6 June 1967.
4. PRO PREM 13/1620, Caradon–FCO, No. 1248, 6 June 1967.
5. PRO PREM 13/1620, Dean–FCO, No. 1649, 6 June 1967.

6. PRO PREM 13/1620, Dean–FCO, No. 1958, 7 June 1967.
7. PRO PREM 13/1620, Caradon–FCO, No. 1260, 7 June 1967.
8. PRO PREM 13/1620, J.A. Thomson memo for Mr Rose, 8 June 1967.
9. Ibid.
10. PRO FCO 17-511, FCO to Washington, No. 6234, 8 June 1967.
11. PRO PREM 13/1621, Amman to FCO, No. 631, 11 June 1967.
12. *Economist*, 10 June 1967. *Daily Telegraph*, 9 June 1967.
13. PRO FCO 17-511 ER 2/11, Mr Rose annotation, 14 June 1967 on Mr Thomson's memo, 8 June 1967.
14. PRO PREM 13/1621, FCO guidance, No. 151, 14 June 1967.
15. PRO FCO 27/5, Memo by the SOSFA, 'Stationing of V-bombers at Masriah', OPD 44, 8 June 1967.
16. Trevelyan, *Middle East in Revolution*, p. 243.
17. Halliday, *Arabia without Sultans*, pp. 217–19.
18. *Times*, 21 June 1967.
19. PRO CAB 128/42, Cabinet Conclusions, 41, No. 3, 22 June 1967. The Israelis at this time were intimating an interest in a land-for-peace deal based on a return to the pre-war frontiers. The plan fell apart. See Bergman and El-Tahri, *Fifty Years War*, pp. 99–101.
20. PRO PREM 13/1622, Jedda to FO, No. 462, 25 June 1967.
21. PRO CAB 128/42, Cabinet Conclusions, 43, 29 June 1967.
22. PRO CAB 129/132 C (67) 123, Memo by the SOSFA, 'Arab Attitudes and British Economic Interests', 11 July 1967.
23. PRO CAB 128/42, Cabinet Conclusions, 47, 11 July 1967.
24. Owing to the development of supertankers, oil demand could be more easily met than in 1956–57. These tankers were too big to go through the Canal. Now, they were used to go around the Cape of Good Hope. Unlike in 1973, the oil embargo proved to be toothless. Production was simply switched to other producers with ease. Yergin, *Prize*, pp. 556–7. Frank Brenchley informed me that Iran provided much of the extra capacity.
25. PRO PREM 13/1622, Amman to FO, No. 867, 17 July 1967. This is a fascinating conversation as Nasser is quoted giving his blessing to Hussein pursuing peace with Israel.
26. This is according to Foreign Secretary Brown in a meeting of the OPD on 10 October 1967. He informed the committee that for the first six months the cost of the Middle East crisis to the UK balance of payments was expected to be of the order of £20 million a month, two-thirds of which was due to the closure of the Suez Canal. PRO CAB 148/30, OPD 67, 32nd meeting, 10 Oct. 1967.
27. PRO PREM 13/1622, Wilson to Brown, PM 67/79, 26 July 1967.
28. PRO PREM 13/1622, FO to Washington, No. 8365, 28 July 1967.
29. USNA, Memcon Dean and Rostow, 28 July 1967, Pol UK–US, DOSCF, Box 2572.
30. USNA, State to AmEmb London, No. 19100, Supplements, US–UK talks on UN affairs, 11 Aug. 1967, Pol UK–US, DOSCF, Box 2572.
31. LBJL, Memo for the President from Rusk, 13 Oct. 1967, United Nations, Vol. 7, 1, NSF Agency File, Box 68.
32. PRO PREM 13/1623, Tel Aviv to London, No. 901, 1 Aug. 1967.
33. Stephens, *Nasser*, p. 523.
34. PRO CAB 128/42, Cabinet Conclusions, 53, 7 Sept. 1967.
35. PRO PREM 13/1623, Washington to FO, No. 3071, 27 Oct. 1967, and New York to FO, No. 2643, 9 Oct. 1967.
36. *Sunday Times*, 10 Sept. 1967.
37. PRO FCO 39/67, Cairo to FO, No. 909, 12 Sept. 1967.

38. See numerous examples in PRO FCO 39/267.
39. PRO PREM 13/1623, PMT 50/67, Brown to Wilson in Washington to FO, No. 2422, 24 Sept. 1967.
40. PRO FCO 39/270, VK 3/23, Gore-Booth to Roberts, 12 Oct. 1967.
41. PRO FCO 39/270, VK 3/23, Cairo to FO, No. 1052, 21 Oct. 1967.
42. This is the central point of Eshkol's message to Wilson, in PRO PREM 13/1623, Tel Aviv to FO, 16 Oct. 1967.
43. PRO PREM 13/1623, Tel Aviv to FO, No. 1114, 12 Oct. 1967, and FO to Tel Aviv, No. 2135, 13 Oct. 1967.
44. PRO CAB 128/42, Cabinet Conclusions, 61, 23 Oct. 1967.
45. PRO CAB 128/42, Cabinet Conclusions, 62, 30 Oct. 1967.
46. Monroe, *Britain's Moment*, p. 215.
47. PRO CAB 129/134, C 172, Memo by the Foreign Secretary, 2 Nov. 1967.
48. PRO CAB 128/42, Cabinet Conclusions, 63, 2 Nov. 1967.
49. Ovendale, *Origins of the Arab–Israeli Wars*, pp. 209–10.
50. PRO, CAB 128/42, Cabinet Conclusions, 68, 24 Nov. 1967.
51. Pickering, *Britain's Withdrawal from East of Suez*, pp. 159, 162–74.
52. Darwin, *Britain and Decolonisation*, p. 293.

—16—

Conclusion

THE CHANGE IN British policy after the devaluation of 1967 was much more profound than after Suez. By withdrawing from the Persian Gulf and Singapore, cutting back on aircraft carriers and abandoning the F-111 fighter-bomber, Britain was abandoning all pretensions to being a world power. The Six Day War demonstrates what a sudden transformation this was as Professor Kennedy points out. During that crisis, Wilson and George Brown 'were still keen to have British aircraft carriers alongside their American counterparts in the Eastern Mediterranean and the Red Sea, as if nothing had changed since the days of Disraeli'.[1] For that reason 1967 marks the end of an era in Anglo-Egyptian relations. A long-term strategy of opposing Nasser came to an end with this shift in policy. Reviewing British policy from 1955 to 1967, there was a remarkable degree of continuity in policy and considerable delusions of grandeur shared by all British governments, Conservative or Labour. However, throughout the story there is a remarkable feeling that British policy-makers knew they were pursuing the wrong policy. Senior ministers from Bevin to George Brown and many senior civil servants all were aware that, by aligning Britain with the conservative forces in the Middle East, they were following an unsustainable even distasteful policy. For instance supporting the repulsive royalists in Yemen involved a considerable amount of holding of noses in Whitehall. However, coming to terms with Arab nationalism, which meant coming to terms with Nasser, proved to be beyond British diplomats and statesmen. In the end the protection of British interests in the Middle East revolved around opposing Nasser. Just as the lessons of the past were of great importance to Nasser, in the case of British statesmen the idea that Nasser was the Arab Hitler seems to have clouded judgements far too much.

Even now the Suez affair strikes one as the most stupid decision taken by British policy-makers in the twentieth century. There is still no justification for Eden's 'Suezside'. However, in mitigation for Eden one can say that some of the ire he felt towards Nasser was justified. Eden had placed his reputation on the line with his party for the deal with Nasser over the Canal base. Nasser's nationalisation just a few weeks after British troops had at last left Egypt not only appeared to threaten British interests, but it made Eden look like a fool. A leader, politically weak, unhealthy and under great strain, was to ruin a reputation built up over a quarter of a century in a little over four months. It is without doubt one of the great political tragedies of our age. However, Eden's central ambition – the reduction or the elimination of Nasser's influence in the Arab world – remained the central tenet of British strategy in the aftermath of Suez.

Macmillan shared his predecessor Anthony Eden's attitude towards the Egyptian President. The key difference was that Macmillan was determined to 'get the Americans in' with the British in this endeavour. The Eisenhower Doctrine, which had the effect of aligning the United States with the conservative monarchies against Nasser, aided Macmillan's strategy, in spite of his initial scepticism about its effect. Primarily, this was because the doctrine alienated Nasser and radical Arab nationalism. They felt that the United States was intervening to prevent the success of the pan-Arab cause. Nasser's hostility towards the Americans in the first half of 1957 brought the latter around to the British way of thinking about Nasser. The pre-Suez hostility to Nasser returned. As the Middle East committee in April 1957 noted, a working group of American and British diplomats set up at the Bermuda Conference agreed that the 'policy of cutting Nasser down to size must continue'. However, Britain's declining power and influence over Egypt and the Middle East was evident in the first half of 1957 when Britain narrowly avoided, thanks to French diplomacy, a potentially damaging vote in the United Nations on an Israeli withdrawal from Sinai. Nasser's ultimate triumph at Suez was confirmed with the interim settlement for the use of the Suez Canal and his forcing through of the terms on which British shipping could use it. Even Macmillan was forced to admit that the settlement was 'damaging in the sense that it recognised the failure of the long struggle to assert our rights and thwart Nasser's ambitions'.[2]

Macmillan's strategy of using the Americans to take action against Nasser came closest to success in the summer and autumn of 1957. The United States, convinced that the radical government of Syria was about to turn Marxist, encouraged the conservative Arab states and Turkey to take action to topple it. Macmillan saw the opportunity to restore Anglo-American co-operation on policy-making in the Middle East, something that was achieved with the setting up of the working group on Syria. More dubiously, he appears to have hoped that an Arab attack on Syria might have the effect of bringing Nasser into a conflict with Iraq, the United States and Britain. A re-run of Suez, this time with the promise of American support, briefly appeared to be within his grasp. Macmillan's memoirs deliberately mislead the reader about this crisis. This book publishes for the first time the extent to which Macmillan saw the crisis as providing an opportunity for getting Nasser with American and other Arab states' aid. The Prime Minister's plans came to nothing. Instead it was Nasser who emerged victorious. The conservative Arab monarchies backed away from action against Syria. Nasser was able to persuade the Americans that only he could save Syria from communism. With some reluctance, the US agreed to give him a free hand in Syria. However, the Americans do not appear to have expected Nasser to have subsumed Syria into the United Arab Republic so quickly. At the Ankara meeting of the Baghdad Pact in January 1958, Dulles, with strong backing from Selwyn Lloyd, promised support for any Arab initiative to prevent the union. On his return to Washington, more informed opinion in the State Department changed the Secretary of State's mind. The true British attitudes to the UAR are revealed here for the first time. Lloyd on his return to London was considering plans to destabilise the UAR. Nuri al-Said, the Iraqi Prime Minister, came up with much the same ideas. On Dulles' change of opinion, Nuri's plans became dangerously vague to the British (Lloyd's plans quickly forgotten about). Indeed, Nuri's Arab Union scheme, with its need for Kuwaiti oil, became as much of a threat to British interests as Nasser. There is evidence that British policy-makers were beginning to tire of Nuri in the first half of 1958. Direct contacts between the British and the Egyptians were limited to the desultory financial talks in Rome, which advanced very slowly. Potential break-throughs and agreements were swiftly dashed by shifts in position by one side or the other. The United States by April 1958 had decided to seek agreement with Nasser to a limited extent.

British and American talks in the winter of 1957 had agreed on the need to keep Lebanon and Jordan out of the Nasserite or communist sphere of influence. In May 1958 a civil war broke out in the Lebanon. While Nasser did supply the rebels with arms, the overwhelming weight of evidence suggests that it was the foolish and unconstitutional behaviour of President Chamoun that occasioned the civil war. The British – blinded by their anti-Nasser prejudice – wanted to launch an immediate Anglo-American operation to save Chamoun and inflict a defeat on the UAR. The files do not tell as yet whether the plans considered an attack on Syria, as well as protecting the Lebanon. As Nigel Ashton and Ritchie Ovendale point out, only the careful analysis of the situation by the American and British Ambassadors, and a marked reluctance on the part of American State and Defence Departments to have joint military operations with the British in the aftermath of Suez, prevented an invasion. The Americans instead sought to compromise with Nasser with the reluctant acquiescence of the British.

This compromise seemed to have resolved the crisis when the Iraqi monarchy was toppled on 14 July 1958. Eisenhower and Dulles, convinced that Nasser was behind the Iraqi revolution, now decided to act. They landed American marines in the Lebanon. Macmillan wanted a wider operation to restore order in the Middle East, an option that was rejected by the Americans on practical and political grounds. Almost as though it was felt that something had to be done, British troops were deployed to Jordan to shore up the monarchy. It was decided not to intervene in Iraq as such an operation was considered too risky. Indeed, Macmillan sought a *modus vivendi* with the new Qasim regime within a couple of days of the revolution. The motivation was a determination to continue to oppose Nasser whom the British held responsible for the latest crisis. The Anglo-American operations were a qualified success. No major fighting took place. Nasser's favoured choice for the presidency of Lebanon, General Chebab, was elected under the protection of the US marine corps. His moderate policies forestalled for a time the drift towards sectarian strife in that country. In the first substantive contact since Suez, Selwyn Lloyd peruaded the Egyptian Foreign Minister, Dr Fawzi, to ease his country's subversive and propaganda attacks on Jordan. They also agreed to restart the stalled financial talks. The meeting appears to have been the start of the Anglo-Egyptian détente.

A twin-track British policy toward Nasser now emerged. On the one hand, it was decided to seek limited accommodation with him. On the other, it was felt necessary to continue support for Qasim in Iraq, who had become dangerously dependent on communist support, because he opposed Nasser. This caused considerable friction with the United States who had begun to move towards the opinion that Nasser might be an anti-communist champion. The Middle East committee of the British Cabinet was torn between two schools of thought. One was that the United Kingdom could never come to terms with Nasser and the other that he was 'not implacably hostile'. In January 1959, Macmillan chose the latter course of action, which was that opposition to Arab unity was no longer to be British policy. He accepted the argument of the previously unpublished 'Points for a Middle East Policy', which had been drafted in the light of the changed strategic situation in the region:

> On all grounds, therefore, it was to our long-term advantage to support it [Arab unity]. It followed, that, while continuing to stand by our friends and maintain our position in the Persian Gulf, we should disengage from Inter-Arab politics and from Palestine and

seek to establish a relationship with the Arab countries based on mutual, commercial and cultural relations with the UAR, supporting the independence of the Sudan, Libya and Tunisia; sustaining the regime in Iraq: and working for increasing United Nations involvement in the area.[3]

It was the logical consequence of events since the Suez crisis. Britain had attempted to maintain its anti-Nasser strategy, but had found it increasingly difficult to sustain. The Iraqi revolution was an important – but by no means the only – factor in making this decision. There had been opinion in Whitehall that British opposition to Arab nationalism was unsustainable well before this event. For a couple of years after the Iraqi revolution, British policy-makers appear to have believed that the new oil discoveries in North Africa and Nigeria had diminished the importance of the Middle East. The exponential growth in oil demand in western Europe did not become a renewed cause of concern until 1963. In the final analysis, access to oil on reasonable terms was all that Britain cared about. The United States, oil self-sufficient at this time, mainly cared about international communism. The apparently diminishing importance of Middle Eastern oil was reflected in a growing British disinterest in the region in the years 1959–62.

The first fruits of the new British policy were the successful negotiation of the Anglo-Egyptian agreement of March 1959. No sooner had it been signed when Egyptian suspicions of British aid to Qasim, and the latter's successful crushing of the Mosul rebellion, set relations back once more. Egypt responded to what they considered British plotting with a refusal to implement the agreement and to restore diplomatic relations. This caused great anger in the British Cabinet and explains the differences of opinion between Britain and the United States over Iraq and Nasser at the March 1959 summit. This rather than an attempt to maintain a balance of power in the Middle East was the reason for British reluctance to abandon Qasim, as is suggested by Nigel Ashton. Thus, when Nasser intimated to the Canadian Ambassador that he was willing to do business with the British, Lloyd took the opportunity to reciprocate. Despite this, Anglo-Egyptian relations proceeded at a very slow pace. Relations at chargé d'affaires level at the end of 1959 were not followed by an exchange of ambassadors until January 1961. This delay was caused by a desultory running argument about Egyptian consular rights in British colonies. A meeting between Nasser and Macmillan at the United Nations finally broke this deadlock.

The years 1961 and 1962 mark the high-water mark of the Anglo-Egyptian détente. The Egyptians and British co-operated in solving the Kuwait crisis in the summer of 1961. The break-up of the UAR did cause some tension but this was resolved in the early months of 1962. An Anglo-Egyptian agreement resolved the outstanding disagreements over the 1959 settlement. The British even agreed to loan the Egyptians money to help them out of an economic crisis. The driving force behind the détente was the United States; President Kennedy and his national security team improved US–UAR relations so much that Britain was carried along in the slipstream. Secondly, Nasser found his Arab unity calls increasingly rejected by other Arab states. He had drawn back from foreign adventurism after the Mosul rebellion failed.

However, when Egypt intervened in support of the Yemen revolution in September, the fragile edifice that was the Anglo-Egyptian détente collapsed. Yemen bordered the British-protected South Arabian protectorate and the post of Aden. The previously unimportant Aden port was now one of the most important British bases in the world. The establishment of a revolutionary government in the Yemen seemed to threaten the base. For this reason, the Colonial Office, the Ministry of Defence and the Prime Minister's Office defeated the Foreign Office and refused to recognise the Yemen Arab Republic. It was, as Oliver Wright, Douglas-Home's private secretary, noted, a 'fundamental mistake'. The deterioration in relations with Egypt which this caused was mitigated by the resumption of relations with Saudi Arabia, who were supporting the royalist cause in Yemen. The importance of Aden had been further increased with the renewed emphasis in the British government on both the east-of-Suez role – owing to the rejection of the UK application for membership of the EEC – and the rediscovery of the vital importance of Middle Eastern oil to the economic vitality of western Europe.

Throughout 1963, relations with Egypt slowly worsened as Nasser's ambition for regional leadership reared its head again. The Americans, determined to protect their vast oil investments in Saudi Arabia and their carefully worked engagement with Nasser, forced both sides to accept a disengagement agreement where the former agreed to halt supplies to the royalists and the latter to begin a withdrawal. The Saudis appear merely to have redirected their supplies outside the view of the United Nations monitors and sent supplies through Beihan, one of the British-protected states. The Egyptians became increasingly concerned about these supplies, to which the British turned a blind eye. The Colonial Office appears to have committed the British to the royalist cause far more than the Foreign Office was aware. The documents only give hints rather than the full picture of the extent of the British commitment to the royalist cause. The British, for their part, were concerned about the failure of Egypt to withdraw any troops. They also raised the issue of Egyptian use of poison gas at the

United Nations. Macmillan had little opportunity to consider Yemen in 1963 as he was overwhelmed by domestic scandal. However, when Sir Alec Douglas-Home assumed office, he immediately ordered a review of British policy. The continued lack of an effective central government in Yemen suited the British government. The Colonial Office, particularly the High Commissioner in Aden, Sir Kennedy Trevakis, believed that, if Nasser succeeded in the Yemen, Aden and the Federation would be next on his list as success bred ambition. This view was not really shared by the Foreign Office.

The British fear that revolutionary violence would spread to Aden and South Arabia came true in December 1963 with the attempted assassination of Trevakis. Nasser – who had previously made little comment on South Arabia – began describing it as 'the Federation of South Britain'. His own position in the Middle East strengthened by the January summit of Arab leaders, he launched a major propaganda offensive against Britain and its Middle Eastern bases, beginning in February with a stinging attack on Douglas-Home. This was coupled with increasing evidence of Egyptian support for subversive activity in South Arabia, and UAR and YAR air attacks on the Federation in early 1964. Britain responded with a retaliatory air attack on Harib, which brought the condemnation of the Arab world upon it, and caused a minor crisis in relations with the United States. Nasser escalated the crisis in April with increased aid for guerrillas and further propaganda attacks on Britain in speeches. There was another split in the British Cabinet with Peter Thorneycroft and Duncan Sandys pressing for heavy retaliations across the border including the assassination of Egyptian intelligence officers. Butler's attempt to enlist the Americans in a campaign against Nasser was rejected in Washington. It is the American rather than the British documents that give a better picture of this conflict, particularly the material in the National Archives. The crisis rumbled on all summer. The Colonial Office authorised aid for the royalists in Yemen and Britain offered aid to the Saudis when it appeared that they might be wavering in their support for the royalists. This again led to disagreements with the Americans confirmed by unproductive talks in September 1964, which demonstrated the growing discord between the allies once more. The extent of the Anglo-American disagreement over Nasser in 1964 has never before been documented.

The incoming Labour party, not burdened by the legacy of Suez, attempted to repair relations with Nasser. A dialogue was started. It was, however, fatally undermined by the deterioration in relations between Nasser and the Americans in December 1964, his clash with West Germany in early 1965 and the continuing violence in South

Arabia that was being encouraged by Egyptian propaganda and supplies. The Labour government did manage to send a minister to Cairo for talks in September 1965. However, the mission was a disaster thanks to the decision to suspend the Aden constitution during the course of the visit. The timing of the suspension was inopportune to say the least. Nasser took the opportunity, offered by the Rhodesian crisis, to break relations with Britain in December 1965. The fact that Britain's cold war with Nasser was more than just the fault of the Conservatives was proved by Labour's failure to come to terms with Nasser.

However, the Aden base had become too costly for Britain to hold, and, in spite of fears that Nasser would claim it as a victory, it was decided to withdraw by 1968. Relations with Egypt continued to deteriorate throughout 1966 despite the withdrawal. Nasser promised to liberate the Federation upon independence, and insisted that Egyptian troops would not leave the Yemen until then. The British lobbied the United States not to give any more food aid to Nasser, something that the Americans were now willing to acquiesce in. They no longer viewed Nasser as a potentially useful influence in the region. Since December 1964, the Egyptian leader had grown increasingly estranged from the West. George Brown, on becoming Foreign Secretary in July 1966, attempted a *rapprochement* with Nasser. The initiative, like all Anglo-Egyptian initiatives, proceeded slowly. Eventually, Nasser agreed to restore relations in July 1967. The future of South Arabia remained the greatest problem. The British remained determined to prevent a Nasserite takeover there. To this end, a British air and naval task force was put in place to protect the Federation in the event of a UAR invasion.

Before relations could be resumed, the crisis leading to the Six Day War broke. The crisis briefly restored Nasser as the undisputed leader of the Arab world. Even his bitterest foes, Kings Faisal and Hussein, were swept along in the rush to polarisation in the Middle East. Harold Wilson and George Brown were the strongest advocates of international action to open the Straits of Tiran. Only the restraints placed upon them by the Cabinet prevented them from making bolder – some might say rasher – moves. The United States was also in favour of international action to prevent war. However, as the crisis developed, it transpired that the safest option for the Western powers was that Nasser would be defeated by the Israelis without help from the West. To force the Straits of Tiran would have led to a potentially devastating economic boycott of Britain by the Arab oil producers, including some that Britain had treaty relationships with, and to acquiesce in a victory for Nasser would have been just as damaging. Therefore, it is of little surprise to discover that British diplomats were letting it be known to the United States that the Israelis going it alone successfully might be the best option. The Americans were giving the Israelis, through back channels, at least the promise of non-intervention. The documents here demonstrate the behind-the-scenes diplomacy of the Six Day War. Most interesting are the American documents – which in many ways are more revealing about the inner workings of the British government than their own documents.

The defeat of Nasser in 1967 was a necessary prerequisite for the withdrawal of British forces from the Gulf. If Nasser had won a diplomatic or military victory, it is hard to see how the withdrawal would have been possible in the short term. The devastating economies demanded by the devaluation of November 1967 were, of course, the key factor, but the knowledge that Nasser would not fill the vacuum eased the decision. There was no longer any reason for Britain and Egypt to continue their cold war.

The beginning of 1968, with the confirmation of Britain's relinquishment of its east-of-Suez role, signified the end of its 'moment' in the Middle East. For Nasser, what should have been a moment of triumph was negated by his catastrophic defeat in the Six Day War. The Suez Canal, his main source of foreign earnings, was blocked, and the Israeli army lay entrenched on its eastern bank; and, at the Khartoum summit in September 1967, he had surrendered his pan-Arab ambitions for the promise of Saudi aid. While the British policy of maintaining its influence in the Middle East through military bases had proved to be unsustainable politically and economically, Nasser's plans to fill the vacuum were equally unsuccessful.

The dominant forces in the Gulf proved to be the conservative monarchies of Iran and Saudi Arabia. The strongest regional power was Israel. The dominant Western power was the United States – now bitterly opposed to Nasser. Its Middle East policy was based firmly on the 'three pillars' of Iran, Israel and Saudi Arabia. It is rather ironic that, after over a decade of struggle to get the Americans to see Nasser as a malign influence, the Americans had come around to the British point of view just when the latter were leaving the Middle East. As the United States moved into a period of tense relations with Egypt, Britain found its relationship with Nasser dramatically improved with the main sources of friction removed. Relations between the two countries have been generally stable since the restoration of relations. This was facilitated by the charting of a pro-Western course by Nasser's successors, Presidents Sadat and Mubarak. In the final analysis, if the protection of oil supplies was the key British objective in the Middle East, the policy must be viewed as a failure. Britain was forced to abandon its positions in the region to a large extent because of the policies of Nasser. He was an inveterate foe. Even when British policies appeared to succeed, such as preventing Qasim being toppled in 1958–59 or by helping the royalists in the Yemen, developments afterwards proved to be just as unhelpful as a victory for Nasser. Qasim proved to be a threat to Kuwait and revolutionary violence became endemic in South Arabia.

A final question that cannot be fully answered is: were the British right? Was Nasser the ambitious demagogue portrayed in the documents and memoirs of British statesmen? Egyptian and Arab archive policies mean we will probably never know the internal story of Egyptian diplomacy of these crucial years. Nasser's biographers have been, in the main, sympathetic but the biographies are based on personal viewpoints and published sources. Viewed from 30 years' distance, Nasser, in comparison to those who have taken on his mantle of 'leader of the Arab world', such as Saddam Hussein and President Gaddafi, seems an almost benign figure. While personal aggrandisement and ambition fuelled his policies to an extent, his concern to free the ordinary Arab from the yoke of oppression, whether it be British or corrupt royal regimes, was not an unworthy goal. In the end, his disaster in June 1967 seems to be as tragic as Eden's a decade before: a career of, in the main, success, ending in avoidable disaster because of momentary stupidity.

NOTES

1. Paul Kennedy, *The Realities behind Diplomacy* (London, Fontana, 1981), p. 376.
2. Macmillan, *Riding the Storm*, p. 233.
3. PRO CAB 134/2230, OME, 1st meeting, 16 Jan. 1959.

Bibliography

UNPUBLISHED PRIMARY SOURCES

BRITAIN

London

Public Record Office, Kew

Cabinet Office Documents:
CAB 128, CAB 129, CAB 130, CAB 134.

Colonial Office:
CO 1055.

Defence:
DEFE 4, DEFE 5, DEFE 13.
Foreign Office and Foreign and Commonwealth Office (FCO title on files after January 1967):
FO 371.
FCO 8, FCO 17, FCO 27, FCO 39.

Prime Minister's Office:
PREM 11 (Macmillan and Douglas-Home), PREM 13 (Wilson).

Oxford

Bodleian Library
Harold Macmillan Diary 1957–63. The available version is a photocopy for some of the years with portions sanitised. The complete original and a typescript are available for 1959 and 1960 at the time of writing.
St Antony's College, Oxford: Middle East Centre
Colin Crowe Manuscript: 'An Account of the Restoration of Relations between the United Kingdom and the United Arab Republic (Egypt) after the Suez Episode', unpublished, written 1964–65.

UNITED STATES OF AMERICA

National Archives, College Park, Maryland
  RG59: Department of State Central Decimal Files 1957–63.
  Lot files: Conference Files 1957–67.
Lyndon Baines Johnson Library, University of Texas at Austin
  National Security Files, Country Files 1963–68.
  Walt Rostow Papers.
  Robert Komer Papers.
  George Ball Papers.
  Oral History Collection: Lucius Battle, Arthur Goldberg, Robert
    Komer and Dean Rusk.
John F. Kennedy Library, Boston (borrowed material)
  Oral History Collection: John Badeau and Dean Rusk.

PUBLISHED DOCUMENTARY COLLECTIONS

BRITAIN

British Documents on the End of Empire Series (HMSO):
Ashton, S.R. and Stockwell, S.E. (eds), *British Documents on the End of
    Empire*, Vol. I, *Imperial Policy and Colonial Practice 1925–1945* (London,
    HMSO, 1996).
Goldsworthy, David (ed.), *British Documents on the End of Empire*, Vols
    I, II, III, *The Conservative Government and the End of Empire 1951–67*
    (London, HMSO, 1994).
Johnson, Douglas H., *British Documents on the End of Empire*, Sudan
    (London, Stationery Office, 1998).
Kent, J. (ed.), *British Documents on the End of Empire: Egypt and the Defence
    of the Middle East*, Parts I, II, III (London, HMSO, 1998).
Other Document Collections:
Aldrich, R.J., *Espionage, Security and Intelligence in Britain 1945–1970*
    (Manchester, Manchester University Press, 1998).
Gorst, A. and Johnman, L. (eds), *The Suez Crisis* (London, Routledge,
    1997).
Lucas, Scott (ed.), *Britain and Suez: The Lion's Last Roar* (Manchester,
    Manchester University Press, 1996).
Porter, A.N. and Stockwell, A. (eds), *British Imperial Policy and Decoloni-
    sation, 1938–64*, Vol. II, *1951–64* (London, Macmillan, 1989).
Hansard, House of Commons Debates (various volumes: 1952–67).

UNITED STATES OF AMERICA

Public Papers of the Presidents of the United States of America (Washington, DC) (1957–67).

Foreign Relations of the United States (FRUS) (Government Printing Office, Washington, DC):

FRUS 1955–57, Vol. XIII, *Near East: Jordan and Yemen* (1988).

FRUS 1955–57, Vol. XVI, *Suez Crisis* (1990).

FRUS 1955–57, Vol. XVII, *Arab–Israeli Dispute* (1990).

FRUS 1955–57, Vol. XXVII, *Western Europe* (1995).

FRUS 1958–60, Vol. XI, *Lebanon and Jordan* (1990).

FRUS 1958–60, Vol. XII, *Near East Region: Iraq, Iran, Arabian Peninsula* (1993).

FRUS 1958–60, Vol. XIII, *Arab–Israeli Dispute, United Arab Republic, North Africa* (1992).

FRUS 1961–63, Vol. XVII, *Near East, 1961–62* (1994).

FRUS 1961–63, Vol. XVIII, *Near East, 1962–63* (1995).

FRUS 1964–68, Vol. XXI, *Near East Region* (2000).

FRUS 1964–68, Vol. XXXIV, *Energy, Diplomacy, and Global Issues* (2000).

DIARIES AND MEMOIRS

Acheson, D., *Present at the Creation* (New York, Norton, 1969).

Brown, G., *In My Way* (London, Gollancz, 1971).

Butler, R.A., *The Art of the Possible* (London, Hamish Hamilton, 1971).

Castle, B., *The Castle Diaries, 1964–70* (London, Macmillan, 1984).

Copeland, M., *The Game of Nations: The Amorality of Power Politics* (New York, Weidenfeld & Nicolson, 1970).

Crossman, R., *The Diaries of a Cabinet Minister*, Vols I, II and III, ed. Janet Morgan (London, Hamish Hamilton, 1975–77).

——*The Backbench Diaries*, ed. Janet Morgan (London, Hamish Hamilton, 1981).

Dayan, M., *The Story of My Life* (London, Weidenfeld & Nicolson, 1976).

Dixon, P. (ed.), *Double Diploma: The Life of Sir Pierson Dixon, Don and Diplomat* (London, Hutchinson, 1968).

Eban, A., *An Autobiography* (London, Weidenfeld & Nicolson, 1978).

Eden, A., *Full Circle* (London, Cassell, 1960).

Eisenhower, D.D., *The White House Years: Mandate for Change, 1953–56* (London, Heinemann, 1963).

——*The White House Years: Waging Peace, 1956–61* (New York, Doubleday, 1965).

Healey, D., *The Time of My Life* (London, Penguin, 1989).

Heath, E., *The Course of My Life* (London, Hodder & Stoughton, 1998).
Johnson, L.B., *The Vantage Point* (London, Weidenfeld & Nicolson, 1971).
Johnston, C., *The View from Steamer Point: Being an Account of Three Years in Aden* (London, Collins, 1964).
——*The Brink of Jordan* (London, Hamish Hamilton, 1972).
Lloyd, J.S., *Suez 1956: A Personal Account* (London, Jonathan Cape, 1978).
Macmillan, H., *Riding the Storm: 1956–59* (London, Macmillan, 1971).
——*Pointing the Way: 1959–61* (1972).
——*At the End of the Day: 1961–63* (1973).
Murphy, R., *Diplomat amongst Warriors* (London, Collins, 1964).
Nasser, G.A., *The Philosophy of the Revolution* (Cairo, Ministry of National Guidance, no date).
Neguib, M., *Egypt's Destiny* (London, Gollancz, 1955).
Nutting, A., *No End of a Lesson* (London, Constable, 1967).
Rusk, D., *As I Saw It* (London, Norton, 1991).
Sadat, A. al-, *Revolution on the Nile* (London, Wingate, 1957).
Shuckburgh, C.A.E., *Descent to Suez: Diaries 1951–56* (London, Weidenfeld & Nicolson, 1986).
Trevakis, K., *Shades of Amber: A South Arabian Episode* (London, Hutchinson, 1968).
Trevelyan, H., *The Middle East in Revolution* (London, Macmillan, 1970).
Wilson, H., *The Labour Government* (London, Weidenfeld & Nicholson/ Michael Joseph, 1971).
Yost, C., *History and Memory* (New York, Norton, 1980).

SECONDARY WORKS

Abadi, J., *Britain's Withdrawal from the Middle East, 1947–1951: The Economic and Strategic Imperatives* (Princeton, NJ, Princeton University Press, 1983).
Aburish, S., *A Brutal Friendship* (London, Gollancz, 1997).
Aldous, R. and Lee, S., *Harold Macmillan and Britain's World Role* (London, Macmillan, 1996).
Aldous, R. and Lee, S. (eds), *Harold Macmillan: Aspects of a Political Life* (London, Macmillan, 1999).
Aldrich, R., *The Hidden Hand: Britain, America and Cold War Secret Intelligence* (London, John Murray, 2001).
Ambrose, Stephen, *Eisenhower the President* (London, Allen & Unwin, 1984).
Ambrose, S. and Immerman, R., *Ike's Spies* (New York, Doubleday, 1981).

Aronson, G., *From Sideshow to Centre Stage: US Policy to Egypt, 1945–56* (Boulder, CO, Lynne Riener, 1996).

Ashton, Nigel John, *Eisenhower, Macmillan and the Problem of Nasser* (London, Macmillan, 1996).

——'Macmillan and the Middle East', in R. Aldous and S. Lee, *Harold Macmillan and Britain's World Role* (London, Macmillan, 1996).

Barbour-Paul, Glen, *The End of Empire in the Middle East: Britain's Relinquishment of Power in her Last Three Arab Dependencies* (Cambridge, Cambridge University Press, 1991).

Bar-Joseph, U., 'Rotem: The Forgotten Crisis on the Road to the 1967 War', *Journal of Contemporary History* (1996).

Barnett, C., *The Lost Victory* (London, Pan, 1995).

——*The Verdict of Peace* (London, Macmillan, 2000).

Bar-On, I.M., *The Gates of Gaza: Israel's Road to Suez and Back* (New York, St Martin's Press, 1994).

Be'eiri, M., *Army Officers in Arab Politics and Society* (London, Praeger, 1970).

Beeley, H., 'The Middle East', in W. Roger Louis and H. Bull (eds), *The Special Relationship* (Oxford, Oxford University Press, 1986).

Bergman, A. and El-Tahri, J., *The Fifty Years War* (London, Penguin, 1998).

Billière, de la, P., *Looking for Trouble* (London, Harper Collins, 1994).

Black, I. and Morris, B., *Israel's Secret Wars: A History of Israel's Intelligence Service* (London, MacDonald Futura, 1992).

Bloch, J. and Fitzgerald, P., *British Intelligence and Covert Action* (Dingle, Brandon, 1983).

Bower, T., *The Perfect English Spy* (London, Mandarin, 1995).

Bowie, R., 'Eisenhower, Dulles and the Suez Crisis', in W. Roger Louis and R. Owen, *Suez 1956: The Crisis and its Consequences* (Oxford, Oxford University Press, 1989).

Brands, H.W., *The Specter of Neutralism: The United States and the Emergence of the Third World 1947–60* (New York, Columbia University Press, 1989).

Bullock, A., *Ernest Bevin, Foreign Secretary* (Oxford, Oxford University Press, 1983).

Burns, W., *Economic Aid and American Policy towards Egypt, 1955–1981* (Albany, NY, State University of New York, 1985).

Carlton, D., *Anthony Eden: A Biography* (London, Allen Lane, 1981).

——*Britain and the Suez Crisis* (Oxford, Blackwell, 1988).

Charmley, J., *Churchill's Grand Alliance* (London, John Curtis, 1995).

Clarke, P., *Hope and Glory* (London, Penguin, 1996).

——*A Question of Leadership from Gladstone to Blair* (London, Penguin, 1999).

Cockett, R. (ed.), *My Dear Max* (London, Historians Press, 1990).

Crosbie, S.K., *A Tacit Alliance: France and Israel from Suez to the Six Day War* (Princeton, NJ, Princeton University Press, 1974).

Daly, M.W., *Imperial Sudan: The Anglo-Egyptian Condominium 1934–36* (Cambridge, Cambridge University Press, 1991).

Dann, Uriel, *King Hussein and the Challenge of Arab Radicalism* (Oxford, Oxford University Press, 1989).

Darby, P., *British Defence Policy East of Suez, 1947–68* (Oxford, RIIA in association with Oxford University Press, 1973).

Darwin, J., 'Imperialism in Decline', *English Historical Review*, 23, 3 (1980).

——*Britain and Decolonisation: The Retreat from Empire in the Post-War World* (London, Macmillan, 1988).

Dawisha, A.I., *Egypt in the Arab World* (London, Macmillan, 1976).

Dekmejian, H., *Patterns of Political Leadership* (Albany, NY, State of New York University Press, 1975).

Dorril, S., *MI6: Fifty Years of Special Operations* (London, Fourth Estate, 2000).

Dutton, D., *Anthony Eden: A Life and Reputation* (London, Arnold, 1997).

Elliot, M., *Independent Iraq* (London, I.B. Tauris, 1996).

Epstein, L., *British Politics in the Suez Crisis* (London, Pall Mall Press, 1964).

Farag, E.S., *Nasser Speaks* (London, Morsset Press, 1972).

Fawzi, M., *Suez 1956: An Egyptian Perspective* (London, Shorouk International, 1987).

Fernea, R. and Roger Louis, W., *The Iraqi Revolution of 1958: The Old Social Classes Revisited* (London, I.B. Tauris, 1991).

Foot, M., *Aneurin Bevan 1945–60*, Vol. II (London, Davis-Poynter, 1974).

Frankel, J., *British Foreign Policy 1945–1973* (Oxford, RIIA/Oxford University Press, 1973).

Freiberger, S.Z., *Dawn over Suez: The Rise of American Power in the Middle East* (Chigago, IL, Ivan R. Dee, 1992).

Fry, M.G. and Hochstein, M., 'The Forgotten Middle Eastern Crisis of 1957: Gaza and Sharm-el-Sheikh', *International History Review, XV* (1993).

Gallagher, J., *The Decline, Revival and Fall of the British Empire* (Cambridge, Cambridge University Press, 1982).

Gallagher, J. and Robinson, R., *The Victorians and Africa* (London, Macmillan, 1981).

Gavin, R.J., *Aden under British Rule 1839–1967* (London, Hurst, 1976).

Gerges, F.A., *The Superpowers and the Middle East, 1955–67* (Boulder, CO, Westview Press, 1994).

Gilbert, M., *Winston S. Churchill, 1945–65*, Vol. 8, *Never Despair* (London, Heinemann, 1988).

Gorst, A. and Lucas, W.S., 'The Other Collusion: Operation Straggle', *Intelligence and National Security*, 3 (1994).

Green, Stephen, *Taking Sides: America's Relations with a Militant Israel 1948–67* (London, Faber, 1983).

Halliday, F., *Arabia without Sultans* (London, Penguin, 1974).

Hasou, T.Y., *The Struggle for the Arab World* (London, Routledge, 1985).

Heikal, M., *Nasser: The Cairo Documents* (London, New English Library, 1972).

——*Cutting the Lion's Tail: Suez through Egyptian Eyes* (London, Andre Deutsch, 1986).

Hennessy, P., *Whitehall* (London, Secker & Warburg, 1989).

——*The Prime Minister* (London, Penguin, 2000).

Hersh, S., *The Samson Option* (London, Sceptre, 1991).

Holland, R.F., *Pursuit of Greatness: Britain and the World Role, 1900–1970* (London, Fontana, 1990).

Hopkins, A.G., 'The Victorians and Africa: A Reconsideration of the Occupation of Egypt 1882', *Journal of African History*, 27 (1986).

Hopwood, D., *Syria: Politics and Society 1945–1990* (London, Allen & Unwin, 1990).

——*Egypt: Politics and Society 1945–1990*, 3rd edn (London, Harper Collins, 1991).

Horne, A., *Macmillan*, Vol. I (London, Macmillan, 1988).

——*Macmillan*, Vol. II (London, Macmillan, 1989).

Howard, A., *RAB* (London, Cape, 1987).

Immerman, R. (ed.), *John Foster Dulles and the Diplomacy of the Cold War* (Princeton, NJ, Princeton University Press, 1990).

Ionides, M., *Divide and Lose: The Arab Revolt of 1955–58* (London, G. Bles, 1960).

James, L., *The Rise and Fall of the British Empire* (London, Abacus, 1995).

Jeffery, K., *The British Army and the Crisis of Empire* (Manchester, Manchester University Press, 1984).

Kaiser, W. and Staerck, G. (eds), *British Foreign Policy 1955–64: Contracting Options* (London, Macmillan, 2000).

Kandiah, M.D., 'British Domestic Politics, the Conservative Party and Foreign Policy Making', in W. Kaiser and G. Staerck (eds), *British Foreign Policy 1955–64: Contracting Options* (London, Macmillan, 2000).

Kelly, S. and Gorst, A. (eds), *Whitehall and the Suez Crisis* (London, Frank Cass, 2000).

Kennedy, P., *The Realities behind Diplomacy* (London, Fontana, 1981).

Kent, J., 'The Egyptian Base and the Defence of the Middle East, 1945–54', *Journal of Imperial and Commonwealth History*, 21, 3 (1993).

Kerr, M., *The Arab Cold War: Gamal Abd-al Nasir and his Rivals, 1958–70* (Oxford, Oxford University Press, 1971).

Khadduri, M., *Political Trends in the Arab World: The Role of Ideas and Ideals in Politics* (Baltimore, Johns Hopkins Press, 1970).

Kolinsky, M., 'Lampson and the Wartime Control of Egypt', in M. Kolinsky and M.J. Cohen (eds), *Demise of the British Empire in the Middle East* (London, Frank Cass, 1998).

Kunz, D., *The Economic Diplomacy of the Suez Crisis* (Chapel Hill, NC, University of North Carolina Press, 1991).

Kyle, K., 'Britain and the Crisis', in W. Roger Louis and R. Owen, *Suez 1956: The Crisis and its Consequences* (Oxford, Oxford University Press, 1989).

——*Suez* (New York, St Martin's Press, 1991).

Lacouture, J., *Nasser* (London, Secker & Warburg, 1975).

LaFeber, W., *America, Russia and the Cold War* (New York, McGraw-Hill, 1993).

Lamb, R., *The Failure of the Eden Government* (London, Sidgwick & Jackson, 1987).

——*The Macmillan Years 1957–63: The Emerging Truth* (London, John Murray, 1995).

Laqueur, W., *The Road to War* (London, Penguin, 1968).

Lesch, D., *Syria and the United States: Eisenhower's Cold War in the Middle East* (Boulder, CO, Westview Press, 1992).

——'Nasser and an Example of Diplomatic Acumen', *Middle Eastern Studies*, 31, 2, Apr. (1995).

Lindsay, T.F. and Harrington, M., *The Conservative Party 1918–1970* (New York, St Martin's Press, 1974).

Little, D., 'The New Frontier on the Nile: JFK, Nasser and Arab Nationalism', *Journal of American History*, 75 (1988), p. 504.

——'Cold War and Covert Action', *Middle East Journal*, 44, 1 (1990).

——'The Making of a Special Relationship: The United States and Israel, 1957–68', *International Journal of Middle East Studies*, XXV (1993).

Little, T., *Modern Egypt* (London, Benn, 1967).

Lucas, W.S., *Divided We Stand* (London, John Curtis, 1991).

——'The Missing Link? Patrick Dean, Chairman of the Joint Intelligence Committee', in S. Kelly and A. Gorst (eds), *Whitehall and the Suez Crisis* (London, Frank Cass, 2000).

Lucas, W.S. and Morey, A., 'The Hidden Alliance: The CIA and MI6 Before and After Suez', in D. Stafford and R. Jeffreys-Jones, *American–British–Canadian Intelligence Relations 1939–2000* (London, Frank Cass, 2000).

Mansfield, P., *Nasser* (London, Methuen, 1969).

——*The British in Egypt* (London, Weidenfeld & Nicolson, 1971).

Marks, F., *Power and Peace: The Diplomacy of John Foster Dulles* (New Haven, CT, Yale University Press, 1993).

Mason, M., 'The Decisive Volley: The Battle of Ismailia and the Decline of British Influence in the Middle East', *Journal of Imperial Commonwealth History*, 19 (1991).

Miller, D.B., *Survey of Commonwealth Affairs: Problems of Attrition and Expansion, 1953–69* (Oxford, Oxford University Press, 1974).

Monroe, E., *Britain's Moment in the Middle East*, 2nd edn (London, Chatto & Windus, 1981).

Mor, B.D., 'Nasser's Decision Making in the 1967 Middle East Crisis: A Rational-Choice Explanation', *Journal of Peace Research*, 28, 4 (1991).

Morsy, L., 'Britain's Wartime Policy in Egypt, 1940–42', *Middle Eastern Studies*, 25 (1989).

Northedge, F.S., *Descent from Power* (London, Minerva, 1974).

Nutting, A., *Nasser* (London, Constable, 1972).

O'Ballance, E., *The War in the Yemen* (London, Faber, 1971).

Onslow, S., *Backbench Debate within the Conservative Party and its Influence on British Foreign Policy, 1948–57* (London, Macmillan, 1997).

Ovendale, R., *The Origins of the Arab–Israeli Wars*, 2nd edn (London, Longman, 1991).

——*Britain, the United States and the Transfer of Power in the Middle East* (Leicester, Leicester University Press, 1996).

Paget, J., *Last Post: Aden 1964–67* (London, Faber, 1969).

Palmer, M., *Guardians of the Gulf: A History of America's Expanding Role in the Persian Gulf, 1833–1992* (New York, Free Press, 1992).

Penrose, E. and Penrose, E.F., *Iraq: International Relations and National Development* (London, Benn, 1978).

Peres, S., *Battling for Peace* (London, Weidenfeld & Nicolson, 1995).

Pickering, J., *Britain's Withdrawal from East of Suez: The Politics of Retrenchment* (London, Macmillan, 1998).

Pieragostini, K., *Britain, Aden and South Arabia: Abandoning Empire* (London, Macmillan, 1991).

Podeh, E., 'The Struggle for Arab Hegemony after the Suez Crisis', *Middle Eastern Studies*, 29, 1 (1993).

——*The Decline of Arab Unity* (Brighton, Sussex Academic Press, 1999).

Pryce Jones, D., *The Closed Circle* (London, Weidenfeld & Nicolson, 1986).

Quandt, W.B., *Peace Process* (Washington, DC, Brookings, 2001).

Ramsden, J., *A History of the Conservative Party: Winds of Change: Macmillan to Heath, 1957–75* (London, Longman, 1996).

Rathmell, A., *Secret War in the Middle East: The Covert Struggle for Syria, 1949–61* (London, I.B. Tauris, 1995).

Reed, B. and Williams, G., *Denis Healey and the Politics of Power* (London, Sidgwick & Jackson, 1971).

Reynolds, David, *Britannia Overruled: British Policy and World Power in the Twentieth Century* (London, Longman, 1991).

Rhodes-James, R., *Anthony Eden* (London, Weidenfeld & Nicolson, 1986).

Richardson, D. and Stone, G. (eds), *Decisions and Diplomacy: Essays in Twentieth-Century International History* (London, Routledge/LSE, 1995).

Roberts, A., *Eminent Churchillians* (London, Phoenix, 1995).

Roger Louis, W., *The British Empire in the Middle East 1945–51: Arab Nationalism, the United States and Postwar Imperialism* (Oxford, Oxford University Press, 1984).

——'The Tragedy of the Anglo Egyptian Settlement 1954', in W. Roger Louis and R. Owen, *Suez 1956: The Crisis and its Consequences* (Oxford, Oxford University Press, 1989).

——'Dulles, Suez and the British', in Richard Immerman (ed.), *John Foster Dulles and the Diplomacy of the Cold War* (Princeton, NJ, Princeton University Press, 1990).

——'Churchill and Egypt', in W. Roger Louis and R. Blake, *Churchill* (Oxford, Oxford University Press, 1994).

——'Macmillan and Middle East Crisis of 1958', *Proceedings of the British Academy*, 94 (1996).

——and Owen, R. (eds), *Suez 1956: The Crisis and its Consequences* (Oxford, Oxford University Press, 1989).

——and Robinson, R., 'The Imperialism of Decolonisation', *Journal of Imperial and Commonwealth History*, XXII (1994).

Said, E., *Orientalism* (London, Penguin, 1977).

Sayyid-Marsot, A.L., 'The British Occupation of Egypt', in A. Porter, *The Oxford History of the British Empire*, Vol. III, *The Nineteenth Century* (Oxford, Oxford University Press, 1999).

Seale, P., *The Struggle for Syria* (Oxford, Oxford University Press, 1965).

Shalom, Z., *The Superpowers, Israel and the Future of Jordan 1960–63* (Brighton, Sussex Academic Press, 1999).

Shlaim, A., *The Iron Wall* (London, Penguin, 2000).

Smith, Simon C., *Kuwait, 1950–65, Britain, the Al-Sabah and Oil* (London, British Academy/Oxford University Press, 1999).

——'Revolution and Reaction: South Arabia in the Aftermath of Yemeni Revolution', in K. Federowich and M. Thomas (eds), *Diplomacy and Colonial Retreat* (London, Frank Cass, 2000).

Stephens, R., *Nasser* (London, Penguin, 1971).

Taykeh, R., *Origins of the Eisenhower Doctrine* (London, Macmillan, 2001).

Thomas, H., *The Suez Affair* (London, Penguin, 1970).

Thornhill, E., 'Alternatives to Nasser: Humphrey Trevelyan, Ambassador to Egypt', in S. Kelly and A. Gorst (eds), *Whitehall and the Suez Crisis* (London, Frank Cass, 2000).

Thorpe, D.R., *Selwyn Lloyd* (London, Cape, 1981).

——*Alec Douglas-Home* (London, Sinclair-Stevenson, 1996).

Troen, S.I. and Shemesh, M. (eds), *The Suez–Sinai Crisis: Retrospective and Reappraisal* (London, Frank Cass, 1990).

Turner, J., *Macmillan: Profiles in Power* (London, Longman, 1994).

Vatikiotis, P.J., *The Egyptian Army in Politics* (Bloomington, IN, Indiana University Press, 1961).

——*Egypt since the Revolution* (London, Allen & Unwin, 1968).

——*The Modern History of Egypt* (London, Weidenfeld & Nicolson, 1969).

——*Nasser and his Generation* (London, Croom Helm, 1978).

Warburg, G.R., *Historical Discord in the Nile Valley* (London, Hurst, 1992).

Willams, P., *Hugh Gaitskell* (London, Cape, 1979).

Wilson, H., *The Chariot of Israel* (London, Weidenfeld & Nicolson, 1981).

Wright, P., *Spycatcher* (New York, Viking, 1987).

Yergin, D., *The Prize* (New York, Simon & Schuster, 1991).

Zeigler, P., *Wilson* (London, Weidenfeld & Nicolson, 1993).

Index